CHANGING LIFE PATTERNS IN
WESTERN INDUSTRIAL SOCIETIES

ADVANCES IN LIFE COURSE RESEARCH

Series Editor: Timothy J. Owens

Recent Volumes:

ADVANCES IN LIFE COURSE RESEARCH   VOLUME 8

CHANGING LIFE PATTERNS IN WESTERN INDUSTRIAL SOCIETIES

EDITED BY

JANET ZOLLINGER GIELE

Heller School, Brandeis University, Waltham, MA, USA

ELKE HOLST

*German Institute for Economic Research (DIW Berlin),
Berlin, Germany*

2004

ELSEVIER
JAI

Amsterdam – Boston – Heidelberg – London – New York – Oxford – Paris
San Diego – San Francisco – Singapore – Sydney – Tokyo

ELSEVIER Ltd
The Boulevard, Langford Lane
Kidlington, Oxford OX5 1GB, UK

First edition 2004

A catalogue record from the British Library has been applied for.

ISBN: 0-7623-1020-0
ISSN: 1040-2608 (Series)

⊗ The paper used in this publication meets the requirements of ANSI/NISO Z39.48-1992 (Permanence of Paper).
Printed in The Netherlands.

CONTENTS

LIST OF CONTRIBUTORS

Sabine Berghahn	Otto-Suhr-institut, The Free University, Germany
Sigrid Betzelt	Department of Gender Policy in the Welfare State, Zentrum für Sozialpolitik, Center for Social Policy Research, University of Bremen, Germany
Suzanne M. Bianchi	Department of Sociology, Maryland Population Research Center, University of Maryland, College Park, MD, USA
Harald Bielenski	Infratest Sozialforschung, München, Germany
Jens Bonke	Danish National Institute of Social Research, Copenhagen, Denmark
Marlis Buchmann	Department of Sociology, University of Zürich, Swiss Federal Institute of Technology, Zürich, Switzerland
Janet Zollinger Giele	Heller School for Social Policy and Management, Brandeis University, Waltham, MA, USA
Janet C. Gornick	Baruch College/City University of New York, New York, USA
Karin Gottschall	Department of Gender Policy in the Welfare State, Center for Social Policy Research, University of Bremen, Bremen, Germany
Catherine Hakim	Department of Sociology, London School of Economics and Political Science, London, UK
Elke Holst	Department of the Socio-Economic Panel Study (SOEP), German Institute for Economic Research (DIW Berlin), Berlin, Germany

Elke Koch-Weser   Department of Statistics, Probability, and Applied
                             Statistics, University of Rome La Sapienza, Rome,
                             Italy

Irene Kriesi   Department of Sociology, University of Zürich,
                             Swiss Federal Institute of Technology, Zürich,
                             Switzerland

Marie-Thérèse Letablier   Research Institute on Employment National Center
                             for Scientific Research (CNRS), Paris, France

Marybeth J. Mattingly   Department of Sociology, University of Maryland,
                             College Park, MD, USA

Marcia K. Meyers   School of Social Work and Evans School of Public
                             Affairs, University of Washington, Seattle, WA,
                             USA

Michael J. Piore   Massachusetts Institute of Technology, Cambridge,
                             MA, USA

Janneke Plantenga   Institute of Economics, University of Utrecht, The
                             Netherlands

Stefan Sacchi   Swiss Federal Institute of Technology, University
                             of Zürich, Zürich, Switzerland

Annemette Sørensen   Department of Sociology, Harvard University,
                             Cambridge, MA, USA

Alexandra Wagner   International Labor Market Research Team,
                             Berlin, Germany

FOREWORD

SERIES PURPOSE AND ORIENTATION

Advances in Life Course Research publishes original theoretical analyses, integrative reviews, policy analyses and position papers, and theory-based empirical papers on issues involving all aspects of the human life course. Adopting a broad conception of the life course, it invites and welcomes contributions from all disciplines and fields of study interested in understanding, describing, and predicting the antecedents of and consequences for the course that human lives take from birth to death, within and across time and cultures, regardless of methodology, theoretical orientation, or disciplinary affiliation. Each volume is organized around a unifying theme. Queries and suggestions for future volumes are most welcome. Please see http://web.ics.purdue.edu/~towens/newsite/advances/ for series details and contact information.

PURPOSE OF THIS VOLUME

The present volume (Number 8) is subtitled *Changing Life Patterns in Western Industrial Societies* and places special emphasis on the intersection of gender and work in the adult life course. The guest editors are Janet Zollinger Giele, a professor of sociology at Brandeis University, and Dr. Elke Holst, a labor economist at the German Institute for Economic Research (DIW Berlin). Taking the gender revolution in Western industrialized societies as its starting point, the editors note that as more and more women have entered the worldwide labor force, a "gender revolution" has emerged. The revolution has provoked unprecedented changes in women's timing of education, marriage, childbearing, and market work as well as more general changes in households and life styles of women and men. Giele and Holst aim to advance the discussion of gender, work, and society by placing the phenomenon of life course change against a larger theoretical and analytic backdrop intended not only to describe the changing life patterns that are emerging in Western industrial societies but also to contemplate their causes, consequences, and likely direction in the future. Such an endeavor necessarily requires a broad and differentiated conceptual framework that takes into account major cultural, political, domestic, and economic forces along with the agency of individual men and women. The array of scholarly contributions in this volume attains that goal while preserving cohesiveness.

Timothy J. Owens
Series Editor

PREFACE

This volume began with a planning meeting in Berlin in July 2000 and with the idea of developing an interdisciplinary conference on changing life patterns in Europe and North America. The committee was a group of women social scientists who wanted to illuminate not only the ways that women's lives were changing but also the impact of changing life patterns on the larger concerns of society.[1] Some members of the group suggested that women use their time differently, have different goals, and want "time to live" that is not easily won from employers and the larger society, in which the dominant work ethic is based on "male values" of profit and competition and the type of narrow focus that is often identified with so-called "male" careers.

Being scholars, the planning group wanted to see whether any of these hypotheses were borne out by the facts. Accordingly, demographers, sociologists, and economists from Denmark, France, Germany, the Netherlands, Switzerland, and the United States were invited to participate in a conference to be held a year later and to present their research findings related to these issues. The conference was sponsored by the German Institute for Economic Research (DIW Berlin), the Social Science Research Center (WZB) Berlin, the Max Planck Institute for Human Development (MPIB), the Berlin School of Economics (FHW Berlin), the Free University Berlin (FUB), the Humboldt University Berlin (HUB), and the Technical University Berlin (TUB) in cooperation with Brandeis University and the Murray Research Center at the Radcliffe Institute for Advanced Study of Harvard University. Sponsorship and financial support came from the central public funding organization for academic research in Germany, the Deutsche Forschungsgemeinschaft (DFG). The conference took place in September 2001 in Berlin at the Social Science Center (WZB). Unfortunately, the events of September 11, 2001 occurred just one week prior to the conference, and two of the presenters from the United States (Suzanne Bianchi and Annemette Sørensen) were unable to attend. Nevertheless, the quality of the conference presentations was so good that the two of us, as members of the Planning Committee and as participants, thought they deserved to be published, and so we decided to undertake the editing of this book.

We were fortunate to persuade Bianchi and Sorensen to contribute chapters to the book even though they had not been present at the conference. In addition, we are indebted to four other authors (Piore, Gornick and Meyers, and Hakim)

xiii

whom we invited to write opening chapters on more general topics related to the change in life patterns in western societies.

For lending their support and encouragement to publish the conference papers, we are particularly grateful to the other members of the Planning Committee who shared with us their vision and the driving force to make the conference a reality. We are indebted to our benefactors, especially the DIW Berlin, for supporting the conference and the work of Holst as editor, and to the Heller School of Brandeis University for similar support to Giele. Special thanks for editorial assistance are due to Madeleine Burry, Donna Einhorn, and Joan Walsh. Finally, we want to express our appreciation to Timothy Owens, our series editor, for his interest and encouragement during the time that was required to transform an assortment of conference papers into published work.

NOTE

1. Members of the Planning Committee were Silke Bothfeld, Claudia Gather, Janet Giele, Elke Holst, Friederike Maier, Birgit Pfau-Effinger, and Heike Trappe.

Janet Zollinger Giele
Elke Holst
Volume Co-Editors

INTRODUCTION: CHANGING LIFE PATTERNS IN WESTERN INDUSTRIAL SOCIETIES

The purpose of this volume is to assemble observations at a macro-social level about the changing nature of lives in western societies. The life course field as a whole, whether anchored in life-span psychology or the sociology of aging, has tended to focus on individual lives as the basic unit of analysis and on the regularities in those lives that result from differences and commonalities by age, sex, race, class, or nationality. To our knowledge, it is an unusual undertaking to examine how lives of women and men may be changing across countries, as part of a more general process of modernization, and to consider the reasons why.

The fourteen chapters in this book are grouped under four main headings that suggest some of the main social forces that lie behind the change in contemporary lives. Part I (Structural Forces that Shape Life Patterns) includes four chapters that address broad economic and cultural trends and developments in social policy. Part II (The Changing Demographics of Time Use) contains three chapters describing changes in time use, working-time policies, and evolving preferences regarding time spent at work and in other pursuits. Part III (Institutional Factors in an International Perspective) assembles four chapters that describe evolving social institutions (the labor market, child care, equality law, and family and welfare regimes) that affect the shape of lives and the allocation of time between employment and private or family life. Part IV (The Role of Individual Agency and Choice) brings the volume to a close with three chapters that describe individual behaviors in more specific contexts: new media professions in Germany, economic relations within married couples, and the changing life patterns of individual women and men who are making specific choices between traditional and new alternative role patterns.

PART I: STRUCTURAL FORCES THAT SHAPE LIFE PATTERNS

In Chapter 1 (New Life Patterns and Changing Gender Roles) Janet Zollinger Giele and Elke Holst present a conceptual framework that provides a theoretical armature for organizing the myriad economic, demographic, and sociological observations that have been made about changing life patterns in North America and Europe. They use this framework to make sense out of the changes that have been observed both in the lives of individuals and in the expectations surrounding gender roles that are coming to be known as the "implicit gender contract." It turns out that increasing flexibility in working times and working arrangements, development of equal rights laws, provision of child care centers, and changing role preferences are all part of a huge secular social trend that has an internal order and logic that the authors attempt to uncover.

In Chapter 2 (The Reconfiguration of Work and Employment Relations in the United States at the Turn of the Century) Michael J. Piore traces the changes in the regime governing relations between employers and employees over the last twenty years. The change is essentially from collective bargaining to a system regulated by law. This change reflects a more fundamental shift from mobilization based on economic identities such as class, profession and enterprise affiliation to mobilization based on social identities such as race, gender, ethnicity, sexual orientation, age and physical disability. Underlying this transformation are still more basic changes in the family as a social unit and the corporate enterprise as an economic institution.

Chapter 3 (Welfare Regimes in Relation to Paid Work and Care) by Janet C. Gornick and Marcia K. Meyers shows how ideologies about work, caregiving, family, and gender relations vary across countries. These various perspectives result in different ways of reconciling the potential conflicts between child well-being, women's caregiving burden, and gender equality. The tensions among these concerns can be resolved in societies that combine intensive parental time for children with a gender-egalitarian division of labor. Social and labor market policies that support such solutions are most developed in the Social Democratic countries, with the Conservative countries of continental Europe and the Liberal English-speaking countries lagging substantially behind.

In Chapter 4 (Lifestyle Preferences vs. Patriarchal Values: Causal and Non-Causal Attitudes) Catherine Hakim provides solid evidence, from longitudinal studies such as the National Longitudinal Surveys and the Panel Study of Income Dynamics, of the significant long-term impact of values and life goals on occupational attainment and earnings. Her preference theory incorporates these findings into sociological and economic explanations of the ways that values and attitudes become important predictors of women's (and men's) behavior. She illustrates her theoretical and methodological distinction between causal and non-causal attitudes and values with data on lifestyle preferences and patriarchal values from comparative surveys in Britain and Spain. The results show that lifestyle preferences have a major impact on women's choices between family work and employment, whereas patriarchal values in the culture are much less closely linked to behaviour.

PART II: THE CHANGING DEMOGRAPHICS OF TIME USE

In Chapter 5 (Time, Work, and Family in the United States), Suzanne M. Bianchi and Marybeth J. Mattingly review changes in family formation and labor force participation that have dramatically altered the activity patterns of U.S. adults. After describing the time use patterns of American parents, especially during the peak childbearing and career years (ages 25–54), they show that as women have markedly increased their time in paid work, they have curtailed their time in housework. On average, women who become mothers do not cut back their time with children, but they engage in "multitasking" when doing child care by combining these activities with doing household chores. Men's lives are changing as well with some increase in housework but a sizable increase in time with children among fathers who live with their children. However, there is a greater sense of time pressure overall, and a gender leisure gap (favoring men) has emerged where none existed before.

The central focus of Chapter 6 (Changing Work and Life Patterns: Examples of New Working-Time Arrangements in the European Member states) by Janneke Plantenga is the interrelationship between flexibilization and equal employment opportunities. Drawing on comparative data, Plantenga wrestles with the different possible ways to categorize the working-time regimes of the EU member states. She is especially interested in whether flexibility of working times increases equality of women and men in employment, as is widely believed. Her analysis shows that the differences in the degree of association between flexibility and gender equality in employment in the European member states are rather large, indicating that there is no fixed relation between the dimensions of flexibility and equality. National differences and political culture do matter and they influence the actual position of each country within the flexibility/equality continuum.

In Chapter 7 (Employment Options of Men and Women in Europe), Harald Bielenski and Alexandra Wagner describe actual and preferred employment rates and working hours by using a representative survey on employment options that was carried out in all 15 member states of the European Union and Norway in 1998. People's own preferences differ in varying degrees from their actual situations. In general, however, the preferences of men and women differ from each other to a much lesser extent than their actual situations do. The same is true for cross-national differences. Thus, the cultural ideals of people in Europe appear to be converging on a standard that is shared between women and men and across the continent.

PART III: INSTITUTIONAL FACTORS IN AN INTERNATIONAL PERSPECTIVE

Chapter 8 (Labor-Market Structures and Women's Paid Work: Opportunities and Constraints in the Swiss Labor Market) by Marlis Buchmann, Irene Kriesi, and Stefan Sacchi argues that previous research on women's changing work patterns has largely ignored the ways in which the employment context shapes the work histories of women. By paying attention to job characteristics and working conditions, they are able to identify the characteristics of the workplace that are most conducive to successful re-entry after an absence from the labor market. Based on an empirical study conducted in Switzerland, they provide evidence that opportunities for continuous employment and labor-force re-entry after quitting paid work vary greatly, depending on occupation and type of firm.

In Chapter 9 (Work and Family Balance: A New Challenge for Politics in France) Marie-Thérèse Letablier shows the central importance of state-supported child care for addressing the issue of work and life balance that has been prominent in public debate in France since the beginning of the 1990s. Families' demands for state support to childcare and workers' demands for more free time for social and family life are emerging in a context where the state has a strong mandate to intervene in family affairs and in work regulations. The use of family policy to restructure childcare policies and working-time policies has become a major tool for public action in France. Of particular interest is the special effort that has been made to reduce the legal number of working hours. It is not yet known what the impact of this change will be on the integration of work and family life.

Chapter 10 (The Influence of European Union Legislation on Labor Market Equality for Women) by Sabine Berghahn describes the legal progress made in European Community law to protect equal rights of women in the workplace. The development of European equal employment laws started in the 1970s and was fostered by the European Court of Justice. As a consequence, the principle of gender equality was incorporated into the legal systems of all the European member states. But the main problem still is to translate these laws into practice. The strategy of gender mainstreaming and the implementation of the new amended "Equal Treatment Directive" could bring further advancements in equality. Structural change, however, continues to be slowed by the continued strength of the male breadwinner family.

In Chapter 11 (The Welfare state and Time Allocation in Sweden, Denmark, France, and Italy), Jens Bonke and Elke Koch-Weser use data from national time-use surveys and the European Community Household Panel to examine the allocation of time from a welfare state perspective, and they ask whether the ordinary welfare regime models are appropriate for the understanding of diversity in everyday life between European countries. The study investigates the time allocation of the working-age population in Sweden, Denmark, France, and Italy and explains the variation as a function of socio-economic characteristics and of differential policy constraints. Family obligations are still more important in southern and middle-European countries than in Scandinavian countries, and, therefore, contribute to continuing tension between women's working-life and family-life in those countries where family demands still command priority.

PART IV: THE ROLE OF INDIVIDUAL AGENCY AND CHOICE

Chapter 12 (Publishing and the New Media Professions as Forerunners of Pioneer Work and Life Patterns) by Sigrid Betzelt and Karin Gottschall focuses on the cultural industries as part of the growing knowledge-based services sector that encourages pioneer work and life patterns. The German publishing and new media professions are characterized by flexible employment and a low degree of gender segregation. The workforce is mostly professional, with a high proportion of well-educated women. Moreover, several innovative collective risk-management strategies have been developed to cope with radicalized market conditions and the needs of a young and mixed-gender labor force. However, the positive image of these occupational fields is only partly justified since such "modernized" strategies are based on gendered understandings of professional work that assume a "male" type of career and make it difficult for workers to be responsive to outside demands such as might come from children and family.

In Chapter 13 (Economic Relations between Women and Men: New Realities and the Re-interpretation of Dependence), Annemette Sørensen shows that women's lives and opportunities in the advanced industrialized countries have changed dramatically during the last decades of the twentieth century. Women's economic power has increased considerably, with women's labor force experience and earnings capacity much closer to that of men's than ever before; and these changes have affected economic relations between men and women who share a household. Women's greater earnings may strengthen rather than weaken their partnership, and their economic contributions to household income may be viewed by their partners as more of an asset than a threat. Sørensen hints at the emergence of a new gender regime, where women's economic dependence no longer has the meaning it did when few women made significant contributions to family income. Now men may be increasingly dependent on women's income.

Finally, in Chapter 14 (Women and Men as Agents of Change in Their Own Lives), Janet Zollinger Giele focuses on the ways that personal biographies of individuals are related to their gender roles. Using biographical methods, she employs a theoretical scheme developed by her and by Glen Elder for study of the life course, which links earlier experience to subsequent life patterns. Modern work-centered women and the new care-oriented men are different from their traditional counterparts in their identity, social networks, goals and ambitions, and strategies for combining education, work, and family life. They are likely to seek out roles that allow them a greater degree of crossover in working and caring. In light of the other chapters in this volume that also touch on changing gender roles, a question for the future is how such preferences form and how they shape the broader gender contract of the larger society.

The chapters presented here underline the massive changes in the public and private spheres of society that result from women's more varied roles and enhanced status. They make clear the need to reform the gender contract based on traditional ascription to make it a more open and egalitarian partnership. Such a change which has already occurred in many households is a logical outcome of the new life course patterns of women and men and calls for supporting structures not only in the family and household but also at work.

Janet Zollinger Giele and Elke Holst
Volume Co-Editors

PART I:
STRUCTURAL FORCES THAT SHAPE LIFE PATTERNS

1. NEW LIFE PATTERNS AND CHANGING GENDER ROLES

Janet Zollinger Giele and Elke Holst

ABSTRACT

This chapter links new life patterns in western industrial societies to societal change and a new division of labor between women and men. Four aspects of this change are shown to parallel the processes of adaptive change that Talcott Parsons outlined in his theory of evolution of modern societies and that Miriam Johnson applied to the gender revolution: (1) technological innovation and new patterns of time use (adaptive upgrading); (2) wider role options for men and women (goal differentiation); (3) new rules and policies about equity and integration of work and family (inclusion and integration); and (4) reframing of values to achieve a better balance between productivity and caregiving (value generalization).

It is not accidental that this book on changing life patterns begins with a discussion of changing gender relations in its very first chapter. The shift in gender expectations is at the very heart of changing life patterns today. Married women's labor force participation has more than doubled since World War II. The preferred life style of women has shifted from full-time homemaker to a dual role of earner and caregiver; and less dramatic changes have also occurred in men's lives such as helping more at home and sharing the breadwinner role with their wives. Yet societal institutions and cultural beliefs lag behind actual life patterns. Similarly, there is a gap between private needs and public willingness to provide social support.

Changing Life Patterns in Western Industrial Societies
Advances in Life Course Research, Volume 8, 3–22
Copyright © 2004 by Elsevier Ltd.
All rights of reproduction in any form reserved
ISSN: 1040-2608/doi:10.1016/S1040-2608(03)08001-8

The purpose of this chapter is to show the underlying order in these changes and to suggest the causes of widespread shifts in time use, life patterns, social institutions, and culture that are described in the rest of this book. We first present a theory of how social systems adapt to change over time that is based on the work of sociologist Talcott Parsons (1966) on societal evolution. We then build on the insights of Miriam Johnson (1989) who applied Parsons' insights to the contemporary revolution in gender roles.

THE PROCESS OF EVOLUTIONARY SOCIAL CHANGE

As Darwin explained in the *Origin of the Species*, survival of a species depends on effective adaptation to the environment and to changing circumstances. So also in the social sciences there is broad agreement that societies are able to survive over the long-term only if they continue to meet basic needs of food production, procreation, internal coordination, and protection from enemies.

In his theory of societal evolution Parsons (1966) outlined the basic types of structural change that have to occur when an old pattern of adaptation is rendered ineffective by changing external or internal circumstances. The key dynamic is structural differentiation in which an established social unit that was effective in the past must break into several specialized units in order to meet new challenges. Such differentiation is characteristic of the modernization process and usually results in a more efficient and complex social organization in which the units become organically interdependent. Parsons identified four hierarchically organized processes that typically help societies evolve toward structures that can successfully meet contemporary challenges. These are adaptive upgrading, goal differentiation, integration, and value generalization. Along the lines suggested by Miriam Johnson (1989), we here further refine these four aspects of structural differentiation to provide a template for describing and analyzing changing life patterns and gender relations. Whether in relation to society as a whole, or life patterns and gender roles, the underlying argument of differentiation theory is that these four processes together lead to greater social efficiency and higher levels of individual well-being.

Adaptive Upgrading

Adaptive upgrading concerns the best use of time, talent, space, information, and material resources. It can be understood as the individual's or society's management of human and material resources that leads to attainment of a greater benefit.

In connection with changing life patterns and the modern gender revolution, for example, home appliances and modern amenities lower the amount of time required for domestic production. Improvements in health, longevity, and reproductive control reduce the portion of a woman's life spent in bearing and rearing children. The gain in time can then be used for other pursuits outside the home.

Goal Differentiation

In the case of life pattern and gender system change, goal differentiation results in greater efficiency and benefit to individuals and society because freedom for self-determination rather than the conformity to prescribed social roles based on age and sex results in a better fit between interests and opportunities. Old-fashioned age and gender categories that are too confining for the variety of individual capacities and interests of women and men give way to expanding choices and opportunities. Thus identity and the sense of self become more flexible and less closely tied to past roles and experience (Johnson, 1989, p. 108).

Integration and Inclusion

Integration refers to the challenge of embracing and coordinating all the newly liberated individual or group options and opportunities in such a way that the social system maintains coherence and integrity. The new role patterns that are experienced by one sex or the other have to be tied into the existing system. In the world of contemporary gender relations, the principal process of inclusion is the acceptance of new role models: for example, the widespread presence of more married women in the labor force and more fathers at home providing care to children. Other examples are the removal of barriers to women's eligibility for educational, professional, and managerial opportunities that were once available only to men, and the gains made by women in seeking and holding political office. For men, comparable changes are seen in the acceptance of them into female-dominated occupations such as nursing, and willingness to provide them with family leave for giving care to children and elders.

Value Generalization

As a system undergoes the three previous types of change, it becomes more complex, with more different parts and more varied and specialized functions

Table 1.   Adaptive Change in Life Patterns and Gender Roles.

Phases in Evolutionary Change	New Life Patterns of Women and Men	Impact on Gender Roles
Adaptive upgrading (resources and facilities)	Greater variety, flexibility, and multi-tasking in the use of time. Expansion of non-standard and part-time work schedules. A "second shift" for doing housework and family care in addition to paid work.	Gender convergence in time schedules and career patterns. Flexibility facilitates women's employment. Time scarcity and overwork result for both sexes, but especially for women.
Goal differentiation (roles within groups)	Expansion of role choices, occupations, and family life styles. Policies to support equal educational opportunity and equal employment opportunity for women.	More crossover between traditional male and female jobs and fields. *More women* in the labor force and in occupations formerly dominated by men. *More men* reliant on wife's help with breadwinning.
Integration and inclusion (institutional level)	Policies to coordinate paid work and family life. Provision of child care, family leave, and work-based social protection by employers and the state.	Gender norms in favor of dual work and family roles. Invention of new household and corporate strategies to accommodate dual roles.
Value generalization (cultural level)	Reframing of cultural priorities to value both care and productivity. Focus on well-being of the population as well as on economic growth	Ideal adult role for both women and men is the capacity to work and to love. For *women*, the frontier is in employment; for *men*, in a commitment to caregiving.

included within it. Yet the challenge for the actors and for the system as a whole is to feel continuity with their initial values and purposes. According to Parsons (1966, p. 23), the "value pattern must be couched at a higher level of *generality* in order to legitimize the wider variety of goals and functions of the sub-units." Thus innovators, by reconciling their new role patterns with their existing values, are able to legitimate their life style as part of established society. This makes them eligible for the social support due any other citizen.

Four Recurring Themes

In the remainder of this chapter we spell out the ways in which the four aspects of the differentiation process can be seen in contemporary life patterns and gender role changes. We also discuss opportunities and challenges connected to these emerging new patterns as well as the difficulties still to be overcome.

Actual changes in the lives of men and women represent four aspects of adaptation as outlined above. In trying out new modes of working and living, individuals begin to experience the benefits of a more complex and varied set of possibilities and discover negative consequences of the traditional roles prescribed for their sex. Changes in individual lives percolate upward to affect the wider social structure, and new norms filter down to reinforce and reward the most adaptive changes in personal life. Changes in both gender roles and gender expectations correspond to the four main aspects of structural differentiation, as outlined in Table 1: (1) greater flexibility in time use and working patterns; (2) more choice in role options; (3) development at work and family policies to support the new roles; and (4) more widespread appreciation of caregiving as well as paid work.

Differentiation theory provides a guide for understanding the connections between the changing ways that individuals arrange their lives at the role level and the structural changes that are also under way in the workplace, the family, social programs and policies, and the broader culture. The succeeding chapters of this book provide insights and examples of these changes as they are indicated by time use and individual preferences and by work and family settings and social policies that differentially reward some life patterns more than others.

TIME USE AND WORKING-TIME PATTERNS

In Western Europe and the United states, achieving flexibility has meant an expansion of the variety of acceptable schedules and adaptive mechanisms for use of time. Common themes are the growing use of part-time, flex-time, family leave, early retirement, career change, re-entry to the labor force, and so on. Flexible scheduling is also associated with an expansion in the categories of persons who can be employed in order to include married women, lone parents, divorced women, mothers of young children, and midlife women returning after an absence. The categories of persons who can give care are also expanded to include men, grandparents, retired persons, and others. The mechanisms for accomplishing this flexibility have to be discovered, and this is the first phase of evolutionary adaptation that Parsons called *adaptive upgrading*.

The locations where people work also undergo differentiation and expansion. Paid work now increasingly takes place in less regimented settings than the office or factory, through consulting and self-employment, or increasingly as free-lance work that may be done by project-teams that work in various locations and come together perhaps only briefly until the project is complete (Piore, 2003; Plantenga,

2003). In their case study of the new German media professions, Betzelt and Gottschall (2003) describe the rapidly shifting and highly complex system of outsourcing. The evolving job structure has meant more opportunity for women but at the same time greater risk and insecurity in putting together a livable wage.

In this climate of increasingly flexible work arrangements, adaptive change can have a variety of effects from increasing the comparative advantage of certain groups to having a leveling effect. Betzelt and Gottschall (2003) comment that the typical worker in the new flexible work setting of the German TV, publishing, and film is in fact young and childless and that professional free-lancing for women is acceptable and attractive only so long as they can match the "male" professional ideal. By contrast, a young mother often prefers a part-time job, but she risks trading off better wages and long-term security for flexibility in the short run (OECD, 2001). A different type of result appears in the U.S., where Bianchi and Mattingly (2003) show how time use of men and women has tended to converge since the 1960s. They report that the newer role combinations of market work and non-market housework and caregiving have brought a steady decline in the proportion of women's hours relative to men's hours in household work. Similarly, using time diary data of 1994 for Denmark, France, Sweden, and Italy, Bonke and Koch-Weser (2003) show that the *sum* (although not the allocation) of women's market work and housework has become very similar to that of men's market work and housework, although women's daily total is still slightly greater.

Changes in working time in turn affect larger societal systems for allocating time and ultimately the types of workers who are channeled into part-time, full-time, and temporary and non-standard work. According to Plantenga (2003) the best systems for assuring women's participation and equality are those where: (1) the proportion of women to men in full-time positions is high; (2) a high proportion of women are in "long" part-time positions; (3) there are few jobs that require more than 45 hours a week; and (4) state regulation rather than collective bargaining is the primary form of labor protection. Flexibility in time use in and of itself, however, does not appear to bring higher benefits to the individual worker or to guarantee gender equality. Plantenga (2003) notes that while both the U.K. and the Netherlands have highly flexible working hours, there is low relative equality between male and female workers in the labor force as a whole.

As experience with flexible working times and their impact on careers has accumulated, it appears that flexible time use patterns may become more widely adopted both by individuals and societies at large. But flexibility takes different forms. One is multi-tasking or engaging in two activities at once, such as shopping and child care. Responsibilities such as child care are now more often doubled up with free time and non-market work. In the U.S. the proportions of child care given during free time or while doing something else rose from 37 to 70% of mothers' child care time between 1975 and 1998 and from 46 to 64% of fathers' child care time over the same period (Bianchi & Mattingly, 2003). On the other hand, flexibility may be understood as making possible a better balance in time spent on work and family. OECD data (2001, 136 ff) show that many couples with young children (aged under 6) would like to work less. Financially well-off parents would prefer to reduce hours more than those who are just getting by. In countries where average hours of couples are longer, they tend to prefer larger reductions in hours.

The elaboration in working-time options and places of work has opened the world of paid work to many who had formerly been excluded, thereby bringing into the labor market talents and skills that enhance productivity of the individual as well as of whole societies. Flexibility is thus a major means for adaptive upgrading that has many implications for men's and women's changing life patterns.

EXPANSION OF ROLE OPPORTUNITIES

Successful response to new challenges requires not only new deployment of time and human capital. It also requires reformulation of specific roles and job definitions to accomplish a goal. In Parsons' theory, this stage of the evolutionary process is referred to as *goal differentiation*, which means the development of several more specialized social units that together accomplish the functions once performed by a single predecessor.

The differentiation in the employers' and workers' goals is reflected in new life patterns that are the result of a proliferation of occupational choices for both women and men. Hakim (2003) emphasizes the expansion of choice that makes possible the greater influence of personal preference (rather than traditional norms) in shaping the individual's career and working schedule. She traces the elaboration of role possibilities to the contraceptive revolution, equal opportunity laws, expansion of white collar occupations, creation of jobs for secondary earners, and sufficient affluence so that preferences rather than necessity become decisive in choice of life style. The change, however, is two-sided: there must be an expansion in the occupational structure along with the expansion of choice.

National differences in the expansion of occupational opportunity are shaped by a combination of market forces, the dominant work-family culture, and the prevailing social welfare regime. Labor markets regulate employment through supply and demand by matching worker characteristics to the jobs available. Thus type of labor market system affects the type of work patterns and household income strategies that emerge. Markets with a high share of low paid and long hours are likely to generate a more unequal dual career pattern in which children are launched while young without the second earner being able to earn enough to contribute much beyond the bare necessities (such as a support for children's further education). At the other extreme are markets with strong incentives for equal participation and for relatively equal contribution by women to the family income. Those markets are characterized by a relatively narrow wage dispersion and a narrow gender pay gap and short full-time and long part-time jobs that encourage mothers to return to the labor force (Plantenga, 2003; Rubery et al., 2001). Influences on career patterns also come from the firm. Buchmann et al. (2003) show for Switzerland that women with opportunities for responsible part-time work in medium-sized firms are much more likely to return to work after an absence than those who worked in large firms. Once having left, the women from large firms were less able to find a reentry portal that allowed them to cross the barriers put up by the strong internal market of segregation that rendered part-time work peripheral and less secure.

A nation's dominant family culture also helps to account for different rates of women's employment. Scandinavian countries with their egalitarian tradition have 70–80% of their women employed, whereas the more patriarchal families of the Mediterranean countries like Italy have only about one-third of their women in the labor force (Bonke & Koch-Weser, 2003).

In Europe legal decisions by the European Court of Justice have further affected opportunity by slowly and consistently turning aside various forms of discrimination against employed women (Berghahn, 2003). These decisions prohibited categorical limits to hiring, promotion, and entitlements that treated women unequally. Similar changes in the law and court decisions in the United states widened occupational opportunity by establishing rights of women to equal pay, promotion, benefits, educational opportunities, and freedom from sexual harassment (Giele & Stebbins, 2003).

These new opportunities are not taken up, however, unless individuals and families are motivated to change by finding novel patterns more rewarding than old familiar ones. Women's rising levels of education raise the opportunity costs of staying at home, and make clear the many advantages of taking paid work. A woman's income raises the family's standard of living. In the U.S., the idea also became widespread, that to maintain households at a middle-class level, both mothers and fathers have to work (Orloff, 2001).

The distinctive life course patterns that result are the product of both changes in occupational structure and expansion of choice. As Giele (2003) shows in her chapter on innovative role patterns of women and men, mothers with careers and involved fathers are atypical in their personal identity, goals, social networks, and adaptive strategies. For the majority of the population (who are not innovators), it is the economic growth and incentives set by each country's economic and social institutions that stimulate a broader range of life choices. Bielenski and Wagner (2003) show the widespread preference on the part of women throughout Europe for more employment rather than less. Presumably it is the absence of the necessary institutional structures that keeps such preferences from being realized.

DEVELOPMENT OF NEW WORK-AND-FAMILY POLICIES

Following the expansion of time use patterns and role opportunities, the creation of new institutional arrangements is the next key challenge. Society must codify, regulate, and integrate the unfamiliar into the established social order. In the Parsonian framework this stage is one of *integration and inclusion*. For example, the greatly increased presence of mothers in the workforce is a challenge to time-honored routines of families, schools, and employers. New arrangements have to be devised, and these are the various programs and entitlements that constitute the burgeoning field of work-and-family policies.

According to Esping-Anderson (2002), contemporary family policy must solve quite different problems from that of the post-war period when the main issues were to protect jobs of male breadwinners and to support families with many children. Today the focus of family policy is on making new work arrangements possible that not only produce income but take childcare into consideration as well. While policies vary across countries; they all touch on three issues: family income support, childcare, and gender policy.

Policies for Family Income Support

Given more divorce, female-headed families, and out-of-wedlock births, governments not only have to shift from relying primarily on traditional family models to assure household welfare; they also must eliminate barriers to women's work that stem from "inadequate work-family reconciliation policies" and labor market discrimination (OECD, 2002, p. 110). Associated with this effort has been a tendency in both Europe and the U.S. to shift emphasis from social protection based on family allowances and welfare assistance to emphasis on work as the main source income (Orloff, 2001; Rubery et al., 2001). This is the emphasis that Rubery (2002, p. 125) refers to as "employment first." European countries are counting on women's increased labor force participation to prevent social exclusion of poor families as well as to raise the European employment rate to 70% (to 60% for women) by 2010 (Rubery, 2002; Rubery et al., 2001). Similarly, in the United states, the 1996 welfare reform law made women's work the key to alleviating poverty of mother-headed families (Orloff, 2001).

The critique of "employment first" comes from the fact that work opportunity is not in itself sufficient for addressing other family functions such as care for children. In addition, these "work first" policies often ignore the intertwining nature of work and family roles, and different countries handle these interconnections differently. While France has historically protected both the working woman and the mother, German legislation has tended to value the traditional mothering role more highly than women's income contributions. Consequently, the Federal Republic of Germany has been quite reluctant to provide public services that would help to reconcile family and work of wives and mothers. Only since 1977 was equity reached in the family. Both spouses were now entitled to do paid work. The division of family work is no longer decided by law. Both spouses can arrange housekeeping by mutual agreement. Since 1994, the constitutional law has encouraged equal opportunities of women and men. Despite this progress, the tax system and the social contributions still support the traditional gendered division of work by encouraging one partner (usually the wife) to remain out of the labor force or to work only part-time (Holst, 2000; OECD, 2001). The problem of reconciling work and family in Germany is thus "solved" by part-time work of the women. But rather than being a preference, it often represents a second choice.[1]

Policies for Child Care

Child care policies have made possible mothers' inclusion into the work force. As Gornick and Meyers (2003) demonstrate, various types of pre-school and after-school programs help to make parenthood compatible with work and careers. In addition, as Esping-Anderson (2002) points out, contemporary threats to the quality of childhood make it more important than ever to invest in children's early education to insure their later life chances.

Letablier (2003) provides a striking illustration of such policies in her description of the French child care system, which is supported by the state and provides a range of child care options from child minders who work in private homes to public facilities outside the home. France is a conservative family-based welfare state, but it differs from west Germany in having a weaker male breadwinner model. The protection of women as workers and mothers is due to the ideology of the Third Republic that made parents (rather than mothers only) the focus of state support. French women also had an early tradition of employment outside the home, and French legislation concerning their protection was drafted before World War I when France had many women in its labor force and their presence was seen as a normal outgrowth of the agricultural and craft economy. The French thus saw the challenge of women's childbearing and paid work as a national issue to be supported by public provision, whereas a number of other countries such as the United states and Britain enshrined the mother-homemaker as the ideal, for whom only private provision of support was thought necessary (Pedersen, 1993).

Gender Policy

New gender expectations have resulted from the fact that women as well as men now support their families. In addition, more child care is now available outside the home. No longer is it only the man's role to bring in the family income. Nor is it only woman who is responsible for the children. These new conditions ultimately bear on widespread gender norms and the implicit social contract (or "gender contract") between women and men throughout the society. At issue is the fairness of the division of labor – whether one sex is overburdened or underpaid, and whether one is more likely to be limited to the workplace and the other to the home.

Women experience inequality at work in being less likely to be employed, in more often working part-time for fewer hours and for lower pay, and in having fewer chances for promotion and opportunities to enter higher paying jobs where men predominate (Gornick, 1999; OECD, 2002). Women feel further injustice in being overburdened by the demands of both paid work and family responsibility. Women consistently report having less free time than men, and in the United states, women's percentage of free time declined 2% between 1965 and 1998, whereas men's free time increased by 3% over the same period (Bianchi & Mattingly, 2003).

The treatment of these questions is what is here referred to as gender policy. Throughout the western industrial world gender policy appears to have two strands. The "sameness" strand is focused on equality of women with men in the workplace; the "difference" strand is focused on the assumption that women's traditional caregiving functions deserve to be valued more highly, to the point that more of them are shared by men. Esping-Anderson (2002, p. 20) alludes to these two dimensions when he says that modern welfare states have to create both a new and more egalitarian equilibrium between men's and women's lives and at the same time make parenthood compatible with a life dedicated to work and careers. Gornick and Myers (2003) in their review of family policies in western industrial nations find that all deal is one way or another with two basic challenges: the definition of who will work and who will give care, and the coordination of these two kinds of activities with each other.

The "work first" policy that focuses on equality of women as workers is only a partial solution to gender injustice because employment and child care policies that help move women into the labor force tend to ignore the gender division of labor in the household and the low value attached to caring work. In arguing the case for a broader approach termed "gender mainstreaming," Rubery and co-authors (2001, p. 166) acknowledge that there is now a new ecology of work, family, and social protection. They call for a general transition to "gender-equal, dual-earner systems" that include opportunities for women to be economically independent of men both outside and inside couple households.

Nations already vary, of course, in how closely they approach this ideal; and many of their differences can be understood in terms of the well known typology of Esping-Anderson (1990, 2002) that contrasts social democratic, liberal, and corporatist states. In the Scandinavian countries, which provide a more gender-equal environment for mothers to participate in the labor force, there appears to be greater potential for individuals and families to realize both employment and family goals and preferences (Bonke & Koch-Weser, 2003). Thus the fertility rate is higher in Denmark and Sweden (where it is easier to reconcile work and family) than in Italy (where it is much more difficult for women to be mothers and to be employed). The liberal regimes, the United Kingdom and the United states, provide positive incentives for women's contribution to family income but at the same time treat workers as detached from family obligations and therefore rely on the private market rather than on government provision of social supports to the family (Blossfeld & Drobnic, 2001). Gornick and Meyers (2003) illustrate these differences with their cross-national comparison of work-family policies. Among the ten countries they describe, the U.K. and U.S. are least advanced in a number of measures of gender equality, extent of available child care, and integration of work and family. Among corporatist welfare regimes such as France and Germany, there are important national differences: French family policy is very supportive of women's employment (as is shown in its child care program) whereas German family law and the taxation system are much less so.

All in all, on the basis of the chapters in this volume, it is fair to say that gender policy is the least developed part of family policy in advanced western societies. There has been considerable progress in exploring a broader range of accepted activity for women in the labor force. Also, as shown in Giele's (2003) chapter, there is a small but growing group of involved fathers who are opening up the potential of men to take a wider range of responsibilities in the home. Overall, however, much of the direction of gender policy is still at the level of rhetoric and visionary projections. Rubery et al. (2001, p. 66) sum up the task ahead: countries must transform a "wide spectrum of social, economic, and institutional arrangements, with the goal of providing a new, coherent model of household organization to replace the outdated and gender unequal male breadwinner model." They add that "a broad strategy for transformation of households and welfare systems or even labor market systems" is also needed.

GENERALIZING THE VALUES OF WORK AND CARE

With respect to the values governing life pattern change, the most problematic issue is the higher relative value, rewards, and legitimacy that are accorded to formal paid work in public settings compared with all of the rest of life such as leisure or civic duties or intimate relationships that require caregiving and continuing effort to sustain them. Because the values surrounding care have historically and symbolically been associated with women, unpaid work, and the private world of the family, the key challenge is to lift the value of care to a more general level so that it has priority for men as well as women, and for work in public settings as well as the family. Thus the culminating challenge to widespread change in life patterns is the problem of value congruence – finding consistency between new forms of action and long-held values. In the present case, the challenge is to reconcile an emphasis on both work and care with the new distribution of paid work and caregiving between men and women and between work and family. Such an undertaking is what Parsons (1966) and Johnson (1989) termed *value generalization*, by which they meant the incorporation of new social patterns into the reigning value system.

Rubery (2002) suggests that such change is already under way. Gender mainstreaming in Europe was a direct response to the 1985 Nairobi International Women's Conference that called for the incorporation of "women's values" into development. The same theme appears in the 1998 Council of Europe statement that recognizes differences between the sexes and calls for more accommodation to the "childbearing functions of women" but also implies that men have rights and duties to care.

Other chapters in this book echo these concerns. In general, there has been more progress in extending the work culture to women and to the private family than in extending care values into the workplace or public life. Although many feminists hope that men will become caregivers to a degree symmetrical with women's involvement in paid employment, this ideal is far from being realized. Nevertheless, there are signs that the generalization of work and care values has made progress at the level of the individual, families and firms, and the nation-state.

Individual Crossovers in Work and Care

One might think of the modern life course as beginning to approach the ideal "to love and to work," a standard most famously expressed by Freud, and now widely recognized as a criterion for healthy adulthood (Smelser & Erikson, 1980). A dual emphasis on both love and work is embedded in changing time use and role patterns, as documented by chapters in this book. Well over half of mothers are now employed in most industrial societies; and according to Bianchi and Mattingly (2003), fathers in the U.S. are also giving somewhat more time to family care than once was the case. Hakim (2003) describes the expanding range of choices available to women that open up the opportunity to combine paid work with family responsibilities. Significantly, the largest group are those women who join family roles with some form of part-time rather than full-time work. Bielenski and Wagner's (2003) cross-national survey of working-time preferences also underlines the overall trend toward a combination of dual work and family responsibilities in the lives of women. If preferences were realized, the differences between working times of men and women would diminish across Europe as well as within countries. Nearly half would opt for an "egalitarian" role pattern with respect to employment. The traditional family breadwinner model would become less common, and one or both partners would work shorter working hours than the current full-time norm.

Men's growing commitment to care is seen in Giele's (2003) review of research on "involved fathers" who as a group give a big place in their lives to caregiving alongside paid work. Conversely, the ambitious and innovative women whom Giele describes are unusually involved in their careers in addition to their family responsibilities. However, despite such examples of more individuals crossing over the boundaries between work and care, the "male" model of career success (which puts greatest value on career achievement and relegates care to much lower priority) is still predominant in the top ranks of business, the professions, and academia (Appelbaum et al., 2002).

The Value of Paid Work to the Family

In the family, the value of equality is being discovered along with growing awareness that the wife's employment is a benefit to the family. In her chapter on mutual dependence in married couples, Sorensen (2003) recasts findings from existing scholarly studies to show the implicit value of a wife's paid work to her husband. Up to now much more emphasis has been put on the wife's employment as a basis for splitting and independence that leads to separation or divorce. Bonke and Koch-Weser's (2003) survey of time use in Denmark,

Sweden, France, and Italy demonstrates that the benefit of a wife's employment and husband's caregiving is well understood in the Scandinavian counties. In Italy where the gender role differentiation and integration of work and family is less advanced, men and women are much more likely to take an either/or position on gainful employment and homemaking rather than sharing these responsibilities by doing both. Gornick and Meyers (2003) reflect the coexistence of several models of family structure in their typology of breadwinner, dual earner part-time, dual earner full-time, and dual earner-dual carer couples. Each nation believes in values of equality and care but realizes them with different degrees of overlap across the boundaries of male and female roles and work and family spheres.

The Value of Care in the Workplace

The frontier of value generalization in the workplace concerns the value of care, particularly the right to working times and leave arrangements that facilitate a worker's absence for giving care to family members. These issues appear in chapters by Piore (2003) and Betzelt and Gottschall (2003) on the changing nature of the workplace. Both chapters mention the new ways of organizing work that rely on project-teams and thereby may involve women workers more easily. The new German media professions do offer greater opportunities for women, but those who work in them nonetheless tend to be young and childless. Buchmann et al. (2003) show that the firms most encouraging to mothers' employment at a managerial or professional level are smaller, probably more personal, and less likely to have the formality and strong internal hierarchies that keep women out. Plantenga (2003) gives a glimpse of the ways that employment arrangements bear on both equality and care. The provision of part-time work opportunities and short full-time positions addresses both concerns. Through flexible work schedules women have a greater chance to be employed (the work dimension). At the same time, the opportunities for flexibility and "mothers' hours" help them be available for their families (the care dimension).

The changed priorities between work and care are eventually reflected in the law. In her review of recent developments in European equality law, Berghahn (2003) recounts the directives and legal precedents for equal hiring of women, provision of equal opportunities for promotion and training, and court decisions prohibiting discrimination based on sex and family status. Piore (2003) also points to the implications of the equal rights movement for employment in the United states. It is no longer easy for unions and internal labor markets to channel men into higher paying primary jobs. The human resources departments of companies are reviewing the hiring records and encouraging openness of the process and attention to diversity of those who are recruited and offered positions. The larger significance of this trend for the generalization of work and care values is contained in the subtle shift in some firms from a primary emphasis on productivity and profit to a concern for larger issues of human resources and diversity. Consistent with this tendency is the increasing attention given by employers in some firms to providing such benefits as family leave and provision for their workers' civic and caregiving obligations which extend beyond the workplace. (It must also be noted, however, that strong economic competition can at the same time reduce job stability, raise the number of non-standard and temporary positions, and thereby weaken the firm's obligation to provide care-related benefits. Betzelt and Gottschall (2003) hint at these potential side effects in their account of growing flexibility in the German film and publishing industries.)

National Variation in the Balance of Work and Care

Gornick and Meyers (2003) provide an overview of the policies that generalize the values of care to society as a whole. The countries where the generalization process has gone the furthest have universal programs of child care, three-week paid vacations, and paid parental and family leaves. Where care is still primarily considered the responsibility of families, the child care programs and parental leaves are much less generous, less nearly universal, and more likely to be a private than a public responsibility. Letablier's (2003) case study of child care provision in France is an excellent example of how the value of care can be generalized to the level of a whole society. Most Western nations, however, put higher priority on the health of the economy and the availability of employment than on the provision of child care, health care, or other forms of social protection (with the understandable rationale that a healthy economy and good jobs are needed first to make the rest possible).

Thus, there is still a long way to go in establishing the value of care at a broad cultural level where every citizen and every organization feels a responsibility for taking care and giving support to care as a public value. Even in the face of huge social costs, the social democratic countries have experienced the greatest success along these lines. The corporatist states retain their social protection provided by unions, employers, and families but at the high cost of losing trade to countries where goods can be produced more cheaply. The liberal capitalist states, on the other hand, with their tendency to turn over care and protection to private families or charities, are more likely to exhibit large disparities in the standard of living between elites and the poor.

Despite these different national profiles, there is increasing pressure to expand public support for caregiving in response to changing life patterns. The major question then becomes how to pay for the costs involved. In the Scandinavian countries this problem is evident in high taxes and threats to social programs when the economy tightens. In the corporatist states, social costs are blamed for jeopardizing national competitiveness by building them into the higher price of goods. In the liberal capitalist nations the problem is the low pay and scarce supply of care workers. Although not treated in this volume, these matters of social costs and who will bear them are the next frontier in balancing the values of work and care.

SUMMARY

The task of this chapter has been to draw together the findings on life pattern change from the subsequent chapters in this book to show recurring themes and their internal logic. The evidence comes from a total of eighteen countries: Norway, the United Kingdom, the United states, and fifteen member states of the European Union. Some chapters are devoted to one country alone; others to cross-national comparisons.

There are four key themes. First is the changing time use of adult men and women. Second are expanding role choices, especially of women. Third is the emergence of work and family policies that incorporate the new role changes into societal institutions. Finally, although not yet fully realized is a coming reconfiguration of the value system to give higher priority to caregiving in relation to productive work. These themes turn out to be cognates of four stages in Talcott Parsons' description of evolutionary upgrading, which he saw as the principal mechanism by which societies modernize. Miriam Johnson built on Parsons' theory to identify the same processes in the gender revolution. *Adaptive upgrading* is the means for reconfiguring time use and other resources. *Goal differentiation* involves the expansion of male and female role choices. *Inclusion and integration* create broader norms and standards to encompass a wider range of masculine and feminine behavior. Lastly, *value generalization* links these changes in life patterns to long-held principles and affirms their integrity. These four processes are arranged in a hierarchy from most concrete to most abstract wherein the greatest change is seen first at the more concrete levels of time use, technology, and role choices. But the change is reciprocal: changes in abstract institutions and values reinforce and help to reproduce new patterns of time use and new role choices of men and women.

At the most concrete level of social life, technological advances and changes in working-time patterns challenge old rigidities and make possible more efficient and competitive organization of resources. Chapters in this book by Bianchi and Mattingly (Chapter 5), Bielenski and Wagner (Chapter 7), and Bonke and

Koch-Weser (Chapter 11) all touch on individual time use and preferences. The overall trend in time use is toward greater flexibility in working schedules and places of work. There is also more multi-tasking and more interpenetration between such domains as childcare and leisure time activity. When work and care responsibilities are added up, men continue to have more leisure time than women.

The expansion of role opportunities has led to a redefinition and broadening of male and female spheres that is especially evident in the widespread employment of mothers with young children. A wider range of role choices is also reflected in the phenomenon of involved fathers who are principal or equal caretakers of their children. Hakim (Chapter 4), Buchmann et al. (Chapter 8), Betzelt and Gottschall (Chapter 12), Sorensen (Chapter 13), and Giele (Chapter 14) all point to these changes and suggest how they have come about. In addition, Piore (Chapter 2), Plantenga (Chapter 6), and Berghahn (Chapter 10) note that part-time work and other more flexible arrangements, as well as laws against sex discrimination have furthered the expansion of women's choices in employment.

Work and family policies help to reconcile the new patterns and role structures with the old. The principal challenge is to assure that socialization and proper care of children and families continue under new conditions where more women are employed outside the home. Chapters by Gornick and Myers (Chapter 3) and Letablier (Chapter 9) show the various national policies by which this can be done with differing levels of state involvement and wide variation in gender expectations regarding breadwinning, caretaking, and household organization.

Finally, all of the preceding changes in use of time and resources, role choice, and family policy are fully established only when they are legitimized by the core values of the society. The key challenge of life pattern change in every nation today is to raise the value and rewards of caregiving. Higher pay and greater respect must be accorded to care workers, and greater priority must be given to care of children and families on each national agenda, while at the same time protecting women's freedom for education and employment and preserving the productive competitiveness of each society as a whole. This challenge is only faintly outlined by chapters in this book, but it appears to be the next major frontier in the establishment of new life patterns in the Western world.

NOTE

1. In the former German Democratic Republic – now east Germany – women were expected to work. Accordingly, child care provision was and still is much higher than in West-Germany. Still different is the higher employment rate of east German women, and their part-time work is often involuntary because few full-time jobs are available. Part-timers

in west Germany, who are used to more conservative attitudes, are mostly happy with reduced employment.

REFERENCES

Appelbaum, E., Bailey, T., Berg, P., & Kalleberg, A. L. (2002). Shared work/valued care: New norms for organizing market work and unpaid care work. In: H. Mosley, J. O'Reilly & K. Schömann (Eds), *Labour Markets, Gender and Institutional Change: Essays in Honour of Günther Schmid* (pp. 136–165). Northampton, MA: Edward Elgar.

Berghahn, S. (2003). The influence of European Union legislation on labor market equality for women. In: J. Z. Giele & E. Holst (Eds), *Advances in Life-course Research: Changing Life Patterns in Western Industrial Societies* (Vol. 8, pp. 211–236). Oxford: Elsevier.

Betzelt, S., & Gottschall, K. (2003). Publishing and the new media professions as forerunners of pioneer work and life patterns. In: J. Z. Giele & E. Holst (Eds), *Advances in Life-course Research: Changing Life Patterns in Western Industrial Societies* (Vol. 8, pp. 257–280). Oxford: Elsevier.

Bianchi, S. M., & Mattingly, M. J. (2003). Time, work, and family in the United States. In: J. Z. Giele & E. Holst (Eds), *Advances in Life-course Research: Changing Life Patterns in Western Industrial Societies* (Vol. 8, pp. 95–118). Oxford: Elsevier.

Bielenski, H., & Wagner, A. (2003). Employment options of men and women in Europe. In: J. Z. Giele & E. Holst (Eds), *Advances in Life-course Research: Changing Life Patterns in Western Industrial Societies* (Vol. 8, pp. 137–162). Oxford: Elsevier.

Blossfeld, H.-P., & Drobnic, S. (2001). *Careers of couples in contemporary societies: From male breadwinner to dual-earner families.* New York: Oxford University Press.

Bonke, J., & Koch-Weser, E. (2003). The welfare state and time allocation in Sweden, Denmark, France, and Italy. In: J. Z. Giele & E. Holst (Eds), *Advances in Life-course Research: Changing Life Patterns in Western Industrial Societies* (Vol. 8, pp. 231–253). Oxford: Elsevier.

Buchmann, M., Kriesi, I., & Sacchi, S. (2003). Labor-market structures and women's paid work: Opportunities and constraints in the Swiss labor market. In: J. Z. Giele & E. Holst (Eds), *Advances in Life-course Research: Changing Life Patterns in Western Industrial Societies* (Vol. 8, pp. 165–180). Oxford: Elsevier.

Esping-Anderson, G. (1990). *The three worlds of welfare capitalism.* Princeton, NJ: Princeton University Press.

Esping-Anderson, G. (2002). Towards the good society, once again? In: G. Esping-Anderson with D. Gallie, A. Hemerijk & J. Myles (Eds), *Why We Need a New Welfare State.* Oxford: Oxford University Press.

Giele, J. Z. (2003). Women and men as agents of change in their own lives. In: J. Z. Giele & E. Holst (Eds), *Advances in Life-course Research: Changing Life Patterns in Western Industrial Societies* (Vol. 8, pp. 299–317). Oxford: Elsevier.

Giele, J. Z., & Stebbins, L. F. (2003). *Women and equality in the workplace.* Santa Barbara, CA: ABC-CLIO.

Gornick, J. C. (1999). Gender equality in the labour market. In: D. Sainsbury (Ed.), *Gender and Welfare State Regimes* (pp. 210–242). New York: Oxford University Press.

Gornick, J. C., & Meyers, M. K. (2003). Welfare regimes in relation to paid work and care. In: J. Z. Giele & E. Holst (Eds), *Advances in Life-course Research: Changing Life Patterns in Western Industrial Societies* (Vol. 8, pp. 45–68). Oxford: Elsevier.

Hakim, C. (2003). Lifestyle preferences vs. patriarchal values: Causal and non-causal attitudes. In: J. Z. Giele & E. Holst (Eds), *Advances in Life-course Research: Changing Life Patterns in Western Industrial Societies* (Vol. 8, pp. 69–92). Oxford: Elsevier.

Holst, E. (2000). *Die stille reserve am arbeitsmarkt. groesse – zusammensetzung – verhalten. (The hidden labor force. size – composition – behaviour)*. Berlin: Edition Sigma.

Johnson, M. M. (1989). Feminism and the theories of Talcott Parsons. In: R. A. Wallace (Ed.), *Feminism and Sociological Theory* (pp. 101–118). Newbury Park, CA: Sage Publications.

Letablier, M.-T. (2003). Work and family balance: A new challenge for politics in France. In: J. Z. Giele & E. Holst (Eds), *Advances in Life-course Research: Changing Life Patterns in Western Industrial Societies* (Vol. 8, pp. 189–210). Oxford: Elsevier.

OECD (2001). Balancing work and family life: Helping parents into paid employment. *OECD Employment Outlook*, 127–165.

OECD (2002). Women at work: Who are they and how are they faring? *OECD Employment Outlook*, 62–125.

Orloff, A. (2001). Ending the entitlements of single mothers: Changing social policies, women's employment, and caregiving in the contemporary United States. In: N. J. Hirschman & U. Liebert (Eds), *Women and Welfare: Theory and Practice in the United States and Europe* (pp. 133–159). New Brunswick, NJ: Rutgers University Press.

Parsons, T. (1966). *Societies; evolutionary and comparative perspectives*. Englewood Cliffs, NJ: Prentice-Hall.

Pedersen, S. (1993). *Family, dependence, and the origins of the welfare state: Britain and France, 1914–1945*. Cambridge: Cambridge University Press.

Piore, M. J. (2003). The reconfiguration of work and employment relations in the United States at the turn of the century. In: J. Z. Giele & E. Holst (Eds), *Advances in Life-course Research: Changing Life Patterns in Western Industrial Societies* (Vol. 8, pp. 23–44). Oxford: Elsevier.

Plantenga, J. (2003). Changing work and life patterns: Examples of new working-time arrangements in the European member states. In: J. Z. Giele & E. Holst (Eds), *Advances in Life-course Research: Changing Life Patterns in Western Industrial Societies* (Vol. 8, pp. 119–136). Oxford: Elsevier.

Rubery, J. (2002). Gender mainstreaming and European employment policy. In: H. Mosley, J. O'Reilly & K. Schömann (Eds), *Labour Markets, Gender, and Institutional Change* (pp. 111–135). Cheltenham, UK: Edward Elgar.

Rubery, J., Smith, M., Anxo, D., & Flood, L. (2001). The future European labor supply: The critical role of the family. *Feminist Economics*, 7, 38–69.

Smelser, N. J., & Erikson, E. H. (1980). *Themes of work and love in adulthood*. Cambridge, MA: Harvard University Press.

Sørensen, A. (2003). Economic relations between women and men: New realities and the re-interpretation of dependence. In: J. Z. Giele & E. Holst (Eds), *Advances in Life-course Research: Changing Life Patterns in Western Industrial Societies* (Vol. 8, pp. 281–297). Oxford: Elsevier.

2. THE RECONFIGURATION OF WORK AND EMPLOYMENT RELATIONS IN THE UNITED STATES AT THE TURN OF THE CENTURY

Michael J. Piore

ABSTRACT

This chapter traces the changes in the regime governing work relations in the United States over the last twenty years. The change is essentially from collective bargaining to a system of regulation through substantive law. The chapter argues that this change reflects a more fundamental shift in the axis of political mobilization from mobilization around economic identities based on class, profession and enterprise affiliation to mobilization around social identities such as race, sex, ethnicity, sexual orientation, age and physical disability. Behind this shift are still more basic changes in the family as a social unit and the corporate enterprise as an economic institution.

NOTE FROM THE EDITORS

Although this chapter is not explicitly focused on changing life patterns, Professor Piore documents the surrounding cultural and economic conditions that have

Changing Life Patterns in Western Industrial Societies
Advances in Life Course Research, Volume 8, 23–44
© 2004 Published by Elsevier Ltd.
ISSN: 1040-2608/doi:10.1016/S1040-2608(03)08002-X

changed the character of work and its relation to family life. His account suggests that there are links between the reconfiguration in employment relations, new working schedules, the evolving family division of labor (between breadwinning and caregiving), and the changing definitions of what men and women do. Under the old structure the primary segment of the labor market had positive functions for assuring security to the worker, continuity in training opportunities, and security for the families that the male worker supported. Since roughly 1970, internal labor markets have been under siege from global competition and the new equality laws. New labor conditions (collapse of unions, the radicalized free market, etc.) have made work insecure and undermined the "family wage" that used to be paid to men as breadwinners. Women's rising labor force participation has filled the gap in family income caused by the rising employment insecurity and falling relative income of male breadwinners. In response to these changing conditions, the U.S. has responded first with more government regulation of employment, especially equal opportunity laws that have implications for women, racial minorities and other identity groups; second, with social programs such as welfare reform that emphasize work for women (even mothers) as well as men; and third, with an evolution in the structure of work itself that is giving ever larger emphasis to a project/team approach. While this chapter is focused on the United States, a question of particular interest for this book is the degree to which the same trends are also found in other Western industrial societies.

INTRODUCTION

The last thirty years have witnessed a major upheaval in national labor relations and labor market policies throughout the world. The United States has been in the vanguard of these changes, initiating many of them itself and pressuring other countries to follow suit through its role in the major organizations that control and direct the international economic order. The changes have been promoted and understood as part of a broader movement toward a competitive market economy. This paper reviews the evolution of labor policy in the United States, and argues that the changes are a reflection of long-term fundamental changes in the evolution of the social structure and the economy. As such, they are difficult to understand as the outcome of a coherent strategy, and they have led to a labor market which, while structured and regulated in a different way, is not in any obvious sense more flexible, open and competitive than it was in the past. Many of the forces which have been playing themselves out in the transformation of the American labor market are also present, albeit to different degrees, in other countries, and the key role of the U.S. in international economic policies suggests that we need to rethink the trends and options in economic development more broadly.

The paper is organized in four broad sections: The first looks at the old structure and the emergent alternative; the second focuses on the changing social structure and the shifting boundary between the society and the economy; the third on new forms of work organization; and a fourth section concludes.

COLLAPSE OF THE OLD STRUCTURE AND EMERGENCE OF NEW ALTERNATIVES

In the early postwar years, there emerged in the United States a fairly well-defined and coherent system of work regulation and employment relations. The system was structured and defined institutionally by legislation, administrative regulations, and managerial practices that grew out of the Great Depression and World War II and were consolidated in the immediate postwar period (Barenberg, 1993, 1994; Kochan et al., 1986; Piore, 1982; Piore & Sabel, 1984; Stone, 1992).

The system was one in which the Government set minimum substantive standards that defined the floor of the labor market. Above that floor, it created a set of procedural standards, but left the substantive terms and conditions of employment to be determined privately within the procedures it had laid out. Essentially, those procedures guaranteed the right of workers to form and join trade unions, and of those unions, once formed, to negotiate wages, hours, and other terms and conditions of employment through collective bargaining.

Below the substantive floor were a series of "uncovered" jobs, largely in agriculture and in certain menial services such as laundries and hospitals. Coverage was extended to most of these jobs in the course of the 1950s and 1960s.

As a result of the government-sanctioned procedures in the broad, middle tier of the wage distribution, employment conditions were effectively set and regulated by collective bargaining. Trade union coverage was extensive and firms that were not actually organized were forced to follow collective bargaining settlements to forestall union organization of the shops. Managerial and professional employees at the top of the wage hierarchy were exempt from coverage and their terms and conditions of employment were determined by the market, albeit a market conditioned by the governmental sector that employed a substantial portion of the highly educated labor force and where employment conditions were set by bureaucratic rules and procedures. In the middle and upper tier, employees had, in effect, long-term job security. For professional and managerial employees this security was virtually absolute, although it was not explicitly recognized. In the middle tier of the labor market, governed by collective bargaining, what tended to evolve was an elaborate system of lay-offs and recalls, in which seniority and carefully delineated jobs played an important role (Doeringer & Piore, 1971; Piore, 1986).

Key Institutions and Underlying Assumptions

This system was built around four key institutions and a series of assumptions about the role they played in an industrial economy: the family; the productive enterprise; the trade union; and the nation-state (in the U.S. context, the Federal government). In the economy itself, the key productive institution was the corporate enterprise. The enterprise was understood to be a stable, well-defined and enduring unit to which employment rights could be attached. The family was the key social institution. Like the enterprise, it was understood to be stable, well-defined and enduring. It was assumed to stand outside the productive economy, but to be represented there by a single, dominant male wage earner whose income was its primary means of support. Conflicts between the social and the economic realm were to be reconciled by adjustments to the terms and conditions of employment of the male wage earner (and family head). Rank-and-file workers were organized into and represented by the third major institution, the trade union, which thus effectively mediated between the social and economic realm by negotiating with the productive enterprise. The employment system was embedded in a relatively closed, national territory, placing the government of that territory (the nation-state) in a position to exert effective control over macro-economic conditions and the competitive environment of individual industries (Osterman et al., 2001).

The implications of this assumption were played out in the design of a variety of other, supplementary, institutions. The system of public assistance to those who did not work was, for example, targeted at female-headed families where, due to widowhood, separation, or divorce, there was no male support.

A final assumption important in the design of the American system of work relations was the idea of mass production as the dominant technological form and one that made it possible, and efficient, to lay out work in terms of a series of well-defined tasks. The tasks were in turn combined into jobs. Those jobs defined the responsibilities of the worker, and the terms and conditions of employment negotiated in collective bargaining were attached to these job definitions (Piore & Sabel, 1984).

The Trade Union Collapse

The proximate cause of the system's decline was the collapse of trade union membership. Membership reached its peak in the mid-1950s, but the decline thereafter was very gradual and did not lead to a perceptible shift in union power until the 1970s. In the second half of the 1970s, union membership declined noticeably, and in the 1980s it virtually collapsed. In the face of that collapse, unions were forced to engage in a process of concession bargaining in which many of the gains of the early postwar decades were relinquished. Indices of strikes and other forms of labor unrest fell to virtually zero, and the direction of determination was reversed, so that the non-union sector began to set the pattern that unions were then forced to follow.

The collapse of collective bargaining in the 1980s ushered in a period of rapidly rising inequality of income (although the causal connection is much disputed). Median earnings stagnated throughout the 1980s, and most of the 1990s as well (the stagnation actually began in the mid-1970s); earnings in the lower half of the distribution fell, and those of higher income workers rose substantially. The premium for education and experience rose. These trends moderated slightly in the two years preceeding the peak of the boom. However, the recession that then developed very rapidly and continued seemed-destined to aggravate them once again (DiNardo et al., 1996; Katz & Autor, 1999; Katz & Murphy, 1995; Levy, 1998).

Income and employment insecurity also increased. The data do not show the impact of job tenure that one might expect, and in this sense, are ambiguous, but the institutional environment changed fundamentally. The de facto guarantees which accompanied professional and managerial jobs were eliminated and the de jure protections for lower levels of workers were widely repealed (Jacoby, 1999; Jaeger & Stevens, 1999; Katz, 2002; Neumark, 2000; Neumark et al., 1999; Osterman, 1996, 1999).

One of the puzzles of the current period is why these trends in income and security have been so little resisted. There has been virtually no protest or general social mobilization. As noted earlier, indices of labor unrest have fallen over the last twenty years to historic lows.

Other Factors in Collapse

More fundamental reasons for the collapse of the old system include: a shift in political power toward management; deregulation and globalization, which increased competitive pressure on wages, particularly at the bottom of the labor market; the breakdown of the enterprise as a stable and enduring institution, as many companies were under threat of bankruptcy and were forced to lay off workers; the development of new organizational structures that called into question the boundaries of the enterprise and with them the structures around which collective bargaining had been organized; and, new production techniques, on the one hand, and the overall instability of the business environment, on the other, which made the well-defined jobs to which employment rights had been linked in collective bargaining increasingly anachronistic and inconsistent with managerial efficiency.

All of these factors have been discussed at length in other writing. They played an important role in virtually all industrialized countries in this period. Three factors may have made the American crisis more acute. First, is the centrality of well-defined and stable jobs to the American system of work regulation through collective bargaining. Second, is the American unitary system of worker representation, rooted in the shop itself, that extends from there to the plant, company, and industry as a whole. Hence, it is not easy to make concessions in the shop without calling into question the institution as a whole. This is very different from the situation in Germany where the works councils in the shop are separate and distinct from the unions, which operate largely outside the company (Thelen, 1991); or even Great Britain, where there is an independent shop steward tradition (Hinton, 1973). Third, is the long American tradition of extreme managerial hostility toward trade unions that is not present in many European countries – or at least not with the same degree of intensity and ideological fervor.

Emergent Alternatives: The High Road/Low Road Dichotomy

The labor market that developed in the wake of the collapse of collective bargaining in the 1980s has been widely viewed as being the result of unilateral employer control, market forces, and/or social anarchy, depending upon one's perspective and political predisposition. Insofar as the new labor situation is the expression of a coherent theory, it is the result of an idealized neoclassical model of a competitive labor market.

At the time, a number of us observing developments in the manufacturing sector predicted that employers exercising the newly achieved discretion in a competitive environment shaped by the new technology, deregulations, and, above all, competitive pressure from the global marketplace, would pursue one of two alternative strategies. We used a shorthand for these two adjustment paths "the low road" "and the high road" (Herzenberg et al., 1998; Kochan et al., 1986; Piore, 1995). One strategy, the "low road," was to compete on the basis of cost. This was likely to result in increased pressure on wages and other employment benefits and a speed-up in the pace of production on the shop floor, but without any fundamental change in the way in which work was organized and managed. The alternative strategy, the "high road," was to move up-market, competing on the basis of quality and product differentiation through an increasing variety of products, more rapid response to changing market conditions, and the like. This second response required the introduction of a variety of new work practices and managerial techniques, many of which had been pioneered in Japan. The new practices required increased commitment on the part of the workforce, greater labor-management cooperation, and a reduction in the distance between managers and workers. We presumed that to achieve this new relationship with the work force, firms would have to maintain wages and offer enhanced employment security, as was the practice at the time in Japan. Blue collar workers, it seemed, would be treated more and more like managerial and professional employees.

As the adjustment process has played out over the last two decades, it has become apparent that the dichotomy was both overdrawn and, given our own values, overly optimistic. The new work practices have spread very widely, although often piecemeal and not in the form of the complete "system" that we envisaged. But they have not been accompanied by either the higher wages or the enhanced employment security we foresaw. If anything, managerial professional workers are treated more like blue collar workers; not the other way around. Indeed, the labor force does not seem to require particular incentives to be drawn into these new cooperative regimes, and the effect of the work practices on employee welfare depends largely on labor market conditions and labor power in the form of union organizations (or the threat thereof). Thus, it would be hard to say that the market constitutes a benign form of social regulation or even that it has the potential in the current period to do so.

An Alternative: Social and Administrative Regulation

But, in fact, the elements of a system of social regulation, not driven by the market, but different from the postwar period, had already begun to emerge in the late 1960s, when the postwar structures were at their apogee. The broad lines of that alternative are now readily apparent (Dobbin & Kelly, 2002; Dobbin & Sutton, 1998; Kelly & Dobbin, 1998; Stone, 2001; Sutton et al., 1994). The key is a series of governmentally imposed substantive terms and conditions of employment which now extend well beyond the floor of the labor market that was regulated under the old system, to the employment hierarchy as a whole. The regulations derive from federal legislation, as detailed and interpreted by a panoply of new administrative structures created to implement them, and have been reviewed by the courts. The courts have also been active in extending direct government regulation and oversight of employment on their own. This process began with Title VII of the Civil Rights Act of 1964, which was designed to prohibit employment discrimination on the basis of race and which created the Equal Employment Opportunities Commission (the EEOC) to enforce that prohibition. Similar protection was extended in the course of the 1970s to other minority and socially stigmatized groups: women and ethnic minorities; people with disabilities (Acemoglu & Angrist, 2001); the aged; and, at the state and local level, gays and lesbians. Substantive regulation of health and safety in the workplace was also expanded in the 1960s and 1970s. The Federal government created a special agency to supervise private pensions plans. Other obligations that were legislatively imposed include advance notice of layoffs and the Family Leave Act (Kelly & Dobbin, 1999). The courts have moved to abrogate the doctrine of employment at will and have become increasingly willing to infer the existence of an individual employment contract and to enforce its provisions (Autor, 2003; Autor et al., 2002; Edelman et al., 1992; Morriss, 1995). Because the outcome of judicial rights created through extensive litigation, was initially very problematic, the first cases concerned only the most lucrative employments at the very top of the wage hierarchy. But as the judicial precedents have accumulated, the rights that are being established have become accessible to workers more generally.

The emergent system of substantive regulation is tremendously cumbersome and economically burdensome to the firms upon which it is imposed. Because the regulations have developed piecemeal, there is no place in the system or point in the process at which their overall burden is assessed and the costs of different regulations weighed against each other or against the economic survival of the enterprise and the value of the jobs that are at stake. Responsibility for the enforcement of the regulations is moreover spread across a number of different administrative agencies and levels of government. Responsibility is divided between these federal agencies, overlapping state and local agencies, and the courts, again at the federal, state, and local levels that are all charged with similar mandates.

Thus, enterprises are faced with multiple reporting requirements and multiple inspectors and site visits. They have responded in two ways. One has been to create internal administrative mechanisms designed to insure compliance and deal with the external institutional environments. These mechanisms are lodged in the human resource departments and in the special groups charged with insuring and managing "diversity." The effect of these developments is to foster the development of internal personnel management codes and insure their enforcement in a way in which they come to substitute for (and where unions still exist, supplement) collective bargaining agreements. The way in which the emergent system of regulation supports such codes and extends to areas of the employment relationship not directly covered by government regulation is suggested by the issue of sexual harassment of women: It is impossible to prove that particular personnel actions which punish women workers do not constitute sexual harassment unless there is a personnel code which establishes these regulations and is applied to male workers as well.

A second reaction which began in the late 1980s and has spread during the 1990s is a form of employment contract in which prospective workers are obliged to agree to take all employment complaints to private arbitration instead of pursuing administrative and judicial remedies (Stone, 1996, 2001). These agreements were initially of very dubious legality. But in a major decision in the spring of 2001, they were upheld by the Supreme Court (Supreme Court, 2001). As a result private arbitration will undoubtedly spread very rapidly. Judging from the evolution of judicial supervision of arbitration in collective bargaining, the courts will now develop a set of standards governing these arbitration proceedings and the judicial review that is likely to follow. A potential outcome is that this new form of private arbitration will become the capstone of the new system of labor regulation. Behind these developments in the social regulation of employment lie a series of more fundamental trends in the evolution of the social and productive structures. We focus on two of those here.

SHIFTS IN THE BORDERS BETWEEN SOCIETY, ECONOMY, AND POLITICS

As noted earlier, the postwar system of work and employment relations assumed a sharp division between the economic and social realms, each with its own characteristic institutions: the enterprise in the economic realm; and the family (or household) in the social. The two were connected by the dominant male wage earner – the pater familius – who moved back and forth between them. In the economic realm, this wage earner had a clear identity as a worker or professional. Other identities, in terms of religious and ethnic affiliations, which have always been quite important in the United States, were social in character. Ira Katznelson (1981) has argued that this division was reflected in politics, and led to a separation between work issues from other political issues (see also Cohen, 1990). This would help explain the rise of the ethnic political machines in large cities of the North and the absence in the United States of a labor party.

The distinction between these different realms, or at least the way in which they are defined, has broken down in the last two decades. The breakdown suggests an explanation of the new system of social regulation in the workplace. It also helps us to understand the tolerance of the society for the increasing dispersion of income and the deteriorating conditions of employment at the bottom of the labor market and the difficulty of union revival.

The most important factor in the breakdown of the old division is the enormous increase in female labor force participation. Now over 60% of women with children under three years of age are currently active labor market participants. Adjustments in the wage of male workers are no longer either necessary or sufficient conditions for adjustments in the welfare of the family. The tension between work and family depends in part on certain kinds of social arrangements such as those for custodial care for children, the sick and the aged, the

remedy for which is not necessarily to be found in the workplace, particularly if the workplace itself is no longer willing or able to provide continuity
of employment.

A second factor, related but distinct, is the way in which women and other
socially stigmatized groups have come to see their problems in the workplace as
related to their social identities and not to their identities as workers. This concep-
tualization actually began, not with women, but with the civil rights movement in
the 1960s. In that period, the leading black organizations made a strategic decision
to model their pursuit of employment opportunity in the workplace on their
experience with desegregation in education. As a result, they chose legislative and
judicial remedies for employment problems rather than strategies which would
have worked directly through workplace organizations, i.e. organizing trade
unions and asserting their political power within the labor movement. The civil
rights movement created the models of action and of institutional arrangements
that all of the other identity groups (women, ethnic minorities, the physically
handicapped, the aged, gays and lesbians, etc.) subsequently used. As a result,
these other groups came to define their problems in the workplace, as black
workers had defined their problems, as an outgrowth of their social status broadly
conceived rather than their status as workers (Greenberg, 1994). (The alternative
strategy was that of the Jewish and Italian labor movements in the garment and
construction industries in the first half of the twentieth century who organized
not on the basis of their ethnic identity but their status as workers (Fraser, 1993).)
Having defined their problems in this way, women, like the blacks, sought
solutions through legislative and judicial remedies rather than union politics and
collective bargaining. This in turn reinforced the shift from the postwar system
where the government created a procedural framework for collectively-bargained
workplace regulations, to the emergent system of the direct substantive regulation
of work by the government (Dobbin & Sutton, 1998; Lichtenstein, 2002;
Stein, 1998).

Economists, by judging economic developments in terms of the original
postwar model (which emphasized social class, rather than the new model, which
emphasizes identity affiliations) may have misunderstood the welfare implications
of the changing work and employment arrangements. Judged in terms of social
class, there has been an enormous deterioration of welfare at the bottom of the
labor market and an apparent regression in worker rights. The result is quite the
opposite when measured in terms of the social welfare of identity groups such
as women and minorities. The vocal identity groups today were all treated as
second-class citizens in the workplace regimes that grew out of the trade union
movement in the 1930s. But, in the last several decades, there have been significant
advances for all of these groups in terms of job access and in the prohibition

against harassment by fellow workers and by managerial supervisors. For women, these advances are reflected in a reduction in the earnings differential. Other groups, particularly blacks and certain ethnic minorities, have not experienced a similar improvement in relative earnings, but they have experienced an enormous improvement in their social position more broadly conceived. To the extent that they do not see work issues as a separate category, but rather as part and parcel of their social position more broadly, any deterioration in wages and working conditions is compensated by gains in other aspects of their lives.

Once people begin to measure progress in terms of such identity groups rather than in terms of social class, the reference point for social comparison began to shift as well. Women and minorities no longer compare themselves to earlier generations of workers in comparable jobs but to earlier members of their own identity group. Thus people who occupy the lower positions in the income distribution are likely to have an enormous sense of progress because the lower positions are increasingly made up of women and immigrants from abroad. Relative to the position of their parents, and, in the case of immigrants, relative to their opportunities at home, their current position in the American labor market now represents considerable upward mobility. Indeed, one can argue that social mobilization in the United States historically should be understood in terms of identity politics rather than working class politics. The two great periods of worker mobilization in the United States, the period of the 1930s and the period of the 1960s, were also the periods in which social mobility relative to earlier generations of the same ethnic and racial groups were blocked. The 1930s was a period when social mobility for the children of immigrants was blocked relative to that of their parents. The 1960s was a similar period for the children of black migrants from the South to the North (Piore, 1979).

In many ways, the most radical change in U.S. social regulation in the last twenty years was the abolition in 1996 of the U.S. system of public assistance which was created as part of the New Deal social legislation in the 1930s. Viewed from a social class perspective, this reform appears as the final victory of neo-liberalism. But in the context of the changing boundary between social and economic life and the reconceptualization of social welfare in terms of identity groups based on race, sex, and ethnicity, this reform appears very differently. The old public assistance system reflected the model of the family as a stable and well-defined institution represented in the labor market by a male head. On that basis it was designed to support single women with small children at home. These women were originally widows who had lost their husbands; in the postwar period, they were increasingly women who had never married or had been deserted or divorced. As both divorce and single motherhood became more and more common and even married women with small children typically worked, the system became increasingly anachronistic. The single women supported by the state at home began to appear as a privileged class. From this perspective, the reform was contradictory. It phased out income support and forced the clients into the labor market. But in an attempt to facilitate the transition, the reform offered the former clients special services, daycare, transportation, and job training. These services reproduce what appears to some to be an inequity of entitlement that is based on family obligation above return to work. In some states (the states were given the freedom to design these services themselves using federal money), the new services generated by the reform process have been made available to all women. It remains to be seen whether these services will survive the current recession, which has placed the budgets of state and local governments under great strain, and if so, whether they will remain generally available. But if they do survive and remain open to all women, the welfare reform will be an important development in moving the focus of identity issues away from the workplace, where such work-related services have been sought in the past, and towards the family and general politics. Once issues at work that affect women have been moved into the political process in this way, the way might ironically open for the revival of workplace organizations narrowly focused on issues that workers (and working parents) have in common (Bane & Ellwood, 1994; Ellwood, 2000).

In the workplace itself, these identity groups play a peculiar role. They do not compete directly with unions, which, where they exist, have increasingly tried to incorporate these other forms of organization within themselves. But the identity groups (or affinity groups, as the employers like to call them) seem to have an episodic existence, becoming active around particular issues, but then seeming to atrophy for relatively long periods until another issue becomes important. Their activities, moreover, focus sometimes on issues within the workplace (such as domestic partner benefits for gays and lesbians) but sometimes on issues related to the politics of the group outside (e.g. an effort to get a company to shift its sales conference out of Denver in protest against a Colorado ballot referendum prohibiting local anti-discrimination laws).

The new arbitration procedures represent a key moment for the evolution of these different groups and the relation between them in the workplace. If the new procedures are to be equitable, they must have provision for independent worker representation. One can imagine this representation as being provided by trade unions; but, as so many of the laws involve equal employment opportunity, it could also be provided by the identity groups, all of which have important legal defense funds modeled on the NAACP (National Association for Advancement of Colored People Legal Defense Fund). Or, the two kinds of organizations through aims as affirmative groups could develop a new kind of working relationship with each other.

WORK ORGANIZATION, EMPLOYMENT SECURITY AND CAREER MOBILITY

Another set of issues in the reconstitution of the system governing work and employment relations concerns changes in the productive establishment. The firm is no longer a stable, enduring and well-defined unit to which employment rights can be attached. In the U.S. context, this poses two distinct, and conceptually separate problems. First, the internal labor markets of large, bureaucratic enterprises in the past served as the fulcrum around which employment continuity and career mobility was organized. Second, the provision of social welfare in the broadest sense was organized around the productive enterprise. Any number of social supports that were not directly related to work, and in fact which often came into play only when work was interrupted, were attached to the enterprise, and provided through its workers to the family. These included old age pensions, supplementary unemployment insurance, and medical insurance. Even as the old system has dissolved in recent years, there has been a tendency to attach new supports to the enterprise such as child care, aged care, and family leave payments.

It is clear that as the enterprise becomes an increasingly problematic institution, these second types of social benefits need to be detached from it and provided directly. Because the family as a stable unit has become problematic as well, and the way in which it is linked to the economy increasing complex, these benefits should be detached not only from the enterprise but from the family and be made directly available to the individual regardless of family status or employment attachment. This is in principle a relatively straightforward adjustment, and the United States has been moving in that direction, albeit very slowly.

The problem which the demise of the enterprise poses for employment security and career mobility cannot be readily resolved in this way. Even if the continuity of income could be assured independently of employment,, workers would still represent a scarce resource: Consideration of economic efficiency, quite independently of concerns about welfare, dictates that we have an institutional structure which facilitates the development of job skills over the course of individual work lives and conserves those skills through continuity of employment. If this can no longer be provided by the internal labor market of large corporate enterprises, we must look for other institutions that will operate to the same ends.

To say this is not necessarily to argue that the government needs to intervene to create these institutions. They might arise spontaneously in a market economy. And indeed, a number of new employment institutions have developed over the last twenty years. But experience suggests that one cannot count on an optimal set of institutions to emerge automatically. In the United States, particularly, concerns about economic efficiency are compounded by the problems of equal employment opportunity and inter-generational mobility, which have driven the evolution of the emergent system of labor market regulation. This suggests that continuous monitoring of the evolving labor market structure is called for.

For this, however, we need a framework of evaluation. Existing frameworks appear to be deficient. While it is not possible to offer an alternative framework here, it is possible to suggest the nature of the problem.

Various accounts have attempted to understand the problem of employment continuity and career mobility in terms of the underlying organization of work and of the shift that has occurred in the principles governing that organization in the 1980s and 1990s As with many of the factors governing the evolution of the postwar system, the principles governing work organization were never fully explicit, but they revolved around a set of ideas that originated in Adam Smith and Karl Marx and were then reasserted and reinforced in the twentieth century by Henry Ford, Fredrick Taylor and the industrial engineering profession that Taylor founded. The central idea is Adam Smith's notion that economic development involves the progressive division of labor, which, in turn, involves the movement exemplified by the shift from the master pin maker to the pin factory. Marx makes a similar distinction between the social division of labor in which there are specialties like that of master pin maker, and the detailed division of labor, in which work is further divided as in the pin factory. Ultimately, this suggests that there are basically two kinds of work: Work which is defined and organized around a set of basic principles (e.g. pin making, plumbing, electricity, the law) and work which can be defined as a series of specific tasks. Ford and Taylor emphasized the latter, and the job defined as a collection of tasks is the central principle around which the U.S. system of job control unionism revolved. The alternative is work organized around the more basic principles from which these tasks derived. This is essentially the craft or professional organization of work.

One can also associate these alternatives with different ways of learning and understanding work. The pin factory workers essentially memorize the operations they perform; given the range of tasks to which they are generally exposed, it is hard to understand the work in any other way. Craft and professional workers might also memorize their tasks, but the range of tasks that they are called upon to perform is generally so wide and so varied that they are more likely to understand them in terms of a set of general principles from which the particular operations they perform are deduced. Because they operate from general principles rather than a repertoire of memorized tasks, craft and professional workers are more flexible than detail workers. Not only are they able to do a wider set of things, but they can also perform novel operations (Berger & Piore, 1980).

In the late 1970s and the early 1980s, when the strains upon the existing system of work regulation first became apparent, economists tried to understand the changes as a shift away from the detailed division of labor back toward a craft/professional organization. The increasing uncertainty and instability associated with the business environment clearly pushed in this direction because it involved a continual change in the products produced and rearrangements of the inputs into the production process that required the flexibility of labor reminiscent of the crafts.

The other major factor impinging on work organization was information technology, and this was a little harder to assimilate into the detail/craft distinction. The routines associated with the detailed division of labor were easy, although often costly, to mechanize, even before computers. But the machines that performed these mechanized tasks tended to be quite rigid, typically dedicated to a particular product and often to a single make and model of that product. When the product changed, the machinery had to be scrapped and replaced. Computers enabled one to shift among routines by changing the software rather than the hardware; hence they introduced a flexibility into mechanization that before was often provided by cross-trained workers or by craft workers, who were not tied to a particular routine. Hence, to some extent, information technology substituted for craft/professional workers as much as for detail workers.

Nonetheless, the fact that the corporate enterprise was no longer a stable, well-defined unit, suggested that the work it performed was changing in a way that shifted work organization toward a craft/professional model. And this conjecture seemed to be confirmed by the trends in the income distribution that since the 1980s have increased the return to education and experience. Moreover, a variety of new labor market intermediaries have emerged in the course of the last two decades that seem to perform exactly the functions of providing employment continuity and career models that the internal labor market had performed under the old system. These include hiring hall arrangements reminiscent of those that have always existed in construction (and also in the entertainment and maritime industries), temporary help services, Web-based bulletin boards, ethnic networks and professional clubs, executive search firms (headhunters), and placement services attached to educational institutions. The most obvious adjustment to the new economic environment would be to evaluate these institutions against a craft/professional model and to impose upon them the obligations previously associated with the productive enterprise itself. Thus, for example, one might expect temporary help services to provide employment security, training and career mobility, equal employment opportunity and the like. And one can actually discern some movement in this direction (Autor, 2001; Autor et al., 1999).

The difficulty with this approach is that there is at least one other employment model that resembles the craft/professional model and utilizes similar institutions but may actually be quite different in terms of the economic and technological forces to which it responds and the institutional supports it requires. This other approach may be termed a *project-team* style of work organization (although this terminology is in no way standard). It can be characterized as follows:

(1) The work is organized in projects.
(2) The workers are organized in teams.
(3) Each team requires a certain set of *competencies*. These competencies are of two qualitatively different kinds. One set of competencies are skills in the traditional sense of the term, and are often, although not always, associated with conventional crafts or professions. A second set of competencies involve experience in applying those skills to a particular domain. Thus, a team may require certain programming skills, but also experience in using those skills in banking, and within banking, in risk management, credit evaluation, and cash dispersal.
(4) The set of competencies is attached to the team and need not adhere to any particular worker. One worker might possess both the programming skills and experience in the domains of application, or only the programming skills, and the domain experiences might be brought to the team by several different workers.
(5) Each worker has a portfolio of competencies. These usually include one professional/craft and experience in one or more domains of application.
(6) A career for the worker involves the broadening and deepening of his/her portfolio of competencies.
(7) The net result of the foregoing characteristics is that matching is highly idiosyncratic. The employer is looking to create a team with a certain set of competencies but no particular worker is expected to provide a particular subset, and thus the team can be constructed in a number of different ways. It is obviously harder to find the right worker to complete the team than to begin it. The employer is also looking for a set of workers who can work together in a team. The literature suggests that the ability to work in this way is itself a well-defined skill (or productive trait). But the interviews we have conducted suggest that it is less a general "skill" or "trait" that is critical and more the fit among the personality types. The worker is looking to develop his portfolio over time but can do so either by deepening his craft/professional skills, deepening his domain skills, or expanding the range of domains in which he has experience.

Project work resembles craft/professional work but it has important differences. If one takes construction as an example of craft work, the typical construction project involves a succession of crafts, each of which works essentially alone on the project for a relatively short period of time. The building is framed by iron workers, then the plumbers install the piping and electricians the wiring; then the masons complete the walls; the carpenters install the woodwork; and finally, the painters do the finishing. Integration across these different crafts is provided by project management. In project/team work, the different competencies are used simultaneously through interaction among members of the team, and the team is held together over a relatively long time, possibly working at several different projects over time, or even at the same time. As a result, project/team work is of much longer duration. The match between the workers and the jobs is much more idiosyncratic as well. And both the idiosyncrasies and the duration of the work mean that there is much more concern in hiring with the quality of the match. Project/team work draws upon many of the same intermediary institutions as craft or professional work, but it uses them in somewhat different ways. For example, for temporary help services in the United States, 25% of the placements are temporary-to-permanent, a kind of placement which belies the term temporary and suggests that workers and employers are placing increased emphasis on the quality of the match.

It is not clear exactly where the project/team organization of work is used or where it is appropriate. But it appears to involve output that is new and unique: the writing of software programs; "investment banking" deals; new product development (Brooks, 1995; Eccles & Crane, 1988; McBreen, 2002). As a result, it does not lend itself to mechanization or mass production. Nor does it involve the standard problem-solving principles that can be easily embedded in software programs. Hence, it resists both the kinds of automation to which detailed labor has been vulnerable and the automation associated with information technology to which craft and professional work is increasingly subject. As these other kinds of work are reduced in this way, it would appear that project/teams are likely to be of increasing relative importance in the economy. For this reason, it would seem important to delay institutionalizing the obligations of labor market intermediaries until the distinction between craft/professional work and project/team work is better understood.

SUMMARY AND CONCLUSIONS

In sum, the U.S. has moved over the course of the last two decades from a system of work regulation organized around trade unions and collective bargaining to one which increasingly revolves around direct government regulation of the terms and conditions of employment. The shift reflects a more fundamental change in the way in which work and the conflicts in the workplace are viewed relative to social conflict more broadly. The collective bargaining system grew out of a perception of work as a separate and distinct realm of activity in which work identity was a distinct axis of social mobilization; and work-based trade unions were viewed as the uniquely appropriate channel for expression of workplace concerns. The axis of social mobilization has now shifted to social identities anchored in sex, race, ethnicity, age, sexual orientation, and physical disability. Workplace problems are more often perceived as the outgrowth of the social stigma associated with these identities, and remedies are conceived in terms of a general strategy to alter the position of the members of these groups in society.

The old system was reinforced by a structure in which social and economic life were sharply distinguished. Economic life was organized around the productive enterprise; social life around the family. The family and the enterprise were linked by a single dominant wage earner who was also the family head and chief support. Conflicts between the two realms could thus be reconciled by adjustments in the worker's wage, negotiated between trade unions (which in this sense represented the worker and through the worker, the social sphere), and the enterprise. The breakdown of the old system was precipitated by the collapse of the trade union movement; but it was also undermined by the disintegration of the family and the enterprise as stable, enduring, and well-defined institutional structures, as the former was plagued by increasing rates of divorce, illegitimacy, and rising rates of female labor force participation, and the latter by subcontracting, mergers, bankruptcies, and strategic alliances.

The narrow economic question of how to conserve and develop human resources in the emergent system remains largely unresolved. In the old system, employment continuity and career development depended heavily upon the personnel policies of the productive enterprise as modified and amended in collective bargaining. As these enterprises have become less stable, and the structure of employment within them subject to more frequent and more radical changes, a variety of intermediary institutions have emerged to guide workers through the labor market and convert irregular jobs into more continuous employment. But these institutions are extremely varied in character, ranging from temporary help services and executive search firms to identity-based networks formed around the social affiliations that structure social mobilization, or networks of alumni of educational institutions, or former employees of prominent corporations. The role these institutions play is similar to that played by craft unions and professional associations in labor markets when these were the dominant form of work organization. This suggests that we are moving toward an organization based on crafts and professions, and that one could impose upon the emergent intermediaries the obligations previously assumed by the productive enterprise itself. Many of these emerging intermediaries, however, have no formal existence. The problem is further complicated by the emergence of a third form of work organization – project/teams. In project/team work, employment is more long lasting and jobs more idiosyncratic; a very high premium is placed on the quality of the match. The same labor market intermediaries sustain project/teams as those which sustained craft/professional work, but because the nature of the match and of careers is so different, it is not clear that they are effectively bearing the same responsibilities in both "markets."

Finally, one might ask about the relevance of these developments in the United States to an understanding of other advanced industrial countries or to the organization of economic activity in general. An answer to that question would require a range of study much broader than any which could be undertaken here. There was enormous variation among countries in the postwar period, but in most countries there were similar forces at work. First, trade unions were extremely strong although they were incorporated into the institutional framework in different ways. Second, countries shared a similar technological base, and, in particular, the influence of mass production as a technological paradigm was pervasive, although in the end its impact also varied from country to country. Third, in virtually every country, the family and the large corporate enterprise were central institutions, although here there was also significant variation.

Insofar as the changes that have emerged are associated with the weakening of the trade union movement and of the stability, durability, and well-defined nature of the corporate enterprise, they have been very similar in all industrial nations. The movement away from mass production and toward a project/team organization of work has been similar as well.

Many of the underlying forces in terms of the organization of the economy, the technology and the key institutional structures have been similar across countries, although they have probably played themselves out with different force and in different ways from one nation to another. In addition, the United States as the hegemonic power in the emerging international order has used its power to pressure for reforms which, in its eyes, give greater weight to the competitive market. The net impact of these reforms has served to further weaken the existing institutional forces and to make way for new institutions to emerge. What seems most problematic outside the United States is the shift from economic class to other forms of social identity as a locus of political mobilization. But this too may actually be more pervasive than it seems, in part because many of the new forms of social identity are rooted in ethnicity and grow out of the process of international migration, and this kind of international migration has been an important factor in virtually all industrial countries and many developing countries throughout the postwar period, although the role of migration is probably nowhere as central to the national identity as it is in the United States. American movies, television, and popular fashion carry a message not only about ethnic identity but about race, sexual orientation, and feminism that have had an influence abroad in creating movements even in countries that were not previously disposed to think in terms of these categories.

REFERENCES

Acemoglu, D., & Angrist, J. (2001). Consequences of employment protection? The case of the Americans with Disabilities Act. *Journal of Political Economy, 109*, 915–957.

Autor, D. H. (2001). Why do temporary help firms provide free general skills training? *Quarterly Journal of Economics, 116*(4), 1409–1448.

Autor, D. H. (2003). Outsourcing at will: Unjust dismissal doctrine and the growth of temporary help employment. *Journal of Labor Economics, 21*(1), 1–42.

Autor, D. H., Donohue, J., & Schwab, S. (2002). *The cost of wrongful-discharge laws*. Massachusetts Institute of Technology, Cambridge, MA: Photocopy.

Autor, D. H., Levy, F., & Murnane, R. (1999). *Skills training in the temporary help sector: Employer motivations and worker impacts*. Massachusetts Institute of Technology, Cambridge, MA: Photocopy.

Bane, M. J., & Ellwood, D. T. (1994). *Welfare realities: From rhetoric to reform*. Cambridge, MA: Harvard University Press.

Barenberg, M. (1993). The political economy of the Wagner act: Power, symbol, and workplace cooperation. *The Harvard Law Review, 106*(7), 1379.

Barenberg, M. (1994). Democracy and domination in the law of workplace cooperation: From bureaucratic to flexible production (Part 1 of 2). *The Columbia Law Review, 94*. L. Rev. 753.

Berger, S., & Piore, M. (1980). *Dualism and discontinuity in industrial society Cambridge*. New York: Cambridge University Press.

Brooks, F. P. (1995). *The mythical man-month: Essays on software engineering*. Boston: Addison-Wesley.

Cohen, L. (1990). *Making a new deal: Industrial workers in Chicago, 1919–1939*. New York: Cambridge University Press.

DiNardo, J., Fortin, N., & Lemieux, T. (1996). Labor market institutions and the distribution of wages, 1973–1992: A semiparametric approach. *Econometrica, 64*(5), 1001–1044.

Dobbin, F., & Kelly, E. (2002). *A tale of two sectors: The spread of anti-harassment remedies among public and private employers*. Princeton University, Princeton, NJ: Photocopy.

Dobbin, F., & Sutton, J. (1998). The strength of a weak state: The rights revolution and the rise of human resources management divisions. *The American Journal of Sociology, 104*(2), 441–476.

Doeringer, P., & Piore, M. (1971). *Internal labor markets and manpower analysis*. Lexington, MA: Heath.

Eccles, R., & Crane, D. (1988). *Doing deals: Investment banks at work*. Boston: Harvard Business School Press.

Edelman, L., Abraham, S., & Erlanger, H. (1992). Professional construction of law: The inflated threat of wrongful discharge. *Law and Society Review, 26*(1), 47–87.

Ellwood, D. T. (Ed.) (2000). *A working nation: Workers, work, and government in the new economy*. New York: Russell Sage Foundation.

Fraser, S. (1993). *Labor will rule: Sidney Hillman and the rise of American labor*. Ithaca: Cornell University Press.

Greenberg, J. (1994). *Crusaders in the courts: How a dedicated band of lawyers fought for the civil rights revolution*. New York: Basic Books.

Herzenberg, S., Alic, J., & Wial, H. (1998). *New rules for a new economy: Employment and opportunity in postindustrial America*. Ithaca: ILR Press.

Hinton, J. (1973). *The first shop stewards' movement*. London: G. Allen & Unwin.

Jacoby, S. (1999). Career jobs: A debate – are career jobs headed for extinction? *California Management Review, 42*(1), 123–145.

Jaeger, D. A., & Stevens, A. H. (1999). Is job stability in the United States falling? Reconciling trends in the Current Population Survey and Panel Study of Income Dynamics. *Journal of Labor Economics, 17*(Suppl. 4), S1–S28.

Katz, H. C. (2002). Working in America: Review symposium: Editor's introduction. *Industrial and Labor Relations Review, 55*(4), 715–716.

Katz, L., & Autor, D. (1999). Changes in the wage structure and earnings inequality. In: O. Ashtenfelter & D. Card (Eds), *Handbook of Labor Economics* (Vol. 3A). Amsterdam: North-Holland.

Katz, L., & Murphy, K. (1995). Changes in relative wages, 1963–1987: Supply and demand factors. *Quarterly Journal of Economics, 107*, 35–78.

Katznelson, I. (1981). *City trenches: Urban politics and the patterning of class in the United States.* Chicago: University of Chicago Press.

Kelly, E., & Dobbin, F. (1998). How affirmative action became diversity management: Employer response to anti-discrimination law, 1961 to 1996. *American Behavioral Scientist, 41*(7), 960–984.

Kelly, E., & Dobbin, F. (1999). Civil rights law at work: Sex discrimination and the rise of maternity leave policies. *The American Journal of Sociology, 105*(2), 455–492.

Kochan, T., Katz, H., & McKersie, R. (1986). *The transformation of American industrial relations.* New York: Basic Books.

Levy, F. (1998). *The new dollars and dreams: American incomes and economic change.* New York: Sage.

Lichtenstein, N. (2002). *State of the union: A century of American labor.* Princeton, NJ: Princeton University Press.

McBreen, P. (2002). *Software craftsmanship, the new imperative.* Boston: Addison-Wesley.

Morriss, A. P. (1995). Developing a framework for empirical research on the common law: General principles and case studies on the decline of employment-at-will. *Case Western Reserve Law Review, 45*(4), 999–1148.

Neumark, D. (Ed.) (2000). *On the job: Is long-term employment a thing of the past.* New York: Russell Sage Foundation.

Neumark, D., Polsky, D., & Hansen, D. (1999). Has job stability declined yet? New evidence for the 1990s. *Journal of Labor Economics, 17*(4), S29–S64.

Osterman, P. (Ed.) (1996). *Broken ladders: Managerial careers in the new economy.* New York: Oxford University Press.

Osterman, P. (1999). *Securing prosperity, the American labor market: How it has changed and what to do about it.* Princeton, NJ: Princeton University Press.

Osterman, P., Kochan, T., Locke, R., & Piore, M. (2001). *Working in America: A blueprint for the new labor market.* Cambridge, MA: MIT Press.

Piore, M. (1979). *Birds of passage: Migrant labor and industrial societies.* Cambridge; New York: Cambridge University Press.

Piore, M. (1982). American labor and the industrial crisis. *Challenge, 25*(1), 5–11.

Piore, M. (1986). The decline of mass production and union survival in the USA. *Industrial Relations Journal, 17*(3), 207–213.

Piore, M. (1995). *Beyond individualism.* Cambridge, MA: Harvard University Press.

Piore, M., & Sabel, C. (1984). *The second industrial divide: Possibilities for prosperity.* New York: Basic Books.

Stein, J. (1998). *Running steel, running America: Race, economic policy, and the decline of liberalism.* Chapel Hill: University of North Carolina Press.

Stone, K. V. W. (1992). The legacy of industrial pluralism: The tension between individual employment rights and the new deal collective bargaining system. *University of Chicago Law Review, 59*(Spring), 575.

Stone, K. V. W. (1996). Mandatory arbitration of individual employment rights: The yellow dog contract of the 1990s. *Denver University Law Review, 73*(4), 1017.

Stone, K. V. W. (2001). The new psychological contract: Implications of the changing workplace for labor and employment law. *UCLA Law Review, 48*(February), 519.

Supreme Court of the United States (2001, March 21). Circuit City Stores, Inc., *Petitioner v. Saint Clair Adams*, No. 99–1379, 532 U.S.

Sutton, J., Dobbin, F., Meyer, J., & Scott, R. (1994). The legalization of the workplace. *The American Journal of Sociology, 99*(4), 944–971.

Thelen, K. A. (1991). *Union of parts: Labor politics in postwar Germany.* Ithaca, NY: Cornell University Press.

3. WELFARE REGIMES IN RELATION TO PAID WORK AND CARE

Janet C. Gornick and Marcia K. Meyers

ABSTRACT

Ideologies about work, caregiving, family, and gender relations vary across countries and over time. Contemporary perspectives typically stress child well-being, women's caregiving burden, or gender equality. The tensions among these can be resolved in societies that combine intensive parental time for children with a gender-egalitarian division of labor. Social and labor market policies that would support such a society are the most developed in the Social Democratic countries, with the Conservative countries of continental Europe and the Liberal English-speaking countries lagging substantially (most markedly, the United states). That policy variation appears to shape cross-country variation in crucial parent and child outcomes.

INTRODUCTION

Parents throughout Europe and the United states share the common challenge of balancing responsibilities in the labor market and at home; mothers and fathers everywhere grapple with establishing a division of labor at home that is equitable and economically viable. Yet despite relatively common problems across contemporary welfare states, social and labor market policies vary dramatically in the level of support that they provide for parents and the extent to which they encourage gender-egalitarian divisions of labor in paid work and care.

Changing Life Patterns in Western Industrial Societies
Advances in Life Course Research, Volume 8, 45–67
ISSN: 1040-2608/doi:10.1016/S1040-2608(03)08003-1

Parents in some countries – especially in northern Europe and, to a lesser degree, on the European continent – benefit from family leave policies that grant them paid time off to care for their young children, labor market regulations that shorten their regular working-time throughout their children's lives, and public programs that guarantee access to high-quality substitute care during the hours that they spend on the job. In some countries, public provisions not only grant parents caregiving supports, they also encourage gender equality, by strengthening mothers' labor market attachment and/or allowing and encouraging fathers to spend more (paid) time caregiving at home. Public financing of these programs distributes the costs of childrearing broadly, spreading the burden across family types, throughout the income distribution, between generations, and among employers. In other countries – most markedly, in the U.S., where childrearing is viewed in exceptionally private terms – parents are largely left to craft market-based solutions to work/family conflicts. For the most part, U.S. parents rely on their employers to voluntarily provide paid family leave and options for reduced-hour work, while turning to consumer markets to obtain child care services.

In this chapter, we consider the links between ideological perspectives, the gendered division of labor, features of the welfare state, and parent and child outcomes. Our goals are three-fold. First, we aim to place policy variation in the context of diverse ideological perspectives on work, caregiving, family, and gender relations. In the next section of this chapter, we identify several ideological perspectives that vary in their degree of concern for child well-being, work/family balance (especially for women), and gender equality, especially in the labor market. The way that these three perspectives are combined correspond to distinctive national models for dividing paid and unpaid work between men and women, ranging from the traditional male-breadwinner/female-carer arrangement to a contemporary model (the "dual-earner/dual-carer" model) defined by symmetrical engagement in both paid work and care in conjunction with ample parental time for children.

Our second aim is to characterize "work/family" policy packages across a group of relatively similar industrialized countries. After considering multiple ideologies and options for the family division of labor, we turn our attention to current policy provisions – comparing the U.S. with nine diverse European welfare states (Belgium, Denmark, Finland, France, Germany, Netherlands, Norway, Sweden, and the United Kingdom). Our goal is to assess the extent to which existing policy packages in these countries support parents' time to care and/or encourage gender-egalitarian divisions of labor. We focus on a policy package that includes three crucial components: public family leave policies, working-time regulations, and public systems of early childhood education and care. Although we argue that policy packages correspond to ideological frameworks, we do not suggest that policies are the direct products of national ideologies. The causal linkages between policy and ideology are complex and multidirectional, in that policy designs both shape, and are shaped by, dominant ideologies.

Third, we link policy variation to variation in family outcomes. Empirical research indicates that the three core policies (family leave, working-time regulation, and early childhood education and care) do indeed shape parent and child outcomes. The countries among these ten with the most generous and most gender-egalitarian policies generally allow parents to spend more time with their children. In addition, mothers and fathers divide paid and unpaid work more equally, and children fare better on crucial outcomes. The evidence is overwhelming that policy matters. The life patterns of parents and children are influenced by the configuration of family, work, and early childhood education and care policies.[1]

IDEOLOGICAL PERSPECTIVES ON EMPLOYMENT, CAREGIVING, AND GENDER RELATIONS

Cross-national comparison shows that ideologies about work, caregiving, family, and gender relations correspond to distinct models for organizing gendered divisions of labor. At least three ideological perspectives are found in several industrialized countries. Although they are not mutually exclusive, they differ fundamentally and the tensions among them are not easily resolved.

One perspective focuses on protecting and enhancing child well-being. In the U.S. and other high-income countries, many researchers, service providers, and advocates in the fields of public health, child development, and education, have focused attention on the role of the family in shaping child outcomes. Although the determinants of children's well-being are widely understood to be multifaceted, analysts and advocates often point to parents' time availability as an important contributing factor. Concerns about parental time available for children have intensified in recent years as maternal employment has grown more common across all of the industrialized countries and, in the U.S., as annual employment hours have risen in recent years.

A second perspective aims to recognize and reward women for their intense engagement in caring work. The "women's caregiver" perspective strives to free up women's time for caregiving by establishing programs, public or private, that allow women both to work for pay and to spend time at home caring for their children. Some strands of the "women's caregiver" perspective are explicitly feminist, calling for radical new conceptions of care, paid work, social citizenship rights, and welfare state obligations (see, e.g. Knijn & Kremer, 1997). Others mainly emphasize the need to "help women balance work and family," linking their analyses and claims to feminism only minimally or not at all. To a large degree, the work/family movement in the U.S. has established weak connections to broader feminist politics. Many U.S. researchers and advocates simply locate the overwhelming share of work/family conflict in women's lives, laying aside larger political questions about the organization of paid work and care as well as the nature of men's economic and familial roles.

A third perspective, with strong roots in feminism, highlights the need for gender parity in the labor market. For the most part, the "women's employment perspective" – or the "universal breadwinner perspective" – envisions achieving gender equality by strengthening women's ties to employment. Since the 1960s, when feminists in the U.S. and elsewhere argued that "the personal is the political," many have taken a hard look at the role of the family in the subjugation of women. Many feminists have concluded that persistent gender inequality in the labor market is both cause and consequence of women's disproportionate assumption of unpaid work in the home. This perspective focuses on the ways in which men's stronger ties to the labor market carry social, political, and economic advantages that are denied to many women, especially those who spend substantial amounts of time caring for children. Many adherents argue (or imply) that when women achieve parity in the labor market, gender inequalities at home will fade away.

There has been surprisingly little meeting of the minds among those representing these varied perspectives, which seem most at odds when they propose public solutions. Research on child well-being stresses the importance of parents' availability and many interpret this research to suggest the need for policies – such as child allowances, caregiver stipends, and maternity leaves – that would allow mothers of young children to opt out of labor market attachments, at least when children are young. Those sympathetic to the "women's caregiver" perspective also stress women's connection to children; solutions focus on policies that allow mothers both to work for pay and to spend substantial time at home – such as part-time work, job sharing, telecommuting, and flextime. Some call for "wages for caring." In contrast, feminists identified with the "employment perspective" typically argue for policies that reduce employment barriers and discrimination; they also advocate for alternatives to maternal child care – such as more and better quality out-of-home child care and an expansion of men's paid leave options.

Variation in the Gendered Division of Labor

These ideological variations correspond to distinct models for dividing labor between women and men. In her recent book, Rosemary Crompton (1999) offers a useful continuum of gendered arrangements – from the traditional male-breadwinner/female-carer arrangement, to current partial modifications, to an idealized dual-earner/dual-carer society. Although largely theoretical in its conception, this continuum provides a framework for envisioning change and serves as a helpful tool when assessing how varied ideological perspectives correspond to social and economic arrangements that exist in practice. We present Crompton's continuum in the upper portion of Fig. 1; in the lower portion of Fig. 1, we link these diverse models to the three ideological emphases that we have identified.

The *first* point on the continuum is the fully-specialized traditional family which prevailed across the industrialized countries from the late nineteenth century until the middle of the twentieth century. Its pure form – men in waged work, women caring for children at home full-time – is now relatively rare in the U.S. and in most of continental and northern Europe as well. The majority of mothers in all ten of the countries included in this chapter are employed; in all but two, Germany and the Netherlands, more than two-thirds of mothers work for pay (Gornick & Meyers, 2003). Mothers of infants constitute an exception to the demise of this highly-specialized arrangement, as many mothers still exit the labor force during their children's youngest years.

The remaining three points on the continuum reflect variations in the political economy of the family that are, to some degree, observable across countries. The *second* point on the continuum – the dual-earner/female part-time carer model – is consistent with an emphasis on child well-being, as it frees up maternal time for children. It also enables some participation in paid work by mothers and, given appropriate policy supports, such as caregiver stipends, it can be consistent with rewarding women as caregivers. This model is represented, for example, by the Netherlands and the U.K. – where many mothers work for pay but part-time and at low weekly hours.

The *third* point on the continuum – the dual-earner model with substitute carers – stresses gender equality in earning. The "state-carer" version was seen in the past in the state socialist countries such as the former German Democratic Republic and is in place, to some extent, in Finland today, where a large share of mothers are employed and mostly full-time. The "market-carer" version is, to some extent, in place in the U.S. today, where as in Finland, a large share of mothers are employed and generally full-time, but without the extensive public child care in place in Finland. Both of these organizational options can be consonant with gender equality in the labor market although they can have inegalitarian consequences if paid care work is highly feminized, especially if it is poorly remunerated (as in the U.S. market-based system). Both of these dual-earner/substitute-carer arrangements can also have gender-inegalitarian consequences if employed women retain the lion's share of unpaid caregiving traditional gender division of labor <------------> less traditional gender division of labor

(continuum from Crompton, 1999)

ideological perspectives on employment, caregiving, and gender relations:	male breadwinner / female carer	dual-earner / female part-time carer	dual-earner / state-carer -- or -- dual-earner / marketized-carer	dual-earner / dual-carer
"child well-being"	emphasized	emphasized	--	emphasized
"helping caregivers blend work and family"	--	emphasized	emphasized	emphasized
"gender equality in the labor market"	--	--	emphasized	emphasized

Fig. 1. Alternative Forms of the Gendered Division of Labor.

at home. That double burden results in both severe time poverty for women and often an erosion in the quality, if not the quantity, of their labor market attachment.

The *fourth* point on the continuum (the dual-earner/dual-carer model) embodies gender equality in both earning and caring. Symmetry in both spheres is a defining feature, and that would require some reduction, on average, in men's current labor market hours. This model also supports favorable child outcomes, assuming that ample parental time with children "produces" child well-being. As such, this social and economic model resolves many of the conflicts among the three ideological perspectives laid out above – in that it is gender egalitarian, it values care work on the part of both men and women, and it emphasizes child well-being (by providing ample parental time for caregiving, especially when children are very young).

This final model of paid work and care has attracted sustained attention in Europe in recent years, especially among feminist welfare state scholars (e.g. Ruth Lister, in the U.K., Birgit Pfau-Effinger in Germany, Anne-Lisa Ellingsæter in Norway, and Diane Sainsbury in Sweden) and, to a lesser extent, in the U.S. (see, e.g. Nancy Fraser's (1994) call for men to become "like women are now"). Whereas no existing society has fully achieved such a gender-egalitarian outcome, some European welfare states have put policy packages in place that strongly encourage it – most notably the social democratic countries of Sweden, Denmark, and Norway. On the continent, new legislation in the Netherlands (*The Work and Care Act of 2000*) articulates the realization of a dual-earner/dual-carer society as its goal. The stated intention of the law is to enable couples to hold "one and a half jobs" between them – with each holding a "three-quarter time job" – thus achieving both time for care and gender equality.

These three overarching ideologies and the gender division of labor to which they correspond can be supported and shaped by specific policies and policy packages. It is important to stress that the nature and generosity of family policies may themselves be influenced by dominant national ideologies about work, family, and gender equality. But such policies often arise in conjunction with other goals as well, such as raising fertility, alleviating labor shortages, attaining full employment, or preventing poverty. In many countries, the factors that motivate family policy formation lack political cohesion and often shift over time. Nevertheless, these ideologies are associated with contemporary policy variation as shown in the ten countries that are compared below.

POLICY VARIATION ACROSS PAID WORK AND CARE REGIMES

At least three areas of family policy influence dominant patterns of parental care-giving, the male-female division of labor, and child well-being. First, *family leave policies* grant parents the right to take time off for caregiving, especially when children are below school-age, and they replace some or all wages during parents' time off. Short-term paid leaves also contribute to gender equality in the labor market by facilitating continuous maternal employment and reducing wage penalties associated with motherhood. Family leave policy designs vary dramatically across countries on at least two core dimensions: the generosity of leave available to new mothers and the degree to which policy designs encourage men's engagement in caregiving.

Second, *working-time regulations* can free up parents' caring time – for both fathers and mothers – by limiting normal employment hours to, say, fewer than 40 per week and by guaranteeing a minimum number of days for annual vacations. Some feminist scholars have concluded, furthermore, that shortening working time may be the most promising tool for achieving a gender-egalitarian redistribution of domestic labor (see, e.g. Mutari & Figart, 2001).

Third, public provisions for *early childhood education and care* further strengthen maternal employment by providing alternatives to full-time maternal caregiving, and high-quality early education and care can also enhance child well-being. Public financing and delivery, rather than a market-based system, alleviates the economic burden of child care costs, especially for low-income families, and raises the wages of the caregiving workforce as well.

In this section, we present the highlights of contemporary policy variation in these three policy arenas as of approximately 2000, using the three-regime typology of Gosta Esping-Anderson (1990) as an organizing framework. Esping-Andersen classified the major welfare states of the industrialized west into three clusters, each characterized by shared principles of social welfare entitlement (with an emphasis on class) and relatively homogeneous outcomes. He characterized social policy in the Nordic countries as generally organized along *Social Democratic* lines, with generous entitlements linked to universal social rights. Social policies in the countries of continental Europe are largely *Conservative*, typically tied to earnings and occupation, with public provisions replicating market-generated distributional outcomes; in these countries, social policies are often shaped by the principle of subsidiarity as well, which stresses the primacy of family and community in providing dependent care and other social supports. Social benefits in the English-speaking countries are described as *Liberal*, that is, organized to reflect and preserve consumer and employer markets, with most entitlements deriving from need based on limited resources.[2]

In the 1990s, many critics (including us) charged Esping-Andersen with ignoring gender issues in the construction of this typology. His primary dimension of variation, decommodification – the extent to which the state protects waged workers from income insecurity – applied poorly to women as a group. In addition, his underlying policy variables excluded most programs targeted on women, such as family leave and child care. Yet, somewhat surprisingly, subsequent empirical efforts to establish new welfare state typologies that did incorporate gender largely corresponded to Esping-Andersen's classification. That suggests that the welfare state principles underlying these categories are highly correlated with factors that shape family policy. In the Nordic countries, the social democratic principles that guide policy design are generally paired with a commitment to gender equality. In the Conservative countries the market-replicating principles are often embedded in socially conservative ideas about family and gender roles. In the Liberal countries, the supremacy of the market system generally drives social welfare designs across all policy arenas.

All told, the Esping-Andersen regime-types provide a fruitful starting point for assessing welfare regimes in relation to paid work and care. We make use of them in this chapter partly because they push us to think theoretically about social policy and partly because they help us to identify empirical patterns across our comparison countries. By working with these well-known groupings, policy comparativists can also situate our findings within the larger literature on the welfare state.

Family Leave Policy

Across these ten countries, family leave policies vary markedly, and on two distinct dimensions. First, there is substantial variation in the total number of weeks of full-time wage replacement available to new mothers, assuming that mothers take all of the leave available to them through existing maternity and parental leave schemes.[3] Second, there is variation in the extent to which family leave policy features are egalitarian with respect to gender: countries vary in the generosity of their provisions for fathers and the extent to which policy designs encourage fathers to take up the leave to which they are entitled (see Fig. 2).[4]

The most generous and most gender-egalitarian family leave policies are found in the Social Democratic countries, where mothers have access to about 30–42 weeks of full-time wage replacement and fathers receive comparatively generous benefits bolstered by incentives for take-up. The Conservative countries provide substantially less generous benefits for mothers – (about 12–16 weeks of fully-paid leave); and provisions and incentives for fathers are generally weak.

Provisions in the U.K. are minimal, but the U.S. stands out as exceptional. It is alone among these ten countries (and one of only a handful of countries in the world) with no national policy of paid maternity leave. In addition, gender-egalitarian provisions in the U.S. are weak. Fathers in the U.S. have some incentive to use the unpaid leave granted to them through national law (the Family and

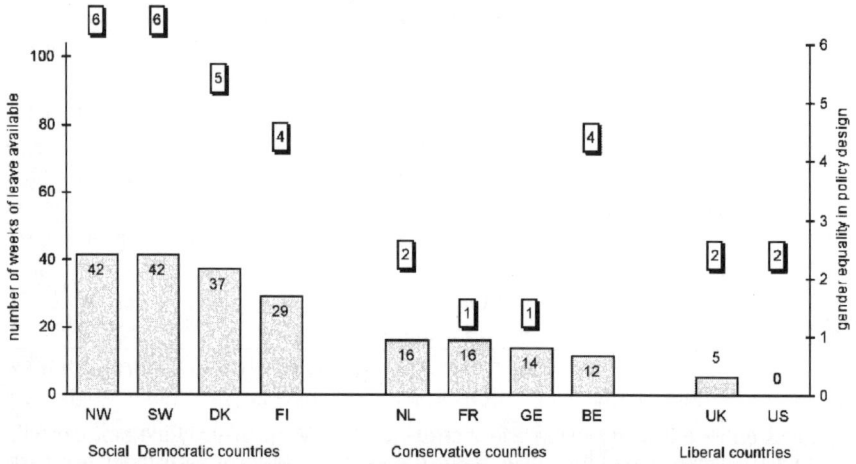

Fig. 2. Family Leave Policy. Generosity of Maternity Leave and Gender Equality in Policy Design (Approximately 2000). *Note:* The values inside the boxes are the scores on the gender equality index. *Source:* Gornick and Meyees (2003).

Medical Leave Act) because their entitlements, if not used, are lost. At the same time, however, the absence of wage replacement constitutes a substantial disincentive because for most men use of the leave would result in a serious loss of income.

Working-Time Regulations

Working-time policies can increase workers' available time at home through at least two mechanisms. Limits on normal weekly employment hours, which are set via direct ceilings on maximum allowable hours or limits on overtime, reduce actual hours worked on a regular basis throughout the year. In addition, guaranteed vacation time grants workers unbroken periods of time that they can spend with their families. Vacation rights also alleviate child care strains during summer months when schools are generally not in session (see Fig. 3).[5]

As of the year 2000, following several years of working-time reductions enacted throughout Europe, all of the countries in this study – both Social Democratic and Conservative – set normal employment hours in the range of 35–39 per week, with the exception of the U.S., where the normal work week remains 40 hours. Efforts to reduce working time even further remain active all across Europe. In both Belgium and Finland, for example, collectively agreed upon hours fell between 2000 and 2002, from about 39 into the range of 35 to 38. Many

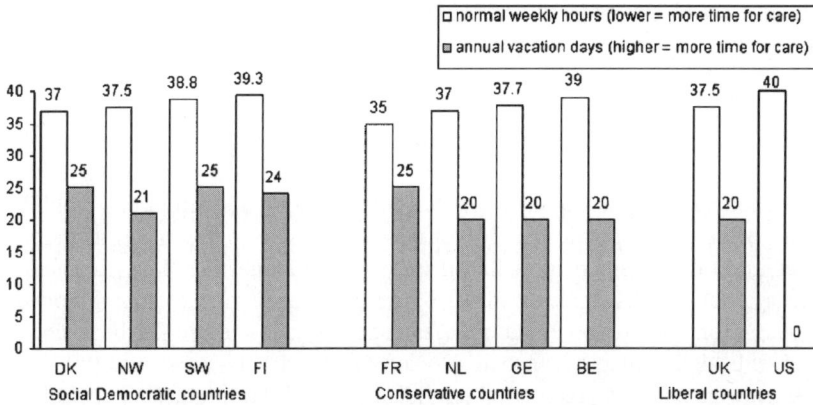

Fig. 3. Working-Time Regulations. Normal Weekly Hours (Overtime Threshold) and Annual Paid Vacation (Minimum Number of Days) (Approximately 2000). *Source:* Gornick and Meyers (2003).

European working-time advocates characterize the ongoing changes seen across these countries as indicative of an unfinished transformation, continent-wide, to a 35-hour work week.

In addition, all of the European countries included in this study provide a minimum of twenty days (approximately four weeks) of vacation. France and three Nordic countries – Denmark, Finland, and Sweden – grant most or all of a fifth week. Intra-European homogeneity is partially explained by the enactment of the 1993 European Union Directive on Working Time,[6] which stipulates that employees be granted not less than four weeks of paid vacation per year, an increase from the three weeks previously in place. In several countries, collective agreements add even more vacation time; agreements in Denmark, Germany, and the Netherlands provide the most generous benefits, about 30 days a year. And, as with normal weekly hours, changes continue to unfold; after 2000, collectively-bargained vacation rights increased in about half of these countries.

Again, the U.S. stands out as the exceptional case. It is the only country among these ten where the normal work week remains at 40 hours (with little ongoing activity aimed at lowering that threshold) and the only one without a nationally-mandated vacation policy. In the U.S., vacation rights and benefits are left to the discretion of employers. In practice, employees at medium and large enterprises are granted an average of about ten days per year during their first five years of service, rising to about 14 days after five years of service and about 17 days after ten years. Workers use about 93% of earned days, with slightly higher take-up reported by non-professionals and by women (Jacobs & Gerson, forthcoming).

Even with the high take-up, the U.S. has been dubbed "the most vacation–starved country in the industrialized world" (Woodward, 2002).[7]

Early Childhood Education and Care

The ten countries in this study also vary markedly in their provision of publicly-provided and/or publicly-financed child care. While public care is limited everywhere for children in the first 12 months of life, many industrialized countries invest substantial public resources in early education and care for children starting at the first birthday, with more extensive provisions for children aged three through five (see Fig. 4).

For the most part, the Social Democratic countries are high providers of public care. The highest providers are Sweden and Denmark, where one half to three-quarters of children aged one and two are in public care, and about 80–90% of children aged three and older. In the Conservative countries, care for the "under threes" is less available – and thus, support for continuous maternal employment is more limited – but universal full-day preschool for the "over threes" is the norm in France and Belgium, with increasing preschool enrollments in recent years in Germany and the Netherlands as well.

Publicly-supported child care for one- and two-year-olds is very restricted in both the U.K. and the U.S., where government subsidies are limited almost

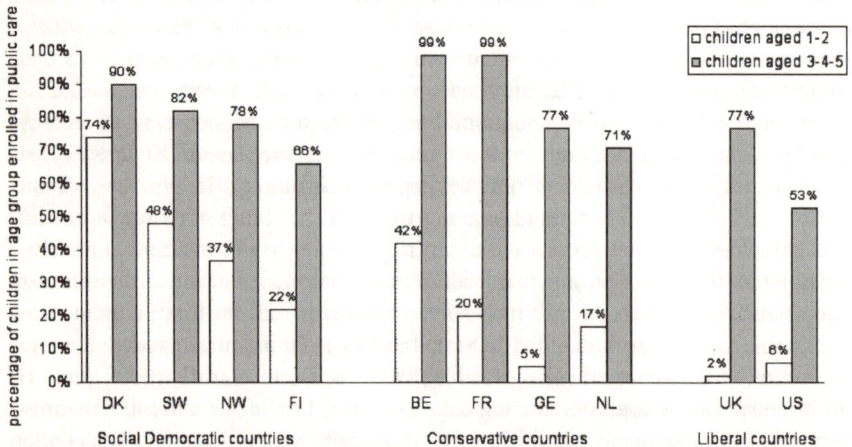

Fig. 4.   Early Childhood Education and Care (Enrollment in Publicly-Provided or Publicly-Financed Care) (Approximately 2000). *Source:* Gornick and Meyers (2003).

entirely to low-income parents. The U.S., in particular, is a cross-national laggard, especially with respect to provisions for the "over threes." In the U.S., just over one-half (53%) of three-, four-, and five-year olds are in publicly-subsidized care. Of those in public care, nearly all are five-year-olds in part-day kindergarten programs.

Policy Packages and Cumulative Effects on Life Patterns

In reality, parents and children do not experience social policies singly, but instead as configurations of policies that interact synergistically. To the extent that policies shape life patterns by supporting parental caring time and gender equality, they do so as holistic packages. Here, we synthesize our policy findings to consider how work/family policy provisions operate across welfare state models to shape parent and child outcomes (see Table 1).

The Social Democratic countries, overall, do the most to support both time for care among employed parents and also gender equality in domestic and paid work. These countries shore up parental time by granting mothers lengthy fully-paid leaves (30–42 weeks) and by limiting normal weekly employment hours to 37–39 hours. They also encourage gender equality at home by offering the most leave time for fathers and encouraging men's take-up (although equal usage is far from achieved). In Denmark and Sweden, especially, extensive publicly-supported child care enables parental employment, primarily of mothers with children as young as age one and two.

The Conservative countries, as a group, are somewhat less supportive on both dimensions: freeing up time for employed parents and encouraging egalitarian divisions of labor between mothers and fathers. With respect to caring time, the Conservative countries offer employed mothers only three or four months of paid leave time, considerably less than their counterparts in the Social Democratic countries. Maternal employment rates, however, are substantially lower than in the Social Democratic countries, so by cross-national comparison, mothers' time at home in the Conservative countries is ample. At the same time, these countries have also reduced weekly employment hours for men and women to well below 40, with France being the most dramatic case since enacting a 35-hour work week in 2000. Gender equality, however, is compromised by the lack of benefits and incentives for male leave-takers, and by the low levels of child care provision for children under age three. Nevertheless, in France and Belgium the operation of universal full-day preschool for the "over threes" encourages mothers' labor market attachment; and not surprisingly, maternal employment in these two countries is the highest among the Conservative countries.

Table 1. Policy Supports by Welfare State Regime Type.

	Support for Time to Care		Support for Gender Equality in Paid and Unpaid Work	
	Family Leave Policy (Frees Time for Mothers of Young Children) (see Fig. 2)	Working Time Policy (Frees Time for both Parents) (see Fig. 3)	Family Leave Policy (Supports Fathers' Caregiving) (see Fig. 2)	Early Childhood Education and Care Policy (Supports Mothers' Employment) (see Fig. 4)
Social democratic countries: DK, FI, NW, SW	High	High/medium	High	High/medium
Conservative countries: BE, FR, GE, NL	Medium	High/medium	Medium/low	High/medium
Liberal countries, Europe: UK	Low	Medium	Low	Medium
Liberal countries, non-Europe: US	Low	Low	Low	Low

The Liberal countries lag on both core dimensions. In the United states especially, current work/family policies do little to grant employed parents time to care
– leave is lacking; weekly hours are long; workers have no guaranteed vacation
days – and virtually nothing to enable, much less encourage, gender-egalitarian
divisions of labor in paid work or in caregiving.

LINKING POLICY CONFIGURATIONS TO
PARENT AND CHILD OUTCOMES

In this section, we consider the question of whether the social and labor market
policies considered here actually shape the life patterns of parents and their children. While our intuition tells us that they do, establishing policy effects is always
a complex task, requiring experimental designs or sophisticated multivariate
methods. A large body of empirical research assesses the impact of the three core
policies outlined here: family leave, working-time regulation, and early childhood
education and care. Drawing from the literature, we summarize key findings here
on a range of parent and child outcomes (see Gornick & Meyers, 2003 for a
detailed review).

First, several empirical studies assess the impact of family leave policy, primarily on mothers' employment patterns. The evidence indicates that access to leave
has the potential to reduce labor market inequalities between men and women by
facilitating continuous employment and reducing wage penalties associated with
motherhood (Glass & Riley, 1998; Hofferth, 1996; Joesch, 1997; OECD, 2001;
Smith et al., 2001). Other research suggests that access to family leave may have
health benefits for children, especially in the form of reduced infant mortality
(Ruhm, 2000; Winegarden & Bracy, 1995). Evidence that very young children do
better on other dimensions when a parent is at home is less consistent, although
the most recent research suggests that high levels of maternal employment during
the first year of life are associated with worse outcomes for at least some groups
of children and that these effects persist well into grade school (see, e.g. Ruhm,
forthcoming).

Second, a small body of research assesses the effects of working-time regulations on working-time patterns; these studies consistently find that lowering the
official overtime threshold reduces actual working-time among employees. Several
empirical studies estimate the proportion of the reduction in standard working
hours that is due to a change in regulations. The magnitude of the effect ranges
from 75% to nearly 100%: 77% in the United Kingdom; 85–100% in Germany;
and close to 100% in France (see Costa, 2000; OECD, 1998 for reviews.)

Third, many researchers have examined the effects of early childhood education and care on women's labor market patterns and on children's well-being. This research has produced substantial evidence that high child care costs depress mothers' employment. Policies that reduce these costs have been shown to increase maternal employment – thereby potentially closing the employment and wage gap between mothers and fathers with young children (see Anderson & Levine, 1999 for a review). A substantial empirical literature has also established the contribution of good quality child care to children's health and positive cognitive and socio-emotional outcomes (see Burchinal, 1999; Vandell & Wolfe, 2000 for reviews).

Parent and Child Outcomes Across Paid Work and Care Regimes

We close this chapter by demonstrating that among the countries included in this study – and among the welfare state types to which they correspond – those with more generous and gender-egalitarian policy designs tend to be the same ones in which parents have more time to spend with their children, mothers and fathers divide paid and unpaid work more equally, and children are doing better on key outcomes. Clearly, correlational results such as these cannot establish a causal link between policies and outcomes. Nor can they rule out reverse causation whereby high levels of female employment create demand for supportive policies. In addition, other unmeasured national characteristics such as cultural values favoring gender equality may explain both high levels of female labor force participation and the provision of supportive public policies. When interpreted, however, in conjunction with the methodologically rigorous studies cited above, many of which correct for these problems, the association between varying policy approaches and different outcomes provides a powerful illustration of likely policy impact.

Table 1 suggested the ways that work/family policies vary across regime types. Those findings are augmented in Table 2, which shows how several critical parent and child outcomes also vary systematically across these country groupings.

Table 2 presents two outcomes that indicate gender equality among parents: first, gender equality in the labor market (indicated by women's share in total employment earnings among married or cohabiting parents) and, second, gender equality in time spent in unpaid work (measured as the ratio of fathers' to mothers' mean daily hours spent doing housework and child care). Another outcome reflects the amount of parents' time available for their children: average joint weekly hours spent in paid work among dual-employed couples with children. Finally, child well-being is indicated by five outcomes: first, the child poverty rate,

Table 2. Parent and Child Outcomes by Welfare State Regime Type.

	Gender Equality in Paid Work	Gender Equality in Unpaid Work	Parental Time for Children		Child Well-Being			
	1	2	3	4	5	6	7	8
	Indicator: female share of labor market earnings	Indicator: ratio of fathers' to mothers' time spent in unpaid work	Indicator: couples' joint time spent in paid work	Indicator: child poverty rate	Indicator: infant and young child mortality rate	Indicator: science achievement scores (8th grade)	Indicator: time spent TV-watching (11 year olds)	Indicator: teenage pregnancy rate
Social democratic countries: DK, FI, NW, SW	Good/moderate	Good/moderate (FI, NW, SW only)	Good/moderate (FI, SW only)	Good	Good	Moderate (FI only)	Moderate	Moderate
Conservative countries: BE, FR, GE, NL	Moderate/poor	Moderate/poor (GE, NL only)	Good/moderate	Moderate	Moderate (BE, FR only)	Good/moderate (BE, NL only)	Good/moderate (BE, FR, GE only)	Good
Liberal countries, Europe: UK	Poor	Moderate	Good	Poor	Moderate	Moderate	Moderate	Moderate
Liberal countries, non-Europe: US	Moderate	Poor	Poor	Poor	Poor	Poor	Poor	Poor

Sources: Outcomes in columns 1, 3, and 4 based on data available through the *Luxembourg Income Study* (LIS). Outcomes in column 2 based on data available through the *Multinational Time Use Study* (MTUS). Outcomes in column 6 based on data from the *Third International Mathematics and Science Study* (TIMSS). Outcomes in columns 5, 7, and 8 from UNICEF (2001), Currie et al. (2000), and Singh and Darroch (2000) respectively. For measurement details, see Gornick and Meyers (2003).

measured as the percentage of children who live in households with post-tax-and-transfer income below their country's median; second, infant and young child mortality rates, represented by the death rates of children below age 1 and age 5, respectively; third, average science achievement scores in the eighth grade; fourth, the percentage of 11-year-olds who watch 4 or more hours of television per day; and finally, the pregnancy rate among young women ages 15–19.[8]

The Social Democratic countries show favorable levels of gender equality both at home and in the labor market; moderate to good parental time for children among dual-employed couples with children; and moderate to good child outcomes. These outcomes suggest that the Social Democratic countries (especially Denmark, Norway, and Sweden) are closest to the dual-earner/dual-carer model situated on the far-right of Fig. 1.

In the Conservative countries, we also observe moderate to good child outcomes; there is more child poverty in these countries (due in part to lower levels of maternal employment) but also lower rates of teenage pregnancy (perhaps not surprising, given the social conservatism). Employed parents, like their counterparts in the Social Democratic countries, have substantial time available to care for their children, but gender equality suffers, as mothers' labor market attachment is much weaker than fathers'. For the most part, current patterns of parental time and gendered labor locate these countries at the crossroads of the "male-breadwinner/female-carer" and the "dual-earner/female part-time carer" models in Fig. 1.

The U.K. is a remarkable case. Parents in dual-employed couples have substantial time to care for their children, because a large share of employed mothers work part-time and at low hours. But the price for that arrangement – the "dual-earner/part-time carer" model from Fig. 1 – is substantial gender inequality in the labor market and at home. Furthermore, children in the U.K. fare less well than children in the Conservative and Social Democratic countries. The moderate child outcomes are perhaps not surprising given the high child poverty rate caused, at least in part, by relatively weak maternal employment in conjunction with comparatively limited cash transfers for families (Meyers & Gornick, 2001).

The U.S. does poorly across the board, with one exception – gender equality in the labor market, as indicated by the share of total parental earnings commanded by mothers. Married or cohabiting mothers in the U.S. take home a substantial share of their families' earnings (on average, about 28%), because a large share of mothers are employed, and mostly full-time; this pattern recalls the characterization of the contemporary U.S. as adhering to a dual-earner (although not dual-carer) model. Comparative scholars have offered several explanations for the high maternal employment rate in the U.S., which is somewhat paradoxical, given the low level of policy support for mothers' labor market engagement. The most persuasive explanations include the "employment-forcing" effects of the lack of alternatives to labor market income; the need for health insurance, which is typically granted in the U.S. through full-time employment; political-cultural factors that stress market involvement; the U.S. feminist movement's longstanding emphasis on employment, and male wages that have fallen more sharply than in most industrialized countries.

With the exception of moderate gender equality in the labor market, all other outcomes in the U.S., among the eight considered here, are poor. Gender equality at home is unimpressive – employed fathers spend 44% as much time as their female counterparts doing housework and child care. Furthermore, employed couples are particularly time-squeezed as they jointly work for pay for 80 hours per week, on average. Finally, children in the U.S. are more likely than children in the other welfare regimes to be poor, to die young, to lag in school, to spend excessive hours in front of the television, and to become pregnant as teenagers. In the U.S., children's well-being, captured at the average, is alarming – in absolute terms and, even more so, in cross-national terms.

CONCLUSION

Welfare states vary widely in the ways in which they support parents in their efforts to balance employment and caregiving responsibilities; they also vary in the extent to which they encourage an egalitarian division of labor between women and men in employment and at home. Family leave policies can grant parents time for caring for their young children; and working-time regulations can increase caregiving time throughout the life cycle. Family leave designs can also both grant men generous paid leave rights and raise the likelihood that they will take them up, while child care policies that ensure available, affordable and high-quality alternatives to maternal care can strengthen women's employment as well as enhance child well-being. Cash benefits, in addition to paid family leave, can shore up family economic security, although their effects on parental caregiving time and gendered labor patterns are ambiguous.

Overall, the Social Democratic countries have enacted policy packages that do the most to support the development of a dual-earner/dual-carer society – that is, a gender-egalitarian society that values both paid work and parental caregiving time and that prizes child well-being. Policies in the Conservative European countries help to secure time for caring and family economic stability, but they do much less to enable or encourage gender equality in paid and unpaid work. Not surprisingly, it is in these countries where inequality between women and men in divisions of labor is still most evident.

In the market-based Liberal countries – the U.K. and especially the U.S. – public policy supports for employed parents are minimal. In these countries, most parents are at the mercy of their employers for paid family leave, reduced-hour options, and vacation time; the vast majority of parents have to turn to private markets to secure care and educational arrangements, especially during the first five years of their children's lives. Considerable evidence suggests that when states do little to help parents with the costs of childrearing – that is, when provisions are distributed via labor and consumer markets – parents and children suffer, on average, as does gender equality. Equally compelling evidence indicates that, when supports for families are not provided publicly, distributional results are also highly regressive within countries. In the U.S., families and workers with the fewest resources have access to the most limited employment-based family leave provisions and the least vacation time; they also spend the largest share of their disposable income on substitute child care while receiving the lowest quality care (Gornick & Meyers, 2003; Heymann, 2001).

What does the future hold for these regimes of paid work and care? In the Social Democratic and Conservative countries of Europe, the foreseeable future seems fairly certain. Despite three decades of political, economic, and demographic strain all across Europe, welfare state retrenchment – contrary to U.S. media accounts – has been quite modest and these welfare states remain intact (Gornick & Meyers, 2001). Whereas some restructuring and rolling-back has taken place in old-age, unemployment, and disability pensions, work/family policies have been singled out for protection and expansion in nearly every European country. Bolstered by policy development at the European Union level throughout the 1990s, provisions for family leave were expanded in several countries and entirely new programs were introduced in others; policy reforms mandated reductions in working time and public investments in early childhood education grew nearly everywhere during this period (Gornick & Meyers, 2001). There is accumulating evidence of continuing growth into the early years of the new century. For the most part, policies in these regimes seem to be expanding in accord with the principles that have long characterized them, with both parental time and family economic security valued everywhere, and gender equality emphasized most strongly in the Social Democratic countries.

In the Liberal countries, especially in the U.S., much less is certain. What is clear is that the development of a package of generous paid work and care policies would require an organized expression of political will. It is possible that broadening the end vision of work/family policy to incorporate the development of a gender-egalitarian world might help to close political cleavages that have hampered the adoption of comprehensive family policies in the past. Formulating leave, working time, and child care policies that explicitly extend benefits to fathers as well as mothers has the potential to engage and intensify men's support for family policy expansion. Designing these policies as supports for both employment and caring, shared equally by women and men, holds promise for closing the schism between feminists oriented to reducing gender differentials, especially in the labor market, and those focused on rewarding caregiving in the home. And advocating for a policy package that enables parents to care for young children at home holds promise for bridging the gap that often separates feminists working toward gender equality from advocates concerned with children's well-being. Embracing the vision of the dual-earner/dual-carer society may help to mobilize broader and more diversified support for family policy expansion in the United states.

NOTES

1. Portions of this chapter are based on material presented in our book: Gornick, Janet C. and Meyers, Marcia K. (2003), *Families That Work: Policies for Reconciling Parenthood and Employment*. New York: Russell Sage Foundation. See the book or contact the first author (janet_gornick@baruch.cuny.edu) for details, and original sources, on the policy measures presented in Figs 2–4 and/or the outcomes presented in Table 2.

2. The ten countries in this study fall into these country groups as follows (with abbreviations used in the exhibits): four *Social Democratic* countries: Denmark (DK), Finland (FI), Norway (NW) and Sweden (SW); four *Conservative* countries: Belgium (BE), France (FR), Germany (GE) and the Netherlands (NL); and two *Liberal* countries: the United Kingdom (U.K.) and the United states (U.S.).

3. "Weeks of leave" presented in Fig. 2 reflects a combination of duration and benefit generosity. In Finland, for example, the 29 weeks reported results from 44 weeks at about two-thirds pay. Figure 2 excludes the U.S. Temporary Disability Insurance programs, which offer some maternity pay, because they operate in only five states. In the other countries, Fig. 2 reports only *earnings-related components* of family leave and assumes earnings below any existing earnings caps. About half of our comparison countries supplement the benefits captured in Fig. 2 with additional periods of leave paid at a low flat-rate – most substantially in Finland, France, and Germany. We exclude these low-paid benefits here because, in some cases (Finland and Germany) the benefits are not conditioned on employment, so characterizing them as wage replacement is not fully accurate. In addition, the program in France is payable only for second and subsequent children. Furthermore, take-up is much lower than in the earnings-related programs, so including them distorts the level of provision upward.

4. The logic of this "gender equality scale" derives from empirical research findings that indicate that male take-up is encouraged by non-transferable rights (rights that cannot be transferred to female partners) combined with high wage replacement. We assigned countries one point on this gender equality scale if they offer any paid paternity leave, two points if fathers have parental leave rights that are non-transferable, and up to three additional points capturing the level of wage replacement (three points if benefits are wage-related and at 80% or higher, two points if benefits are wage-related but at less than 80%, and one point if benefits are paid but at a flat rate).

5. In Fig. 3, normal weekly hours indicate the shorter of normal hours set by statute or by standard collective agreements. Vacation time captures the minimum number of days required by national statute.

6. European Union Directives are binding for EU-member countries. Norway, the one non-member among these nine European countries, voluntarily implements EU Directives.

7. Working-time regulations can also aim to increase the feasibility of reduced-hour work by raising its quality. The 1997 European Union Directive on Part-Time Work, for example, required member countries to enact measures that prohibit discrimination against part-time workers, thus aiming at parity in pay, benefits, and working conditions, relative to comparable full-time workers.

8. These outcomes were coded into categories as follows. Gender equality in the labor market, indicated by women's share in total employment earnings among married or cohabiting parents: good = 35% or more, moderate = 25–34%, poor $\leq$ 25%. Gender equality in time spent in paid work at home, measured as the ratio of fathers' to mothers' mean daily hours spent doing unpaid work, including housework and child care: good = 55% or more, moderate = 45–54%, poor $\leq$ 45%. Average joint weekly hours spent working for pay among dual-employed couples with children: good $\leq$ 75, moderate = 75–79, poor = 80 or more. The child poverty rate, measured as the percentage of children who live in households with post-tax-and-transfer income below their country's median: good $\leq$ 5%, moderate = 5–10%, poor = 15% or more. Infant and young child mortality rates, captured in the death rates of child below age 1 and age 5, respectively: good $\leq$ 5 per 100,000, moderate = 5–6 per 100,000, poor = 7–8 per 100,000. Average science achievement scores in the eighth grade: good = 550 and above, moderate = 520–549, poor $\leq$ 520. Percentage of 11 year-olds who watch 4+ hours of television per day: good $\leq$ 15, moderate = 15–30%, poor = 35% or more. The pregnancy rate among women aged 15 to 19: good = 20 or fewer per 1000, moderate = 21–50 per 1000, poor = 70 or more per 1000.

REFERENCES

Anderson, P. M., & Levine, P. (1999). Child care and mother's employment decisions. Working Paper No. W7058. Cambridge, MA: National Bureau of Economic Research.

Burchinal, M. (1999). Child care experiences and developmental outcomes. *Annals of the American Academy of Political and Social Science, 563*, 73–97.

Costa, D. (2000). Hours of work and the fair labor standard act: A study of retail and wholesale trade, 1938–1950. *Industrial and Labor Relations Review, 53*, 648–664.

Crompton, R. (Ed.) (1999). *Restructuring gender relations and employment: The decline of the male breadwinner*. Oxford, UK: Oxford University Press.

Currie, C., Hurrelmann, K., Settertobulte, W., Smith, R., & Todd, J. (Eds) (2000). *Health and health behavior among young people*. Copenhagan, Denmark: World Health Organization Regional Office for Europe.

Esping-Anderson, G. (1990). *The three worlds of welfare capitalism*. Princeton, NJ: Princeton University Press.

Fraser, N. (1994). After the family wage: Gender equity and the welfare state. *Political Theory, 22*(4), 591–618.

Glass, J., & Riley, L. (1998). Family responsive policies and employee retention following childbirth. *Social Forces, 76*, 1401–1435.

Gornick, J. C., & Meyers, M. K. (2001). Lesson-drawing in family policy: Media reports and empirical evidence about European developments. *Journal of Comparative Policy Analysis: Research and Practice, 3,* 31–57.

Gornick, J. C., & Meyers, M. K. (2003). *Families that work: Policies for reconciling parenthood and employment.* New York: Sage.

Heymann, J. (2001). *The widening gap: Why America's working families are in jeopardy – and what can be done about it.* New York: Basic Books.

Hofferth, S. L. (1996). Effects of public and private policies on working after childbirth. *Work and Occupations, 23,* 378–404.

Jacobs, J., & Gerson, K. (forthcoming). *The time divide: Work, family, and social policy.* Cambridge, MA: Harvard University Press.

Joesch, J. M. (1997). Paid leave and the timing of women's employment before and after birth. *Journal of Marriage and The Family, 58,* 1008–1021.

Knijn, T., & Kremer, M. (1997). Gender and the caring dimension of welfare states: Towards inclusive citizenship. *Social Politics, 4,* 328–362.

Meyers, M. K., & Gornick, J. C. (2001). Gendering welfare state variation: Income transfers, employment supports, and family poverty. In: N. Hirschmann & U. Liebert (Eds), *Women and Welfare: Theory and Practice in the United States and Europe* (pp. 215–243). New Jersey: Rutgers University Press.

Mutari, E., & Figart, D. M. (2001). Europe at a crossroads: Harmonization, liberalization, and the gender of work time. *Social Politics, 8,* 36–64.

OECD [Organization for Economic Cooperation and Development] (1998). Working hours: Latest trends and policy initiatives. *Employment Outlook,* 153–188.

OECD [Organization for Economic Cooperation and Development] (2001). Balancing work and family life: Helping parents into paid employment. *Employment Outlook,* 129–166.

Ruhm, C. J. (2000). Parental leave and child health. *Journal of Health Economics, 19,* 931–960.

Ruhm, C. J. (forthcoming). Parental employment and child cognitive development. *Journal of Human Resources.*

Singh, S., & Darroch, J. (2000). Adolescent pregnancy and childbearing: Levels and trends across developed countries. *Family Planning Perspectives, 32,* 14–23.

Smith, K., Downs, B., & O' Cornell, M. (2001). Maternity leave and employment patterns: 1961–1995. Current Population Reports P70–79. Washington, DC: U.S. Census Bureau.

UNICEF (2001). *The state of the world's children.* Downloaded from: http://www.unicef.org/sowc01/pdf/fullsowc.pdf on August 12, 2002.

Vandell, D. L., & Wolfe, B. (2000). Child care quality: Does it matter and does it need to be improved? Institute for Research on Poverty Special Report. Madison, WI: University of Wisconsin.

Winegarden, C. R., & Bracy, P. (1995). Demographic consequences of maternal leave programs in industrial countries from fixed effects models. *Southern Economic Journal, 61,* 1020–1035.

Woodward, E. (2002). *Are Americans 'vacation starved'?* Downloaded from: http://www.accuracy.org/ipam081601.htm on December 2, 2002.

4. LIFESTYLE PREFERENCES VERSUS PATRIARCHAL VALUES: CAUSAL AND NON-CAUSAL ATTITUDES

Catherine Hakim

ABSTRACT

There is solid evidence, from longitudinal studies such as the NLS and PSID, of the significant long-term impact of values and life goals on occupational attainment and earnings. So far, these findings have not been incorporated into sociological and economic theory. Preference theory does this, identifying the social and economic context in which values and attitudes can become important predictors of women's (and men's) behaviour. A theoretical and methodological distinction between causal and non-causal attitudes and values is made, illustrated by data on lifestyle preferences and patriarchal values from comparative surveys in Britain and Spain. The results show that lifestyle preferences have a major impact on women's choices between family work and employment, whereas patriarchal values are only tenuously linked to behaviour.

INTRODUCTION

Academic social scientists have been slow to recognise the importance of attitudes and values as causal factors in their own right. There are several reasons for this.

Changing Life Patterns in Western Industrial Societies
Advances in Life Course Research, Volume 8, 69–91
© 2004 Published by Elsevier Ltd.
ISSN: 1040-2608/doi:10.1016/S1040-2608(03)08004-3

One is the relative invisibility of core attitudes and values – as illustrated by the desire to have, or not have, children. In both cases, people rarely discuss their preference, either because it is obvious and taken-for-granted, or else because it is odd or deviant. Second, there is an old research literature showing only a weak association between attitudes and behaviour. The third reason is organisational: most research on attitudes is done by social psychologists, while sociologists, economists and demographers generally focus on behaviour. A fourth reason is technical. Many methods textbooks are written by social statisticians, who typically advise that attitudes should be measured by a series of questions making up a scale rather than by single items. Researchers are discouraged from using their substantive expertise to identify just two or three key diagnostic questions on values and preferences. Fifth, it is well known that political attitudes are highly volatile and responsive to public events. This prompts the false conclusion that all attitudes and values are moulded by the contemporary situation, and that none have independent causal powers.

This chapter demonstrates that we already have solid evidence from longitudinal studies on the long-term impact of personal values and life goals. This evidence has been ignored because of the technical difficulty of differentiating between causal and non-causal values. We identify theoretical and methodological distinctions between causal and non-causal attitudes and values, and then present a new theory that sets out the social, economic and institutional context in which core values start to impact heavily on women's choices. Preference theory reveals the impact of lifestyle preferences as a causal factor of increasing importance in modern societies. Survey data for Britain and Spain show that lifestyle preferences already shape labour force participation and fertility. We also show that acceptance or rejection of patriarchal values has little or no impact on behaviour, because these are public morality attitudes (and non-causal in relation to private choices), rather than personal preferences (which are causal).

THE LONG-TERM IMPACT OF VALUES AND PERSONAL GOALS

From the 1960s onwards, the National Longitudinal Surveys (NLS) in the USA provided longitudinal data that revealed the long-term impact of work orientations and work plans. Of particular interest is the cohort of young women aged 14–24 in 1968 who were interviewed almost every year up to 1983 when aged 29–39 years. This cohort was asked in 1968, and again at every subsequent interview, what they would like to be doing when they were 35 years old, whether they planned to be working at age 35 or whether they planned to marry, keep house and raise a family at age 35.[1] Compared to the length and complexity of work commitment questions included in some surveys (Bielby & Bielby, 1984), the question is crude, and conflates preferences and plans. But because it asked about women's personal plans, rather than generalised approval/disapproval attitudes, the question turned out to have astonishing analytical and predictive power.

There are a number of independent analyses of the extent to which early workplans were fulfilled by age 35 in the USA in the 1980s. They all show that women achieved their objectives for the most part, resulting in dramatic gains to career planners in terms of occupational grade and earnings (Mott, 1982; Rexroat & Shehan, 1984; Shaw & Shapiro, 1987). Furthermore, career planners were more likely to choose typically-male jobs, had lower job satisfaction than other women and adapted their fertility behaviour to their workplans (Spitze & Waite, 1980; Stolzenberg & Waite, 1977; Waite & Stolzenberg, 1976). Workplans were a significant independent predictor of actual work behaviour. After controlling for other factors affecting labour force participation, a woman who consistently planned to work had a probability of working that was 30 percentage points higher than did a woman who consistently planned not to work. Of the women who held consistently to their work plans, four-fifths were actually working in 1980, at age 35, compared to only half of the women who consistently intended to devote themselves exclusively to home-maker activities. Women who had planned a "marriage career" nevertheless were obliged to work by economic factors in half the cases: their husband's low income, divorce, or the opportunity cost of not working led half to be in work despite aiming for a full-time homemaker role.

Planning to work yielded a significant wage advantage. Women who had consistently planned to work had wages 30% higher than those of women who never planned to work. Those women who had planned to work in the occupation they actually held at age 35 had even higher wages than women whose occupational plans were not realised. Women who made realistic plans and acquired necessary skills fared best in the labour market. However career planners were a small minority of one-quarter of the young women cohort; the vast majority of the cohort had unplanned careers (Table 1).

Factors which have long been held to determine women's labour force participation, such as other family income, educational qualifications, marital status, and age of youngest child were revealed as being most important in relation to women with little or no work commitment, who have so far been in the majority. Women with definite career plans manifested a rather inelastic labour supply, similar to that of men (Shaw & Shapiro, 1987).

Overall the NLS results have repeatedly shown the importance of motivations, values and attitudes as key determinants of labour market behaviour, occupational status and even earnings, an influence that is independent of conventional

Table 1.   Young Women's Work Plans and Outcomes in the USA.

	Distribution of Sample (%)	% Working at Age 35
Homemaker career: consistently indicate no plans for work; aim is marriage, family and homemaking activities	28	49
Drifters and unplanned careers	47	64
(a) Highly variable responses over time, no clear pattern in plans for age 35	35	
(b) Switch to having future work expectations at some point in their twenties	12	
Career planners: consistently anticipate working at age 35 throughout their twenties	25	82

Source: Derived from Tables 2 and 3, reporting National Longitudinal Surveys data for the cohort of
young women first interviewed in 1968, when aged 14–24 years, in Shaw and Shapiro (1987,
pp. 8–9).

human capital factors, and frequently exceeds the influence of behavioural factors (Andrisani, 1978; Mott, 1982; Parnes, 1975; Sproat et al., 1985). These "psychological" variables are usually omitted from sociological and economic research, so their importance has been overlooked.

Similar results emerge from other longitudinal studies, on the rare occasions when researchers address the long-term impact of values and life goals. Attitudes have a specially strong impact on women's behaviour today, because they have gained genuine choices regarding employment vs. homemaking. But attitudes and values have also been shown to have a major impact on men as well. For example, Szekelyi and Tardos analysed 20 years of PSID microdata for 1968–1988 to show that people who plan ahead and express confidence and optimism about their plans subsequently earn significantly higher incomes than those who do not, after controlling for other factors. The long-term effects of attitudes were stronger than short-term effects (Szekelyi & Tardos, 1993).

Similar results are reported by Duncan and Dunifon (1998), from another analysis of 24 years of PSID data, this time covering men only. Motivation (as measured in the early twenties) had a large impact on long-term success (as measured by hourly earnings 16–20 years later), and the effect remained after controlling for other factors. Only a small part of the impact of motivation worked through its effect on greater investment in training and education; a substantial part remained after this control. The study showed that values commonly found among women, such as religiosity and a preference for affiliation (as measured by a preference for friendly and sociable work settings rather than challenging work settings) both had a negative effect on earnings. Work orientations that emphasised challenge rather than affiliation and a clear sense of personal efficacy boosted earnings in the early forties.

In sum, there is already solid evidence that attitudes, values and life goals have an important impact on outcomes in adult life, for men as well as women in modern societies. Some social scientists are exploring the pivotal role of values in modern societies, often using person-centred analysis, as illustrated by Szakolczai and Füstös (1998). However there has so far been no attempt to integrate this new knowledge into sociological theory, and empirical studies routinely ignore these substantive findings.[2] One specific problem has been the difficulty of differentiating between causal and non-causal attitudes and values within the attitudinal data collected in surveys.

CAUSAL AND NON-CAUSAL ATTITUDES AND VALUES

A review of empirical studies in the 1960s concluded that attitudes were generally "unrelated or only slightly related to overt behaviours" (Wicker, 1969, p. 65). Alwin (1973) concluded that it is rarely possible to determine to what extent attitudes cause behaviour or behaviour causes attitudes. This old literature, showing a weak association between attitudes and behaviour, has become received wisdom, despite the fact that a new stream of research in the 1990s exposed methodological weaknesses in early studies, and revealed that *some* attitudes have a causal impact on behaviour.

A meta-analysis of 88 attitude-behaviour studies concluded that attitudes predict future behaviour to a substantial degree, but the link is only revealed when data measures specific, rather than general attitudes (Kraus, 1995; see also Ajzen & Fishbein, 1977). A cross-national comparative study by political scientists confirmed the substantive and analytical primacy of values as an independent variable shaping behaviour; underlined the fragmentation and pluralisation of values in the 1990s; and concluded that values now have a larger impact on choice of political party than social differences (Van Deth & Scarbrough, 1995, pp. 18, 533–538). Further, international bodies such as the OECD are beginning to accept that labour market behaviour is strongly shaped by work orientations, in particular women's marked preference for part-time jobs in all advanced economies (OECD, 1999, Table 1.13). Attitudes can have important short-term and long-term impacts, even if their influence disappears among social structural factors in many studies, like water in sand. Beliefs and values may be intangible, but people act on them.

There is an important theoretical and methodological distinction between personal goals and preferences (which are causal in relation to individual behaviour) and general social attitudes and views on public morality at the broad level (which are usually non-causal). Hofstede (1980, p. 21, 1991) was the first to make the distinction between *choice* and *approval*, between personal goals and public beliefs, between what is desired by the survey respondent for their own life and what is considered desirable in society in general. The strong link between attitudes and behaviour only occurs in the case of personal preferences and goals (Hakim, 2002).

Opinion polls and social attitude surveys, such as the General Social Survey in the USA, the British Social Attitudes Survey (BSAS), the World Values Survey, the International Social Survey Programme (ISSP), and the European Social Survey, mainly collect data on public support for selected public morality statements. They almost never ask people about their personal preferences for their own life. As the designers of the BSAS and ISSP point out, these sorts of social attitudes cannot be read as predictions of individual behaviour (Jowell & Witherspoon, 1985, pp. 58, 124).

Surprisingly, specially-designed social surveys in the USA and Europe also collect data on public morality far more often than on personal preferences and goals, even when they seek to explain behaviour, leading to the inevitable conclusion of a weak association at best (Agassi, 1979, 1982; Bielby & Bielby, 1984; Hakim, 2000, pp. 72–82). The British 1980 Women and Employment Survey collected public morality data almost exclusively, and several analyses of the data showed only weak associations between general approval for women's employment and women's own employment choices (Dex, 1988, p. 124; Hakim, 1991, p. 105; Martin & Roberts, 1984, pp. 172–176).

On the rare occasion when studies collect data on personal preferences, they find strong correlations with behaviour. For example Geerken and Gove (1983, pp. 64–66) found that women's responses to general sex-role attitude statements were not associated with employment decisions, whereas their personal preference for and commitment to having a job was a powerful determinant of being in work or not, stronger than social structural factors, especially when the husband's attitudes were also taken into account. Geerken and Gove show that these two factors in combination produced a 50–70 percentage point increase in wives' economic activity rates in the USA.

PREFERENCE THEORY

Preference theory identifies the type of values that have the greatest causal impact on behaviour. Preference theory is a new theory for explaining and predicting women's choices between market work and family work, a theory that is historically-informed, empirically-based, multidisciplinary, prospective rather than retrospective in orientation, and applicable in all rich modern societies (Hakim, 2000). Lifestyle preferences are defined as increasingly important causal factors which thus need to be monitored in modern societies. In contrast, other social attitudes are either unimportant as predictors of behaviour, or else have only a marginal impact in creating a particular climate of public opinion on women's roles.

Preference theory specifies the historical context in which core values become important predictors of behaviour. It notes that five historical changes collectively produce a qualitatively new scenario for women in rich modern societies in the 21st century, giving them opportunities and choices that were not previously available to them. The five conditions that create a new scenario are:

- the contraceptive revolution which, from the 1960s onwards, gave sexually active women reliable and independent control over their own fertility for the first time in history;
- the equal opportunities revolution, which ensured that for the first time in history women obtained equal access to all positions, occupations and careers in the labour market. Sometimes, this was extended to posts in the public sphere more generally. In some countries, legislation prohibiting sex discrimination goes much wider than just the labour market, giving women equal access to housing, financial services, and other public services;
- the expansion of white-collar occupations, which are far more attractive to women that most blue-collar occupations;
- the creation of jobs for secondary earners, people who do not give priority to paid work at the expense of other life interests; and
- the increasing importance of attitudes, values and personal preferences in the lifestyle choices of people in prosperous, liberal modern societies.

The five changes are historically-specific developments in any society. They are not automatic, and do not necessarily occur in all modern societies. They may not occur together, at a single point in time in a country. The timing of the five changes varies greatly between countries. The effects of the five changes are cumulative. The two revolutions are essential and constitute the core of the social revolution for women. The five changes collectively are necessary to create a new scenario in which women have genuine choices and female heterogeneity is revealed to its full extent.

In western Europe, north America, and other modern societies, these five changes only took place from the 1960s onwards. The timing and pace of change has varied, even between countries in Europe. All five changes were completed early in the USA and Britain, so that the new scenario was well established by the last two decades of the 20th century in these two countries, unlike the rest of Europe. Within Europe, the Netherlands may be the only other country that had achieved the new scenario by the year 2000. Sweden has so far failed to implement the last two conditions, so genuine choices are still not a reality in that country. Our analysis of Scandinavian social policy (Hakim, 2000, pp. 232–243) clarifies that gender equality is in reality no further advanced than in other modern societies, and that social policy, in Sweden particularly, favours a single, uniform adaptive lifestyle for women that disregards the diversity of lifestyle preferences. As Bielenski and Wagner show (in this volume), half of all employees in western Europe would prefer to work fewer hours, so actual hours worked are constrained by inflexible employment structures. However the Netherlands has the highest level of satisfaction with working hours, especially among women, and Sweden has one of the lowest levels of satisfaction with working hours.

A review of recent research evidence (Hakim, 2000) shows that once genuine choices are open to them, women choose three different lifestyles: adaptive, work-centred or home-centred (Table 2). These divergent preferences are found at all levels of education, and in all social classes.

Adaptive women prefer to combine employment and family work without giving a fixed priority to either. They want to enjoy the best of both worlds. Adaptive women are generally the largest group among women, and will be found in substantial numbers in most occupations. Certain occupations, such as schoolteaching, are attractive to women because they facilitate an even work-family balance. The great majority of women who transfer to part-time work after they have children are adaptive women, who seek to devote as much time and effort to their family work as to their jobs. In some countries (such as the USA and southern European countries), and in certain occupations, part-time jobs are still rare, so other types of job are chosen. For example seasonal jobs, temporary work, or school-term-time jobs all offer a better work-family balance than the typical full-time job, especially if commuting is also involved. Because adaptive women are in the majority, they give rise to the idea that all women's priorities (or preferences) change over the life course. However the two minority groups of women have lifestyle preferences and priorities that are stable over the life course.

Work-centred women are in a minority, despite the massive influx of women into higher education and into professional and managerial occupations in the last three decades. Work-centred people (men and women) are focused on competitive activities in the public sphere – in careers, sport, politics, or the arts. Family life is fitted around their work, and many of these women remain childless, even when married. Qualifications and training are obtained as a career investment rather than as an insurance policy, as in the adaptive group. The majority of men are

Table 2. Classification of Women's Work-Lifestyle Preferences
in the 21st Century.

Home-Centred 20% of Women Varies 10–30%	Adaptive 60% of Women Varies 40–80%	Work-Centred 20% of Women Varies 10–30%
Family life and children are the main priorities throughout life.	This group is most diverse and includes women who want to combine work and family, plus drifters and unplanned careers.	Childless women are concentrated here. Main priority in life is employment or equivalent activities in the public arena: politics, sport, art, etc.
Prefer *not* to work.	Want to work, but *not* totally committed to work career.	Committed to work or equivalent activities.
Qualifications obtained as cultural capital.	Qualifications obtained with the intention of working.	Large investment in qualifications/training for employment or other activities.
Number of children is affected by government social policy, family wealth, etc.	This group is *very responsive* to government social policy, employment policy, equal opportunities policy/propaganda, economic cycle/recession/ growth, etc.	Responsive to economic opportunity, political opportunity, artistic opportunity, etc.
Not responsive to employment policy.	Such as: Income tax and social welfare benefits Educational policies School timetables Child care services Public attitude towards working women Legislation promoting female employment Trade union attitudes to working women Availability of part-time work and similar work flexibility Economic growth and prosperity And institutional factors generally.	Not responsive to social/family policy.

Source: Hakim (2000).

work-centred, compared to only a minority of women. Preference theory predicts that men will retain their dominance in the labour market, politics and other competitive activities, because only a minority of women are prepared to prioritise their jobs (or other activities in the public sphere) in the same way as men. This is unwelcome news to many feminists, who have assumed that women would be just as likely as men to be work-centred once opportunities were opened to them, and that sex discrimination alone has so far held women back from the top jobs in any society.

The third group, *home-centred women*, is also a minority, and a relatively invisible one, given the current political and media focus on working women and high achievers. Home-centred women prefer to give priority to private life and family life after they marry. They are most inclined to have larger families, and these women avoid paid work after marriage unless the family is experiencing a financial emergency. They do not necessarily invest less in qualifications, because the educational system functions as a marriage market as well as a training institution. Despite the elimination of the sex differential in educational attainment, an increasing proportion of wives in the USA and Europe are now marrying a man with substantially better qualifications, and the likelihood of marrying a graduate spouse is hugely increased if the woman herself has obtained a degree (Hakim, 2000, pp. 193–222). However these women are less likely to choose vocational courses with a direct economic value, and are more likely to take courses in the arts, humanities or languages, which provide cultural capital but have lower earnings potential.

The three preference groups are set out as sociological ideal-types in Table 2. As argued in detail elsewhere (Hakim, 2000), Britain and the USA provide examples of countries where public policy does not bias the distribution of preference groups, and estimates of the relative sizes of the three groups are based on research evidence for these countries. In this case, the distribution of women across the three groups corresponds to a "normal" distribution of responses to the family-work conflict. In practice, in most societies, public policy, and associated rhetoric, are biased towards one group or another, by accident or by design, so that the exact percentages vary across modern societies. As Heath et al. (1991) point out, ideas and core values that do not have elite backing and institutional support generally do not have the same force and coherence in public opinion as those benefitting from intellectual pedigrees and institutional support. In countries such as France, social policies developed alternately by socialist and conservative governments have produced a wider span of support for all three lifestyle preferences, whereas in Germany, for example, there is a clearer bias towards support for home-centred women. Thus, within each country, the welfare regime and fiscal policy combine to amplify or dampen the expression and implementation of preferences. Choices are not made in a vacuum. Social and economic factors still matter, and will produce national variations in employment patterns and lifestyle choices. As a result, there will always be differences between the new scenario countries in work rates, patterns of employment, and fertility levels.

In sum, lifestyle preferences determine:

- women's fertility: the incidence of childlessness and, for the majority who do have children, family sizes;
- women's employment pattern over the lifecycle: choices between careers and jobs, full-time and part-time work, and associated job values; and
- women's responsiveness to public policies, employer policies, economic and social circumstances.

Preferences do not predict outcomes with complete certainty, even when women have genuine choices, because of variations in individual abilities and factors in the social and economic environment. However in prosperous modern societies, preferences become a much more important determinant, sometimes even the main determinant of women's employment patterns.

The three lifestyle preference groups differ in values, goals and aspirations. That is, they are defined by their contrasting lifestyle preferences rather than by behavioural outcomes. The three groups also differ in *consistency* of aspirations and values, not by strong vs. weak preferences. Critics who argue that women's choices are shaped by external events and that an individual's preferences change over the life course immediately define themselves as adaptives. The distinctive feature of the two extreme groups of women (and equivalent men) is that they do *not* waver in their goals, even when they fail to achieve them. Work-centred people are defined by prioritising market work (or equivalent activities in the public sphere) over family work and family life, *not* by exceptional success in the public sphere.

LIFESTYLE PREFERENCES VERSUS PATRIARCHAL VALUES: CAUSAL AND NON-CAUSAL VALUES

Two surveys, in Britain and Spain, were used to test and compare the relative impact of lifestyle preferences, which we classify as core values that shape behaviour, and the type of public morality attitudes that are typically collected by opinion polls and social attitude surveys.[3] Britain illustrates the impact of lifestyle preferences in the new scenario. In contrast, Spain is a modern country that has not yet fully achieved the new scenario, so we expected weaker links between attitudes and behaviour in the Spanish survey results.

The British survey was carried out as part of the Economic and Social Research Council (ESRC) five-year Research Programme on the Future of Work 1998–2003. The interview survey was carried out for the author by the Office of National Statistics (ONS) in Britain in January and February 1999. The survey was based on a probability random sample of households, and face-to-face interviews with one person aged 16 and over chosen randomly within each household. The proportion of households in which the selected informant was the head of household or spouse was 81% in our sample. From a sample of 5,388 eligible addresses, an overall response rate of 68% was achieved, producing data for a nationally representative sample of 3,651 persons aged 16 and over in Britain. Refusals accounted for 24% of the initial sample, and non-contacts for another 8%. The final sample included 1,691 men and 1,960 women, with a substantial proportion (20%) aged 65 and over. Excluding the pensioners reduces the sample for the population of working age to 2,900, including 2,345 married and cohabiting couples.

The Spanish survey was carried out towards the end of 1999 by Análisis Sociológicos, Económicos y Políticos (ASEP) in collaboration with the Director, Professor Juan Díez-Nicolas. The survey was designed to obtain a nationally representative random sample of adults aged 18 or over living in private households in Spain, including the Balearic Islands and the Canary Islands, but excluding Ceuta and Melilla (two enclaves in north Africa). Sampling was based on proportional distribution by region and size of place within each region. Within each sampling cluster, individuals were selected according to random routes and Kish tables for members of the household. Personal interviews were conducted with respondents at their homes. Refusals were only 2%. The completed sample of 1,211 people aged 18 and over included 595 men and 616 women. The Spanish sample is much smaller than the British sample, with a corresponding reduction in the scope and detail of analyses. Excluding people aged 60 and over (27%), reduces the sample for the population aged 20–59 to 837. Students in full-time education were excluded from all analyses, as for Britain. Two-thirds of the sample consisted of married and cohabiting couples, of whom 541 were aged 20–59. Due to much lower work rates in Spain, for men as well as women, only 493 people aged 20–59 had a job of any kind, 320 men and 173 women.

In both surveys, three questions were used to operationalise lifestyle preferences (Table 3). A question on the respondent's personal ideal model of the family was taken from the Eurobarometer series. This identified home-centred women, whose ideal was the complete separation of roles, with the husband as breadwinner and the wife as full-time homemaker. Another Eurobarometer question was used to identify people who regard themselves as primary earners in their household, rather than secondary earners who are financially dependent in large part. The third question was a widely-used question on people's commitment to paid work, even if this were not financially necessary, as in the case of winning the lottery. There are national lotteries in Britain and Spain, so that the idea of winning enough money to allow one to quit employment is a concrete notion in both countries. The work commitment question and the question differentiating primary and secondary

Table 3.   Lifestyle Preferences and Patriarchal Values.

	Britain			Spain		
	All	Men	Women	All	Men	Women
1. Ideal family model						
Symmetrical roles	44	46	42	66	65	67
Compromise	39	35	41	20	20	19
Role segregation	17	19	17	14	15	14
2. % Who would still work even without economic necessity	60	62	58	50	52	48
3. Main income-earner in your household						
Self	50	69	33	40	65	18
Both equally	11	12	10	13	12	13
Partner	27	6	46	28	3	50
Other person	12	14	11	19	20	19
4. Lifestyle preferences (calculated for women only)						
Home-centred			17			17
Adaptive			69			70
Work-centred			14			13
5. Even when women work, man is still main breadwinner % who agree/are indifferent	56	58	54	39	40	38
6. In high unemployment, wives should stay home % who agree/are indifferent	34	35	33	32	33	32
7. Patriarchal values						
Accept	29	31	27	28	28	27
Ambivalent	32	30	33	19	19	19
Reject	39	39	40	53	53	54
Base = 100%	3,651	1,691	1,960	1,211	595	616

Notes: The 3% of respondents saying Don't know or rejecting all three family models are excluded from responses to question 1. Tiny numbers of people giving a Don't know response to questions 3, 5 and 6 are grouped with the "quit work" group and the agree/indifferent group respectively.
Source: Hakim (2003a, Table 3.1).

earners were combined to identify work-centred women. In both surveys, work-centred women were defined as those who, like men, have adopted the primary earner identity (irrespective of current income level) and whose commitment to their work outside the home went beyond the purely financial. Other women were classified as adaptives, who all held mixed and/or contradictory values on the three key questions. In Britain, women aged 20–59 who had completed their full-time education were distributed 14%, 70% and 16% across the home-centred, adaptive and work-centred groups respectively, with a similar pattern in Spain.

Public morality attitudes are illustrated by the patriarchy index in our surveys. Patriarchy is a feminist concept that has been given many different meanings (Hakim, 1996, pp. 5–13; Lerner, 1986, p. 239; Walby, 1990). We use the term to refer to the institutionalisation of male dominance over women in society as a whole as well as in the family (Hakim, 2000, p. 281). Male dominance remains acceptable to many women in modern society, because they obtain direct and concrete benefits from it, which presumably outweigh the disbenefits (Hakim, 1996, pp. 113–118, 2000, pp. 281–283).

The patriarchy index is a combination of two questions. Both are typical of the statements that appear in social attitude surveys on women's position in society, with people invited to agree or disagree with each statement on a five-point scale. The first was: "Even when women work, the man should still be the *main* breadwinner in the family." This item is an indicator of acceptance of patriarchy in the family, in that it insists on men's main breadwinner role (and the informal power that often goes with it) even when women have paid employment. It suggests that a wife's earnings should have only a minor impact on male dominance in the family. The second was: "In times of high unemployment, married women should stay at home." This item is an indicator of acceptance of patriarchy in public life – specifically in the labour market and, by implication, other public spheres such as politics. If men have priority for jobs in the labour market, they will always hold dominant positions in the workforce – and hence also in politics and public life more generally. This second item was chosen because it offers a modern version of the now unlawful *marriage bar*, the custom that women should resign from their jobs on marriage, which was widespread in the USA and Europe before equal opportunities legislation.

Admittedly, these two items provide a limited index of patriarchy. There are other aspects of the concept that are not covered. Nonetheless, the index is useful in summarising two attitudes that provoked relatively strong reactions in both countries. With the five-point scales reduced to two codes (accept/indifferent or reject), gamma values average 0.90 for Spain (0.89 for men and 0.90 for women) and 0.80 for Britain (0.86 for men and 0.75 for women). The two indicators are strongly associated.

The patriarchy index revealed remarkable similarities in values in Britain and Spain, and there are virtually no sex differences in either country, in either the younger or older generations (people aged under 40, and people aged 40 and over). One-quarter (27%) of Spaniards accept patriarchy in private and public life; half (55%) reject patriarchy completely; a bare one-fifth (18%) are ambivalent, usually because they regard men as retaining the main breadwinner role even if women work. In Britain, two-fifths (39%) of adults reject patriarchy, one-quarter (29%) fully accept it, and one-third are ambivalent, almost always because they accept that men remain the main breadwinner in a family, but no longer accept that this allows men to have priority for jobs. Hardly anyone accepts the modern version of the now-unlawful marriage bar in the labour market, even though the idea of men as main breadwinners is still accepted by many people. Surprisingly, Spaniards are most likely to reject patriarchy. This result reflects a political correctness bias that pervades responses to attitude surveys in Spain (Hakim, 2003a, pp. 62–68). Responsiveness to the social context is generally greater on the patriarchy index than on our measure of personal lifestyle preferences. For example, patriarchal values vary hugely across education levels, whereas education has little impact on lifestyle preferences in Britain (Table 4). Similarly, there is a link between political and religious ideology and patriarchal values, whereas there is no link at all with lifestyle preferences (Hakim, 2003a, pp. 191–208).

These results for Britain and Spain reflect attitudes across Europe. A 1996 Eurobarometer survey found that one-third of men and women in Britain and Spain (and in the EU generally) agreed that "when jobs are scarce" men should have priority over women for the available jobs. Across the EU, sex differences in responses were small or non-existent, and seem to be due primarily to sex differences in employment rates in each country. Differences between working and non-working women were relatively tiny: 20% and 35% respectively believed men should have priority for scarce jobs, implying a very weak link with behaviour. In contrast, there were enormous variations in responses across the EU: only one in ten people in Scandinavia agreed, compared to over half of the Greeks and Belgians (European Commission, 1998, pp. 26–27). Clearly, the socio-political context has the biggest influence on public morality attitudes.

In both surveys, the patriarchy index displayed substantial variation, across ages and social groups, but it had only a weak association with behaviour. In contrast, lifestyle preferences varied less across groups, and were strongly associated with behaviour. In line with preference theory, Table 4 shows that lifestyle choices differ very substantially between the three preference groups. In Britain, two-thirds of work-centred women are in full-time employment, while two-thirds of adaptive women work part-time or not at all. Almost half of the home-centred women are not in employment, and a small minority have never had a job. A relatively high 40% of home-centred women have full-time jobs. The reasons for this unexpected result are explored in the full report, and show that in certain circumstances, economic necessity overrides personal preferences (Hakim, 2003a, pp. 141–143, 211–233).

Home-centred and adaptive women are most likely to marry or cohabit, and to stay married. This is not surprising, as their preferred lifestyle is heavily dependent on having a breadwinner spouse who is in regular employment. Work-centred

Table 4.   Characteristics of Women in the Three Lifestyle Preference Groups.

	Home-Centred	Adaptive	Work-Centred
Britain			
% Employed			
Full-time	40	35	63
Part-time	16	37	15
% Not in employment	44	28	22
% Married/cohabiting	71	80	45
Average number of dependent children aged 0–16 at home	1.28	1.02	0.61
% Left full-time education			
By age 16	54	55	42
17–20 years	28	28	32
Age 21+	18	17	26
Base = 100%	171	870	194
National distribution of the three groups	14%	70%	16%
Spain			
% Employed			
Full-time	13	30	72
Part-time	4	12	8
% Not in employment	83	58	20
% Married/cohabiting	87	77	57
% With children (any age) at home	74	82	63
Household composition: 2+ adults, with children	66	76	50
% With education at each level			
Primary	45	31	17
Secondary	51	56	37
Higher	4	13	47
Base = 100%	47	273	61
National distribution of the three groups	12%	72%	16%

Notes: Women aged 20–59 who have completed their full-time education. The fertility indicator for
    British women is shown for married and cohabiting women aged 20–55 years.
Source: Hakim (2003a, Tables 9.2 and 9.4).

women are least likely to marry, and most likely to be separated or divorced. Women who regard themselves as financially independent anyway have less motive to marry and to stay married. Finally, home-centred women in Britain have twice as many children as work-centred women, many of whom seem to be childless. The fertility measure here is demographers' "own-child" measure: the average number of children aged 0–16 living at home per woman aged 20–55 years. It does not include older children and those who have left home, so it understates total fertility. Nonetheless, it shows clearly that fertility levels vary dramatically between the three preference groups in Britain, along with marriage rates and employment patterns.

Educational standards differ little between the three lifestyle preference groups in Britain. Work-centred women are slightly more likely to have higher education: 26% compared to 18% in the other two groups. The difference is small enough to be explained by differential self-selection into higher education. These results undermine, and even overturn, human capital theory: educational differences between the three lifestyle groups are far too small to justify the thesis that education is normally undertaken as an investment in future careers. This may be true for most men, but it is not true for many women. As predicted by preference theory, lifestyle preferences cut across education groups.

Overall, all the key features of the three preference groups in Britain are in line with preference theory. Preferences are a major predictor of outcomes. Other analyses show that lifestyle preferences predict the decision to work full-time very precisely, but have no impact on women's choice of occupation (Hakim, 2002, 2003a).

In Spain, there is also a strong association between lifestyle preferences and employment, but this is due in part to dramatic changes in values and behaviour between the older and younger generations of women in Spain. The older generation (aged 40 and over) had very limited education, lived under the conservative Franco dictatorship, had narrow Catholic values, and had low rates of female employment. The younger generation (aged under 40) has lived all their adult lives under democracy, benefits from free access to higher education, has accepted the new values and attitudes of democracy and freedom of choice for women, and has high rates of female employment. After controlling for age, there is a weaker link between preferences and behaviour in Spain, and the tenuous link between patriarchal values and behaviour disappears completely (Table 5). There are also no differences between the three preference groups in marital status and fertility that are not due entirely to age differences. So the results for Spain are generally weaker, although they also reveal a clear impact of lifestyle preferences on behaviour.

In line with the results of longitudinal studies, detailed analysis of the new surveys shows that preferences predict behaviour, but behaviour does not predict preferences (Hakim, 2003a, pp. 134–141, 153–156, 158–160). That is, lifestyle preferences are not a post hoc rationalisation of choices already made.

Table 6 summarises the results, and shows the relative importance of practical constraints, such as parental responsibilities, vs. lifestyle preferences as determinants of female full-time work rates in Britain. (The much smaller Spanish dataset does not permit a similar analysis.) The aim in Table 6 is to identify the factors

Table 5. Causal and Non-Causal Values by Age, Spain.

% of Women Working Full-Time in Each Group	<40	40+	All Ages
Lifestyle preferences			
Work-centred	73	70	72
Adaptive	38	22	30
Home-centred	21	4	13
Patriarchal values			
Accept/ambivalent	41	10	24
Reject	44	35	40
All women aged 20–59	43	26	34

Source: Hakim (2003a, Table 5.21).

that cumulatively push up wives' full-time work rates, up to the same level as husbands' full-time work rates, or that depress their work rates down to nothing. For illustrative purposes, the exercise is repeated for all men and women aged 20–59. However this exercise is theoretically less meaningful. Women's attitudes and values predate, and anticipate, marriage and childbearing, but women only make hard choices between a career and a family-centred life if, and when, they actually marry and have children. We already know that higher education raises female work rates, so the analysis focuses on non-graduates, who are the vast majority. The analysis here is person-centred rather than variable-centred (Cairns, Bergman & Kagan, 1998; Magnusson, 1998; Magnusson & Bergman, 1988). A

Table 6. Ideological Influences on Full-Time Work Rates (%) Among Non-Graduates in Britain.

Cumulative Impact of 3–4 Factors Added in Ascending/Descending Order	Wives	Husbands	Women	Men
+4 has a mortgage to pay off	100	83	88	87
+3 not a parent of child(ren) aged <17	72	77	72	80
+2 rejects patriarchal values	72	82	62	83
+1 work-centred lifestyle preference	64	76	56	76
Average for all women aged 20–59	32	84	36	80
+1 home-centred lifestyle preference	31	74	37	65
+2 parent of child(ren) aged 0–16	9	76	10	71
+3 in public rented housing	0	43	7	41

Notes: People aged 20–59 who completed their full-time education before the age of 21 and are not currently studying and are almost certainly non-graduates.
Source: Hakim (2003a, Table 5.10).

key feature of this approach is that it reveals how variables may have a hugely different impact, depending on the context (social group or situation) where they occur. Person-centred analysis recognises the heterogeneity of respondents; denies that people are homogenous in their responses to social and economic influences and experiences; and often focuses on extreme cases, which can amount to 20% at either end of a distribution.

Table 6 shows that a combination of lifestyle preferences plus two contextual factors can push women's work rates up to 100% or down to 0% among non-graduate wives. Results are a little weaker for all women aged 20–59 (graduates and non-graduates combined). Compared to the average for all non-graduate women aged 20–59, a work-centred lifestyle preference doubles non-graduate wives' full-time work rates, from 32% to 64%. In contrast, patriarchal values have very little impact, and childcare responsibilities have no impact at all on work rates among these work-centred women. Having a mortgage to pay off has a substantial additional impact, raising work rates from 72% to 100%. The reasons for this are discussed in the main report (Hakim, 2003a, pp. 141–143, 211–233), but include selection effects as well as motivational factors. The social and financial attractions of home-ownership, and the financial burdens of associated mortgages, have had a significant impact in raising wives' employment in recent decades in Britain.

Full-time work rates among home-centred women are no lower than the average for all non-graduate women, although they are lower among adaptive women. Children, however, have a large impact, depressing work rates from 31% to 9% among home-centred non-graduate women, with a weaker impact on adaptive women, depressing full-time work rates to 17%. Housing has only a tiny impact: living in public rented housing depresses wives' work rates a little further from 9% to 0% among home-centred women, but it has no impact at all on adaptive women. These results demonstrate that lifestyle preferences are never the sole determinant of behaviour, but also that lifestyle preferences determine *which* social and economic contextual factors women respond to.

These results corroborate the NLS results for the USA reviewed earlier and summarised in Table 1. Wives who work only if their childcare responsibilities allow them to do so are in effect fulfilling a prior choice of emphasis on homemaking as life's central activity. Childcare responsibilities have no impact on employment rates among work-centred women. Similarly, housing can have a major or minor impact depending on which lifestyle preference group is looked at. These results demonstrate how any particular factor can be important, or unimportant, when case study projects focus narrowly on one or another group of women. The heterogeneity of women's lifestyle preferences renders it impossible to produce universally valid statements about which social factors determine female work rates. It is essential to differentiate between the three preference groups among women.

Sex-role ideology has no impact on men's full-time work rates. Parental responsibilities also have no effect, because men's role in most families is primarily as income-earner, not as carer. Table 6 confirms the lack of genuine choices in men's lives, as compared with women's lives in the 21st century.

In sum, a close link between lifestyle preferences and behaviour emerges clearly in modern countries which have achieved the new scenario for women. In these societies, the link is specifically between lifestyle preferences, a core personal value, and behaviour. It does not extend to a general link between all and any social attitudes and behaviour. The index of patriarchal values, which combines typical social attitude statements on women's role, shows almost no link with behaviour in two European countries.

CONCLUSIONS

Lifestyle preferences are core values that are stable rather than volatile, unlike other sex-role attitudes. Most important, they refer to *personal* preferences and life goals rather than to opinion on general rules of public morality and appropriate behaviour.

Life goals matter. Women vary in their goals, and they tend to differ from men (Hakim, 1998, pp. 221–234). The heterogeneity of women's preferences has so far been poorly acknowledged in social science theory and research (Hakim, 1996). If we want to understand changing life patterns in western industrial societies, we need to do two things. First, we must investigate women's lifestyle preferences in each country rather than assuming we know in advance what women's aims are. The surveys conducted in Britain and Spain demonstrate that it is feasible to assess women's lifestyle preferences with just three questions in national surveys. Our two surveys also confirm the expected impact of lifestyle preferences on (full-time) work rates and fertility in Britain and Spain.

Second, we have to consider which modern societies have implemented the institutional, social and economic changes that create the new scenario for women, and which are still on the way, because it is only in the new context that core personal values become important predictors of behaviour. As argued elsewhere (Hakim, 2000), Britain and the USA, probably also the Netherlands, have all completed the five social and economic changes that produce a new scenario of options and opportunities for women. In our judgement, Spain in 1999 had some way to go down that road (Hakim, 2003a, pp. 12–28). In countries that have not yet achieved the new scenario for women, lifestyle preferences can be expected to have a weaker impact on choices and behaviour. Modern societies are not all the same, and the differences do not consist exclusively of differences in the character of welfare states. If we want to understand women's changing lives, we must undertake sharper analyses of the character of the social and economic environment as it affects women. In some countries, this is a liberating environment, permitting diversity; in others, the social environment is still the main determinant of choices and produces uniformity in behaviour.

Finally, relatively few attitudes and values are causal. As we illustrated in relation to patriarchal values, social attitude surveys collect data on many topics concerning women's position in society that have the responsiveness and variability of political attitudes and values. These attitudes and values have little or no association with behaviour; they certainly do not predict it in any reliable way. There is a vast difference between core personal values and life goals, and generalised public morality attitudes (Hakim, 2000, pp. 72–82). Unfortunately, at present, most survey research is focused on the latter. In Britain, the desire to achieve comparability with the landmark 1980 Women and Employment Survey or the British Social Attitudes Survey has led many researchers to use attitude items from these surveys in their own surveys.[4] This has had the unfortunate effect of promoting public morality attitude questions at the expense of personal choice questions, even in surveys that seek to elucidate the interaction between attitudes and values and behaviour. Asking the right questions is crucial.

NOTES

1. Two versions of the question have been used in the NLS. In the initial 1968 survey respondents were asked "Now I would like to talk to you about your future plans. What would you like to be doing when you are 35 years old?" From 1969 onwards the question was modified to read "Now I would like to talk to you about your future job plans. What kind of work would you like to be doing when you are 35 years old?" In both versions, keeping house or raising a family was a possible response.

2. For example, recent NLS analyses continue to treat childcare responsibilities as a key determinant of women's labour force participation, as illustrated by Charles et al. (2001).

3. The report here is a summary of a much fuller report in Hakim (2003a).

4. Just one example is McRae's longitudinal study of maternity rights beneficiaries in Britain. From 1988 to 2000 she surveyed women who had been in employment (usually full-time) immediately before a birth in 1988, tracking changes in attitudes and employment patterns (McRae, 2003). As usual, she found that attitudes were volatile, and had only the weakest connection with employment decisions, because all her attitude items were taken from the 1980 Women and Employment Survey and were of the public morality type rather than measures of personal preferences and choices (Hakim, 2003b). Such studies are not a comment on the validity and utility of preference theory.

REFERENCES

Agassi, J. B. (1979). *Women on the job: The attitudes of women to their work*. Lexington, MA: Lexington Books.

Agassi, J. B. (1982). *Comparing the work attitudes of women and men*. Lexington, MA: Lexington Books.

Ajzen, I., & Fishbein, M. (1977). Attitude-behaviour relations: Theoretical analysis and review of empirical research. *Psychological Bulletin, 84*, 888–918.

Alwin, D. F. (1973). Making inferences from attitude-behaviour correlations. *Sociometry, 36*, 139–181.

Andrisani, P. J. (1978). *Work attitudes and labor market experience: Evidence from the national longitudinal surveys*. New York/London: Praeger.

Bielby, D. D. V., & Bielby, W. T. (1984). Work commitment, sex-role attitudes and women's employment. *American Sociological Review, 49*, 234–247.

Cairns, R. B., Bergman, L. R., & Kagan, J. (Eds) (1998). *Methods and models for studying the individual*. London/Thousand Oaks, CA: Sage.

Charles, M., Buchmann, M., Halebsky, S., Powers, J. M., & Smith, M. M. (2001). The context of women's market careers: A cross-national study. *Work and Occupations, 28*, 371–396.

Dex, S. (1988). *Women's attitudes towards work*. London: Macmillan.

Duncan, G. J., & Dunifon, R. (1998). Soft skills and long run labor market success. *Research in Labor Economics, 17*, 123–149.

European Commission (1998). *Equal opportunities for women and men in Europe? Eurobarometer No. 44.3*. Luxembourg: OOPEC.

Geerken, M., & Gove, W. R. (1983). *At home and at work: The family's allocation of labour*. Beverly Hills, CA: Sage.

Hakim, C. (1991). Grateful slaves and self-made women: Fact and fantasy in women's work orientations. *European Sociological Review, 7*, 101–121.

Hakim, C. (1996). *Key issues in women's work: Female heterogeneity and the polarisation of women's employment*. London: Continuum Press.

Hakim, C. (1998). *Social change and innovation in the labour market*. Oxford: Oxford University Press.

Hakim, C. (2000). *Work-lifestyle choices in the 21st century: Preference theory*. Oxford: Oxford University Press.

Hakim, C. (2002). Lifestyle preferences as determinants of women's differentiated labour market careers. *Work and Occupations, 29*, 428–459.

Hakim, C. (2003a). *Models of the family in Europe: Ideals and realities*. Aldershot: Ashgate.

Hakim, C. (2003b). Public morality vs. personal choice: The failure of social attitude surveys. *British Journal of Sociology, 54*, 499–505.

Heath, A., Evans, G., Lalljee, M., Martin, J., & Witherspoon, S. (1991). The measurement of core beliefs and values. Working Paper No. 2, Joint Unit for the Study of Social Trends. Oxford: Nuffield College.

Hofstede, G. (1980). *Culture's consequences: International differences in work-related values*. New York/London: Sage.

Hofstede, G. (1991). *Cultures and organisations*. London: HarperCollins.

Jowell, R., & Witherspoon, S. (Eds) (1985). *British social attitudes – the 1985 report*. Aldershot: Gower.

Kraus, S. J. (1995). Attitudes and the prediction of behaviour: A meta-analysis of the empirical literature. *Personality and Social Psychology Bulletin, 21*, 58–75.

Lerner, G. (1986). *The creation of patriarchy*. New York: Oxford University Press.

Magnusson, D. (1998). The logic and implications of a person-oriented approach. In: R. B. Cairns, L. R. Bergamn & J. Kagan (Eds), *Methods and Models for Studying the Individual* (pp. 33–64). Thousand Oaks, CA: Sage.

Magnusson, D., & Bergman, L. R. (1988). Individual and variable-based approaches to longitudinal research on early risk factors. In: M. Rutter (Ed.), *Studies of Psychosocial Risk: The Power of Longitudinal Data* (pp. 45–61). Cambridge/New York: Cambridge University Press.

Martin, J., & Roberts, C. (1984). *Women and employment: A lifetime perspective.* London: HMSO for the Department of Employment.

McRae, S. (2003). Constraints and choices in mothers' employment careers: A consideration of Hakim's preference theory. *British Journal of Sociology, 54*, 472–498.

Mott, F. L. (Ed.) (1982). *The employment revolution: Young American women of the 1970s.* Cambridge, MA: MIT Press.

OECD (1999). *Employment outlook.* Paris: OECD.

Parnes, H. S. (1975). The national longitudinal surveys: New vistas for labour market research. *American Economic Review, 65*, 244–249.

Rexroat, C., & Shehan, C. (1984). Expected vs. actual work roles of women. *American Sociological Review, 49*, 349–358.

Shaw, L. B., & Shapiro, D. (1987). Women's work plans: Contrasting expectations and actual work experience. *Monthly Labor Review, 110/11*, 7–13.

Spitze, G. D., & Waite, L. J. (1980). Labor force and work attitudes. *Work and Occupations, 7*, 3–32.

Sproat, K. V., Churchill, H., & Sheets, C. (Eds) (1985). *The national longitudinal surveys of labor market experience – An annotated bibliography of research.* Lexington, MA: Lexington Books.

Stolzenberg, R. M., & Waite, L. J. (1977). Age, fertility expectations and plans for employment. *American Sociological Review, 42*, 769–783.

Szakolczai, A., & Füstös, L. (1998). Value systems in axial moments: A comparative analysis of 24 European countries. *European Sociological Review, 14*, 211–229.

Szekelyi, M., & Tardos, R. (1993). Attitudes that make a difference: Expectancies and economic progress. Discussion papers of the Institute for Research on Poverty. Madison, WI: University of Wisconsin.

Van Deth, J. W., & Scarbrough, E. (Eds) (1995). *The impact of values.* Oxford: Oxford University Press.

Waite, L. J., & Stolzenberg, R. M. (1976). Intended childbearing and labor force participation of young women: Insights from nonrecursive models. *American Sociological Review, 41*, 235–252.

Walby, S. (1990). *Theorising patriarchy.* Oxford: Blackwell.

Wicker, A. (1969). Attitudes vs. actions: The relationship of verbal and overt behavioral responses to attitude objects. *Journal of Social Issues, 25*, 41–78.

PART II:
THE CHANGING DEMOGRAPHICS
OF TIME USE

5. TIME, WORK, AND FAMILY
IN THE UNITED STATES

Suzanne M. Bianchi and Marybeth J. Mattingly

ABSTRACT

We review changes in family formation and labor force participation that have dramatically altered the activity patterns of U.S. adults. We then discuss the time use patterns of American parents, focusing on those in the peak childbearing and career years (ages 25–54). As women have markedly increased their time in paid work, they have curtailed their time in housework. Surprisingly, those who become mothers have not cut back their time with children, on average, but they may be "multitasking" when doing child care and this may add to their increased sense of time pressure. Men are changing as well: with some increase in housework and a sizable increase in time with children among fathers who live with their children. However, a gender leisure gap (favoring men) has emerged where none existed before.

INTRODUCTION

Large scale socioeconomic shifts have altered the backdrop of family life in the U.S. in recent decades. One such factor is the increase in income inequality after 1970. Another is the steady upgrading of educational attainment across birth cohorts over the 20th century and the changing nature of work in the U.S. that places a premium on higher education. Each generation of parents is better educated, with higher educational aspirations for their children.

Changing Life Patterns in Western Industrial Societies
Advances in Life Course Research, Volume 8, 95–118
ISSN: 1040-2608/doi:10.1016/S1040-2608(03)08005-5

Higher educational attainment and expectations for children go hand in hand with changes in marriage and fertility that alter parenting in U.S. society – marriage and childbearing are increasingly delayed, albeit more so among the highly educated than among the less educated. This delay, combined with smaller families and increased life expectancy, circumscribes the proportion of adulthood spent caring for very young children. However, delayed childbearing often results in the coincidence of the most "intense" childrearing years with years when adults also need to invest heavily in their labor market careers in order to secure their future trajectory. These life course timing issues can add to individuals' perceived time pressure. In addition, although parents have fewer children on average, they nurture each individual child for longer periods, often financially supporting children well into their twenties as children complete more education and enter adulthood more slowly than in the past.

In the latter half of the 20th century, gender norms and behaviors shifted dramatically, altering what is expected of American fathers and mothers. Today there is greater gender similarity in adult roles as more women complete higher education, continue their market involvement throughout their childrearing years, and increasingly become co-breadwinners when they are married, sole breadwinners when they are not. Not surprisingly, as women's breadwinning roles within the family change, norms about what men should be doing in the family – how involved they should be in domestic activities and the more nurturant dimensions of family life – are evolving as well. However, as the labor force roles of mothers expand, the ideal of the good mother as "ever available, ever attentive to her child's needs" has not disappeared. Indeed, it is only slowly being modified. At the same time, fathers continue to be expected to be good providers but increasingly are also charged with being involved parents who spend "quality" time with their children and share with mothers in the day-to-day tasks of childrearing. In fewer and fewer families is there a "wife" to attend to the myriad activities of family life. The U.S., like most developed countries where the market roles of women have expanded greatly, is only beginning to come to grips with this loss of "person-time" in the home.

The end result is that one hears constantly about the fast-paced life and stress on American families. The popular press and much of the social science literature assumes that parental time with children has diminished in quantity and quality, given the changes in the family. The presumption is also that women, but not men, are doing a double shift by adding paid work hours onto extensive domestic responsibilities. If time in activities such as housework and child care is becoming more similar across gender, it is often argued that this is only because women are "shedding load" as men remain relatively untransformed by the considerable changes in the family.

In this chapter, we place these assumptions about parenting and the gender division in work and family life "under the microscope." We expand the assessment of changing activity patterns of American parents using data collections designed to account for the full array of time expenditures. What reallocation of time, particularly on the part of American parents, leads to the sense of time pressure and contributes to the ongoing assessment that American women, but not American men, are overburdened by work and family responsibilities? We show that, if anything, investment of time in children and childrearing is on the increase among those who choose parenting. The gender division of labor in the home has also changed. Increasingly, men and women face family pressures that are more similar than dissimilar. There is a "second shift" in American family life but it is increasingly confined to those who parent and it is often experienced by fathers as well as mothers though we show that a gender leisure gap (favoring men) emerged by the end of the 20th century.

Our primary focus in the chapter is on the "work and family" years when children are present in the household and both parents are of prime labor force age. However, we begin with a general overview of women and men's time use, followed by a short section on the changes that characterize young adulthood. Then we move to the topics of work and family balance, particularly in households with children. Throughout the chapter, our perspective on change is demographic: In the latter half of the 20th century, particularly rapid social change occurred in the U.S. as large Baby Boom cohorts came of age and embarked on gender arrangements in the workplace and the family that were quite distinct from their parents' generation. The preliminary evidence from recent cohorts suggests that many of these changes were quite permanent (e.g. women's increased commitment of time to market work) while others are still unfolding (e.g. changes in married father's time with children).

DATA FROM THE CURRENT POPULATION SURVEY AND TIME DIARIES

In this chapter, we rely upon a number of data sources. First, at points we draw on family, fertility, and labor force trends that are captured in the major labor force survey in the U.S., the Current Population Survey (CPS). Many of the trends that form the backdrop for this chapter are analyzed in depth in a recent book, co-authored by the first author of this paper, and we draw liberally on the same data used for that book, *Continuity and Change in the American Family* (Casper & Bianchi, 2002).

This chapter also draws on two new time diary data collections, one completed in 1998–1999 (with funding from the National Science Foundation) and the other in

1999–2000 (with funding from the Alfred P. Sloan Foundation's Working Families Program). These new data are contrasted with earlier time diary data collections (the first one done in 1965) to assess changes in time allocation that relate directly to the quality of family life in America. A subtext throughout the examination of time use of American parents is the relationship of gender to change. Gender differentiation in paid work, housework, child care, and leisure continues; yet gender norms and behaviors are undergoing metamorphosis. The time diary collections offer a unique picture of the array of domains and activities undergoing transformation.

In the 1999–2000 National Survey of Parents (NSOP), we interviewed a national probability sample of 1,200 parents living with children under age 18. Parents were asked an array of attitudinal questions about their activities with children and their feelings about the time they spent with their children, spouse, and on themselves. Embedded in the study was a one-day, yesterday diary of time expenditures. The data were collected in computer assisted telephone interviews, with a 64% response rate.

The 1999–2000 NSOP followed closely upon another data collection, a 1998–1999 national study of adults, age 18 and over, in which 1,151 adults were interviewed by telephone and completed a one-day, yesterday diary. The overall response rate was 56%. This study, conducted with funding from the National Science Foundation, was designed to be comparable to national time diary data collections that had been done at roughly 10-year intervals in 1965 and 1975 at the University of Michigan and in 1985 at the University of Maryland. The earlier data collections are described in detail in *Time for Life* (Robinson & Godbey, 1999, Chapter 4).

Our data collections are the first in the U.S. since 1985 that, in addition to primary activity, ask adult respondents about simultaneous or secondary activities and "with whom" they spent their time on the diary day. Interviews for both studies were done over the phone using the same survey procedures and survey organization (the Survey Research Center of the University of Maryland). Questions around the time diary in the NSF-funded study were more limited, less focused on childrearing, and more methodological in nature. Yet similar demographic information was collected in both studies.

Considerable research has established that estimates from time diary studies are more accurate than estimates from stylized survey questions (Juster, 1985; Marini & Shelton, 1993; Robinson & Godbey, 1999). Stylized estimates are higher than estimates from time-diaries, and the difference is larger for activities that occur with some frequency and intermittence, such as many housework and child care tasks. Data from time-diary surveys have been shown to have three advantages compared to stylized estimates. First, in time diary surveys, respondents report all activities within a 24-hour period. This format minimizes reporting burden on respondents because they are allowed to report their time use in a way that is natural to them. From childhood, people gain experience in reconstructing their days, first for parents, and then for spouses and friends. In contrast, "stylized" estimates are not a natural category for most people, and hence it is difficult for people to determine accurately how much time they spend on market and non-market tasks (Gershuny et al., 1994; Robinson & Godbey, 1999). Moreover, respondents may have different interpretations of what activities comprise housework, child care, or leisure, and hence estimates of time in these global categories may be based on different sets of tasks. Second, time diaries minimize the possibility of respondents presenting themselves in a more socially desirable light, since to do so they would have to fabricate the bulk of the account of their day (Robinson & Godbey, 1999; Stinson, 1999). In contrast, respondents may answer stylized questions (consciously or not) so as to present their activities in the best or most socially appropriate way, either by adding or subtracting time from certain activities. For example, because reading to children is an activity in which "good" parents are normatively supposed to engage, parents may respond to questions about the frequency with which they read to their children with inflated estimates (Hofferth, 1999). Third, since all minutes of the day must be accounted for, time diary estimates allow more accurate assessments of change over time, since an increase of time in one activity must be balanced by a decrease of time in another activity (Robinson & Godbey, 1999).

Overview of Trends in Time Use

How has adult time use changed in the U.S.? On average, across the population of adults age 18 to 64, men currently do less market work than they did in 1965, primarily because they retire earlier and enter the labor force more slowly (see next section on young adulthood). American men have increased their time in household work and child care activities and their leisure time was slightly higher in 1998 than in 1965.

During the same period, women increased the time they allocated to market work, decreased the time they spent in non-market work, especially housework, and their leisure time diminished as more experienced the "second shift" that came with increased market work but continued demands at home. This "broad brush" picture of time use introduces the time use topics we focus on in this chapter: market work, non-market work (both housework and child care), free time or leisure, and perceptions of time pressure.

Figures 1 and 2 illustrate change in time allocation (excluding personal care time much of which is sleep) of men and women. Average time use patterns of

1965

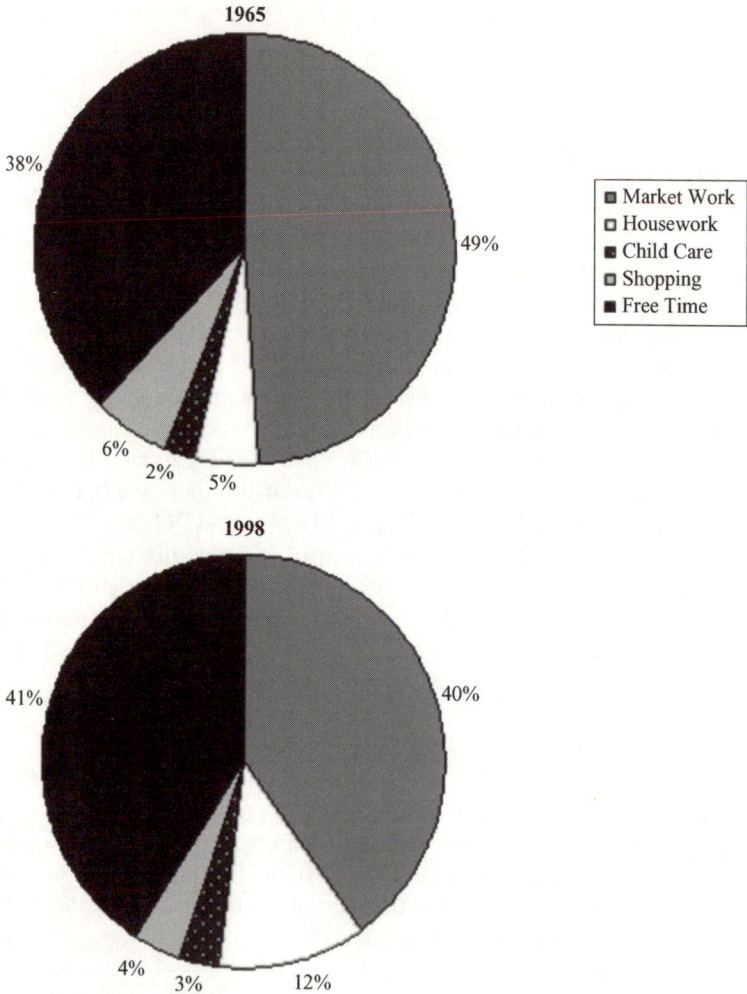

1998

Fig. 1. Distribution of Men's Time in Market Work, Housework, Child Care, Shopping and Free Time in 1965 and 1998. *Note:* Time devoted to personal care activities is excluded from these charts. *Source:* Reprinted with permission from Sayer (2001, Fig. 6.1).

American women and men in 1965 and 1998 document declining, but persistent differences between how women and men spend their days. In 1965, men devoted a large portion of their waking hours to market work (49%); the corresponding figure for women was only 17%. Women's days were largely consumed by

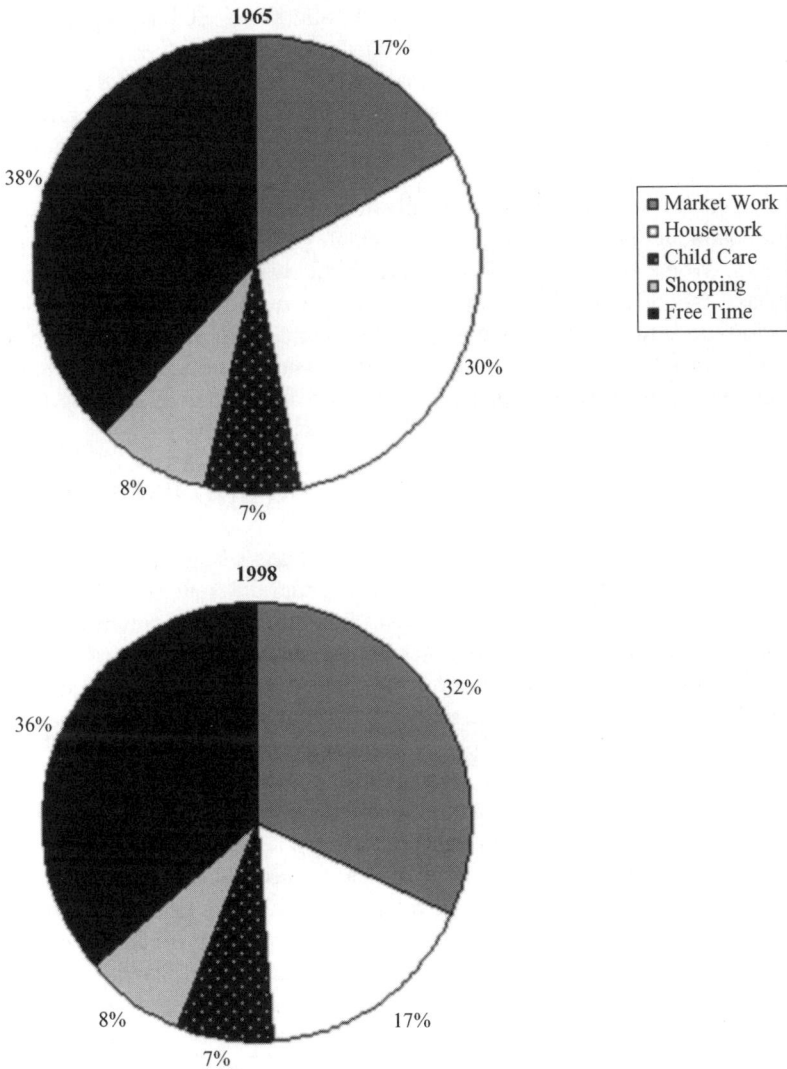

1965

17%

38%

30%

8%

7%

■ Market Work
□ Housework
■ Child Care
□ Shopping
■ Free Time

1998

32%

36%

8%

7%

17%

Fig. 2. Distribution of Women's Time in Market Work, Housework, ChildCare, Shopping and Free Time in 1965 and 1998. *Note:* Time devoted to personal care activities is excluded from these charts. *Source:* Reprinted with permission from Sayer (2001, Fig. 6.1).

housework and child care, which comprised 38% of their activity time, whereas men devoted only 7% of their time to such tasks.

Progressive change is evident such that by 1998, we see that only 8 percentage points separate men and women's time devoted to market work (compared with a 32 percentage point gap in 1965). The gap in housework time has also declined because men have expanded their time somewhat and women have dramatically curtailed their time in this activity. Finally, whereas free time activities consumed the same amount of time for men and women in 1965, a gender gap had emerged by 1998. Women spent 36% of their time in activities labeled as "free time" whereas 41% of men's hours were in these activities.[1] Hence, there is some basis for concerns about the "second shift" falling disproportionately on women. However, in other ways men's and women's time is becoming more similar, though perhaps more so at some points of the life course than others.

DELAYED ENTRY INTO MARRIAGE AND PARENTING

Time allocation is greatly affected by gender and one's stage in the life course. In young adulthood, there are relatively small gender differences as, increasingly in the U.S., both men and women allocate time to finishing school, frequently extending schooling to include post-secondary education. Nearly two-thirds of those who graduate from secondary school enroll in college after high school graduation and college attendance rates are now actually higher for women than for men in the U.S. (Bianchi & Spain, 1996, Table 3).

Subsequent to leaving school, young men and women in their mid-to-late twenties establish themselves in the labor market. Valerie Oppenheimer and her colleagues have documented that it is taking young men, particularly those without a college-education, a number of years to secure full-time employment. She argues that the difficulty young men are having gaining a secure hold in the U.S. labor market is part of the reason that other family formation behaviors are being delayed (Oppenheimer, 2000; Oppenheimer et al., 1997). Rones et al. (1997) have shown that among both male and female youth and young adults, aged 16 to 24, the percentage of workers working less than full-time hours increased between the 1970s and 1990s: from 34 to 40% for men and from 44 to 51% for women. Therefore, young people in the U.S. are taking longer to enter the "adult" roles of full-time work, marriage and parenting.

There is variation in these trends by social class but the delay in marriage and experimentation with other types of living arrangements, particularly cohabitation, is widespread. For example, it is estimated that now over half of marriages in the U.S. are preceded by cohabitation (Bumpass & Lu, 2000). Women still marry at a somewhat younger age than men but the median age at first marriage rose from 20 to 25 years for women between 1960 and 2000 and the comparable increase for men was from 23 to 27 years of age. Teenage marriages are almost non-existent (97% of women and 99% of men, age 15–19, have never married) and most young adults in their early twenties have also not yet married (70% of women and 83% of men age 20–24) (Casper & Bianchi, 2002, Table 1.3). Childbearing in the U.S. is not being delayed as long as marriage, at least among some subgroups of the population. Hence, almost one-quarter of women, even in the most recent cohorts, have a birth by age 20 and about 50% of American women become mothers by age 25 (Casper & Bianchi, 2002, Table 3.1). However, these are far lower percentages than in the middle of the 20th century when one-third of women had a first birth before age 20 and three-quarters become mothers before age 25.

As the events that tend to differentiate men's and women's time use, marriage and childrearing, are postponed, time allocations become more similar for men and women in their (early) twenties. Young women (and men) focus on work and time for themselves with relatively small portions of the population taking on obligations to a spouse or children at early ages. Changes in young adulthood in the U.S. parallel those in other Western economies.

Market Work During the Childrearing Years

Part of the reason that time use data show a decline in time men allocate to market work is compositional: young men are less likely to work full-time than in the past (as just described) and older men retire earlier than in the past. But what about those in the prime working ages, age 25 to 54, those most likely to be combining work with family? Here average weekly work hours have changed little for workers and average around 41 hours per week for men and 35 hours for women workers. However these stable averages mask increased bifurcation in work hours: some work few hours, probably less than they desire. At the same time, there has been a growth in the percentage of men and women working more than 40 hours per week. Among 25 to 54 year old workers, Rones et al. (1997) estimate that the percentage of men working more than 40 hours per week increased from 22 to 29% between the 1970s and 1990s. The comparable increase for women was from 6 to 12%. Average *annual* hours of market work have also increased because the number of weeks worked per year has gone up, particularly for women: American men are working an additional 100 hours per year and women a more dramatic increase of 233 hours per year (capturing both increasing percentages employed and more weeks worked per year among the employed). Hence, one reason there may be a greater perception of time squeeze and "overwork" (Schor, 1991) is that

Table 1.   Total (Joint) Weekly Market Hours of U.S. Husbands and Wives.

	1970	1997	Change
Mean hours			
All couples	52.5	62.5	+10.0
Dual earners with children	76.9	80.4	+3.5
Dual earners without children	79.5	82.5	+3.0
% Working more than 100 hours			
All couples	3.1	8.6	+5.5
Dual earners with children	8.2	12.8	+4.6
Dual earners without children	9.5	14.4	+5.7

Source: Derived from Jacobs and Gerson (2001), Tables 1 and 4.

large Baby Boom cohorts are passing through the point in the life course when work and family demands are highest and, among this cohort, more workers are working long hours in the U.S.

Why individuals feel time squeezed, even when average weekly work hours do not suggest much change and time diary data suggest men may actually be devoting a declining portion of adulthood to market work as they retire earlier and enter the labor force later is a question that has generated substantial debate (Robinson & Godbey, 1999; Schor, 1991). Jacobs and Gerson (2001) point to the fact that more households with children have all adults in the labor force and this creates a feeling of "time poverty." As more married women have entered the labor force and more households include only one parent, families face increased constraints on the hours available for family caregiving. Figure 3 illustrates this family compositional change. In 1978, the majority (59%) of families with children already faced a situation in which all parents present in the household were employed. But by 1998, three-quarters of all families with children had both parents employed or were single parent families where the lone parent was employed.

Jacobs and Gerson (2001) make a compelling case for examining the family's rather than the individual's time commitment to market work. Over time, the joint hours of market work among married couples has increased. As shown in Table 1, across all couples, the combined hours of market work (taking both husbands' and wives' work hours into account) jumped from 52.5 to 62.5 hours per week between 1970 and 1997 as wives' labor force participation rose. Further, Jacobs and Gerson (2001) estimate that the proportion of dual-earner couples with children where the combined work hours of the mother and father exceeded 100 hours increased from 8 to 13% between 1970 and 1997. Most families do not work these exceedingly long hours but an increasing proportion do. Also, dual-earner two-parent families average 80 hours of market work

1978

31%

45%

59%
Time Poor
Familes

2%

3%

7%

12%

1998

49%

16%

75%
Time
Poor

5%

4%

3%

20%

- ▨ Single Mother, Not Employed
- ▨ Other
- ☐ Two Parent, Only Father Employed
- ▨ Two Parent, Both Employed
- ■ Single Father, Employed
- ☐ Single Mother, Employed

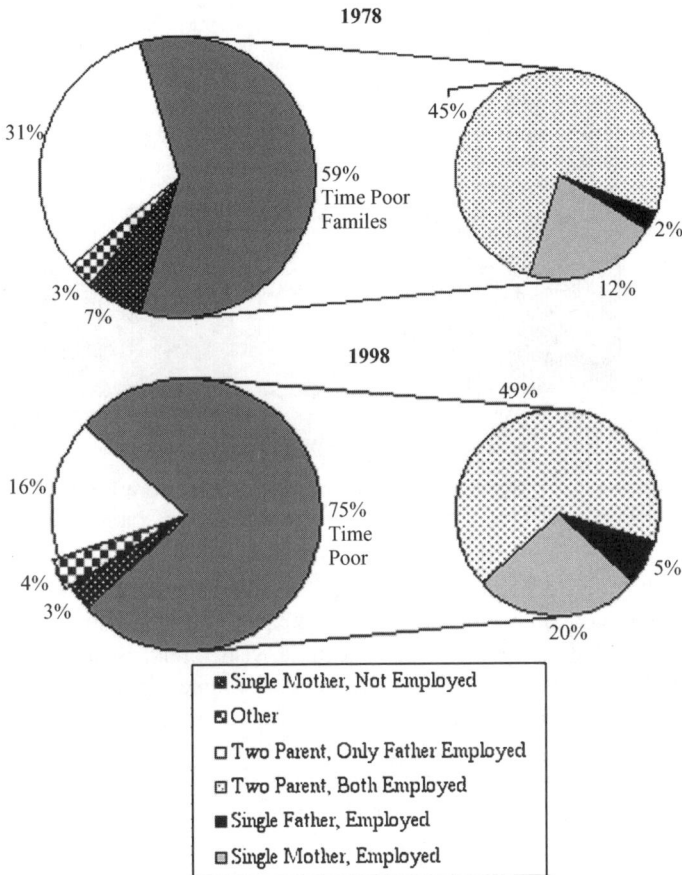

Fig. 3. Family Composition in 1978 and 1998: More Families with Children are "Time Poor" Due to Increase in Single Parenting and Dual Earning. *Source:* Current Population Survey, March Supplement, 1978 and 1998.

(wife plus husband combined), a sizable commitment to weekly market activity that typically removes parents from the home for a large number of hours each day.

Despite the increased representation of mothers in the labor force, there remains a wage penalty for mothers. For example, Budig and England (2001, p. 219) estimate that mothers pay a wage penalty of about 7% per child. About one-third of this "motherhood penalty" is explained by the fact that mothers have more employment breaks and part-time employment, and therefore accumulate fewer

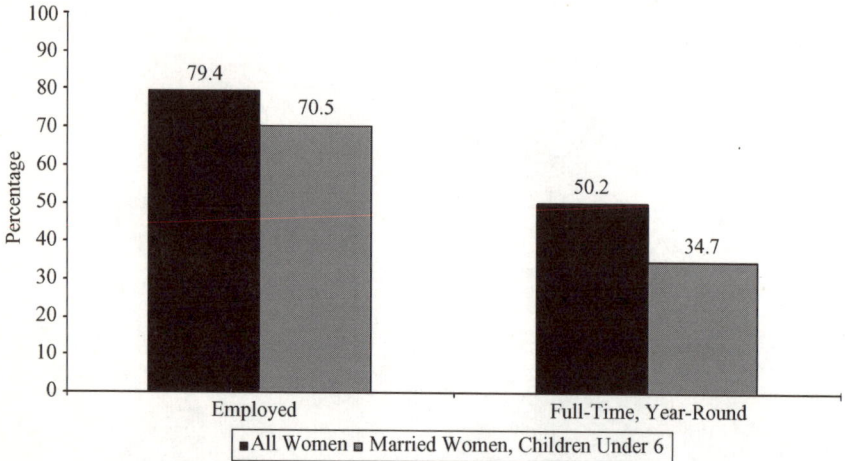

Fig. 4. Percent of U.S. Mothers who are Employed and who work for Pay Year Round, Full Time: 1998. *Source:* Current Population Survey, March Supplement, 1998.

years of job experience and seniority than childless women. Figure 4 illustrates that, although more than 70% of married mothers of preschoolers are employed, less than half of these women work full-time, year round. Becker and Moen's (1999) findings from in-depth interviews with couples in upstate New York suggest that women scale back market work effort more than men when children arrive, despite egalitarian gender ideologies. Some scaling back is common for both women and men during the early years of childrearing. Their definition of scaling back includes limiting time and devotion to work, characterizing work as a job rather than a career, and trading off between job and career over the life course. Since women more than men use these measures to balance their work and family lives, it is perhaps not surprising that women suffer an income penalty. Yet it is not clear why two-thirds of the penalty remains unexplained after taking into account mothers' interrupted labor force careers.

NON-MARKET WORK

Accompanying dramatic changes in the time American parents spend at work are shifts in other aspects of time use including time devoted to non-market work activities. As shown in Table 2, American mothers have dramatically curtailed the time they spend in housework tasks. Mothers' hours of housework (exclusive of child care) fell from an average of 32 hours per week in the mid-1960s to about

Table 2. Trends in Average Weekly Housework Hours by Gender for Parents.

	All Mothers					All Fathers					Ratio of Mother's Time to Father's Time				
	1965	1975	1985	1995	2000	1965	1975	1985	1995	2000	1965	1975	1985	1995	2000
Total housework	32.1	23.7	20.5	18.8	18.6	4.4	7.5	10.3	10.8	9.5	7.3	3.1	2.0	1.7	2.0
Core housework	29.2	21.7	17.6	15.0	14.8	1.6	1.8	4.0	3.9	4.4	18.5	12.3	4.4	3.9	3.4
Cooking meals	10.1	8.7	7.5	5.3	5.4	0.7	0.9	1.8	1.5	2.2	13.8	10.0	4.2	3.5	2.5
Meal cleanup	4.8	2.5	1.9	0.8	1.3	0.3	0.2	0.4	0.1	0.3	14.0	11.4	4.6	6.8	4.9
Housecleaning	8.1	7.1	5.5	6.5	4.8	0.4	0.5	1.5	1.6	1.6	23.0	14.8	3.7	4.0	2.9
Laundry and ironing	6.2	3.4	2.7	2.4	3.3	0.2	0.2	0.3	0.6	0.4	34.5	17.6	8.7	3.8	9.4
Other housework	3.0	2.0	2.9	3.8	3.8	2.8	5.8	6.3	6.9	5.1	1.0	0.3	0.5	0.6	0.7
Outdoor chores	0.3	0.4	0.4	0.7	0.7	0.6	1.0	1.3	2.3	2.0	0.5	0.3	0.3	0.3	0.3
Repairs	0.4	0.6	0.5	0.7	1.0	1.3	3.2	2.3	1.9	1.4	0.3	0.2	0.2	0.3	0.7
Garden and animal care	0.5	0.4	0.6	0.5	0.7	0.2	0.4	0.9	1.1	0.4	2.4	1.0	0.7	0.4	1.6
Bills, other financial	1.8	0.7	1.4	2.0	1.5	0.7	1.1	1.8	1.6	1.3	2.4	0.6	0.8	1.2	1.1
Sample size	405	607	913	312	728	337	480	699	181	472					

Source: 1965, 1975, 1985, 1995 and 2000 time diary surveys.

19 hours per week in 2000. In the early part of this period, fathers' participation in housework chores increased from 4 to around 10 hours per week; however their participation in household chores has remained relatively constant at this 1985 level, perhaps even dipping a bit in 2000. In 2000, mothers spent roughly twice as long as fathers did engaged in household chores. Although this ratio is dramatically lower than in 1965 when the ratio of mothers' to fathers' housework time was 7.3, there has not been a constant decline in the ratio and the ratio is considerably above unity.

Time With Children

Time diary data allow for three measures of mother's and father's participation in child care: the time parents spend primarily engaged in a direct child care activity, the time they spend either directly focusing on child care or doing a child care activity in conjunction with something else, and finally, the overall time they spend with their children whether engaged in child care or not (the most inclusive category). Table 3 shows estimates of mothers and fathers' hours per day with their children and the ratio of (married) mothers' and fathers' time with children.

Despite the increase in maternal employment, on average, mothers' overall time with children has remained at 1965 levels (at around five and one-half hours per day). Fathers have significantly increased their time with children from an average

Table 3. Change in Parents' Daily Hours of Child Care and Time with Children.

	1965	1998
Primary child care time		
Mothers	1.5	1.7
Fathers	0.4	1.0
Ratio (fathers/mothers)	0.27	0.59
Primary or secondary Child care time		
Mothers	2.2	2.8
Fathers	0.7	1.3
Ratio (fathers/mothers)	0.32	0.46
Any time with children		
Mothers	5.3	5.5
Fathers	2.8	3.8
Ratio (fathers/mothers)	0.53	0.69

Source: 1965 and 1998 time diary surveys.

of 2.8 to 3.8 hours per day spent with children. Therefore, the gap between mothers' and fathers' time spent with children has declined. In 1965, fathers did about one-quarter the amount of child care that mothers did and only spent half as much time with their children as mothers. By 1998, fathers were doing about half as much child care as mothers and were spending two-thirds as much time as mothers with their children each day. Sandberg and Hofferth (2001) show parallel findings of increased father time with children, at least among married fathers, and no substantial decline in mothers' time with children, on average. One caveat is that some of this time with children is "double counted" in that both mother and father can be present. Fathers remain much more likely to have their spouse present when with their children whereas mothers spend more "solo" time with children (Sayer et al., 2002).

While most research shows that employed mothers spend less time with their children relative to non-employed mothers, the difference is not dramatic except perhaps for very young children. The differences in time with children may be minimized between employed and non-employed mothers because working mothers curtail work hours when children are young, try to synchronize work hours with children's school schedules when children are older, "tag-team" work hours with a spouse so as to maximize parental availability to children, and curtail time spent in other activities such as housework outside of child care, volunteer work, personal care, and free-time pursuits (Bianchi, 2000).

With respect to fathers, one large gap in knowledge is the involvement of non-residential fathers in their children's lives. There is evidence that step-fathers spend less time with children than biological fathers. "Fathers" who cohabit with a partner and her children spend more time with those children than step-fathers, on average, but still less than biological fathers (Hofferth et al., 2002).

Another dramatic shift in the ways mothers and fathers spend time with their children is a trend toward multitasking. Sayer (2001) documents that both men and women have increased the amount of their child care time that is spent while they are also doing something else. Figure 5 shows that in 1965, child care was the sole activity about 63% of the time a child care activity was reported by mothers whereas 31% of mother's child care time in 1998 is focused solely on providing care to her children. Similar trends characterize men's child care time. While some of the increase for women is in doing non-market work while also caring for children, most is in having children with them while they engage in "free time" or more discretionary activities. This trend may raise questions about the quality of time spent with children, given that parents increasingly have other things on their mind during the time they devote to child care. It also raises questions about how "refreshing" leisure activities are for parents who spend more of it dealing with the demands of young children.

SUZANNE M. BIANCHI AND MARYBETH J. MATTINGLY

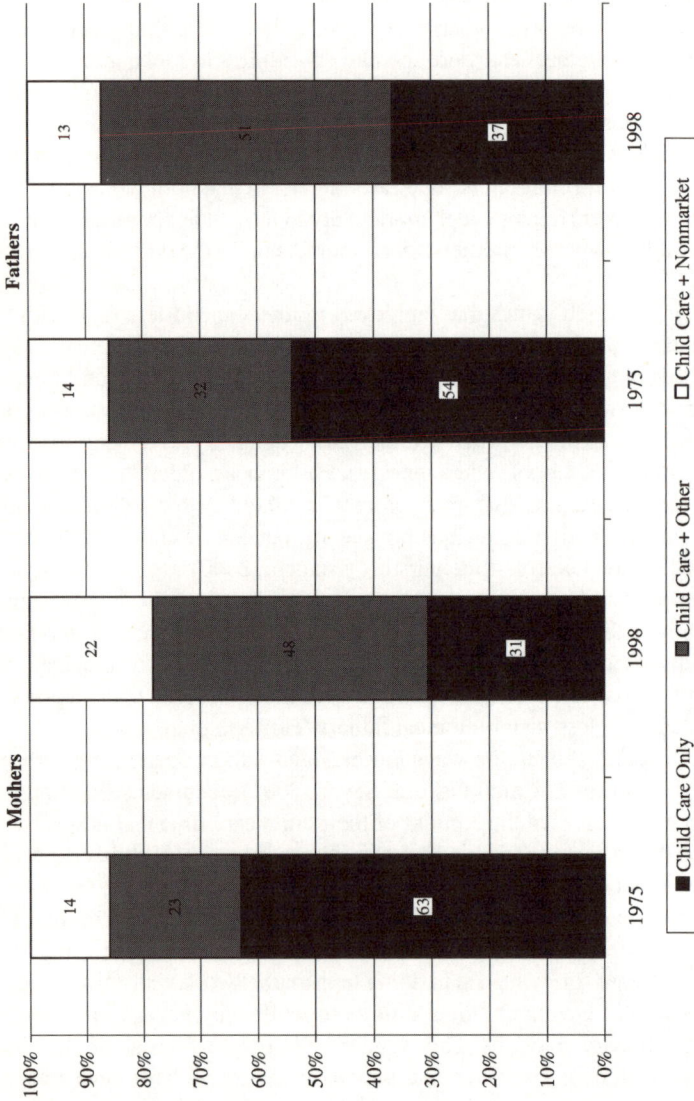

Fig. 5. Primary Child Care in 1975 and 1998: Child Care is More Often Combined with Free Time or Non-market Work in 1998. *Source:* Reprinted with permission from Sayer (2001, Fig. 7.3).

FREE TIME

American men have more free time than do women: we estimate nearly a half an hour more per day (Mattingly & Bianchi, 2003). This estimate is an average difference across respondents surveyed throughout the year on every day of the week. If accurate, men experience approximately 164 more hours of free time over the course of a year. This is equivalent to more than four weeks of paid vacation (at 40 hours per week), or to 6.8 extra 24-hour days each year.

Mattingly and Bianchi (2003) also document gender differences in the experience of leisure time among U.S. parents. Although the total number of minutes fathers and mothers report spending in free time activities with children is quite similar: fathers report 1 hour, 16 minutes a day, while mothers report 1 hour, 15 minutes of free time in activities they share with children, fathers more often report having others present when spending free time with children whereas mothers spend more free time alone with children (35 minutes of free time alone with children per day for mothers, on average, as compared to an average 22 minutes per day for fathers), as shown in Table 4. The percentage of respondents spending any leisure time alone with children reveals that significantly more mothers than fathers spend at least some of their free time alone with children (44% for mothers vs. 28% for fathers). Whereas overall gender similarity characterizes the amount of leisure time with children for married parents, estimates suggest that single, custodial fathers may spend somewhat more time in leisure pursuits with children than single mothers; however, this sample includes only 20 single fathers, a sample much too small to be confident in the estimate and too small to be able to detect whether this is a significant gender difference.

In addition to the permeation of parents' free time with childrearing activities, a larger question is whether the combination of market work, which is increasing for women, and family caregiving, which seems to be increasing for men, curtails time for the active community involvement of adults. Sayer (2001) has classified free time activities that constitute community and organizational involvement into a category she terms "caring civic" leisure and free time activities that build informal social ties, into a category she labels "social leisure." She estimates that the percent of women who report a "caring civic" activity on the diary day decreased by half between 1975 and 1998 (declining from 19 to 9%). There was no change for men, with 12% reporting "caring civic" activities at both points. In terms of "social leisure" (e.g. getting together with friends, eating meals with others, etc.), there remained high levels of such reported activity (87% for women and 75% for men in 1998). However, the percent reporting such activities declined for both men and women, but especially men where 93% had reported this type of activity in 1975.

Table 4.   1998 Time Diary Estimates of Gender Differences in "With Whom"
Parents With Children Under 18 in the Household Spend Their Free Time
(Hours:Minutes Per Day).

	Free Time as Primary Activity[a]		
	Fathers	Mothers	Difference (Men-Women) & Significance
All parents			
Free time spent with children (total)	1:16	1:15	0:01
Free time spent with children only	0:22	0:35	−0:13[**]
% Who spend any free time alone with children	28	44	−17[**]
Free time spent with others and children	0:41	0:23	0:17[**]
Sample size	159	270	
Married parents			
Free time spent with children (total)	1:16	1:19	−0:02
Free time spent with children only	0:20	0:34	−0:13[**]
% Who spend any free time alone with children	26	41	−15[*]
Free time spent with others and children	0:43	0:28	0:15[**]
Sample size	139	192	
Custodial single parents			
Free time spent with children (total)	1:22	1:05	0:16
Free time spent with children only	0:45	0:42	0:03
% Who spend any free time alone with children	46	55	−9
Free time spent with others and children	0:17	0:08	0:09
Sample size	20	78	

Note: Gender comparisons are based upon the results of weighted two-tailed *t*-tests.
Source: Reprinted with permission from Mattingly and Bianchi (2003), Table 2.
[a] This category includes all of the time individuals reported a free time activity as their main activity;
extremely high values on the dependent variable (total free time) were recoded to the 95th percentile
value for that variable.
[*] $p \leq 0.05$.
[**] $p \leq 0.01$.

This may be another reason why time pressures are so keenly felt by working
families in the U.S. today.

SUBJECTIVE FEELINGS ABOUT TIME

Changes such as delayed childbearing and the increased labor force participation
of mothers have dramatic implications for how daily life is lived. Not surprisingly,
these changes affect public perceptions of family life and have differential impacts

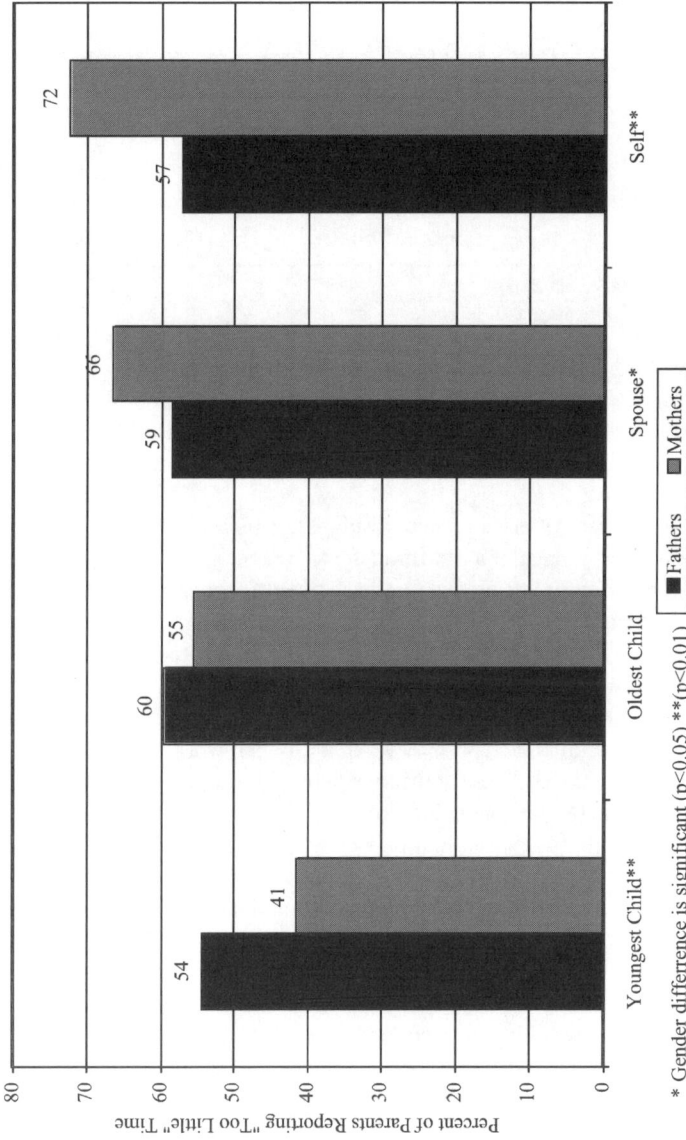

Fig. 6. Percent of Parents Reporting "Too Little" Time with Youngest Child, Oldest Child, Spouse, and "Too Little" Time for Oneself.

Source: National Survey of Parents (2000).

* Gender differrence is significant (p<0.05) **(p<0.01)

Table 5.   Women's and Men's Subjective Perceptions of Feeling Rushed, 1975 and 1998.

	All		Women		Men	
	1975	1998	1975	1998	1975	1998
Feeling rushed (%)	100.0	100.0	100.0	100.0	100.0	100.0
Always (%)	27.0	35.1*	27.8	39.1*	26.0	30.8
Sometimes (%)	52.6	54.5	51.3	53.3	54.3	55.9
Never (%)	20.4	10.4*	20.9	7.7*	19.8	13.4*
Sample size	751	964	456	547	295	417

Source: Mattingly and Sayer (2003).
*Change over time significant at 0.01 level.

on both how parents feel about their time and on fathers' and mothers' time use. What is most interesting about data on subjective assessments of the adequacy of time with children is that, despite increases in actual time with children, U.S. parents express strong feelings that they do not spend enough time with their children.

Figure 6 illustrates American parents' subjective feelings about their time with family members. Evidence of a time crunch is apparent given the large proportion of mothers and fathers reporting that they have too little time with their children and spouse and not enough time for themselves. Not surprisingly, more mothers than fathers report that they have less than the ideal amount of time for themselves and their spouses. However, fathers more than mothers report that they would like more time with their children. This gender difference is explained by the fact that mothers spend more time with their children whereas longer work hours limit fathers' time with children. Indeed, these subjective perceptions are highly correlated with parental work hours (Milkie et al., 2002b). But they may also signify the changing ideals of fatherhood. Today, familial expectations of fathers are changing. More and more men and women want fathers to be equally involved in child care yet the division of labor is typically such that mothers shoulder a disproportionate amount of the day to day child care responsibilities (Milkie et al., 2002a).

Another indicator of the heightened sense of time pressure among adults in the U.S. today is captured by a question on frequency of feeling rushed, asked in 1975 and repeated in the 1998 NSF-funded time diary collection. As shown in Table 5, in 1998, 39% of women reported always feeling rushed, a significant increase over the 28% who felt this way in 1975. The comparable percentages for men were 31% in 1998, up (though not significantly) from 26% in 1975. In both years, the vast majority of Americans reported either sometimes or always feeling rushed and the proportion reporting that they never felt rushed was cut in half between the two years (from 20 to 10%). The decline in those who reported never feeling rushed was much greater for women, perhaps not surprisingly given that it was women who dramatically increased their rates of paid work during this period but also continued to be more likely than men to combine paid work with substantial amounts of unpaid family work and caregiving. (see Mattingly & Sayer, 2003).

CONCLUSION

In this chapter, we have chronicled the changing work and family patterns in the U.S. and also documented the widely shared feeling of "too little time" for family (children and spouse) and for oneself and an increase in feeling rushed in late 20th century America. To summarize, we showed that women in the U.S. have dramatically increased their time in the paid workforce, and, at the same time, cut back their time in housework. Perhaps surprisingly, those who become mothers have not increased market work at the expense of time with children: average time with children was quite similar for mothers in 1965 and 1998. However, mothers may be accomplishing this by increasingly "multitasking" when with their children, combining child care with other activities. This may in part explain why more women report always feeling rushed in 1998 than in 1975. Further, we do not know the effects on the quality of time mothers spend with their children.

We show that men are changing too, with a somewhat lower percent of adult men's lives spent doing market work. This largely reflects later labor market entry and earlier retirement. Men, especially fathers, in their prime "work and family" years almost always work full time. This high level of labor market attachment, combined with their spouse's increased market hours, has resulted in a rising combined paid workload in families and an increased share of dual-earner couples with children who work very long combined work weeks (100 hours or more).

Despite their continued commitment of hours to market work, men are adding domestic duties to their day. This is most clear for fathers who live with their children – their child care activities and overall time with children has increased substantially. Mothers still do more child care than do fathers, but the allocation of time to these activities was much more equal in 1998 than in 1965. Gender inequality remains but the gender gap in most uses of time is narrowing. The one exception is an emergence of a gender leisure gap in the U.S. where there was none in earlier time diary collections (Robinson & Godbey, 1999).

Where does this leave American men, women and children at the beginning of the 21st century? Becoming a parent has far reaching implications for how women and men spend their days and children continue to curtail women's labor force participation. Women cut back on their time commitment to market work, which has implications for their later career trajectories. Further they cut back on their leisure. In addition to being more responsible for children, mothers maintain a higher commitment to household labor than do fathers whereas fathers continue to shoulder more of the breadwinning responsibilities in families.

Women have assumed the breadwinner role in families more rapidly than men have assumed the caregiver role. Yet there is evidence that the latter movement on the part of men, at least those who live with their children, is beginning. It is unclear whether or not gender gaps in time allocation that surround childrearing will ever disappear but fathers are becoming more actively involved in child care and report wanting to spend more time with their children. Some specialization within the household seems foreseeable and researchers need to closely monitor what it is that men and women do in the home and in the workplace as well as what they prefer to do. We also must remain cognizant of the long-term consequences – for men, women, and children – of the constrained choices individuals and families make to meet the dual responsibilities of work and family.

Finally, the subjective dimension of work-family time pressures warrants much further examination. The data presented herein suggest "feeling time pressured" is widespread and perhaps not all that reflective of changes in actual time allocation. For example, many parents report feeling like they spend too little time with their children, despite stability in time with children for mothers and increases for fathers. It is possible that parents' expectations for the amount and quality of time with their children may be rising at the same time that pressures to do many things at once, to multitask, may be diminishing their sense that the time they spend with their children is of sufficient quantity or quality.

NOTES

1. In the time use literature, time is typically divided into contracted time (paid work), committed time (including housework and child care), personal time (self-care), and a residual category of discretionary time (free time) (see Robinson & Godbey, 1999 for more detail). Free time captures all activities that are not included in the other three categories. Travel is generally included with the activity with which it is associated; hence, for example, commuting to work is considered with market time (Robinson & Godbey, 1999, pp. 11–13). Since free time is a residual, it captures all activities that individuals chose to engage in during time other than that committed to paid work, domestic work and family care, and self-care or personal hygiene. Some of the activities coded as "free time" activities such as attending classes or Parent-Teacher Association meetings may not be considered truly elective uses of time. However, Robinson and Godbey (1999, p. 13) argue that "While educational and organizational activities may be 'forced' on the individual by other role obligations, these are also activities that most people feel they have some degree of choice in, as supported by empirical study."

REFERENCES

Becker, P. E., & Moen, P. (1999). Scaling back: 'Dual-earner couples' work-family strategies. *Journal of Marriage and the Family, 61,* 995–1007.

Bianchi, S. M. (2000). Maternal employment and time with children: Dramatic change or surprising continuity? *Demography, 37,* 401–414.

Bianchi, S. M., & Spain, D. (1996). Women, work, and family in America. *Population Bulletin, 51,* 1–46.

Budig, M. J., & England, P. (2001). The wage penalty for mothers. *American Sociological Review, 66,* 204–225.

Bumpass, L., & Lu, H. (2000). Trends in cohabitation and implications for children's family contexts in the United States. *Population Studies, 54,* 29–41.

Casper, L. M., & Bianchi, S. M. (2002). *Continuity and change in the American family.* Thousand Oaks, CA: Sage.

Gershuny, J., Godwin, M., & Jones, S. (1994). Domestic labour revolution: A process of lagged adaptation? In: M. Anderson, F. Bechhofer & J. Gershuny (Eds), *The Social and Political Economy of the Household* (pp. 151–197). Oxford: Oxford University Press.

Hofferth, S. (1999). Family reading to young children: Social desirability and cultural biases in reporting. Presented at the Workshop on Measurement and Research on Time Use, sponsored by the Committee on National Statistics, National Research Council, May, Washington, DC.

Hofferth, S., Pleck, J. H., Stueve, J. L., Bianchi, S. M., & Sayer, L. C. (2002). The demography of fathers: What fathers do. In: C. Tamis-LaMonda & N. Carera (Eds), *Handbook of Fathers Involvement: Multidisciplinary Perspectives* (pp. 63–90). Rahwah, NJ: Lawrence Erlbaum.

Jacobs, J. A., & Gerson, K. (2001). Overworked individuals or overworked families? *Work and Occupations, 28,* 40–63.

Juster, F. T. (1985). The validity and quality of time use estimates obtained from recall diaries. In: F. T. Juster & F. P. Stafford (Eds), *Time, Goods, and Well-Being* (pp. 63–91). Ann Arbor, MI: Survey Research Center, Institute for Social Research, University of Michigan.

Marini, M. M., & Shelton, B. A. (1993). Measuring household work: Recent experience in the United States. *Social Science Research, 22,* 361–382.

Mattingly, M. J., & Bianchi, S. M. (2003). Gender differences in the quantity and quality of free time: The U.S. experience. *Social Forces, 81,* 999–1030.

Mattingly, M. J., & Sayer, L. C. (2003). *Gender differences and changes over time in the relationship between free time and individuals' perceived time pressure.* Unpublished manuscript, University of Maryland, College Park, MD.

Milkie, M. A., Bianchi, S. M., Mattingly, M. J., & Robinson, J. P. (2002a). Gendered division of childrearing: Ideals, realities, and the relationship to parental well-being. *Sex Roles, 47,* 21–38.

Milkie, M. A., Nomaguchi, K., & Bianchi, S. M. (2002b). *Feelings of time deficits for children, spouse and oneself among dual-earner parents: Do mothers and fathers differ?* Unpublished manuscript, University of Maryland, College Park, MD.

National Survey of Parents (2000). Collected for J. P. Robinson & S. M. Bianchi by the Survey Research Center with funding from the Alfred P. Sloan Foundations. College Park, MD: University of Maryland.

Oppenheimer, V. K. (2000). The continuing importance of men's economic position in marriage formation. In: L. J. Waite (Ed.), *Ties that Bind: Perspectives on Marriage and Cohabitation* (pp. 283–301). New York: Aldine de Gruyter.

Oppenheimer, V., Kalmijn, M., & Lim, N. (1997). Men's career development and marriage timing during a period of rising inequality. *Demography, 34,* 311–330.

Robinson, J. P., & Godbey, G. (1999). *Time for life* (2nd ed.). University Park, PA: Pennsylvania State University Press.

Rones, P. L., Ilg, R. E., & Gardner, J. M. (1997). Trends in hours of work since the mid-1970s. *Monthly Labor Review, 120*, 2–14.

Sandberg, J. F., & Hofferth, S. L. (2001). Changes in parental time with children, United States 1981–1997. *Demography, 38*, 423–436.

Sayer, L. C. (2001). *Time use, gender and inequality: Differences in men's and women's market, non-market, and leisure time.* Unpublished manuscript, University of Maryland, College Park, MD.

Sayer, L. C., Bianchi, S. M., & Robinson, J. P. (2002). *Are parents investing less in children?* Unpublished manuscript, University of Maryland, College Park, MD.

Schor, J. B. (1991). *The overworked American.* New York, NY: Basic Books.

Stinson, L. L. (1999). Measuring how people spend their time. Paper prepared for the August 1999 Joint Statistical Meetings, Baltimore, Maryland.

6. CHANGING WORK AND LIFE PATTERNS: EXAMPLES OF NEW WORKING-TIME ARRANGEMENTS IN THE EUROPEAN MEMBER STATES

Janneke Plantenga

ABSTRACT

The central focus of this chapter is the interrelationship between flexibilization and equal opportunities. Drawing on comparative data, the chapter focuses on different ways to categorize the working-time regimes of the EU member states and to assess the different realities from an equal opportunities point of view. It appears that the differences in this respect between the European member states are rather large, indicating that there is no fixed relation between the flexibility and equality dimensions. Politics do matter and influence the actual position taken within the flexibility/equality spectrum.

INTRODUCTION

The organization of work and working times is changing rather rapidly. There are at least two important trends. Firstly, all over Europe, there is a shift from jobs organized on a relatively permanent and full-time basis, towards less standard, flexible and part-time employment. At the end of the 1990s the part-time rate for

Changing Life Patterns in Western Industrial Societies
Advances in Life Course Research, Volume 8, 119–135
© 2004 Published by Elsevier Ltd.
ISSN: 1040-2608/doi:10.1016/S1040-2608(03)08006-7

men was more than 6%, whereas the temporary employment rate was approximately 10%. For women, in particular, the figures are quite impressive, indicating that the trend towards flexibility has a clear gender dimension: throughout Europe, the female part-time rate is more than 33% and the temporary employment rate is more than 12%. Secondly, there is a trend towards greater flexibility in the allocation of working time over the working week and working year. The boundaries of the normal working day have expanded and work on Saturday and Sunday is becoming more frequent. Of course, the two trends are interconnected, as part-time and temporary workers match the variations in demand during the day, the week or the year, partly covering hours outside the normal working time, like evenings and weekends. At the same time, the permanent, full-time worker is also involved in the growing flexibility in allocation of working times. Annualized hours schemes are perhaps the most illustrative example of a trend towards a more flexible scheduling of standard full-time hours (Bettio et al., 1998; Rubery et al., 1995).

This trend towards more flexible and more individualized working hours is the result of several developments. A shortening and de-standardization of working hours has been claimed to be a prerequisite for attaining a significant decline in unemployment. Economists may be skeptical about the idea that work can be redistributed by shortening the full-time working week or by increasing part-time work. Yet, working-time policy, emphasizing the importance of labor market flexibility, has become a vital element of the efforts to reduce Europe's unemployment. Shorter working hours may also be seen as a response to the growing demand of employees for (leisure and/or caring) time. This trend is connected with the growing diversity in life styles and the rise of dual earner families. Women especially have expressed their interest in tailor-made working hours matching their personal needs for flexibility.

There is, however, not an easy relationship between gender equality and flexible working hours. A high part-time rate, for example, might on the one hand be seen as a factor which contributes to a differentiated economy, thereby stimulating women to engage in paid work. Yet, if women engage disproportionately in part-time work (or other non-standard working-time arrangements), the result might be enduring gender inequality in terms of income, responsibility and power. Feminist writers in particular have pointed to the fact that the various flexibilization strategies seem to exploit and confirm the unequal position of women and men on the labor market. Flexible arrangements do not actually affect the prevalent social division of labor; in contrast to their male counterparts women on flexible working arrangements have little prospect of building a career and thus continue to combine their household and caring tasks with a paid job in a manner that is likely to keep them in the secondary labor market (Blossfeld & Hakim, 1997; Maruani, 1995; Perrons, 1998).

This discussion, about the interrelationship between flexibilization and equal opportunities is the central theme of this chapter. This article first documents the new working-time arrangements taking into account several dimensions of working-time flexibility. Second, drawing on comparative data, the article focuses on different ways to categorize the working-time regimes of the EU member states and to assess the different realities from an equal opportunities point of view. An important point of departure in the analysis is that no a priori answer can be given to the question of whether flexibilization offers women real opportunities or whether it should rather be interpreted as a development which makes use of their weak labor market position, and thus does no more than perpetuate it. The concern here is an empirical one. Flexibilization can offer opportunities, but also take them away. An analysis of the actual situation should determine which aspect dominates.

MAJOR TRENDS

Individualized Working Hours

The rise of individualized and flexible working times is primarily a matter of supply and demand. Employers attempt to cut back on labor costs, to cope with seasonal and other fluctuations in demand, or to extend operating hours. Employees want choices other than the all-or-nothing option on the labor market and are experimenting with more tailored working-time patterns. The adjustment process of supply and demand, however, does not occur in a vacuum. The matching of preferences takes place against a backdrop of legislative and regulatory measures, which make specific options more or less attractive. As a result, the actual distribution of working hours is heavily influenced by the statutory framework and the system of collective bargaining (Anxo & O'Reilly, 2000; Evans et al., 2000).

The actual variety in working-time profiles throughout Europe is illustrated by Fig. 1a–c, comparing the working-time profiles for 1993 and 1999 for male and female employees in three European countries. It appears that in France working hours of men are still concentrated around 36–40 hours; changes in this respect have been fairly limited. This mirrors the strong influence of state regulation, and the rather subordinate role of collective bargaining. Anxo and O'Reilly (2000, pp. 71–72) argue in this respect that the introduction of the 35-hour week in 2000 should be seen as an example of adaptation and continuity within the "dirigiste" tradition. Although the new legislation seeks to encourage the social partners (employers and employees) to reach agreement on the flexible implementation of reduced working time at the industry and firm level, the state remains the main architect and the final arbitrator. At the other end of the spectrum is the U.K. in

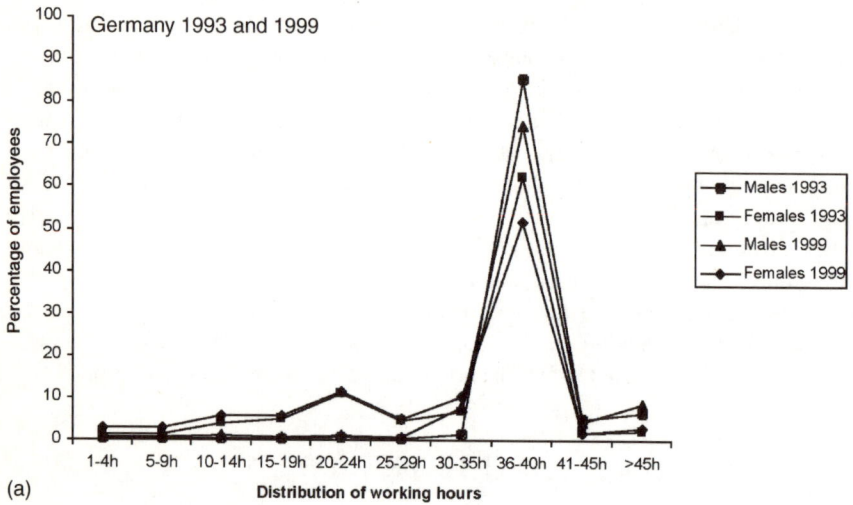

(a)

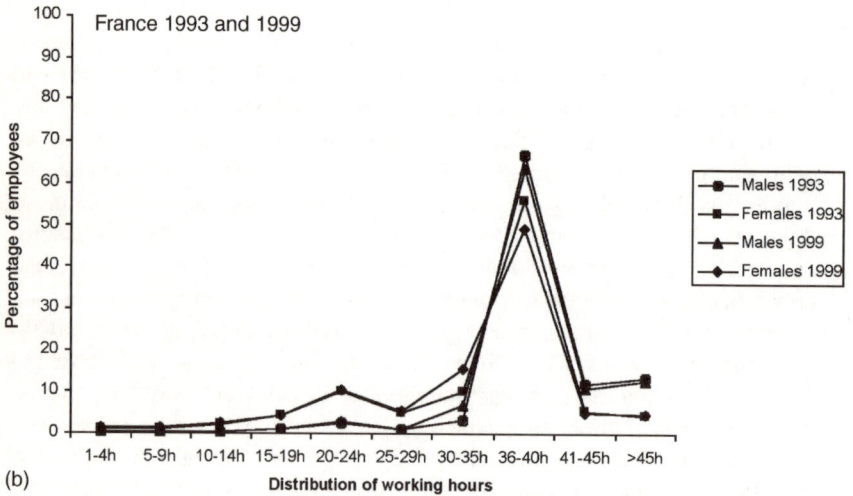

(b)

Fig. 1.   Working-Time Pattern of Men and Women. *Source:* Eurostat, Labor Force Survey
1993, 1999.

which any collective norm seems to have disappeared; the concept of standard
working time simply does not appear to exist in this country anymore. The highly
diversified working-time pattern – in combination with the high percentage of
men working 46 hours or more a week – seems in line with the strong emphasis

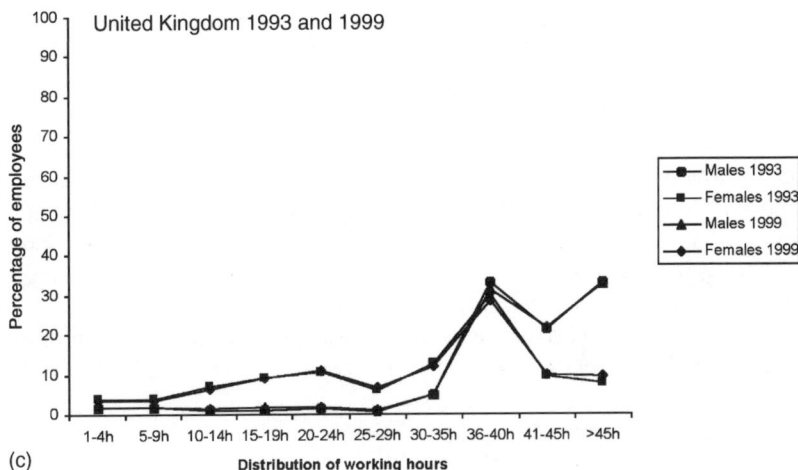

United Kingdom 1993 and 1999

Males 1993
Females 1993
Males 1999
Females 1999

(c)

Distribution of working hours

Fig. 1. (*Continued*)

on uncoordinated, decentralized collective bargaining. Finally, in Germany, the percentage of the labour force usually working 36–40 hours has decreased quite substantially, although there seems to be a trend towards standardization of the workweek. Indeed, in the period between 1993 and 1999, the percentage of the workforce working 40 hours a week has significantly increased, at the expense of the percentage of the workforce working 38 hours a week, which has dropped. The increased preponderance of the 40-hour workweek might be (partly) attributed to the unfavorable economic situation in Germany during that period.

What cannot be observed from these charts is that the peak at the 36–40 hour workweek interval is "broader" in Germany than in France. In Germany, the 40-hour workweek is prevailing, yet the 38-hour workweek is still very common (even though its frequency has been decreasing). In France, on the other hand, the peak in the 36–40 hour interval can be attributed entirely to the unparalleled popularity of the 39-hour week. Furthermore, in England the peak is approximately uniformly distributed, due to the aforementioned idiosyncratic nature of the English labor market.

Figure 1 also illustrates that both male and female working hour profiles show large similarities and that a typical "national" pattern can be ascertained for both men and women. In France, for example, the differences seem relatively small. Even in the U.K. de-standardization seems to have affected both the male and female working hours patterns. Yet, for all countries the working-time distribution of women is more concentrated in shorter working hours, with men working considerably longer hours than women. A simple index of working hours segregation confirms these differences. The *s index*, also called the *index of dissimilarity*, is often applied in research on occupational segregation (Rubery & Fagan, 1993), but can also be used to illustrate the extent of working hours segregation. The index can be interpreted as the sum of the percentage of male and/or female labor force that would have to change their jobs (or – in this case – working hours) in order to eliminate all segregation. It appears that there are large differences in this respect. Finland, Portugal, Greece and Germany have lower rates of dissimilarity with scores below 20%, whereas Belgium, the UK, and the Netherlands have scores higher than 35%. In fact, the Netherlands scores highest with a score of 51%; this means that 51% of the male/female population would need to change their working hours to reach an equal distribution. The liberal working-time regime of the U.K. comes in second, with a score of 38%.

Flexible Working-Time Arrangements

In principle, flexible working-time arrangements refer to a flexible matching of labor inputs over the day, week, and year. A well known example is the annualization of working time, in which actual working times are spread over a specified sub-period of the year, for example, three or six months. Annualized hour schemes can be combined with other non-standard working-time schedules and are often introduced in tandem with reduced working time. Other examples include the compressed, four-day working week, and "swingtime" arrangements in which employees are able to work a few hours a day less, so long as they catch up on these hours within the same week. Working-time practices which provide employees with real autonomy over their working times (variable start and finishing hours) are still infrequent, but may increase due to the introduction of new information technology and the concomitant move towards more output-oriented management styles.

Whereas the rise in individual working hours can be rather easily documented on the basis of labor force survey data, the rise in flexible working-time arrangements is much more difficult to ascertain. This is partly attributable to the fact that flexible working-time arrangements are negotiated at the level of the firm, rather independently of statutory regulation and/or the system of collective bargaining. As a result, the statistical processing of these developments is far from complete. Eurostat data, for example, give information about the number of people usually (or sometimes) working in the evening, night, Saturday, Sunday or at home. This information is very incomplete because high percentages of persons working on weekends for instance might just as easily indicate the rise of the 24-hour economy, as a rather traditional economy in which agriculture and retail are

Table 1. Flexible Working Time Arrangements in 15 European
Countries (in %).

	Usually Working in the Evening				Usually Working From Home			
	Males		Females		Males		Females	
	1993	1999	1993	1999	1993	1999	1993	1999
Greece	30.7	29.5	29.1	28.0	1.6	1.2	3.4	2.6
Spain		10.3		8.4	0.4	0.4	1.1	1.5
Italy	12.8	14.5	9.3	10.4	4.9	3.8	5.6	4.4
Portugal	0.7		0.6		2.0	1.6	6.2	3.9
UK	16.6	36.3	14.9	28.3	1.4	1.4	4.3	3.6
Ireland	12.6	12.9	12.6	9.6	25.2	9.0	9.6	4.7
Denmark	19.3	21.8	16.9	19.9	10.7	11.0	9.9	10.3
Finland		25.1		23.2		10.0		10.6
Belgium	13.8	5.5	10.7	4.7	10.9	5.8	12.0	6.7
France	3.5	9.9	2.6	6.9	2.3	4.4	2.9	4.5
The Netherlands	15.8	16.7	15.3	17.3	6.6	6.5	6.3	5.8
Germany	16.0	20.1	12.1	16.4	4.5	3.9	6.0	4.4
Austria		17.1		11.8		10.4		13.0
Sweden		21.7		23.3		8.9		7.7
Luxembourg	10.5	9.1	11.7	9.4	6.4	7.5	7.9	10.1
EU 12	12.1	14.3	10.0	11.5	3.7	4.1	5.0	4.7
EU 15		18.5		15.4		3.8		4.6

Source: Eurostat, Labor Force Survey 1993, 1999.

still important sources of employment, because such an economy also requires
weekend work and flexible times.

Given the difficulties in interpreting the available data, Table 1 only gives
information about the percentage of persons in employment who are usually
working in the evening, and usually working at home. Evening work, according
to Eurostat, may be considered to be work done after the usual working hours, but
before the usual hours of sleep; it implies the opportunity to sleep at normal times.
Homeworking applies to many self-employed persons, for example, who are
practicing an artistic or liberal profession. In the case of employees, homework
should be interpreted strictly on the basis of formal agreements concluded with
the employer, in which both parties, employee and employer, agree that part of
the work is to be done at home. A person is usually considered to work at home
if, for a reference period of four weeks before the interview, the hours worked at
home amount to at least half of the total hours worked during the period. On the
basis of Table 1 it appears that the data are rather unstable, with wide variations
between two years. Presumably these jumps mirror the difficulties in statistical
processing. Nevertheless, some general trends can be ascertained, for example,

that evening work is much more frequent in Denmark than in France for both the male and female labor force. It also appears that the incidence of evening work has increased in most countries. For work at home Ireland (with a rather extreme score in 1993), Denmark, and Belgium show the highest percentages; home work seems to be rather infrequent in Spain, Greece, Portugal, and the U.K. with marks below 1%. From the table it also appears that the percentages have been rather stable – home working is clearly not a booming business. The overall data might, however, conceal important changes in the different categories.

Summarizing this section, it can be concluded that the de-standardization of working times – although a world-wide phenomenon – is mediated by the national systems for regulating working time. Gender differences appear to be large in the U.K. and especially the Netherlands. There is only limited statistical evidence about the extent to which flexible working time has been developing over recent years. Whenever evidence is available, the data seem to suggest that the magnitude of change should not be exaggerated. The data do indicate, however, that there are huge country differences in this respect.

CATEGORIZING WORKING-TIME REGIMES

Unequal working times are an important indication of labor market inequality between men and women. Yet the relationship between unequal working hours and gender inequality is not very straightforward as many industrialized countries have promoted part-time work as a strategy for reconciling paid and unpaid work. Furthermore, job sharing and the ability to distribute time optimally over the working week seem important elements of a more female-friendly working-times regime (Rubery et al., 1998). Innovative working-time schemes therefore imply both threats and opportunities for a more equal distribution of paid and unpaid work, depending on the specific form of the innovation and the economic and societal environment in which these innovations occur.

The Mutari and Figart Model

The complex relationship between gender equality and working times has been elaborated by Mutari and Figart (2001), measuring the gender friendliness and flexibility of fifteen national labor markets. High labor force participation of married women and a small gender pay gap are identified with high gender equality. Flexibility is measured more extensively by a total of six indicators.

Flexibility indicators include the full-time modes of working hours of both men and women, the kurtosis (based on the modes) that provides information about the distribution of average weekly working hours of both men and women, and the percentage of married women working part-time and men working overtime.

On the basis of these indicators, Denmark and France are classified as examples of "solidaristic" gender equity work-time regimes. Both countries have made strides towards gender equity by changing social norms concerning work time; policies focusing on a shorter full-time working week have changed the male model of full-time employment, enabling men and women to participate in the labor market on a more nearly equal basis. At the same time, these countries do not rank high with regard to flexibility. The full-time men's and women's mode is relatively low, and there is no strong reliance on overtime or part-time work. The U.K. seems a quintessential example of a liberal and flexibilized working-time regime. In this case, a relatively self-regulated or laissez faire market economy, relying heavily on overtime and part-time work, seems to pose severe difficulties for gender equity: even among full-timers women's hours are substantially lower than men's. Spain on the other hand is an example of the male breadwinner working-time regime. Full-time work is still structured on the male model of long hours. The part-time rate is rather low and so is men's overtime. No country is yet classified as a high road flexibilization working-time regime, described by Mutari and Figart (2001, p. 41) as "providing the institutional basis for a restructuring of gender relations by utilizing a variety of approaches to working hours and the work week in order to balance paid and unpaid work." The low road or "mean" version relies on a cheap and disposable labor force in a deregulated environment; the high road provides workers as well as employers with control over their schedules and input into the production process. The Netherlands and Germany are designed as "transitional," meaning that these countries are at a fork in the road with the potential to implement flexibility following either the high or the low road. The Netherlands resembles the male breadwinner model in the sense that the distribution of full-time workers is peaked around a 40-hour mode for full-time workers. Yet the small number of men working long hours and the large proportion of part-time work among women forces the Netherlands into a distinct model. Germany, according to Mutari and Figart, is clearly on the road to some form of flexibilization, as a wide range of working-time alternatives becomes accepted.

The Mutari and Figart model is an intriguing attempt to rate the fifteen EU national labor markets on the levels of gender equality and flexibility. When one examines the authors' sub-division of countries more closely, however, some questions regarding the ratings spring to mind.

The main weakness of the model is that the two dimensions that stand central in this research, flexibility and gender equality, are not measured independently from each other. The authors have chosen certain flexibility indicators in order to obtain concomitant information on gender equality. The flexibility indicators, married women's part-time rate and men's overtime, are not used to measure flexibility of work time alone, but also to measure gendered working time specifically. A large percentage of men working overtime combined with a large percentage of women working part-time, for example, indicates a flexible as well as a segregated labor market that is reflected in a low score on gender equity. A second weakness relates to the fact that two indicators that measure flexibility are confounded. Full-time men's kurtosis and men's overtime overlap. A simple correlation indicates a Pearson correlation level of -0.526, with a significance of 0.044, which means that the correlation is indeed statistically significant (at conventional levels). This was to be expected, as a high percentage of men working overtime will necessarily lead to a low kurtosis. A third critique deals with the fact that Mutari and Figart use only two indicators to measure gender equality. This renders the ranking of a country on the gender friendliness scale quite sensitive. For instance, Mutari and Figart have placed the U.K. under the heading of a liberal flexibilization regime. In fact, the U.K. scores relatively high on the labor force participation of married women – one of the two gender equity indicators – which makes the case of the U.K. less clear cut.

An Alternative Model

Based on the above-mentioned critique, we propose six new indicators to rank countries in the two dimensional equality-flexibility framework. In order to scale countries on *gender equality* we use the following three indicators: (1) the standardized gender gap in employment; (2) the gender pay gap; and (3) the working-time segregation index. Flexibility is charted by using an additional three indicators: (1) the shape of the working-time distribution (kurtosis) of all employees; (2) the percentage of persons usually working in the evening; and (3) persons usually working at home.

Equality Indicators

The gender gap between men and women in employment is measured by calculating the standardised gender employment gap for all countries; that is by calculating the difference between the male and the female participation rates, divided by the male participation rate. Paid labor is an important precondition of economic independence and as such an indispensable dimension in any gender equality measure. The standardized gender gap in employment is an excellent indicator of gender equality as it shows the gender gap in participation rates. A high labor force participation of women might still disguise a large gender gap if the participation of men is much higher. The standardized employment gender gap should be preferred over the absolute gap as the relative gap neutralizes the impact of differences between countries in absolute levels of employment. Thus male and female employment rates of 70 and 80% produce a smaller gender gap in employment rates than rates of respectively 50 and 60%. The age category, 25–55, will be used, as this category has the greatest potential for an increase in employment.

The second indicator, the gender pay gap, refers to the ratio of women's gross hourly earnings to men's. Unfortunately, reliable data on pay are extremely scarce. Nevertheless, pay should be deemed an indispensable aspect of women's relative equality in the labor market, and as such should be included in any gender equality measure. For this chapter, we have made use of ECHP (European Community Household Panel)[1] data of 1998, referring to the average gross hourly earnings of female paid employees as a percentage of average gross hourly earnings of male paid employees. The population consists of all paid employees aged 16–64 that are at work 15+ hours per week.

The third indicator to measure gender equality scales countries on the segregation in working hours between both sexes. As explained earlier, the segregation index refers to percentage of the male and/or female labor force that would have to change their working hours in order to eliminate all segregation. A high score on this indicator implies that men and women are employed at different levels of working hours and is thereby a sign of gender inequality in working time.

Flexibility Indicators

With regard to the flexibility dimension, we first use the kurtosis indicator. Kurtosis measures the peakedness of a distribution. When a distribution is normal, the value of kurtosis is zero. Kurtosis values above zero indicate a distribution that is more sharply peaked (compared to a standard normal distribution) and has long tails, while kurtosis values below zero indicate a distribution that is flatter than the normal distribution. We have used a data file provided by Eurostat that includes absolute figures for both men and women working as employees. In order to make it a gender independent indicator, we measure the kurtosis over the working-time distribution of all employees (men and women). A high kurtosis means that employees are mostly clustered in one (or few) working-time routines (in almost all cases this time pattern is 36–40 hours). A low kurtosis, on the other hand, indicates that the employees in a given country are rather spread out over the alternative working-time schedules, while a negative kurtosis indicates that this effect is even bigger.

Another important indicator to measure flexibility is the percentage of persons working during hours that fall outside the standard workweek. Ideally, we would like to select indicators that measure the prevalence of a 24-hour economy. However, the best available indicator is percentage of persons usually working during evening hours. The percentage of women and men usually working at home (based on the number of total in employment) is a third indicator of flexibility, because home working is often seen as an important and innovative strategy with regard to the organization of work and working times in which distance and place no longer constitute restrictions.

Categorization of Countries in Relation to Equality and Flexibility

In order to be able to determine the ranking of the countries we have computed the standardized z-scores of each country on the six indicators. z-Scores are transformed data that change any set of scores to a new set with a mean of 0 and a standard deviation of 1. A z-score thus equals the number of standard deviations a score is from the mean. A positive z-score implies that the observed score is above the sample mean, a negative z-score means that the observation is below the sample mean. z-Scores facilitate the comparison of scores on different measurement items as they reveal where scores are placed in their distributions. Cumulative z-scores, which are obtained by adding up the z-scores on three flexibility and three equality indicators, are thus a means of summarizing the information on a country's relative flexibility and equality. The details of the country scores are found in Tables 2 and 3.

The summary results of indexing the fifteen countries on their aggregated z-scores are displayed in Fig. 2. On the horizontal axis, countries are arrayed according to their aggregated z-scores on gender equality. The vertical axis indicates the relative flexibility of the different working-time regimes. The Nordic countries Finland, Denmark and Sweden have positive scores on both the gender equality and the flexibility indicators and can thus be found in the upper-right quadrant. The upper left quadrant, with high flexibility and low equality, is occupied by Austria, Ireland, and the more extreme cases of the United Kingdom and the Netherlands. The position of the United Kingdom clearly reflects the ideosyncratic nature of the British labor market. More striking is the position of the Netherlands, which has by far the lowest score on gender equality, whereas it does obtain a relatively high score on flexibility (Plantenga, 2002). Luxembourg and Spain have negative

Table 2. Country Scores on Three Equality Indicators.

Country	Standardized Gender Employment Gap, 2000	Gross Gender Pay Gap, 1998	Working Hour Segregation, 1999 (Employees and Self Employed)	Cumulative z-Scores
Greece	−0.42	87	18.48	0.092
Spain	−0.42	86	20.51	−0.24
Italy	−0.41	91	21.95	0.021
Portugal	−0.21	94	17.98	1.02
UK	−0.17	76	37.75	−0.65
Ireland	−0.29	80	29.67	−0.47
Denmark	−0.11	90	28.86	0.64
Finland	−0.09	82[a]	12.83	0.75
Belgium	−0.26	93	36.37	0.096
France	−0.20	88	27.77	0.30
The Netherlands	−0.23	79	51.20	−1.11
Germany	−0.20	81	18.48	−0.22
Austria	−0.23	79	28.38	−0.37
Sweden	−0.05	82	28.56	0.32
Luxembourg	−0.33	88	30.47	−0.19

Source: Eurostat, Labor Force Survey 1999, 2000, ECHP (1998).
[a] This statistic is based on Finland's index of wage and salary earnings for 1999.

scores on flexibility as well as equality and are therefore in the lower left quadrant, with Spain having by far the lowest score on flexibility. The lower right quadrant is occupied by Portugal, France, Belgium, and Greece since they all score positively on equality and negatively on flexibility. Portugal has in interesting position, scoring high on equality but performing relatively poorly on flexibility. Finally, Germany and Italy are borderline cases, since they are close to the mean on the equality and the flexibility axes, with Italy falling between the lower right and the lower left quadrant and Germany falling between the upper left and the lower left quadrant.

It is extremely tempting, now that the fifteen countries are grouped in four different quadrants, to give normative labels to these quadrants. Given the limited nature of this exercise and the difficulties with regard to the statistical data, it is important to be rather cautious in this respect. Presumably the most important message of Fig. 2 is that there are large differences between European member states with regard to their record on equality and flexibility. Apparently, a relatively high score on flexibility is not by definition connected with a low score on gender equality. At the same time, a relatively high score on gender equality may be combined with a working-time regime that is a more or less flexible. The

Table 3.   Country Scores on Three Flexibility Indicators.

Country	Kurtosis	Persons Usually Working in the Evening, 1999	Persons Usually Working From Home, 1999	Cumulative z-Scores
Greece	2.307	29	1.7	−0.083
Spain	5.883	9.6	0.8	−1.123
Italy	4.367	13	4.0	−0.451
Portugal	4.820	16.7[a]	2.6	−0.506
UK	−0.057	32.7	2.4	0.848
Ireland	2.936	11.6	7.3	0.025
Denmark	3.314	20.9	10.7	0.666
Finland	7.904	24.2	10.3	0.069
Belgium	1.812	5.1	6.2	−0.169
France	3.175	6.5	4.4	−0.489
The Netherlands	0.596	17	6.2	0.490
Germany	2.862	18.5	4.1	0.005
Austria	6.392	14.8	11.5	0.038
Sweden	4.519	22.5	8.3	0.322
Luxembourg	4.231	9.2	9.1	−0.093

Source: Eurostat, Labor Force Survey 1999, 2000.

[a] Data for people "usually working in the evening" are extremely unreliable according to Eurostat. In order to compensate for questionable data, the European average (16.7%) was substituted for Portugal.

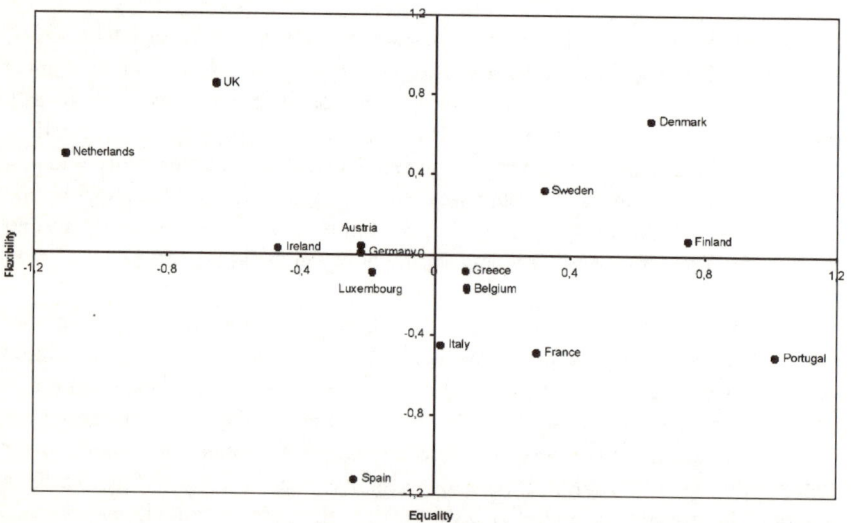

Fig. 2.   Country Scores on Equality and Flexibility (Cumulative z-Scores). *Source:* See Tables 2 and 3.

bottom line is that there is no fixed relation between the two dimensions. This is an important message from a policy point of view as it indicates that countries still have a variety of options. Politics do matter and influence the actual position taken within the flexibility/equality spectrum.

FUTURE DEVELOPMENTS

Improving the participation rate is the main goal of the European Employment Strategy. An important milestone in this respect is the agreement on quantitative targets at the Lisbon summit in March 2000. It was agreed that the employment rate in the EU should be raised from an average of 61% today, to as close as possible to 70% by 2010, and the percentage of women in employment should increase from the current 51% to more than 60% in 2010. In Stockholm in March 2001, the EU political leaders agreed upon intermediate targets (67% total and 57% for women) and an employment rate target for persons ages 55–65 to increase their participation rate to 50% in 2010.

The European employment strategy also favors more flexible working-time patterns. In fact, one of the four pillars focuses especially on encouraging adaptability of businesses to the needs of their employees. Social partners are invited to negotiate and implement agreements at all appropriate levels to modernize the organization of work, including flexible working arrangements, with the aim of making businesses productive and competitive, achieving the required balance between flexibility and security, and increasing the quality of jobs. Areas to be covered may, for example, include the introduction of new technologies, new forms of work and working-time issues such as the expression of working time as an annual figure, the reduction of working hours, the reduction of overtime, the development of part-time work, access to career breaks and associated job security issues (Pillar 3 of the European Employment Strategy). See for an overview of policy initiatives JER (2000, 2001).

At this moment it is not yet clear whether the combined result of these two strategies (raising employment and increasing flexibility) favors gender equality or undermines it. From a more general point of view it seems likely that the lives of ordinary men and women will become less linear, and will be more oriented towards combining work, care, and education over a life time. This life-time approach emphasizes the importance of new solutions like annual time credit arrangements to facilitate the reconciliation of work and family life. Working times seem to lose more and more of their implicit meaning as standards and become subject to negotiation and trade. This development also gives a new meaning to the well known phrase "time is money" as time acquires qualities commonly attributed to money. Time can be stored for example; be held in reserve to meet unanticipated demand, be used as a medium of exchange, etc. In all the current discussions and the debates yet to come, we should be aware that the issue of working time should not be analyzed too narrowly, or too objectively as simply time during which work is actually performed. We should also take into account a more subjective and broader perspective and conceive working time as time in the life of a worker (Supiot, 1999). Recent innovations with regard to working times have made it abundantly clear that the organization of working time has important implications for the public good, be it the ability of the individual to come to terms with domestic responsibilities or the ability of the society to protect its collective time.

NOTE

1. *The European Community Household Panel* (ECHP) is an annual longitudinal survey of a representative panel of households launched in 1994. The survey is based on a standardized questionnaire covering a wide range of topics: income, including the various social benefits, health, education, housing, socio-demographic characteristics including employment, etc. More information is available at http://www.iccr-international.org/echp/main.html

ACKNOWLEDGMENTS

The author thanks Jules Korsten and Bob Rijkers for their research assistance and the editors of this book for their support in finishing this article.

REFERENCES

Anxo, D., & O'Reilly, J. (2000). Working-time regimes and transitions in comparative perspective. In: J. O'Reilly, I. Cebrian & M. Lallement (Eds), *Working-Time Changes. Social Integration Through Transitional Labour Markets*. Cheltenham: Edward Elgar.
Bettio, F., Del Bono, E., & Smith, M. (1998). *Working-time patterns in the European Union, policies and innovations from a gender perspective*. Report of the European Commission's Group of Experts on Gender and Employment, Employment and social affairs.
Blossfeld, H.-P., & Hakim, C. (1997). Introduction: A comparative perspective on part-time work. In: H.-P. Blossfeld & C. Hakim (Eds), *Between Equalization and Marginalization*. New York: Oxford University Press.
Evans, J. M., Lippoldt, D. C., & Marianne, P. (2000). *Trends in working hours in OECD countries*. Labour market and social policy. Occasional papers No. 45.
Eurostat (1994). *Labour force survey 1993*. Luxembourg: Office for Official Publications of the European Communities.

Eurostat (2000). *Labour force survey 1999*. Luxembourg: Office for Official Publications of the European Communities.

Eurostat (2001). *Labour force survey 2000*. Luxembourg: Office for Official Publications of the European Communities.

JER (Joint Employment Report) (2000). Downloadable from http://europa.eu.int/comm/employment_social/employment_strategy//report_2000/jer2000_en.pdf

JER (Joint Employment Report) (2001). Downloadable from http://europa.eu.int/comm/employment_social/employment_strategy//report_2001/jer2001_en.pdf

Maruani, M. (1995). Inequalities and flexibility. In: *Equal Opportunities for Men and Women: Follow up to the White Paper on Growth, Competitiveness and Employment*. Report to the European Commission's Employment Task Force (DGV) (February).

Mutari, E., & Figart, D. M. (2001). Europe at a crossroads: Harmonisation, liberalisation and the gender of work time. *Social Politics, 8*(1), 36–64.

Perrons, D. (Ed.) (1998). *Flexible working and the reconciliation of work and family life – or a new form of precariousness*. Final Report. European Commission. Directorate-General for Employment, Industrial Relations and Social Affairs, Unit V/D.5

Plantenga, J. (2002). Combining work and care in the polder model: An assessment of the Dutch part-time strategy. *Critical Social Policy, 22*(1), 53–71.

Rubery, J., & Fagan, C. (1993). *Occupational segregation of women and men in the European community*. Social Europe, supplement 3/93. Luxembourg: Office for Official Publications of the European Communities.

Rubery, J., Smith, M., & Fagan, C. (1995). *Changing patterns of work and working time in the European Communities and the impact of gender divisions*. Report for the network of experts on the situation of women in the labor market. Equal opportunities unit, DGV, Commission of the European Union.

Rubery, J., Smith, M., & Fagan, C. (1998). National working time regimes and equal opportunities. *Feminist Economics, 4*(1), 71–101.

Supiot, A. (1999). The transformation of work and the future of labor law in Europe; a multidisciplinary perspective. *International Labor Review, 138*(1), 31–46.

7. EMPLOYMENT OPTIONS OF MEN AND WOMEN IN EUROPE

Harald Bielenski and Alexandra Wagner

ABSTRACT

The article describes actual and preferred employment rates and working hours. Empirical data come from a representative survey about "Employment Options of the Future" which was carried out in all 15 member states of the European Union (EU) and in Norway in 1998. There are great differences between men and women and among the 16 countries as far as actual employment rates and actual working hours are concerned. There are also very different patterns in the way that work is shared between men and women within couples. People's own preferences differ in varying degrees from their actual situations. Remarkably, however, the preferences of men and women differ to a much lesser extent than their actual situations do. The same is true for the cross-national differences. In other words, cultural ideals of people in Europe are much more homogeneous with respect to gender and national background than is today's reality.

INTRODUCTION

This article has a special focus on work life in Europe. In the different European countries one finds a broad variety of patterns. Labour market participation and employment rates – especially of women – and working hours of both sexes vary to a large extent. On one hand, the variance reflects the different legal and

Changing Life Patterns in Western Industrial Societies
Advances in Life Course Research, Volume 8, 137–162
Copyright © 2004 by Elsevier Ltd.
All rights of reproduction in any form reserved
ISSN: 1040-2608/doi:10.1016/S1040-2608(03)08007-9

institutional systems (e.g. labour law, tax law, social security legislation, provision of childcare facilities) that promote or prevent high employment rates or long working hours in general and the egalitarian division of paid work among men and women in particular. On the other hand, changing patterns of work life may induce adaptations in the legal and institutional framework.

The most significant change of work life in Europe over the past five decades has been the increasing labour market participation of women and the decreasing number of weekly working hours of those who are in paid work. This happened in all European countries – although there are large differences as far as speed and outcome is concerned. In some countries (Denmark, Norway, Sweden) female employment rates rose nearly as high as male employment rates whereas in other countries (Greece, Italy, Spain) there is still a large gap between male and female employment rates. Standard weekly working hours range from 35 to 40 depending on country and sector of activity. In some countries (the Netherlands, Sweden, U.K., Germany, Norway) part-time work is widespread whereas in others (Finland, Portugal, Italy, Greece, Spain) it is relatively rare. All these differences in actual work life patterns can be explained by a number of factors (cf. Bielenski et al., 2002a, b; Bonke & Koch-Weser, 2003).

This chapter focuses on what is likely in the future. To this end we do not extrapolate the past trends nor do we compare present reality with our own ideas about how things should develop. We look at peoples' own preferences as far as participation in paid work and working hours are concerned. A comparison of the preferences with the actual situation shows where political action is necessary in order to make reality better fit the way that people want to organise their working lives.

We will show that – despite the large national and gender differences which characterise the present situation – there is a convergence in Europe in the preferences regarding working time. This is true at three different levels: among the European countries, between both sexes in general, and between men and women living together as a couple. Their preferences are much more similar with respect to participation in paid work and working hours than are their actual situations. Something like a new European standard seems to be emerging. The data suggest that it is not only desirable but also possible to establish a joint European labour market and working-time policy in order to support people in making their preferences become reality.

PREFERENCES AND FUTURE TRENDS

This chapter presents some results of the survey "Employment Options for the Future," which was conducted in 1998 on behalf of the European Foundation for the Improvement of Living and Working Conditions.[1] The Foundation is a tripartite body of the European Union (EU), whose role is to provide key actors in social policy making (governments, employers and trade unions at a national and EU level) with findings, knowledge and advice drawn from comparative research. The Employment Options Survey was launched in order to find out more about which working-time arrangements will be asked for in the future by those who are in paid work already and by those who are likely to enter or re-enter the labour market in the near future. Survey results should enable employers, trade unions and governments to make the necessary provisions for a better match of the supply and the demand side of the labour market. Apart from that the survey revealed some general trends which go beyond short-term policy making.

In the Employment Options Survey questions were asked not only about actual participation in employment and working times but also, and in particular, about employment preferences and working-time preferences. In investigating working-time preferences, a more wide-ranging procedure was adopted than in many other studies, which tend to question only the currently employed about their working-time preferences. First, data were gathered not only on employees' working-time preferences but also on the employment and working-time preferences of people not currently employed. By extending the range of questioning in this way, the study takes account of the fact that working times will in the future be influenced not only by the preferences of those currently in employment but also by the inflows of currently inactive people into the labour market and, conversely, by the outflows of employed people into inactivity. Secondly, interviewees who lived together with a partner were asked not only about their own working-time preferences but also about whether their partners worked and, where applicable, how many hours they worked. These questions enable us to identify the various combinations of employment and working-time preferences at the household level and to compare them with the situation that currently exists. Radical changes at the household level are to be expected as increasing numbers of women enter the labour market. The questions about working time and employment preferences make it possible to identify the actions that employers, the social partners (trade unions and employers' organisations), national governments, and the EU will need to take in future. The EU, for example, is arguing for an increase in the employment rate in order to reduce unemployment; as we shall see, the results of this survey provide impressive support for this position. At the same time, the results also show that the EU's demand for equal employment opportunities for men and women is in accordance with the preferences of most men and women in the EU (European Commission, 2000, p. 5).

It seems to us legitimate to draw conclusions about the need for action from the results of the study. Although recent research shows that preferences can be good predictors of future behaviour (cf. Hakim, 2003), some caution is necessary. On the one hand, preferences express individual desires for change; on the other hand, these desires are influenced by objective constraints within which individuals plan their lives. Thus, preferences are usually compromises between what is desirable and what is feasible. When the objective conditions change, preferences may change as well. If individuals' room for manoeuvre is extended, what was previously "unthinkable" becomes desirable and possible; if, however, that room for manoeuvre is reduced, then preferences expressed earlier may be sacrificed to individual perceptions of what is feasible. Thus, preferences are not static; rather, they evolve in close interaction with the actual circumstances of the individuals concerned. This interaction between preferences and individual circumstances can be truly understood only from a dynamic perspective, with employment policy conclusions being drawn accordingly. Thus, it is now known that women's employment preferences are shaped to some extent by public childcare provision and are influenced by changes in such provision. Similarly, employment preferences are not formulated independently of the actual labour market situation in a given country. In a bad labour market situation, people wishing to work may well be discouraged from seeking employment. Conversely, in a favourable labour market situation, their latent employment preferences may be reawakened.

Preferences can be expressed without any consideration of the monetary and non-monetary costs of realising them. However, if the time comes to take them seriously, then more careful consideration may be given to costs and, under certain circumstances, preferences may be sacrificed as a result. Reduced working time usually means a drop in income. However, it is uncertain whether respondents would actually be prepared to forego earnings if there was a serious possibility that their expressed preferences for shorter time at work might be realised. Under such circumstances, it may well be important whether a second person in the household can offset the income foregone by increasing his or her working time. However, even preferences for longer working hours or, in the case of non-active workers, for labour market entry are not without their costs. Some of the benefits of longer working hours are higher earnings and greater financial independence. The costs include a loss of free time, and possibly additional expenditure on childcare or the non-realisation of certain aspirations (having children, getting further education or training, etc.). These very complex cost-benefit considerations that have to be carefully weighed in real-life situations are not fully taken into account when answering a survey questionnaire, but are only thought through when there is a serious possibility of realising the preferences.

Preferences are probably better indicators of actual behaviour if those surveyed have a very high degree of freedom in their employment and working-time choices. In societies with high levels of freedom (high incomes, good social security, institutionalised rights to flexibility, such as parental leave schemes, flexible work organisation systems, high educational levels with correspondingly high employability, all-day schools and a highly developed childcare infrastructure), preferences can be more easily realised than in societies with little freedom in these respects. In such countries, however, differences between actual working times and working-time preferences point to a high level of dissatisfaction, which could also be interpreted as an invitation to policymakers to act.

Thus, working-time preferences may go unrealised because of the costs likely to be incurred and the environment in which working and family life takes place; furthermore, they have to be negotiated with other employees and household members. To that extent, it cannot be expected that working-time preferences can ever be realised in full. However, the cost calculations and the external conditions shaping working-time decisions can be influenced. Similarly, rules can be established for bargaining processes in the workplace, and household members can be given greater freedom when making their working-time decisions (for example, by improving the public provision of childcare). Changes in these areas will in turn influence working-time preferences. We need to be conscious of the fact that, in investigating working-time preferences, we are dealing to some extent with a moving target that is very much influenced by the economic and social conditions that are either given or expected. For this reason, the observed discrepancy between current and preferred working times should be interpreted not simply as an individual desire for change but also as a challenge to policymakers, since the reasons for this discrepancy can, in part at least, be influenced by policy.

DATA BASE

All figures quoted in this article are drawn from the Employment Options Survey which was conducted in summer 1998. Data are representative for the residential population aged 16–64 years in all 15 Member states of the EU and in Norway. Data collection was made on the basis of representative samples in each of the 16 countries involved in the survey.[2] In total 30,557 interviews are available for analysis.

Gross samples were drawn at random from the national telephone directories in each country. In order to cope with the problem of non-listed numbers in some countries artificial telephone numbers were created (Random Digit Dialling method, RDD). If there were more than one person belonging to the universe in one household (i.e. eligible for an interview), selection of the interviewee was also made at random (mainly by using the last birthday method).

Fieldwork was co-ordinated by Infratest Sozialforschung in Munich, Germany, and carried out between May and September 1998 by national fieldwork institutes.

Data collection was made by computer-assisted telephone interviews (CATI). In order to provide cross-nationally comparable data an English master version of the CATI questionnaire was developed and translated into the different languages of the countries involved in the survey.[3]

A series of publications resulted from the Employment Options Survey.[4] This article is mainly based on a comprehensive analysis of the data from a cross-national perspective (Bielenski et al., 2002a, b). Additional analyses were made for this article.

Actual and Preferred Employment Rates

Employment rates vary greatly between the 16 countries involved in our survey. In Europe on average 63% of the residential population aged 16–64 are in paid work.[5] Employment rates vary between 48% in Spain and 82% in Norway. The differences can mainly be explained by the different levels of female employment rates. The range between the country with the highest and the country with the lowest male employment rate is 23 percentage points, whereas the range is as high as 50 percentage points between female employment rates. Apart from the female labour market participation there are some other factors which also have a positive or negative influence on national employment rates, such as the level of unemployment, the number of years people normally spend in general education before they join the workforce, and the different social security systems and their impact on retirement age.

If we look at the preferences we see that in all countries more people would like to be in paid work than there are at present. According to these preferences, the employment rate in Europe as a whole would have to rise by as much as 11 percentage points from 63 to 74%. This means that people in Europe would like to have an employment rate which the United states already has. This is also in line with the official policies of the European Union (European Commission, 2000, p. 5). Making employment rates rise by 11 percentage points is a huge challenge for employers, social partners who are negotiating the collective bargaining contracts, national governments, and the EU.

Again, there are large differences among countries and between the sexes. As a general rule the difference between actual and preferred employment rate is larger, the lower the present employment rate. In the Scandinavian countries where employment rates are already very high, preferences would induce only a very moderate increase in overall employment, by less than 10 percentage points. In Italy and Spain, however, employment rates would have to rise by 15 or 20 percentage points on order to come into line with the wishes of the population of working age.

The gap between preferences and reality is much larger for women than for men (see Figs 1 and 2). Across Europe female employment rates would have to rise by 13 percentage points on average, male employment rates by only 8 percentage points. In countries like Denmark or Norway practically all women who prefer to work are in paid employment already. Female employment rates would have to rise only very moderately. In other countries, however, dramatic changes are necessary. In Greece, Italy, and Spain the preferences of women of working age imply employment rates that are 20 percentage points or more above the present level. In Greece and Italy this means that the preferred level is one and a half times as high as at present, in Spain it is twice as high.

If the preferences would become reality, the differences between the countries would become smaller. At present the range between the highest and the lowest overall employment rate is 34 percentage points (Norway: 82%, Spain: 48%). Regarding preferences the range shrinks to 23 percentage points (Norway: 88%, Italy: 65%). This convergence of employment rates in Europe is due only to the preferences of women. The range of the male employment rates remains almost unaffected if one compares today's reality with peoples' preferences (23 vs. 22 percentage points difference between the highest and the lowest national male employment rate). Women's preferences, however, are much more homogeneous across Europe than their actual situation is: the range would be almost halved from 50 percentage points in actual employment rates to 27 percentage points in preferred employment rates. The range would then be not much higher than the range we observe among the national male employment rates; national differences would become smaller but would not disappear.

The large gender-specific differences between the European countries show that at present the legal, institutional, and cultural framework have much more influence on women than on men as far as labour market participation as such is concerned. At the same time the survey data show that the present situation is not in line with people's preferences – in particular with respect to female employment rates in those countries where still relatively few women are in paid employment. Political action might therefore focus on the creation of additional job opportunities especially for women and on the necessary adaptations of the legal and institutional framework (such as provision of adequate childcare facilities and removal of tax regulations which prevent married women from taking up paid work).

Actual and Preferred Weekly Working Hours

At present typical employees in Europe work 37.7 hours per week. According to their preferences they would like to work 34.0 hours, or 3.7 hours less than they actually do.

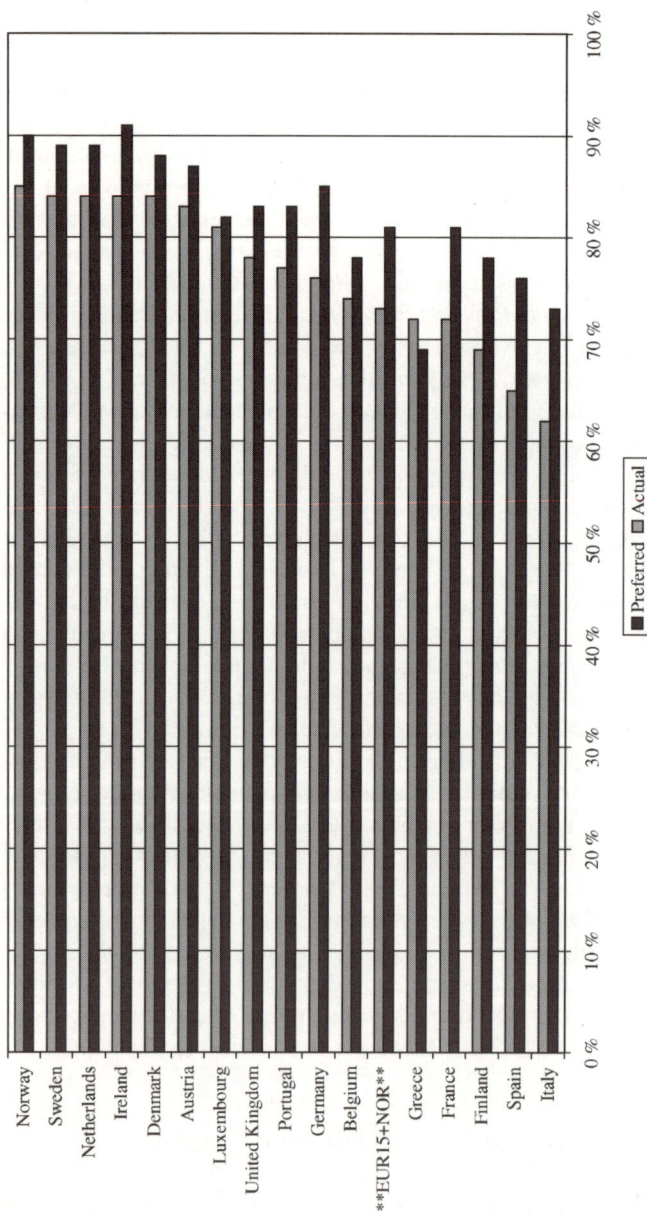

Fig. 1. Employment Rates of Men. *Source:* Employment Options Survey 1998.

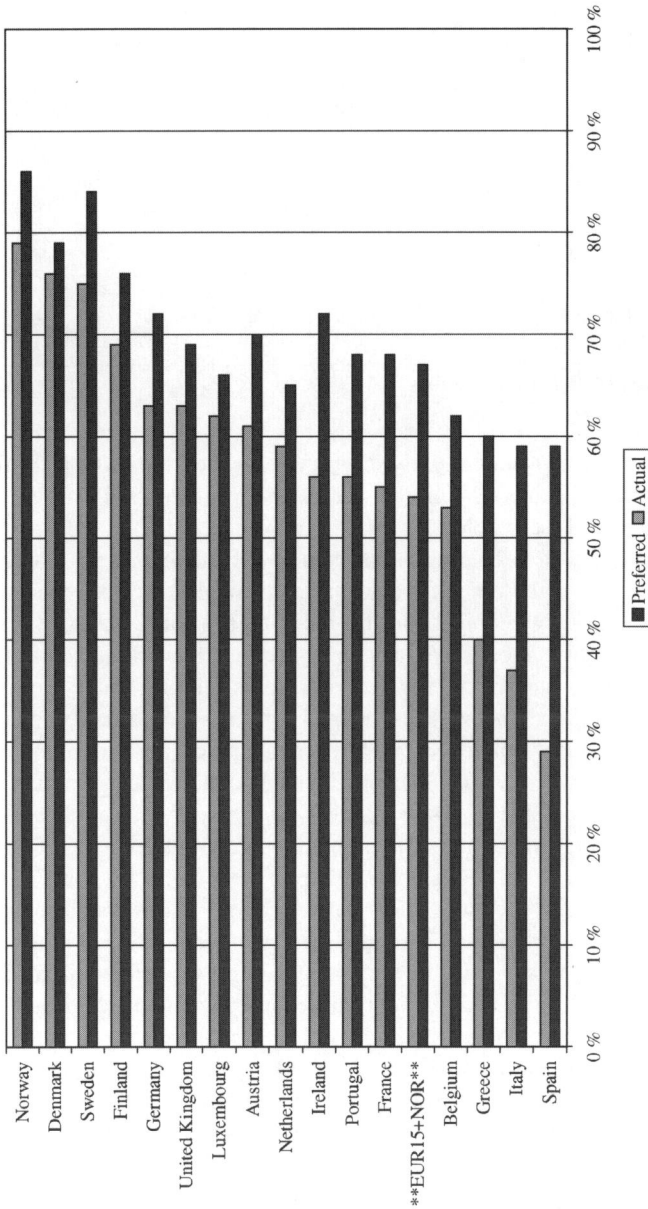

Fig. 2. Employment Rates of Women. *Source:* Employment Options Survey 1998.

Table 1. Difference Between Actual and Preferred Weekly Working Hours of Employees at an Individual Level (in %).

	Respondent Prefers to Work ...					Total
	More Than 5 Hours Less	1–5 Hours Less	Approx. Same Hours	1–5 Hours More	More Than 5 Hours More	
All employees	33	16	39	4	8	100
Women	30	12	42	4	11	100
Men	34	20	37	3	6	100
Employees who currently work 45 h or more	69	9	19	1	2	100
Employees who currently work 20 h or less	2	3	48	7	41	100

Source: Employment Options Survey 1998.

The overall trend towards slightly shorter weekly working hours is the result of extremely heterogeneous relations between actual and preferred working times at the individual level (see Table 1).

Only two out of five employees are happy with their present working-time arrangements. As many as half would prefer to work less: 33% would like to reduce their weekly working hours by more than 5 hours per week, 16% by 1–5 hours. A minority would like to have longer weekly working hours (12%).

Employees who have very long working hours tend to prefer shorter hours whereas many of those who work less than 20 hours per week would prefer to work more hours. As a result employees' preferences are much more concentrated in the medium range between 20 and 40 hours than are actual working hours at present (85% vs. 64%, see Table 2). Only relatively few employees say that they want to work long hours (more than 40 hours), although at present a significant share of the workforce have such long hours (9% preferred vs. 28% actual). Very short weekly working hours (below 20) are relatively rare, as far as both actual practice and preferences are concerned. There are a number of reasons for working very long or very short hours. If wages are low, very long working times may still seem necessary. On the other hand, a high-earning partner and poor public childcare facilities might make very short working hours attractive for married women with children.

Men tend to have clear preferences for working hours that cluster around the present full-time standard, i.e. between 35 and 40 hours; but a substantial minority of men would also be interested in weekly working hours between 20 and 34, which might be a reduced full-time standard or a part-time arrangement close to the present full-time standard. As Fig. 3 shows men mainly express a preference for weekly working hours of 40, 35, or 30 hours (in that order).

Table 2. Actual and Preferred Weekly Working Hours of Employees (in %).

	Less Than 20 Hours	20–34 Hours	35–40 Hours	More Than 40 Hours	Total
All employees					
Actual	8	15	49	28	100
Preferred	6	31	54	9	100
Women					
Actual	14	25	47	15	100
Preferred	10	45	41	4	100
Men					
Actual	4	6	51	39	100
Preferred	3	20	63	14	100

Source: Employment Options Survey 1998.

Among women working-time preferences are more heterogeneous. While working hours around the full-time standard are still the predominant working-time arrangement for women, most of the presently employed women in Europe would prefer a 30-hour week. The 40-hour week only comes second as far as preferences are concerned; it is closely followed by 35 hours, 20 hours and, much less frequently, 25 hours (Fig. 4).

If we compare current and preferred working hours between the 16 countries involved in the Employment Options Survey we can see a clear convergence. The range between the country with the longest average weekly working hours of employees and the one with the shortest is 7.4 hours at present but only 5.1 hours if we look at the preferences. This trend is true for both, female and male employees (see Table 3).

Regression analyses show that the influence of gender on actual working times in all the countries (with the exception of Portugal and Greece) is significantly positive: men work longer hours than women. Nevertheless, the extent of the difference between the sexes varies considerably from country to country. The average difference across Europe of 8.5 hours actually conceals very different national patterns (see Table 4). Whereas in Finland women work only 4.2 hours per week less than their male colleagues, in the Netherlands women work as much as 13.4 hours less than men.

The greater heterogeneity of women's working times is reflected particularly in the very diverse female part-time rates, which vary from 13% in Finland to 60% in the Netherlands. These very different part-time rates are attributable in turn to the very different social environments with which women and mothers seeking paid work have to contend. Women's working times are consequently much less

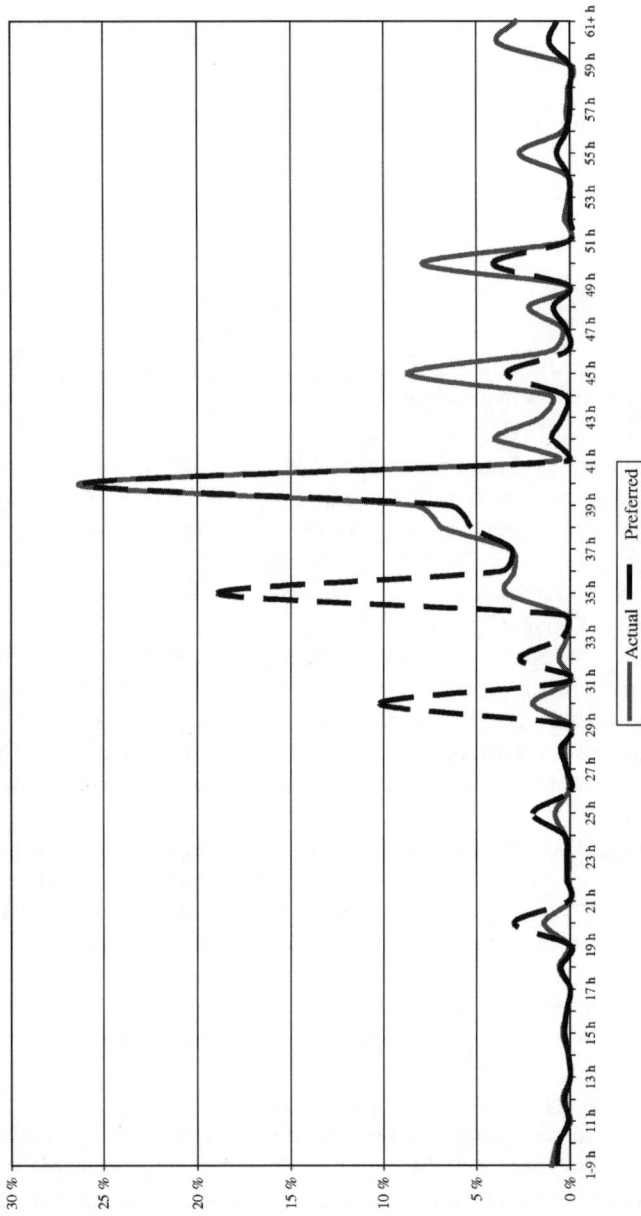

Fig. 3. Actual and Preferred Weekly Working Hours of Men. *Source:* Employment Options Survey 1998.

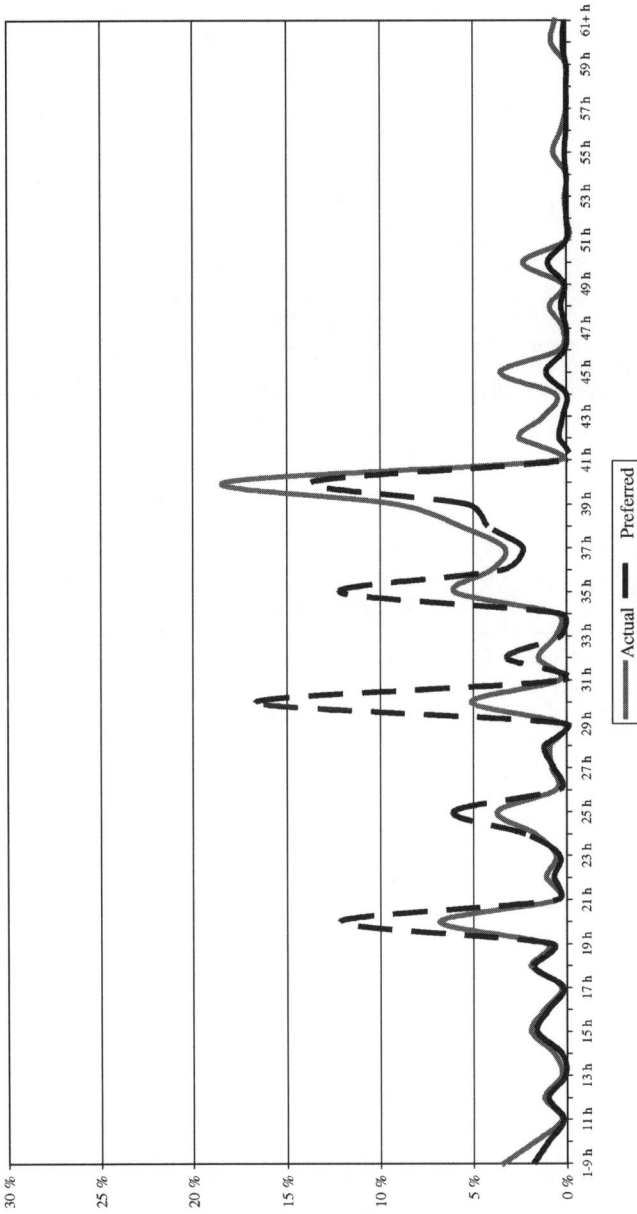

Fig. 4. Actual and Preferred Weekly Working Hours of Women. *Source:* Employment Options Survey 1998.

Table 3. Range of Actual and Preferred Weekly Working Hours of Employees.

	Average Weekly Working Hours Range . . .	Range[a]
All employees		
Actual	from 33.7 h in the Netherlands to 41.1 h in Austria	7.4 h
Preferred	from 31.5 h in the Netherlands to 36.6 h in Greece	5.1 h
Women		
Actual	from 25.9 h in the Netherlands to 37.3 h in Finland	11.4 h
Preferred	from 25.6 h in the Netherlands to 34.2 h in Spain	8.6 h
Men		
Actual	from 38.8 h in Denmark to 45.2 h in Austria	6.4 h
Preferred	from 34.9 h in Denmark to 39.6 h in Austria	4.7 h

Source: Employment Options Survey 1998.
[a] Difference between the country with the longest and the country with the shortest average weekly working hours.

Table 4. The Gender Gap[a] in Actual and Preferred Weekly Working Hours of Employees (in Hours Per Week).

	Gender Gap in Actual Working Hours (Col. 1)	Gender Gap in Preferred Working Hours (Col. 2)	Difference (Col. 2 − Col. 1)
Austria	9.5	7.5	−2.0
Belgium	6.9	5.7	−1.2
Denmark	5.0	5.2	0.2
Finland	4.2	2.9	−1.3
France	6.3	3.8	−2.5
Germany	9.9	5.7	−4.2
Great Britain	12.0	9.1	−2.9
Greece	6.7	4.9	−1.8
Ireland	7.9	6.8	−1.1
Italy	5.3	6.3	1.0
Luxembourg	6.8	7.7	0.9
Netherlands	13.4	10.1	−3.3
Norway	8.8	5.6	−3.2
Portugal	6.4	4.8	−1.6
Spain	6.2	2.7	−3.5
Sweden	6.2	4.0	−2.2
EU and Norway	8.5	6.4	−2.1

Source: Employment Options Survey 1998.
[a] Difference between average weekly working hours of men and women.

influenced than men's by the prevailing statutory or collectively agreed working-time norm. The main reason for this is that, in all the countries, albeit to varying extents, women still shoulder the main responsibility for unpaid domestic work and childcare and therefore often work part-time, if they do any paid work at all. It is also true that men's hourly rates of pay are generally higher, so that with the same number of hours they are able to contribute more to the household's earnings than their wives. On the other hand, traditional roles enable men not only to work full-time for the most part but also to work a considerable amount of overtime as well.

If working-time preferences of men and women were realised, the gender gap in working hours would become smaller in most of the countries (as shown in column 3 of Table 4).

The preferences of employed men and women differ least in Spain and Finland. In both countries women's actual and preferred working times are rather long, although for very different reasons. Finland has a high female employment rate and women are able to combine paid work and domestic and family responsi-bilities with relatively little difficulty; therefore they are oriented predominantly to full-time work. In Spain, on the other hand, childcare facilities are rather poor and at the same time there are very few part-time jobs only; consequently the female employment rate is low and the few women who are in paid work favour full-time work.

Men's and women's preferences differ most in the Netherlands as a result of women's pronounced inclination towards part-time work; the same applies to Great Britain, where men additionally favour longer-than-average working times. In Denmark, the difference between men's and women's working times would remain more or less unchanged if preferences were realised, since both sexes would like to reduce their working hours by virtually the same amount.

If preferences were realised, the differences between the working times of men and women in dependent employment (as shown in the third column of Table 4) would be considerably reduced, not only across Europe as a whole but also within most of the countries considered here. This convergence both within and across countries is one of the most important findings of our study.

THE WORKING TIMES OF MEN AND WOMEN WITH CHILDREN

Only in some countries does the presence of children in a household influence working time; when it does, the effect is gender-specific, with women working shorter hours and men working longer hours.

In countries in which the conditions for combining paid work and family responsibilities are unfavourable, the traditional division of labour is still very stable. This can be illustrated by taking the example of *Germany*, a country that in many respects retains a traditional gendered division of labour. A woman of 35 in Germany with a child up to age 5 works on average 23.3 hours if she is in paid work at all, while a 35-year old man with a child up to age 5 works 39.5 hours. On the other hand, a 35-year old woman with no children works 33.2 hours and a 35-year old man with no children works 37.2 hours. Over and above the existing difference of around 4 hours between men's and women's working times, women in households with a child aged up to 5 reduce their working time by almost 10 hours and men increase theirs by more than 2 hours, thereby extending the gender gap to more than 16 hours.

In *Denmark*, however, which here typifies those countries with relatively egalitarian employment and working-time structures and good social support for parents, there is no such dramatic effect. The difference between men's and women's working-times rises by only one hour when there is a young child in the household.

In Belgium, Denmark, Finland, France, Norway and Spain, working times are not significantly affected by the presence of children in the household. In the Scandinavian countries, as well as in Belgium and France, adequate childcare facilities make it possible to combine paid work and family responsibilities. In the Scandinavian countries, moreover, the taxation and social security systems offer incentives for women to participate in paid work on an equal footing with men. The influence of children on working times is also very slight in Spain and Italy, but for different reasons. Low wage rates, on the one hand, and family-based solutions to the childcare problem, on the other, may well induce women – and make it possible for them – to maintain their working times even after the birth of children, if they do not give up paid work altogether. In these countries, it is primarily those mothers who find individual solutions to the childcare problem who remain in the labour market once they have children to look after.

In Denmark, France, and Norway, the public provision of childcare facilities means that the conditions for combining paid work and family responsibilities are good. Nevertheless, parents in these countries would prefer to work significantly shorter hours than men and women without children. This shows that a good supply of public childcare facilities does not in itself create the optimal conditions for combining paid work and childrearing. Parents would also like to work shorter hours in order to reduce their heavy burden of paid and unpaid work or simply to have more time for their children.

HOW FAR IS REALITY FROM THE PREFERENCES?

In the previous sections we looked only at working-time preferences of those men and women who are already in paid work (as employees). However, in all European countries there are lots of people who are not employed at the moment but would like to be so: unemployed persons, women who want to return to paid work after a more or less long break due to family duties, or young people who want to enter the labour market for the first time after having completed their studies. Those who are not employed at present but would like to be so on average would prefer to work 33.1 hours per week, i.e. a bit less than those who are already in paid work.

The key figure which takes into account both, employment rates and working hours, is the "volume of work." It is normally given as the sum of all hours worked by all people in gainful employment in a certain period of time (per year or per week). This figure not only depends on employment rates and individual working hours but also on the absolute size of the population of working age. In large countries the volume of work therefore is ceteris paribus bigger than in small countries. For the purpose of this article we want to compare countries by the combined effect of different employment rates and weekly working hours regardless of the absolute size of the population. We therefore use a "standardised volume of work," i.e. the average volume of work per person of working age (in hours per week).

Across all 16 European countries involved in the Employment Options Survey the standardised volume of work is 23.7 hours per week at present.[6] According to the preferences it should rise to a level of 25.0 hours. This is the balanced effect of an increased employment rate (74% instead of 63%) and a reduced weekly working time of those who are already in paid work.

The difference between actual and preferred volume of work is calculated on an aggregated level and shows the balance of those who want to work more and those who want to work less. Therefore small differences between actual and preferred volume of work do not necessarily indicate that preferences are close to reality, i.e. that people are fairly happy with their actual situation. If half the people want to work 10 hours more and the other half 10 hours less, the actual and the preferred volume of work are exactly the same, but nobody is happy with the present situation.

In order to check for which groups of persons and in which countries reality is close to the preferences and where this is not the case we use another indicator: the absolute difference between preferred and actual working time at an individual level (see Table 5). Unlike the figures shown in Table 1, here we integrate those who are not employed or who don't want to be employed; in these cases actual or preferred working time is zero.[7] If a person is not employed at present but would like to work 20 hours a week the difference is 20 hours. The same applies

Table 5.   Absolute Difference Between Actual and Preferred Volume of Work[a] at an Individual Level (including the currently not employed).

	Absolute Difference Between Actual and Preferred WT[b] (Hours Per Week)	In % (Total = 100%)		
		Want to Work Less	Are Happy with WT	Want to Work More
All persons in working age	9.0 h	32	48	20
Women	8.4 h	22	54	24
Men	9.7 h	41	43	17
Presently employed	7.7 h	51	37	12
Presently not employed	11.3 h	–	66	34
Presently employed men	8.3 h	56	35	9
Presently employed women	6.9 h	44	41	15
Presently not employed men	13.5 h	–	64	37
Presently not employed women	10.0 h	–	68	32

Source: Employment Options Survey 1998.
[a] Not employed = 0 hours.
[b] Preferences for longer working hours do not compensate preferences for shorter working hours as any differences between preferences and reality are cumulated – irrespective of the direction of the deviation.

for a person who works 25 hours and wants to reduce his or her working time to 5 hours; again the absolute difference is 20 hours.

Table 5 shows that on average people in working age in the 16 European countries surveyed want to change their involvement in paid work by 9 hours per week, be it less or more. Some 48% are happy with their present employment status and working hours while 32% want to reduce their involvement in paid work and another 20% want to increase it.

Despite the fact that there are a considerable number of presently not employed women who want to take up paid work, women on average more often accept their present employment status and working hours than men. For 54% of the women but only 43% of the men their present situation is in line with their preferences. It seems as if women more often than men have already achieved what they consider feasible under the given circumstances. On average women of working age want to change labour market involvement by 8.4 hours, men by 9.7 hours. However, the direction of the preferred changes differs largely between men and women. Among women there are almost as many who want to reduce working hours (22%) as there are who want to work more hours or take up paid work (24%) whereas men rather want to reduce their involvement in paid work than increase it (41% vs.

17%). Unlike women, men who would like to work reduced hours often-times do not actively pursue this preference – on one hand because they fear that this would not be accepted by their employers and might negatively affect their careers, on the other hand because they less often have to combine paid work and family duties.

Of the presently employed persons 37% are happy with the present situation. Half of the presently employed want to reduce their involvement in paid work, most by reducing weekly working hours, only a very few by giving up paid work totally, while 12% want to increase the number of working hours. On average, presently employed people in Europe would like to change their involvement in paid work by 7.7 hours per week. Two-thirds of those who are not in paid work at present are happy with their situation (66%). However, the other third would prefer to be employed.

If we sort the 16 countries involved in our survey by the degree to which actual employment and working hours differ from the preferences we find a wide range, as shown in Fig. 5. In Greece and Spain there is the largest gap between reality and preferences. On average people of working age want to change their labour market involvement by 12.6 hours per week in Greece and by 11.0 hours per week in Spain. Greece and Spain are the countries where women are most unhappy with their actual situation; female employment rates are very low but many women would prefer to be employed. Additionally, in Greece very long working times of men are widespread (because of the high share of self-employed), consequently there is a preference of men for shorter working hours, whereas in Spain the unemployment among men is very high so that preferences to change are due to intended labour market entry not only of women but also of men.

In Luxembourg and Belgium people on average are already closest to their preferences. In these two countries there is a relatively high satisfaction with the existing employment rates. Also the average difference between actual and preferred working time is relatively low with 5.7 hours in Luxembourg and 6.7 hours per week in Belgium. Both men and women in these two countries report the highest degree of satisfaction with their actual employment situation of all 16 countries – with one exception: In the Netherlands women on average are even closer to their preferences. On one hand they seem to be quite happy with the actual employment rate which is slightly above the European average but far from the high levels in the Scandinavian countries. On the other hand they also seem to accept the low share of women in the volume of paid work which is due to the high rates of short part-time work. This means that in the Netherlands the traditional division of labour between men and women is still widespread and well accepted.

It is a bit surprising that it is not the Scandinavian countries with their high female employment rates that rank highest in the scale calculated above. If we look at all persons in working age, Denmark ranks third, Norway fifth, and

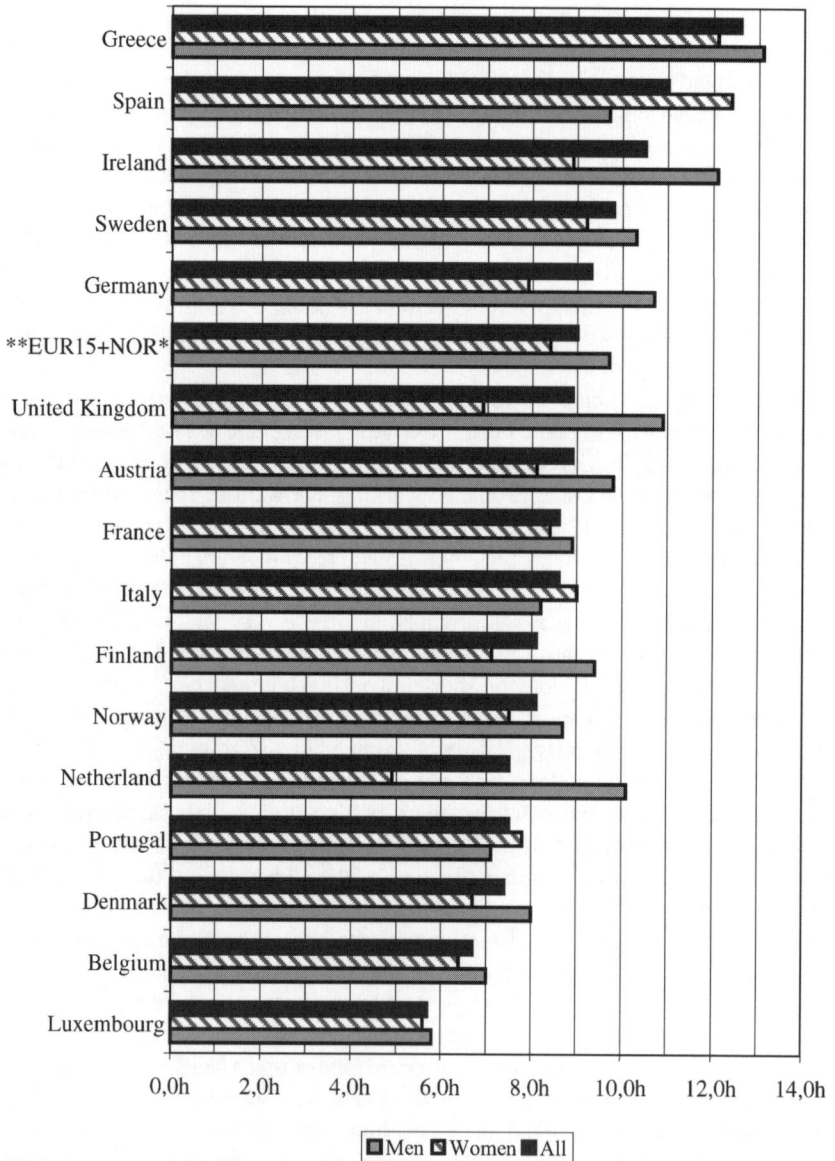

Fig. 5. Absolute Difference Between Actual and Preferred Weekly Working Hours of All Persons in Working Age (Not Employed = 0 h). *Source:* Employment Options Survey 1998.

Finland sixth among the 16 countries – all of them with degrees of satisfaction above the European average. Sweden, however, only ranks thirteenth.

The rank order of countries shows that there seems to be more than one model which is likely to meet people's wishes best. One should bear in mind that probably nowhere and never can a complete correspondence between reality and preferences be achieved since preferences always express the wish to improve the actual situation. Therefore the difference between preferences and reality always has a historical dimension. Swedish women would be very dissatisfied not only with the present Spanish model but also with the employment rates and working hours Spanish women would prefer (much more than with their own Swedish model) whereas the Spanish women – at least at present – probably would be very happy if they had the opportunities provided by the Swedish model.

All in all people seem to be closer to their preferences in the Scandinavian countries than in the Mediterranean countries. High female employment rates and many part-time job opportunities make it likely that people are happy with their actual situation (as for example in Denmark), but these conditions do not guarantee satisfaction (as in the case of Sweden). On the other hand, low female employment rates and few part-time jobs or limited chances of choice with regard to working hours often induce a high level of dissatisfaction with the actual situation as is the case in Greece and Spain.

ACTUAL AND PREFERRED WORKING TIMES OF PARTNERS IN A COUPLE

So far this paper has examined actual situation and the preferences of individuals or of groups of individuals by gender and by country. Now we want to look at couples, i.e. men and women who live together with a partner. In these cases decisions on labour market participation and working hours are usually not made on an individual basis exclusively, but the actual situation and the preferences of the partners are also taken into consideration or have at least a strong influence on both the actual situation and the preferences. Although in real life mutual-decision making is the normal situation for the majority of the working population (69% of the employed share their lives with a male or female partner, while 31% are single), scientific research about labour market issues very seldom takes this perspective (Bonke & Koch-Weser, 2003 or Bielenski & Hartmann, 2000).

If we add up the individual working hours of both partners,[8] couples in Europe on average spend 62 hours per week in paid work. According to the preferences the total time spent for paid work would remain almost unchanged (61 hours) but the distribution among both partners would have to change dramatically.[9]

At present in Europe the difference in working hours between both partners in a couple is 25.4 hours per week, i.e. the partner who works more hours (mostly the man) on average spends 25.4 hours more in paid work than the partner who works less or not at all. There is a wide range across the countries surveyed. The smallest difference was found in Denmark (13.7 hours), the largest in Ireland (30.8 hours). The differences between both partners in a couple are due to a wide range of reasons. They may reflect differences in actual working time, e.g. if one partner works full-time and the other one part-time, or one of them regularly works overtime. They may also be due to the fact that one of the partners is not in paid work with various reasons for this, including unemployment, education/training, retirement, parental leave, voluntary inactivity, etc. A large part of the working-time differences, however, is probably due to the gender division of labour. Evidence for this interpretation is to be found in the relatively small working-time differences between partners in the Scandinavian countries (universal breadwinner model) and the relatively large differences in those countries with a strong attachment to the male breadwinner model (Ireland, Greece, Spain).

In all 16 countries there is a preference for a less unequal distribution of working time between men and women living as couples. It is true that even if preferences were realised, participation in paid work and working time would still be unequally distributed among both partners. However, the average working-time difference in Europe would fall by almost half from its present level of 25.4 hours to 13.1 hours per week. Again we find a strong convergence (here: between men's and women's involvement in paid work) if we compare the actual situation with people's preferences. Differences would become considerably smaller but would still exist.

There are different models of how to share paid work among men and women who live together as couple:

- The traditional male breadwinner mode of distribution (men in full-time employment, women economically inactive) is still the most widespread form of the gender division of participation in paid work in Europe. It is currently found in 35% of the couples with at least one person in paid work. This model is predominant among couples in Spain, Luxembourg, Italy, Greece, Ireland and, to a lesser extent, in Germany.
- In the second place we find the model that both partners work full-time (32%). This is the dominant mode of distribution in the Scandinavian countries and in Portugal, Belgium, France, the U.K., and Austria.
- In 21% of the couples the man works full-time and the women part-time. In Luxembourg, Ireland and Germany this modernised form of the male bread-winner model plays a quantitatively significant role but only in the Netherlands

is the male full-time/female part-time combination the most widespread mode of distribution.
- The model of both partners working part-time is practised very seldom in Europe (2%).
- The same applies to other forms of sharing work where the woman works more hours than the man (10%).

The preferred modes of distribution confirm the trend identified above, that couples express a preference for a more equal distribution of paid work. Attachment to the single (male) breadwinner model is weak: It is preferred by an average of only 15% of couples in Europe as a whole (but is the practice among 35%). Conversely its modernised form (man in full-time/woman in part-time) is preferred by significantly more couples (32%) than actually practise it (21%). The share of households with two full-time workers would remain unchanged if preferences were realised (32% actual and preferred). Although only 2% of two-adult households in Europe currently practise the combination of two part-time jobs, 16% declare a preference for it; this form of the division of paid work is particularly attractive in the Scandinavian countries and the Netherlands where experience of part-time work is already widespread.

If it is assumed that the combination of two full-time jobs and that of two part-time jobs are both "egalitarian" forms of the division of paid work, then the share of egalitarian forms of the gender division of paid work at the household level rises from its actual level of 34% to almost half at the level of preferences.

Table 6. The Distribution of Paid Work Between Men and Women in Two-Adult Households with at Least One Economically Active Person with Respect to the Existence of Children (in %).

	Actual			Preferred		
	Age of the Youngest Child		No Children	Age of the Youngest Child		No Children
	Under 6	6 or over		Under 6	6 or over	
Both partners full-time	24	32	40	26	33	38
Man full-time, woman part-time	24	23	15	39	34	21
Only man economically active	47	35	27	15	14	14
Both partners part-time	1	2	2	18	14	17
Other patterns	4	8	4	2	4	9
Total	100	100	100	100	100	100

Source: Bielenski and Hartmann (2000, p. 6).

The way in which couples divide up paid and unpaid work is only partially influenced by the presence of young children (for further details, see Fagan et al., 2001). The preference for the single male breadwinner model and the desire for both partners to work part-time only are not dependent on whether or not there are young children to be cared for. However, the presence of children and the age of the youngest child do influence the form of paid work the partners of full-time male workers would enter if preferences were realised. Women with children, particularly young children, would be more likely to seek part-time rather than full-time employment, (39% part-time vs. 26% full-time) if they were to work at all (see Table 6).

CONCLUSIONS

Employment rates and average working hours of men differ much less between countries than employment rates and working hours of women. The national legal, institutional, and cultural framework has much more influence on women than on men as far as participation in paid work is concerned. Women's working times are considerably more heterogeneous and differ to a significantly greater extent than men's from the prevailing full-time norm. The main reason for this is that women still shoulder the main responsibility for unpaid domestic work, which explains why many of them work part-time, if indeed they are economically active at all. This is also the reason why the gap between preferences and reality is much larger for women than for men.

Considerable differences between men's and women's actual working times are found in those countries in which part-time work is widespread and often the only possible form of labour market participation for women, mainly because of an inadequate supply of childcare facilities. The differences are smaller both in countries with low female employment rates where women either work full-time or are not employed at all and in countries where the social environment is favourable to combining paid work – even full-time – and parenthood. So childcare facilities do influence employment rates and working times of women. Only in a few countries does the presence of children in a household influence working times. When it does, the influence is gender-specific, with mothers working shorter hours than childless women and fathers working longer hours than childless men.

The survey results show that employed men and women in all 15 EU member states and Norway feel a need for shorter and more flexible working-time options. One of the main findings of our study is that working-time *preferences* in general, and those of men and women in particular, are more similar than actual working times, both within and across countries. The differences in working time between men and women would shrink considerably if preferences were realised. However, working-time preferences are still influenced by the prevailing models of male and female labour market behaviour and the wider social environment in each country. For these reasons, there would still be differences between men and women in this respect, albeit at a lower level, if preferences were realised.

Working-time preferences converge strongly towards a weekly working time of between 30 and 40 hours. More than three-quarters of men and almost two-thirds of women would like working times within this range. If working-time preferences were realised, the boundary between full and part-time work would become fluid. "Short" part-time jobs and excessively long working hours would virtually disappear, while working times close to the current "long" part-time and "short" full-time hours would become more widespread.

The unremitting task of providing for a family's material needs can be shared if both partners are economically active. This makes shorter individual working hours possible. Paid work for both partners and shorter working hours both accord with the wishes of men and women in the 16 countries investigated. If their preferences were realised, the current difference in hours worked between the partners in a household could be reduced by about half. There is a clear preference for a less uneven distribution of paid work between partners. The traditional family breadwinner model would become less widespread while working times below the current full-time norm for one or both partners would become more common.

The role of part-time work is ambiguous. In countries which offer poor public childcare facilities, part-time work often times is the only form of labour market access for women with family duties, i.e. they only have the choice between part-time work and not participating in paid work. In countries with a well developed childcare infrastructure parents have genuine choices whether and to what extent they want to take up paid work; women working reduced hours in such countries tend to be doing so because they do not want to work full-time.

NOTES

1. Methodological details are set out the next section.

2. In each of the five large countries (France, Germany, Italy, Spain and U.K.) approximately 3,000 persons were interviewed, in Luxembourg 800 and in each of the other countries 1,500. In the weighting process the actual ratio of the different country sizes was re-established in order to allow analyses representative for the whole population of working age in all 16 countries together.

3. The English master version of the questionnaire is available on the homepage of Infratest Sozialforschung under http://www.infratest-sofo.de/downloads/fragebogen_01.pdf.

4. For details please refer to homepage of the European Foundation (http://www.eurofound.eu.int).

5. All figures in this article are drawn from the Employment Options Survey. Other sources might report slightly different data about employment rates or working hours (for details cf. Bielenski et al., 2002a, 8 ff.). In order to allow a consistent comparison of the actual situation and the preferences we decided to use data from one single source. The Employment Options Survey enables us to compare present reality and preferences not only at an aggregate level but also on an individual level.

6. This figure also includes self-employed people and family workers and their working hours.

7. Table 1 is restricted to dependent employees whereas Table 5 includes all persons in gainful employment, i.e. also self-employed people.

8. Not employed = 0 hours.

9. Respondents with a partner were not only asked for their own actual and preferred working hours but also for the actual working hours of the partner and the number of hours the respondent would prefer for his/her partner.

REFERENCES

Bielenski, H., Bosch, G., & Wagner, A. (2002a). *Working time preferences in sixteen European countries*. Luxembourg: Office for Official Publications of the European Communities.

Bielenski, H., Bosch, G., & Wagner, A. (2002b). *Wie die Europäer arbeiten wollen. Erwerbs- und Arbeitszeitwünsche in 16 Ländern*. Frankfurt/Main: Campus.

Bielenski, H., & Hartmann, J. (2000). *Combining family and work: The working arrangements of women and men*. Dublin: European Foundation for the Improvement of Living and Working Conditions (EN00/25).

Bonke, J., & Koch-Weser, E. (2003). The welfare state and time allocation in Sweden, Denmark, France, and Italy. In: J. Z. Giele & E. Holst (Eds), *Advances in Life-course Research: Changing Life Patterns in Western Industrial Societies* (Vol. 8, pp. 165–188). Oxford: Elsevier.

European Commission (2000). *Employment in Europe 2000*. Luxembourg: Office for Official Publications of the European Communities.

Fagan, C., with Warren, T., & McAllister, I. (2001). *Gender, employment and working time preferences in Europe*. Luxembourg: Office for Official Publications of the European Communities.

Hakim, C. (2003). Lifestyle preferences versus patriarchal values: Causal and non-causal attitudes. In: J. Z. Giele & E. Holst (Eds), *Advances in Life-course Research: Changing Life Patterns in Westerns Industrial Societies* (Vol. 8, pp. 69–92). Oxford: Elsevier.

PART III:
INSTITUTIONAL FACTORS IN AN
INTERNATIONAL PERSPECTIVE

8. LABOR-MARKET STRUCTURES AND WOMEN'S PAID WORK: OPPORTUNITIES AND CONSTRAINTS IN THE SWISS LABOR MARKET

Marlis Buchmann[*], Irene Kriesi and Stefan Sacchi

ABSTRACT

Previous research on women's changing work patterns has greatly neglected the ways in which the work context shapes their profiles of labor-force participation. By paying attention to job characteristics and working conditions, we discuss the opportunities and constraints associated with emerging new work patterns. Based on an empirical study conducted in Switzerland, we provide evidence that opportunities for continuous employment and labor-force re-entry after quitting paid work greatly vary with job characteristics and working conditions. Areas of further research are discussed and the implications are shown for policies at the firm level.

* The first listed author worked on this contribution while she was a Fellow at the Center for Advanced Study in the Behavioral Sciences, Stanford, CA. She is grateful for the financial support provided by The William and Flora Hewlett Grant #2000-5633.

Changing Life Patterns in Western Industrial Societies
Advances in Life Course Research, Volume 8, 165–188
© 2004 Published by Elsevier Ltd.
ISSN: 1040-2608/doi:10.1016/S1040-2608(03)08008-0

INTRODUCTION

Over recent decades, labor markets in most Western industrial countries, including Switzerland, have undergone swift and profound changes, thoroughly affecting men's and women's work patterns across the life course. The introduction of new working-time models, such as annualized hours or working-time accounts, and flexible employment contracts, such as temporary employment or work on call, are just a few illustrations of the changes likely to modify employment patterns. The rapid increase of part-time work and the broad dissemination of multiple forms of under-employment are other important developments. Given that people's social position greatly depends on their access to paid work, how do labor-market characteristics affect women's chances of *obtaining* market work and *continuously participating* in paid work? What *facilitates* and what *impedes continuous employment, withdrawal* from paid work, and *re-entry* into employment?

These issues are particularly salient for *women*. Despite the substantial increase in female labor-force participation over recent decades in most Western industrial societies, women's work patterns still vary considerably *within* and *across* countries as amply documented in other chapters of this book (Bianchi & Mattingly for the U.S., 2003; Plantenga, 2003; as well as Bielenski & Wagner for EU countries, 2003) and in the literature (Buchmann et al., 2002; Charles, 2002; van der Lippe & van Dijk, 2002). Whereas some women remain continuously employed over their entire work life, others interrupt their employment careers and resume them after shorter or longer periods. Some women, however, leave the labor market and never return. Furthermore, some women hold full-time jobs, whereas others work part-time, sometimes a few hours per week only.

Despite the profound changes in labor markets of Western industrial countries over recent decades, research on women's employment careers has focused primarily on their family situation and their human capital. Numerous studies have shown that women's employment careers are greatly affected by marriage and especially childbirth, often resulting in labor-force withdrawal (Drew et al., 1998; van der Lippe & van Dijk, 2001) or reduced working hours (Blossfeld, 1997). Likewise, research has piled up evidence that women's schooling influences their employment careers (Buchmann et al., 2002; Drobnic et al., 1999; Lauterbach, 1994). By giving preference to *supply-side* factors, previous research has greatly neglected *demand-side* factors, that is, workplace and job characteristics and their respective significance for women's integration into the labor market. This is a serious shortcoming. We therefore attempt to fill this gap in part by discussing how the *employment context* shapes women's profiles of labor-force participation. Our contribution asks how labor-market structures affect women's work patterns, women's *employment exit* and *re-entry*, in particular.

Although our contribution attempts to delineate the larger relevance of *work context* to women's profiles of labor-force participation, the immediate context of application is Switzerland. To put our arguments in context, we begin by describing how women's work patterns in Switzerland have changed over the last decades. We focus on changes in women's full-time and part-time employment and discuss their generalizability beyond the Swiss context.

RISE IN WOMEN'S PART-TIME EMPLOYMENT

Contributors to several other chapters in this book have shown that women's labor-force participation in many industrialized countries has increased considerably since the 1970s. The same holds for Switzerland: The female rate of employment has climbed from approximately 33% in 1971 to 45% in 2000.[1] Despite the sizable increase, women's labor-force integration is still far below men's employment rate, which was 62% in 2000. Compared to other Western industrial countries, the overall rate of female employment in Switzerland is still on the low side (Plantenga, 2003).[2] This is especially true for women's full-time employment. One of the most striking developments in Swiss women's labor market behavior since the 1970s is the steady decline of full-time employment and the rise of part-time work. Although the figures are not directly comparable, Plantenga also documents in her contribution to this book the impressive increase in part-time work for women in the EU countries. In the case of Switzerland, about 60% of employed women in 1970 declared that they worked full-time, only about 50% did so in 1990. These figures are based on Swiss Census data and represent women's self-declaration (Federal Office of Statistics, 1970, 1990). Unfortunately, the comparable data of the 2000 Swiss Census have not yet been released. For recent years, we have to resort to the Swiss Labor-Force Survey (SAKE), which dates back only to 1991.[3] Moreover, this survey measures female full-time and part-time employment as a percentage of normal weekly working hours within a particular industry.[4] Activity rates above 89% are defined as full-time work, those between 50% and 89% as substantial part-time work, and below 50% as marginal part-time work.

Including annual figures for the decades of the 1990s, Fig. 1 shows that female full-time work has further declined from 51% in 1991 to about 45% in the year 2001. By contrast, substantial part-time work has increased to about 28% (from about 22% in 1991), whereas marginal part-time work lingers around 28%.

Overall, these figures confirm that, at the outset of the 21st century, paid work has become almost an integral part of women's lives in Switzerland. But gainful employment sustaining a financially independent life does not yet characterize the great majority of women's work careers. The rise of female part-time work over

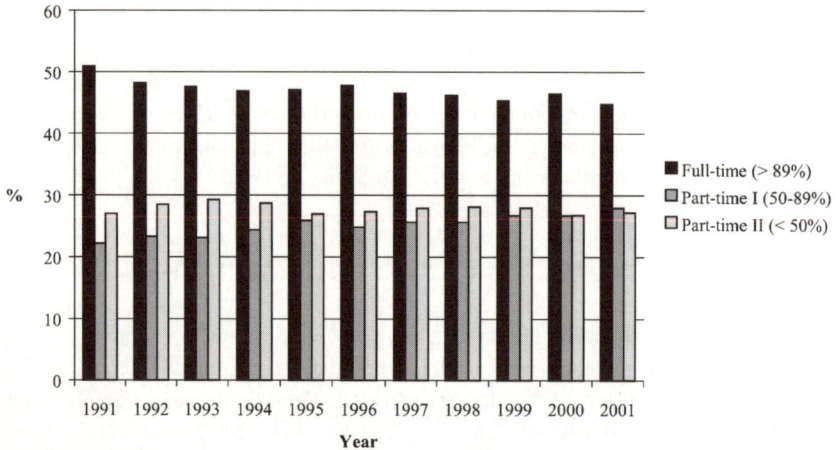

Fig. 1. Female Full-Time and Part-Time Employment in Switzerland, 1991–2001.
Source: Swiss Labor-Force Survey (SAKE), 1991–2001. Conducted annually by the Swiss
Federal Office of Statistics. Unpublished data, own computations.

the last decades of the 20th century bears great responsibility for women's lower
occupational positions, lower wages, and lower chances for upward mobility
(Blossfeld & Hakim, 1997; Fagan & Rubery, 1996; Rosenfeld & Birkelund,
1995).[5] Women who do not participate at all in the labor market are excluded from
one of the most relevant social realms, greatly affecting their opportunities for
engaging in diversified social interactions. Against this background, the answers
to the questions of what facilitates and, vice versa, impedes women's labor-force
attachment are of great relevance with regard to gender-egalitarian opportunities
both in the labor market and in society at large.

Before providing some answers to these questions, we present several descriptive findings related to changes in female labor-force participation *by age* since the
1970s in Switzerland.[6] It is well known that, whereas men's engagement in (full-
time) gainful employment does not alter much with age, women's labor-force participation is greatly affected by life course events and, hence, by age. It is also well
known that the increase in female employment over the last decades in many industrial nations is mostly due to women who do not withdraw from the labor market
when they become wives and especially mothers or who, if they do withdraw, return
more often and more rapidly to paid jobs (Charles et al., 2001; Drew et al., 1998;
Jenson et al., 1988). This general picture also holds for Switzerland (see Fig. 2).

These aggregate-level statistics show that, in 1970, 1980, and 1990, roughly
80% of 20-year-old women in Switzerland were employed. In 1970, after the age

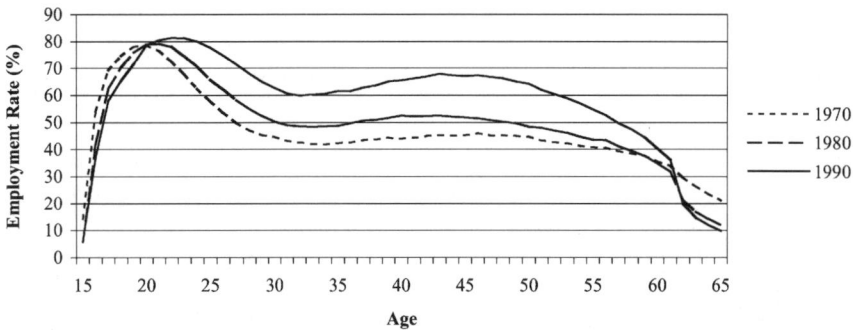

Fig. 2. Women's Employment Rate by Age in Switzerland, 1970, 1980, 1990. *Source:* Swiss Census Data, 1970, 1980, 1990. Unpublished data, own computations.

of 20, the employment rate started to decline; it was lowest (approximately 40%) at the age of 35 and grew only modestly for women in the age bracket of 35–50. The age-related employment rate for 1980 documents slightly higher levels of labor-force participation for women of *all ages*, suggesting women's greater labor-market attachment compared to 1970. By contrast, in 1990, the employment rate was substantially higher for all ages (except for women above age 62). In that year, women's age-related employment behavior resulted in a characteristic two-peak curve with increasing employment rates to the age of 24, declining rates in the age bracket between 25 and 35, and fairly steeply rising rates up to the age of 45. This aggregate-level pattern suggests that a sizable proportion of women withdraw from the labor force during the family-formation years and rejoin the labor force after the time-demanding years of raising children. Unfortunately, for the year 2001, we can rely on employment rates only for *age groups* (i.e. 15–24, 25–39, 40–54, and 55–64-year-old women). The classification by age *group* renders the two-peak curve invisible. Nevertheless, a recent study based on the Swiss Labor-Force Survey 1991–1999 and conducted by the Federal Office of Statistics reveals that, in the 1990s, women in Switzerland became less likely to exit employment when they gave birth to a child (see SAKE-News, 2000). During the 1990s and on average, 60% of the women who had their first baby continued to be employed, compared to approximately 25% in 1970 and 1980.[7] Among women who worked *full-time* before having a baby, one third did not change their employment status, another third changed to part-time work, and the last third withdrew from the labor force. Among those who worked *part-time* before having their first child, 50% continued to work part-time and the other 50% quit their jobs. Evidence for other industrial nations has documented the increasing labor-force attachment of wives and mothers. The spread of part-time work in

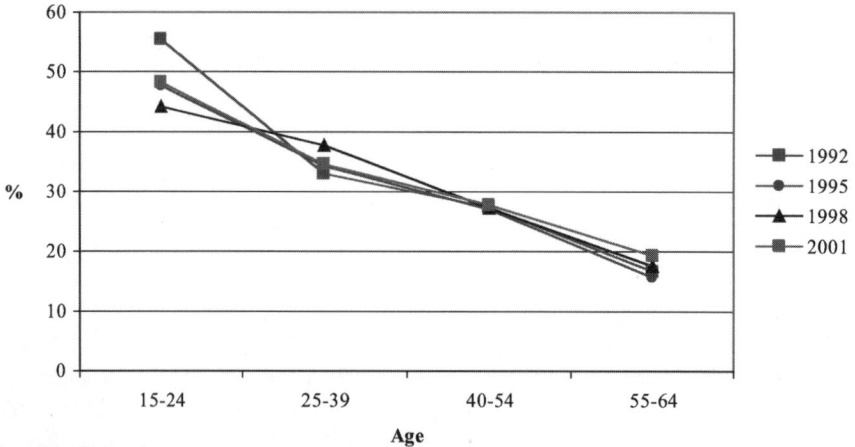

Fig. 3. Women's Full-Time Employment Rate by Age Group in Switzerland, 1992, 1995, 1998, 2001. *Source:* Swiss Labor-Force Survey (SAKE), 1992, 1995, 1998, 2001. Unpublished data, own computations.

Switzerland over the last years suggests that women's market behavior in this country tends to follow the trend observed for other Western industrial countries.

With regard to *full-time employment* broken down by age groups for the years 1992, 1995, 1998, and 2002, the youngest age group (i.e. 15–24-year-old women) shows the highest rate of full-time jobs (Fig. 3).[8] After the age of 24, the rate drops dramatically and never resumes higher levels.[9]

According to these descriptive statistics, the overall decline in full-time employment in the decade of the 1990s is mostly attributable to the decreasing engagement in full-time jobs among women of the youngest age group. The expansion of the educational system is responsible for this trend, postponing labor-force entry of an ever-increasing proportion of a given birth cohort. The *stable* rate of full-time employment for the other age groups implies that the overall increase in female employment observed in the 1990s is due to the spread of part-time work. In other words, many previously non-employed women would engage in part-time work in the decade of the 1990s. Overall, these findings attest to the still rather low labor-force attachment of women in Switzerland during the years when they are most likely burdened by family obligations. These are also the years when crucial changes take place in their work careers.

These age-related findings raise once more the question of what pushes women, wives and mothers especially, out of the labor force and, vice versa, what facilitates the compatibility of family and work. Informed answers to this question are of utmost importance for understanding the changing work and life patterns in Western industrialized societies. The great impact of women's family situation and their human capital on their labor-market behavior is well documented. Amazingly little attention has been paid, however, to the *opportunities* the labor market offers for women's continuous employment and the *constraints* it imposes on their market behavior. To date, little is yet known about how the demand side of the labor market (women's working conditions and job opportunities) shapes women's work trajectories and, ultimately, their life patterns. In order to better understand the significance of demand-side characteristics on women's labor-market careers, we present some theoretical considerations below.

IMPORTANCE OF DEMAND-SIDE FACTORS

The relative neglect of labor-market opportunities for women's labor-market careers is not only attributable to the dominance of individual-centered theorizing (as exemplified by neoclassical and functionalist paradigms) (see Charles et al., 2001). It is also related to the difficulties of measuring contextual factors.[10] We attempt to overcome some of the existing limitations in conceptualizing labor-market-related opportunities for women's employment exit and re-entry in two ways. First, we theoretically explore the ways in which jobs assigned to particular *labor-market segments* have an impact on women's labor-force attachment. Second, we probe the significance of *organizational characteristics* of jobs for women's work patterns.[11]

Labor-Market Segmentation Theory

The starting point of theories of labor-market segmentation is that firms value their employees according to the amount of not easily substitutable skills, such as scarce abilities, firm-specific skills, and productivity. Firms attempt to secure employees who cannot easily be replaced by offering them higher salaries, favorable upward mobility chances, and better working conditions. The property that emerges from the recruitment and reward policies pursued by individual firms is the partition of the labor market into several segments with differing work conditions and strong mobility barriers that prevent workers from moving freely between segments. Income inequalities and unequal upward mobility chances are thus regarded as the aggregate outcome of individual firms' recruitment and reward policies.

In this context, how do the properties associated with different labor-market segments shape women's market behavior, especially with regard to labor-force withdrawal and re-entry? We assume that two mechanisms are at work. *First*, costs of labor-force withdrawals vary across labor-market segments. When firms need to fill vacancies, both the recruitment of (comparable) replacements and the new employees' adjustment to the new jobs generate costs. *Second*, the quality of employment differs across labor-market segments, especially with regard to work-family compatibility, but also with regard to employment rewards (e.g. wages, prestige, mobility chances). To specify these general assumptions, we choose Sengenberger's theory of the tripartite labor market (Sengenberger, 1987; for Switzerland, see Levy et al., 1997). Among the various strands of segmentation theory it captures best the particularities of the Swiss labor market, referring to the differentiated and vocationally oriented educational system and its systematic and tight links to the labor market.[12] These characteristics result in a strong segmentation of the labor market along skill lines. Below, we briefly outline the basic tenets of Sengenberger's approach.

The *tripartite* labor market is subdivided into three main segments: the internal labor market, the occupation-specific labor market, and the peripheral labor market for unskilled labor.

- *Internal labor markets* exist in large companies only. Recruited for entry to the lower levels of the organizational hierarchy, skilled workers climb up institutionalized career ladders, acquiring firm-specific knowledge. Hence, the ties between workers and firms become strong as firms provide good career advancement chances and workers acquire firm-specific skills, which are not easily transferable to other companies. Under these conditions, the costs of labor-force withdrawal are high and family-work compatibility low. Employers' recruitment and reward policies for jobs in this labor-market segment focus on minimizing the replacement costs of employees. Employers thus expect *continuous* and *full-time* employment.[13] Hence employment interruption (with the possible prospect of resuming the job) and working-hour reduction are not likely options for women holding jobs in this labor-market segment. With these prospects, the *propensity to exit* the internal labor-market segment tends to be *high*, resulting in permanent exclusion from this attractive labor-market segment and inflicting substantial costs related to income loss, de-skilling, and the loss of an attractive occupational position (Blossfeld, 1991). Labor-force *re-entry* of women previously employed in this segment may be severely restricted because of the great likelihood of experiencing downward mobility, either from relegation to an entry-level position in the internal labor market or from referral to an occupation-specific segment of the labor market (Borkowsky & Streckeisen, 1982). As both options are unappealing, women may opt not to return to the labor market.

- Access to the *occupation-specific labor market* is predicated on the appropriate educational certificate. This labor-market segment is thus subdivided into numerous sub-segments. For example, the sub-segment for kindergarten teachers, car mechanics, or for carpenters, etc. *Within* particular occupation-specific sub-segments, skills can be easily transferred between firms. Mobility *between* the sub-segments is limited, however, as it requires the acquisition of an additional occupation-specific credential. The occupation-specific labor market also tends to discriminate against women, as it is closely linked to gender segregation of the occupational structure.[14] Under these circumstances, the rates of both *employment exits* and *re-entry* depend on the occupation-inherent work-family compatibility. Occupations with flexible work arrangements and ample part-time opportunities are likely to lower the rate of women's employment exits and for the same reason increase the rate of women's employment re-entry.
- The *peripheral labor market* has to do with unskilled tasks to be performed by workers with no specific educational credentials. These include, for example, charwomen or manufacturing laborers). The exchange of workers does not result in substantial replacement costs. Hence working conditions are not very attractive and salaries are generally low. Women are often relegated to this segment because of statistical discrimination. Out of economic necessity, they are often forced to stay in these jobs. Both the absence of entry barriers and the provision of a big pool of unskilled (part-time) work with flexible working arrangements lower women's work exits and, if they do occur, help increase employment re-entries.

Additional Labor-Market Segmentation Arguments

If we take into account that employed women are strongly over-represented in the *service* and the *public* sectors of the economy,[15] do jobs assigned to these two sectors provide different opportunities or impose different constraints with respect to women's labor-force attachment compared to those in the *industrial* and the *private* sectors? When attempting to answer this question from the perspective of labor-market segmentation, we should be able to identify segment-specific recruitment and reward policies pursued by employers as well as mobility barriers between the private and public sectors, and between the *industrial* and *service* sectors of the economy.

Many studies have shown that, compared to the private sector, *public sector* employment is secure and, hence, occupational careers are stable (e.g. Becker, 1993 for Germany). Public service careers follow institutionalized rules pertaining to seniority, internal recruitment, and well-defined (lifelong) career ladders. In this respect, they resemble occupational careers located in the internal labor market of private firms. In stark contrast to the private sector, however, institutionalized rules regarding employment conditions and career advancement opportunities are not limited to individual establishments. Rather, they apply to all branches of a given public service institution. Hence it makes sense to conceive of the public sector as a separate segment of the labor market embracing all public service branches. Besides greater employment stability, the public sector distinguishes itself from the private sector by ample part-time opportunities as well as better work-family compatibility. Jobs assigned to the public sector should thus help keep women in the labor force and offer better opportunities for re-entry in case of labor-force withdrawal.

There are two major differences between the *industrial* and *service* sectors when one analyzes opportunities and constraints in women's labor-force attachment. *First*, employment opportunities in general, and for women in particular, have rapidly increased in the service sector over the last decades.[16] *Second*, flextime arrangement and part-time work are much more prevalent in the service sector, attributable in part to organizational changes, in part to the shortage of skilled labor. This development is mostly responsible for the increase in women's labor-force participation and hence women's changing life patterns. Flextime work is particularly widespread in office jobs where the organization of work depends to a lesser degree on technological constraints (Hoepflinger et al., 1991). This means that – even *within* given occupations – flextime work is more widespread in the service sector than in industry (and agriculture). Greater job opportunities coupled with ample flextime-work offers help to *lower* women's employment interruptions and to *increase* work re-entry in case of labor-force withdrawal.

Organization Theory

We now turn to the *organizational context* of employment and explore how organizational characteristics of firms affect women's labor-force attachment over the life course. Baron and Bielby (1980) have forcefully argued that firm-level processes are responsible for the unequal distribution of employment opportunities. According to these authors, job opportunities, income, and mobility chances depend on the firm-specific division of labor and the concomitant recruitment and reward policies. Arguments provided by organization theory thus offer an additional perspective on how demand-side factors may affect women's profiles of labor-force attachment. We focus our discussion on two organizational characteristics: *firm size* and *position in the organizational hierarchy* (Bruederl et al., 1993; Carroll et al., 1990; Stewman & Konda, 1983).

The significance of *firm size* for women's work patterns may be conceived in two different ways. On the one hand, *job-turnover rate* varies by firm size. Workers employed in small firms run a greater risk of losing their jobs because they are exposed to strong structural fluctuations. This is so because the survival rate of jobs is rather low, although the number of jobs created by small firms is large.[17] On the other hand, big firms show a higher level of *hierarchical differentiation*, they offer more *higher-level vacancies* and *institutionalized career ladders*, and provide more *opportunities for skill up-dating*. These characteristics are relevant for upward mobility chances and higher income.[18] Accordingly, incentives for continuous employment increase as the size of the organization grows. Both arguments suggest that employment in big firms helps to keep women in the labor market.[19]

The propensity of working women to withdraw from the labor force is also affected by their *position in the organizational hierarchy*. There are two sides to the coin, however. One side implies that the costs of employment exits increase with rank in the organizational hierarchy. The higher the position, the less likely women are to give up their jobs. Should they nevertheless exit the labor force, a great proportion of these women are likely to re-enter employment rapidly. The other side implies that jobs in the higher echelons of the organizational ladder typically show a "male profile." Gendered organizations (see Acker, 1991; Heintz & Nadai, 1998; Mueller, 1993) implicitly presuppose a traditional division of labor between the sexes, enabling men to concentrate fully on their jobs while women care for the family. Hence higher positions offer few opportunities for flextime and part-time work or job sharing, which should increase the exit rate from these jobs. And when women formerly employed in high status jobs re-enter the labor force, they must fear downward mobility.

Still, these assumptions need to be qualified in several respects. First, employees in high status jobs enjoy considerable autonomy regarding working hours. This helps women to juggle their work and family obligations. Second, the high salaries that come along with jobs in the higher echelons of the organizational hierarchy allow women to hire domestic help and pay for their small children's day care. Despite the various counteracting factors involved, such attributes of high status jobs as high salaries coupled with the financial ability to hire domestic help, autonomous working hours, and interesting work should outweigh long working hours and male job profiles and help to keep women in the labor force. By and large, work exits should go down as job status increases. Because employment re-entry may result in downward mobility for women formerly working in high status jobs, work re-entry should occur less often and be *slower* the higher the position of the former job was.

RESEARCH ON SWISS WOMEN'S WORK
EXITS AND RE-ENTRIES

A recent study, conducted in Switzerland, is used to show the relevance of demand-side characteristics on women's profile of labor-force participation. In order to make the empirical part of our contribution accessible to all readers, we keep the description of data and methods to a minimum. For detailed information, we refer the readers to the book publication of this study (Buchmann et al., 2002).

The *data* are taken from a mailed retrospective life history survey carried out in 1989 (Buchmann & Sacchi, 1997). It is representative for Swiss citizens in the German-speaking part of Switzerland, born 1949–1951 and 1959–1961.[20] We define women's employment exit as a labor-force withdrawal lasting a full year or more and limit our analysis to *first* employment exit and, consequently, to *first* employment re-entry.[21] To estimate the impact of the work context on the occurrence of these two events, we employ *event history analysis* using a Cox regression model (Allison, 1984). We describe the measurement of the work-context characteristics as we present the respective findings.[22] We ran separate analyses for work exit and re-entry to test whether the opportunities for women's continuous employment differ by such contextual factors as *occupation, industry, type of firm, firm size*, and *organizational position*.

THE IMPACT OF THE WORK CONTEXT ON WOMEN'S
PROFILE OF LABOR-FORCE ATTACHMENT

The results in Table 1 are easy to read. For *employment exit*, the table presents a figure and a sign. The figure. is a *percentage number*, indicating how much the risks of exiting the labor force increase or, in case of a *negative* sign, decrease for women holding jobs with the attribute in question. The sign is a *star* and indicates whether the increasing or decreasing risks of labor-force exits associated with the job attribute in question reach the level of statistical significance.[23] For *employment* re-entry, the same parameters are presented. Hence the *percentage number* indicates how much the chances of re-entering the labor market increase or, in the case of a *negative* sign, decrease for women holding jobs with the attribute in question *before* their first labor-force exit. One additional comment is necessary for an easy understanding of Table 1. For job characteristics with more than two categories (*occupations, employment level, and firm size*), the *reference category* displayed in Table 1 represents the baseline against which the increasing

Table 1. Size and Direction of Regression Coefficients for Average Propensity for Employment Exit and Re-Entry in Switzerland.

	Exit % Sig.	Re-Entry % Sig.
Labor market context		
Occupation[b] (Reference: office clerks)		
Teachers – secondary level upwards	183[*]	−63[d]
Professions	170[*]	−41
Finance associate professionals	318[***]	−70[d]
Customer service clerks	17	60
Teachers – Kindergarten/element school	133[*]	−52[d]
Modern health and nursing AP's	14	−36
Cosmetic body care	−39	−32
Personal health and child care	119[**]	−52[d]
Physical/engineering science AP's	11	−64[*]
Restaurant service workers	−40[d]	−16
Sales people	−4	−46[*]
Trade/artisans	23	28
Skilled agricultural workers	−21	41
Machine operators	44	25
Unskilled laborers	−50[d]	34
Other occupations	0	−53[d]
Part-time opportunities[a,b]	−15[*]	2
Sector: service sector[b,c]	8	21
Type of firm: public service[c,b]	44[**]	17
Position: job authority[b]	−58[d]	350[**]
Occupational status[b]	−8[**]	8[*]
Employment level[b] (Reference: full-time)[d]		
Part-time	−30[*]	9
Missing values	−4	−15
Firm size[b] (Reference: 1–9 employees)[d]		
10–49 employees	17	1
50–99 employees	−11	73[*]
≥100 employees	−3	−13
Cohort		
Birth cohort: 1959–1961[c]	−64[***]	75[**]

Source: Swiss Life History Survey (Buchmann & Sacchi, 1997); full Table 1 published in (Buchmann et al., 2002).

[a] In occupations.
[b] Time dependent.
[c] Dichotomous variable.
[d] $p = 0.10$.
[*] $p = 0.05$.
[**] $p = 0.01$.
[***] $p = 0.001$.

or decreasing risks of labor-force exit or re-entry associated with a given job attribute (e.g. working in the professions) is assessed.

We begin our discussion with the *four* job characteristics that we associate with *labor-market segmentation*. These are *occupational groups, part-time opportunities offered by occupations*, job allocation in the *service sector* vs. the *industrial and agricultural sectors*, and in the *public sector* vs. the *private sector*. The *occupation* to which a job belongs is an indicator of *occupation-specific* labor-market segments. We distinguish 17 occupational groups and choose *office clerks* as reference category. In case of employment exit, the opportunities for continuous employment vary considerably between occupational groups as the two stars in the first row of this covariate indicate.[24] Compared to the reference group of office clerks, most occupation-specific labor-market segments provide fewer opportunities for attaching women to paid work. This can be gathered from the large number of *positive* signs shown for various occupational groups in the exit model (i.e. *greater* propensity to exit) and the large number of *negative* signs in the re-entry model (i.e. *lower* propensity to re-enter). The better opportunities provided by jobs as office clerks can be traced back to the relatively favorable conditions for combining work and family due to the large number of job offers and the broad distribution of flextime work. We will illustrate the varying opportunities for women's continuous employment by selecting two particular sub-segments of the occupation-specific labor market. To discuss all 16 occupational groups individually would be far beyond the scope of this chapter. We choose *physical/engineering science associate professionals* (APs) and *personal health care*.

• The propensity to exit the labor market does not differ between *physical/engineering science associate professionals* (e.g. technical draftswoman, laboratory assistant) and office clerks: To work in the labor-market segment of *physical/engineering science AP's* increases the risk of exiting employment by 11% only (relative to clerical work). By contrast, former work as a *physical/engineering science AP* (i.e. before giving up paid work) lowers the chances of employment re-entry by 64%. Extended absence from these rapidly changing technical jobs is likely to result in considerable de-skilling (Weck-Hannemann, 1993; Weck-Hannemann & Frey, 1989). The return to the labor market is therefore much more difficult. Women are confronted with the options of continuous skill up-grading or the prospect of less demanding jobs with lower salaries when they return to paid work. Given these options, women may decide not to re-enter the labor market.
• Relative to clerical work, *personal health care* jobs (e.g. child-care workers, nursing aides) show high risks for employment exit and low chances for

employment re-entry: The risks of quitting paid work increase by 119% and the chances of re-entering the labor market decrease by 52%. The high level of psychological stress encountered in these relatively low-skilled jobs may account for the high exit rate. Moreover, irregular working hours make family-work compatibility difficult, thus increasing the propensity to withdraw from the labor market. The norms of femininity ingrained in the occupational image may define the self-image of the job incumbents, resulting in strong concentration on the family role. For these reasons, women formerly employed in personal health care jobs may not return to the labor market despite lower salaries and the absence of skill depreciation.

Part-time work opportunities define another dimension of occupation-specific opportunity structures. Occupation-specific part-time opportunities are measured as the proportion of women within a given occupation holding jobs characterized by employment levels of less than 90%.[25] Women remain more often continuously employed in occupational fields that provide a sizable share of part-time jobs. These occupational fields, especially, enhance the opportunities to switch to part-time work when women expect children. Further analyses (not presented here) corroborate these findings by showing that the chances of engaging in part-time work (i.e. the independent variable) greatly depend on the labor-market context. This amounts to saying that the opportunities provided by the labor market play an even greater role for the employment chances of women who, for family reasons, cannot engage in full-time work. Our result also indicates that the rising number of part-time jobs over the last 30 years is closely linked to changing female employment patterns. As for employment re-entry, not surprisingly, the part-time work opportunities offered by the occupations in which women worked before they withdrew from the labor market are irrelevant.

Does job allocation to the *industrial or service sectors* influence the risks of employment exit or the chances of re-entering paid labor? The answer is no. Women working in service sector jobs are as likely to withdraw from the labor force as their counterparts holding either industrial or agricultural jobs. The same holds for re-entering the labor force after an extended period of non-employment. How about women employed in *public sector* jobs? They are even more likely to withdraw from the labor force than their colleagues in the *private sector*: The exit risks of public sector employees increase by 44%. This finding may be attributable to civil servants' anticipation of fewer difficulties when re-entering employment. The greater efforts made by the public sector to establish gender-egalitarian work opportunities may even encourage women to exit employment temporarily because they can more firmly count on equivalent jobs when they resume paid work. Because these women don't have to fear large skill depreciation and income losses often associated with extended periods out of paid labor, it might be easier for them to interrupt employment than for their counterparts in the private sector. If this argument holds, the re-entry rate observed for women previously employed in the public sector should be higher than the rate for women who worked in the private sector. The difference shown in Table 1 is not statistically significant, however.

In Table 1, the *organizational context* of employment is represented by *four* job characteristics. These are jobs with *formal authority, occupational status, employment level (full-time or part-time)*, and *firm-size*. Women working in jobs vested with *authority* or in *high-status* jobs are much less likely to withdraw from the labor force than their less fortunate counterparts holding jobs without formal authority or low-status jobs.[26] If they nonetheless interrupt their work careers, they re-enter employment much more often than women previously holding low-status jobs or jobs without formal authority. For example, former employment in jobs with *authority* increases women's chances to return to paid work by 350%. We suspect that their strong work commitment brings them back to the labor force despite the danger of downward mobility coupled with income losses.[27] These findings support our arguments that higher positions in the organizational hierarchy, be it formal authority or be it high occupational status, enhance women's labor-force participation by offering not only greater prestige and responsibility but also interesting work, as well as considerable flexibility and autonomy as regards working hours. Compared to these incentives, the constraints implied by the 'male profile' of these jobs apparently carry less weight in affecting women's continuous employment. Perhaps these positions are reserved exclusively for women who are not burdened with family obligations, or these women have learned to reduce their household obligations. These findings provide evidence that women's rising level of education and employers' increasing willingness to hire women for high-status jobs are conducive to women's stronger labor-force integration, thus promoting changing life patterns.

Employment level refers to women's actual *engagement* in part-time work and is distinct from the part-time job opportunities characteristic of the respondent's *occupation* discussed above. Women working in part-time jobs are less likely to withdraw from the labor force than women holding full-time jobs. Part-time work gives more leeway for combining work and family obligations. Our findings thus show that both the part-time opportunities provided by the *occupation* and the *individual engagement* in part-time work affect the risks of exiting the labor market. There is no relationship, however, between employment level and re-entry into paid work. This finding is in line with those reported by Lauterbach (1994) as well as Klein and Braun (1995). According to Hakim's (1997) expectations of low work commitment associated with part-time work, the rate of employment exit among women working part-time should be higher and, vice versa, the rate of employment re-entry of women previously employed in part-time work should be lower. Apparently this is not the case (for similar findings, see Kurz, 1998).

Does the *size of the firm* in which women are employed have anything to do with their labor-force attachment? According to our findings, the answer is no. For women who exited the labor force, however, the size of the firm in which they worked last facilitates employment re-entry. The chances of returning to paid work increase by 73% for those previously employed in medium-sized firms (50–99 employees), relative to their counterparts who held jobs in small firms of less than 10 employees (reference group). We argue that larger firms provide more favorable conditions for skill updating. As a result, women previously employed in such firms may be attractive to future employers, thus encouraging their employment re-entry. In addition, the recruitment policies of medium-sized firms are likely to be less institutionalized and to depend more on personal relationships than those of large firms. This difference may ease the re-employment of former employees whose cost of adjustment to their work place tends to be low. To complicate matters, however, this does not hold for firms with more than 100 employees. The chances of returning to paid work for women previously employed in large firms (compared to the average size of Swiss enterprises) is about the same as those observed for women coming from small firms (1–9 employees). This speaks for an interpretation based on segmentation arguments. In large firms, entry barriers may keep women away from returning to the internal labor markets. After an extended period out of the labor force, these women may fear they will be relegated to the entry ports of internal labor markets or experience downward mobility to the occupation-specific segment of the labor market. As both options are unappealing, women who formerly held jobs in large firms with internal labor markets may decide to stay away from paid work.

Before we draw any conclusions about the larger relevance of *work context* to women's profiles of labor-force participation, we would like to comment on the stronger labor-force attachment among women of the younger cohort (1959–1961) shown in the last row of Table 1. Compared to their counterparts born between 1949–1951, women of the younger cohort are less likely to exit employment – the risks are reduced by 64% – and if they do, they re-enter paid work more often – the chances increase by 75%. These findings indicate an *intergenerational change* in employment patterns and a substantial increase in women's labor-force integration. They provide crucial evidence for changing *work patterns* and, ultimately, changing life patterns in this country. Women have undoubtedly gained ground with regard to continuous labor-force partici-pation. The aggregate-level statistics presented at the beginning of this chapter remind us, however, that women's increasing integration into the labor force is accompanied by declining rates of full-time employment. The rise in female part-time employment opportunities has eased women's inroads into continuous paid work – in many instances at the price of holding jobs that offer lower wages, fewer training opportunities, and lower upward mobility chances than full-time jobs.

CONCLUSIONS: REFRAMING KEY RESEARCH AND POLICY QUESTIONS ON WORK PATTERNS

Both the aggregate-level observations on Swiss women's labor-force participation and the findings on their work attachment based on our life-course data confirm the increasing salience of paid work for female life patterns over recent decades. However, higher rates of female employment and stronger work attachment over the life course go hand in hand with declining rates of full-time work. Although ample part-time work opportunities facilitate women's labor-force attachment, especially during the time when they are most burdened by family responsibilities, they also bear the danger of relegating women to the margins of the labor market as many part-time jobs offer lower prestige, lower salaries, fewer training opportunities, and lower chances for upward mobility than full-time jobs. These recent developments document the importance of paying close attention to the *characteristics of jobs* women hold and the *working conditions* they are exposed to in order to better understand the opportunities and constraints associated with the emerging new work and life patterns. From the vantage point of gender-egalitarian opportunities in the labor market, solid knowledge about job characteristics and working conditions is of the utmost importance. It not only helps to keep women in the labor market or avoid being pushed out; it also helps them keep jobs with good salaries, training opportunities, and chances for upward mobility. By paying attention to the *work and employment context*, we were able to detect inequalities in employment opportunities that are beyond the control of individual women. Women's changing work and life pattern are strongly influenced by *employers' recruitment and reward policies*. Whether women have access to attractive jobs or are relegated to less attractive ones depends on how employers and personnel recruitment managers judge women and their long-term work commitment. Deep-rooted gender-stereotypical views on women's lack of work commitment are more and more out of sync with the reality of women's stronger work attachment over the life course. Interestingly enough, our findings document that women employed in *high-status* jobs and those vested with *formal authority* indeed are less likely to interrupt their work careers. Future research should pay more attention to the criteria employers and personnel recruitment managers apply when hiring new workers, female employees especially.

Women's work patterns over the life course are also shaped by *occupation-specific constraints*. Our findings provide convincing evidence that some occupations offer better opportunities for continuous employment than others. Likewise, the propensity to exit and re-enter the labor market varies considerably by occupation-specific labor markets. To date, however, the salient characteristics of occupations that help to keep women in employment or, vice versa, are responsible for pushing them out, are not well understood. For example: What exactly are the characteristics of *personal health care* jobs or *elementary-school teaching* jobs that increase the risks of quitting paid work and lower the chances of returning to the labor market? Future research should engage in-depth studies of occupations to come up with informed answers to these salient questions. *Organization-specific characteristics*, such as firm size, provide further evidence of the importance of the work context for women's work patterns. Apparently, smaller and larger firms offer quite different opportunities for continuous employment. Again, much more research is needed to disentangle the underlying causes that produce these outcomes.

All in all, our findings bear implications for policies at the *firm level* that would enhance gender-egalitarian opportunities at the work place. Companies should devote much more attention to designing working conditions, especially at the higher echelons of the organizational hierarchy, that will be compatible with family responsibilities. This concern implies, among other things, the creation of part-time jobs and job-sharing opportunities at the higher levels of the organizational hierarchy. Our recommendation necessitates profound changes in employers' attitudes regarding the evaluation of paid and unpaid work. As long as women's family responsibilities and related employment interruptions are interpreted solely as indications of deskilling and lack of work commitment, women's labor-market opportunities will be severely hampered. Likewise, the under-appreciation of typically female tasks, such as nursing, caring, tending, and cleaning, result in low wages and low opportunities for upward mobility, which, in turn, affects women's labor-force attachment.

NOTES

1. The labor-force participation rate reported here is defined as the number of employed women (plus the number of registered unemployed women) relative to the total population of working age (15–65 years of age). Employment is defined by a minimum of six weekly working hours.

2. For further comparative data on various sets of countries, see Charles (2002), Schulze Buschoff (1999) and van der Lippe and van Dijk (2001, 2002).

3. The Swiss Labor Force Survey is based on a random sample of permanent residents in Switzerland of age 15 and above. The sample includes 18,000 cases.

4. The reference points are the regular weekly working hours within given firms and industries, respectively. In the labor-force survey, respondents are first asked to answer whether they work full-time or part-time. Next, they are asked to indicate the percentage of regular weekly working hours their jobs represent.

5. Compared to women, men's rate of part-time work is very low and hasn't changed much in most Western industrial countries (Plantenga, 2003).

6. For the same reasons as mentioned above, we rely on Swiss Census data for the time period from 1970 to 1990 and on the Swiss Labor-Force Survey for the decade of the 1990s.

7. The figures referring to 1970 and 1980 are based on Swiss Census data.

8. These rates are based on the total population of the respective age groups.

9. It is noteworthy that the low full-time employment rate for the age group of the 15–24-year-old women in the year 1998 goes along with a rather high unemployment rate in the same year.

10. For a brief discussion of measurement problems, see Buchmann et al. (2002). The few studies that account for labor-market opportunities and constraints in assessing women's labor-market behavior have limited themselves to such relatively easy-to-measure attributes as work-time regulations, working conditions, private or public sector employment (see Born, 1991; Krueger & Born, 1991; Kurz, 1998; Lauterbach, 1994). There are a few exceptions, however. Glass and Riley (1998), for example, include various job characteristics into their empirical analysis. Studies conducted by Desai and Waite (1991), Rexroat (1992) and Glass and Riley (1998) assess the effects of occupational sex-typing on women's labor- force attachment.

11. Theories on labor-market segmentation and those referring to organizations have not been developed primarily to account for women's labor-force attachment. Their arguments may provide, however, important insights into the relationship between labor-market opportunity structures and women's employment behavior.

12. For international variability in school-to-work transitions, see Shavit and Mueller (1998); for the Swiss educational context, see Buchmann and Sacchi (1998).

13. This is the major source of gender inequality in access to jobs in the internal labor market. Women are likely to be confronted with statistical discrimination as employers stereotype women as having low aspirations and exhibiting low labor-force attachment because of anticipated family responsibilities (Blossfeld & Mayer, 1988; Bornschier, 1982).

14. Women are almost completely cut off from a substantial number of industrial and crafts-related sub-segments of the occupation-specific labor market because apprenticeships are strongly dominated by men (e.g. mechanics). Vice versa, men are excluded from some female-dominated sub-segments of the occupation-specific labor market (e.g. nursing).

15. In 2000, 83.1% of employed women held jobs in the service sector compared to 58.9% of men (Swiss Census 2000: Federal Office of Statistics). The figures for 1998 in the public sector are 19.6% of employed women compared to 15.5% of men (Federal Office of Statistics: Swiss Establishment Census 1998).

16. The growth of the service sector greatly spurred women's employment opportunities. The supply of typically female jobs increased rapidly in education, administration, sales, and services, in the health sector and in social work (see Hoepflinger et al., 1991).

17. For figures, see, for example, OECD (1994).

18. Empirical evidence supports the expected link between firm size and opportunity costs in so far as income, upward mobility chances, and employment stability increase with organizational size (see Preisendoerfer, 1987; for Switzerland, see Bundesamt füer Statistik, 1996; Lewin, 1982).

19. It is still disputed, however, whether the expected link is to be attributed to *organizational processes*. Sengenberger's *segmentation theory* offers an alternative rationale for the same link. *Internal labor markets*, typical of big firms, create strong ties between workers and the organization because of the acquisition of firm-specific skills and the offering of good career advancement prospects. Although the opportunity costs of exiting the labor market increase, segmentation theory suggests that women employed in internal labor markets of big firms are *more* likely to exit the labor force.

20. The survey includes detailed biographical information on education, occupation, and family, providing exact dates of family and labor-force transitions. Consideration of employment histories is limited to jobs held after the completion of formal education. Moreover, respondents were directed to report only jobs that lasted at least four months.

21. Over the observation period (i.e. first labor-force entry after completion of formal education to the time of the survey), 40% of the women in our sample were continuously employed ($N = 309$) and 60% left the labor market at least once ($N = 481$).

22. Our full analysis also takes into account individual-level characteristics referring to the *family situation, human capital (i.e. schooling and labor-force experience)*, and *financial circumstances*. The list is comprehensive in that it considers most supply-side factors that the literature suggests as relevant for women's market behavior.

23. For the methodologically interested reader, the percentage numbers are based on the regression coefficients of the Cox regression model, using the following conversion formula (expB-1) × 100. They refer to a one-unit change of the respective covariate. Since the measurement level varies between covariates, the *size* of the absolute percentage change does not give any indication of whether a result reaches statistical significance.

24. Although the differences between occupational groups are similar in magnitude with respect to *employment re-entry*, they are not significant, because of the smaller sample of episodes, which reduces the power of the statistical test.

25. These computations are based on the 1990 Swiss Census data.

26. *Occupational status* of a job is measured by Treiman's occupational prestige scale (Treiman, 1977). The finding shown in Table 1 reads as follows: A one-point increase in the occupational prestige of a job reduces the risks of exiting employment by 8% and increases the chances of re-entry by 8%.

27. Our full model (not shown in Table 1) controls for women's human capital (see note 22). For this reason, we do not relate women's strong work commitment to their educational attainment.

REFERENCES

Acker, J. (1991). Hierarchies, jobs, bodies: A theory of gendered organizations. In: J. Lorber & S. A. Farrell (Eds), *The Social Construction of Gender* (pp. 162–179). London: Sage.

Allison, P. D. (1984). *Event history analysis: Regression for longitudinal event data*. Beverly Hills, London; New Delhi: Sage.

Baron, J. N., & Bielby, W. T. (1980). Bringing the firm back in stratification, segmentation, and the organization of work. *American Sociological Review, 45*, 737–767.

Becker, R. (1993). *Staatsexpansion und Karrierechancen: Berufsverlaeufe im oeffentlichen Dienst und in der Privatwirtschaft.* Frankfurt: Campus.

Blossfeld, H.-P. (1991). Der Wandel von Ausbildung und Berufseinstieg bei Frauen. In: K. U. Mayer, J. Allmendinger & J. Huinink (Eds), *Vom Regen in die Traufe: Frauen zwischen Beruf und Familie* (pp. 1–22). Frankfurt: Campus.

Blossfeld, H.-P. (1997). Women's part-time employment and the family cycle: A cross-national comparison. In: H.-P. Blossfeld & C. Hakim (Eds), *Between Equalization and Marginalization: Women Working Part-Time in Europe and in the United States of America* (pp. 312–324). Oxford: Oxford University Press.

Blossfeld, H.-P., & Hakim, C. (Eds) (1997). *Between equalization and marginalization: Women working part-time in Europe and the United States of America.* Oxford: Oxford University Press.

Blossfeld, H.-P., & Mayer, K.-U. (1988). Arbeitsmarktsegmentation in der Bundesrepublik Deutschland. Eine empirische Ueberpruefung von Segmentationstheorien aus der Perspektive des Lebenslaufs. *Koelner Zeitschrift fuer Soziologie und Sozialpsychologie, 40*, 262–283.

Borkowsky, A., & Streckeisen, U. (1982). Wiedereinstieg von Frauen in den Beruf: Theoretische Ueberlegungen zu Determinanten im domestikalen Arbeitsbereich und im Lohnarbeitsbereich. *Schweizerische Zeitschrift fuer Soziologie, 8*, 279–310.

Born, C. (1991). Zur Bedeutung der beruflichen Erstausbildung bei der Verbindung von Familien- und Erwerbsarbeit in weiblichen Lebenslaeaeufen. In: C. Gather (Ed.), *Lebenslaeufe von Frauen und ihre Benachteiligung im Alter* (pp. 19–31). Berlin: Edition Sigma.

Bornschier, V. (1982). Segmentierung der Unternehmen in der Wirtschaft und personelle Einkommensverteilung. *Schweizerische Zeitschrift fuer Soziologie, 8*, 519–539.

Bruederl, J., Preisendoerfer, P., & Ziegler, R. (1993). Upward mobility in organizations: The effects of hierarchy and opportunity structure. *European Sociological Review, 9*, 173–188.

Buchmann, M., Kriesi, I., Pfeifer, A., & Sacchi, S. (2002). *Halb drinnen – halb draussen. Analysen zur Arbeitsmarktintegration von Frauen in der Schweiz.* Zurich/Chur: Rueegger.

Buchmann, M., & Sacchi, S. (1997). *Berufsverlauf und berufsidentitaet im sozio-technischen Wandel: Konzeption, methodik und repraesentativitaet einer retrospektiven befragung der geburtsjahrgaenge 1949–1951 und 1959–1961.* Zurich: Eidgenoessische Technische Hochschule (ETH).

Buchmann, M., & Sacchi, S. (1998). The transition from school to work in Switzerland: Do characteristics of the educational system and class barriers matter? In: Y. Shavit & W. Mueller (Eds), *From School to Work. A Comparative Study of Educational Qualifications and Occupational Destinations* (pp. 407–442). Oxford: Clarendon Press.

Bundesamt füer Statistik (Ed.) (1996). *Die schweizerische lohnstrukturerhebung 1994. Kommentierte Ergebnisse und Tabellen.* Bern: Bundesamt füer Statistik.

Carroll, G. R., Havemann, H., & Swaminathan, A. (1990). Karrieren in Organisationen. Eine oekologische Perspektive. In: K. U. Mayer (Ed.), *Lebensverlaeufe und sozialer Wandel. Koelner Zeitschrift fuer Soziologie und Sozialpsychologie*, Sonderheft 31 (pp. 146–178). Opladen: Westdeutscher Verlag.

Charles, M. (2002). Schweizerische Besonderheiten im Vergleich mit andren westlichen Laendern. In: M. Buchmann, I. Kriesi, A. Pfeifer & S. Sacchi (Eds), *Halb drinnen – halb draussen* (pp. 207–228). Zurich/Chur: Rueegger.

Charles, M., Buchmann, M., Halebsky, S., Powers, J., & Smith, M. (2001). The context of women's market careers: A cross-national study. *Work and Occupations, 28*, 371–396.

Desai, S., & Waite, L. J. (1991). Women's employment during pregnancy and after the first birth: Occupational characteristics and work commitment. *American Sociological Review, 56,* 551–566.

Drew, E., Emerek, R., & Mahon, E. (1998). *Women's work and the family in Europe.* London: Routledge.

Drobnic, S., Blossfeld, H.-P., & Rohwer, G. (1999). Dynamics of women's employment patterns over the family life course: A comparison of the United States and Germany. *Journal of Marriage and the Family, 61,* 133–159.

Fagan, C., & Rubery, J. (1996). The salience of the part-time divide in the European Union. *European Sociological Review, 12,* 227–250.

Federal Office of Statistics (1970). *Swiss census data.* Berne: Federal Office of Statistics.

Federal Office of Statistics (1990). *Swiss census data.* Berne: Federal Office of Statistics.

Federal Office of Statistics (1998). *Swiss establishment census.* Berne: Federal Office of Statistics.

Glass, J. L., & Riley, L. (1998). Family responsive policies and employee retention following childbirth. *Social Forces, 76,* 1401–1435.

Hakim, C. (1997). A sociological perspective on part-time work. In: H.-P. Blossfeld & C. Hakim (Eds), *Between Equalization and Marginalization: Women Working Part-Time in Europe and the United States of America* (pp. 22–70). Oxford: Oxford University Press.

Heintz, B., & Nadai, E. (1998). Geschlecht und Kontext: De-Institutionalisierungsprozesse und geschlechtliche Differenzierung. *Zeitschrift fuer Soziologie, 27,* 75–93.

Hoepflinger, F., Charles, M., & Debrunner A. (1991). *Familienleben und berufsarbeit: Zum wechselverhaeltnis zweier lebensbereiche.* Zurich: Seismo.

Jenson, J., Hagan, E., & Reddy, C. (Eds) (1988). *Feminization of the labor force.* Padstow: Polity.

Klein, T., & Braun, U. (1995). Der berufliche wiedereinstieg von muettern. *Zeitschrift fuer Soziologie, 24,* 58–68.

Krueger, H., & Born, C. (1991). Unterbrochene erwerbskarrieren und berufsspezifik: Zum arbeitsmarkt- und familienpuzzle im weiblichen lebenslauf. In: K. U. Mayer, J. Allmendinger & J. Huinink (Eds), *Vom Regen in die Traufe: Frauen zwischen Beruf und Familie* (pp. 142–161). Frankfurt: Campus.

Kurz, K. (1998). *Das Erwerbsverhalten von Frauen in der intensiven Familienphase: Ein Vergleich zwischen Muettern in der Bundesrepublik und in den USA.* Opladen: Leske und Budrich.

Lauterbach, W. (1994). *Berufsverlaeufe von Frauen: Erwerbstaetigkeit, Unterbrechung und Wiedereintritt.* Frankfurt: Campus.

Levy, R., Joye, D., Guye, O., & Kaufmann, V. (1997). *Tous egaux? De la stratification aux representations?* Zurich: Seismo.

Lewin, R. (1982). *Arbeitsmarktsegmentierung und Lohnstruktur: Theoretische Ansaetze und Hauptergebnisse einer Ueberpruefung am Beispiel der Schweiz.* Zurich: Schulthess.

Mueller, U. (1993). Sexualitaet, organisation und kontrolle. In: B. Aulenbacher & M. Goldmann (Eds), *Transformationen im Geschlechterverhaeltnis: Beitraege zur industriellen und gesellschaftlichen Entwicklung* (pp. 97–114). Frankfurt: Campus.

OECD (Organisation for Economic Cooperation and Development) (1994). Job gains and job losses in firms. *Employment Outlook, 12,* 103–134.

Preisendoerfer, P. (1987). Organisationale Determinanten beruflicher Karrieremuster. *Soziale Welt, 38,* 211–226.

Rexroat, C. (1992). Changes in the employment continuity of succeeding cohorts of young women. *Work and Occupations, 19,* 18–34.

Rosenfeld, R., & Birkelund, G. E. (1995). Women's part-time work: A cross-national comparison. *European Sociological Review, 11,* 111–134.

Shavit, Y., & Mueller, W. (Eds) (1998). *From school to work: A comparative study of educational qualifications and occupational destinations.* Oxford: Clarendon Press.

SAKE-News (2000). *Maternité, mariage et divorce dans les années 90: quelles conséquences sur la vie professionnelle des femmes? Une étude basée sur l'enquêtes suisse sur la population active.* Berne: Federal Office of Statistics.

Schulze Buschoff, K. (1999). *Teilzeit im europaeischen Vergleich: Individuelle Dynamik, Haushaltskontext, Wohlfahrtsertraege.* Duesseldorf: Boeckler Stiftung.

Sengenberger, W. (1987). *Struktur und Funktionsweise von Arbeitsmaerkten: Die Bundesrepublik Deutschland im internationalen Vergleich.* Frankfurt: Campus.

Stewman, S., & Konda, S. L. (1983). Careers and organizational labor markets: Demographic models of organizational behaviour. *American Journal of Sociology, 88*, 637–685.

Treiman, D. J. (1977). *Occupational prestige in comparative perspective.* New York: Academic Press.

van der Lippe, T., & van Dijk, L. (2001). *Women's employment in a comparative perspective.* New York: Aldine de Gruyter.

van der Lippe, T., & van Dijk, L. (2002). Comparative research on women's employment. *Annual Review of Sociology, 28*, 221–241.

Weck-Hannemann, H. (1993). Krankenpfleger und Ingenieurin: Die Berufswahl von Frauen und Maenner aus oekonomischer Sicht. In: G. Groetzinger, R. Schubert & J. Backhaus (Eds), *Jenseits von Diskriminierung: Zu den institutionellen Bedingungen weiblicher Arbeit in Beruf und Familie* (pp. 54–79). Marburg: Metropolis Verlag.

Weck-Hannemann, H., & Frey, B. S. (1989). Frauen und arbeit: Eine oekonomische Betrachtung. *Wirtschaftliches Studium, 18*, 562–568.

9. WORK AND FAMILY BALANCE: A NEW CHALLENGE FOR POLICIES IN FRANCE

Marie-Thérèse Letablier

ABSTRACT

The issue of work and life balance has become more prominent in public debate in France since the beginning of the 1990s. In this chapter we explore the policy responses to families' demand for state support to childcare and to workers' demand for more free time for social and family life. This happens in a context where the state has a strong legitimacy to intervene in family affairs and in work regulations. First, we examine the changing family policy that is a major domain for public action in France. Then, we look at the restructuring of childcare policies and at working-time policies. Of particular interest is the special effort that has been made to reduce the legal number of working hours and the impact of this change on the integration of work and family life.

INTRODUCTION

In France, the issue of work and life balance emerged in public debate from the 1990s onwards. Up to that time, the focus had been limited to the smooth integration of work and family life, though family was always a major policy area and a source of debates. The change in the government in 1997 undoubtedly contributed

Changing Life Patterns in Western Industrial Societies
Advances in Life Course Research, Volume 8, 189–209
Copyright © 2004 by Elsevier Ltd.
All rights of reproduction in any form reserved
ISSN: 1040-2608/doi:10.1016/S1040-2608(03)08009-2

to pushing the issue to the forefront because work and life balance had a major place in the political program of the left. In this chapter, the focus is on policy responses to the gender revolution, i.e. the growing number of women in employment and changing gender roles. The intent is to note the connection between changing household structure and lifestyles and their consequences for public policies, including family policies as well as working-time policies. Emphasis here is put on the changing life patterns that are emerging, and on their consequences for the formulation of policies and the principles of public action. Handling of these questions is highly determined by the role of the state in the regulation of family affairs, and especially its role in the reconciliation of work and family life, and in the regulation of work.

Policy responses to changes in work and life patterns vary among countries according to types of arrangements between the state, the companies, the market, the civil society, and the family. In most European Union countries, the restructuring of social care over recent decades has been characterised by shifts in policy goals, in the entitlement to benefits, and in the eligibility of the recipients. Since the 1970s, institutional reforms in EU countries have tended to converge in response to similar socio-demographic trends and to European Union recommendations. But each country shapes the reforms according to its own welfare regime and its historical tradition. In France, the issue of work and life balance is mainly a public policy matter. Work and life balance is at the crossroads of several policy areas among which family policies have been representing the main domain of intervention by the state for more than half a century. The reconciliation of work and family life has been on the policy agenda since the family policy was institutionalised just after the Second World War. The well-being of families that was a major objective of state support to families was expected to result from a gender division of work between paid work of the male breadwinner and unpaid work of his wife and the mother of his children. Nowadays, however, most women are in the labour market, and the question of how to meet both work and family demands has become a priority for French family policies since the late 1970s. In the meantime, the political rhetoric has changed and the forms of state support as well. Gender equality has become a major principle guiding public policies, according to the European Union recommendations. In this chapter, we examine how French policies have attempted to implement the principle of gender equality in family policies and in working-time policies, and in the process to improve work and life balance. First, we examine the historical background that explains the role of the state in the regulation of the welfare of families. Although France cannot be characterised as a "caring state" as are the Nordic countries, it differs deeply from the other "conservative corporatist" states as defined by Esping-Andersen (1990) in his classification of welfare regimes in Europe. Whereas the French welfare state is family-based as in other continental welfare states in Europe, the male breadwinner model is weaker in France than in Germany or Austria for example. Since the nineteenth century, women have been protected by the state in France, both as workers and as mothers (Lanquetin et al., 2000). Next we examine policies aimed at improving the balance of work and family: state support to childcare and state regulations of working-time. Childcare policies respond to the social demand for more diversified childcare facilities, for improving the reconciliation of work and family life, for caring rights for families, and the emancipation of women, not only as workers or as mothers but as citizens. These new social demands are not limited to social services but also include a call for relief of time pressure on families, and a demand for gender equity in the share of caring obligations. *"Du temps pour vivre!"* ["Time to live!"] was the slogan of this demand, and *"l'articulation des temps de vie"* ["work and life balance"] was the issue for policies (Gauvin & Jacot, 1999).

HISTORICAL BACKGROUND: STATE SUPPORT TO FAMILIES

In France, the state recognises the family rather than the individual. This is different from the Nordic welfare regimes. As a consequence, family is a major issue for public policies. France has an explicit and institutionalised family policy that implies legal recognition of the family as a social institution that plays a major role in the maintenance of social cohesion (Hantrais & Letablier, 1996). The family policy of France was institutionalised in 1938 when the Family Code was introduced. It became an independent component of public policy in the years following the Second World War, with a budget mostly paid for by employers from social contribution on salaries (that constitute 65% of the family policy budget). In addition, there are specific organisations to administer the policy: a ministry devoted to family affairs, a national fund, and a policy decision process involving economic and social actors as partners. Beginning in the late nineteenth century, allowances were added to worker's salaries by employers with the aim of improving the workers' family life. Since that time a number of laws were introduced in order to protect mothers and children. Motherhood was considered to need attention from the state for demographic reasons, to increase the population by raising the birth rate. Maternity leave was introduced in the labour law as a right for working women at the beginning of the twentieth century. In 1945, when the welfare state was settled, support to families was transferred from enterprises and charities to the state. Family policy became a main component of public action.

From the post-war period up until the late 1970s, French family policy has been aimed at protecting the family as a norm and as a value. It explicitly supported the traditional "male breadwinner model." Single-earner families were provided with a "Single Salary Allowance" or a "housewife allowance" aimed at supporting women's care work at home. The impact of this scheme was to confine women to the role of full-time mothers and housewives because it was assumed that this would contribute to the welfare of young children and to the rise of fertility. Accordingly, the labour force participation rate of mothers remained low until the mid-1960s, even lower than in the beginning of the twentieth century. That particular form of work and family balance resulted in a gender division of labour, institutionalised by family policy, and tied to demographic objectives. Maternity was encouraged by various benefits and allowances given to families to compensate the direct costs of children, and mothering was recognised by the state as being of value for the society as a whole. Mothers of numerous children were honoured as "good citizens" for giving children to the nation. Family was symbolically linked to civic values, and motherhood to citizenship (Knibiehler, 1997). Housewives and children were entitled to social rights as dependants of the male breadwinner, making the French welfare regime a "conservative corporatist" one, according to the Esping-Andersen classification (1990, op. cit.).

Family policy was also inspired by the idea that children are a collective investment, and hence that the state has to share responsibility and costs of childcare. As part of the intergenerational contract, children will work and pay for pensions of the elderly. Therefore a family is not supposed to be the sole support of its children because they bring future benefits to the whole society as well as individuals. This idea underlies the horizontal solidarity and redistributive nature of the French family policy which is still the fundamental mechanism of state support to families.

From the 1970s onwards, family policy had to adapt to changing family forms and the increase in working mothers. The level of the "Single Salary Allowance" was progressively reduced and restricted to low-income families, and was finally abolished by 1978. Against the background of an acute labour shortage, the French government began to set up community-funded day care centres in an attempt to attract women into the work force (Norvez, 1990). The demand for the expansion of public day care facilities and other social services was actively supported by the women's movement by putting strong emphasis on equality issues in the labour market, as well as by the main trade unions. These factors provided a strong impetus for family policy change: French family policy began to incorporate the model of the "working mother." There followed a progressive transfer of a growing proportion of unpaid private care-giving responsibility into paid public provision. In the 1980s, family policy was characterised by a far reaching neutrality with respect to family forms and to women's decision to work or to mother. The political rhetoric was "freedom of choice" for mothers to be in employment or not. Funding allocated by both local authorities and the National Family Allowance Fund (*Caisse nationale des allocations familiales, CNAF*) for the construction of daycare centres substantially increased. Part-time work was encouraged, both on the supply and demand sides. And allowances aimed at reducing costs of private childcare were introduced. They were supplemented by tax reductions for care expenses and by reductions of social contributions for the employment of a childminder or a family helper.

State intervention in childcare is highly legitimised in France and is still linked to a conception of the state as a protector of childhood and a guarantor of equal opportunities for children. This conception of childhood and the upbringing of children is rooted in the principles of the Third Republic (Rollet-Echallier, 1990) according to which children are a "common good" and the wealth of the nation, which obligates society to care for them in return. Childcare has become an even more important area of family policy. It is viewed as state support for families, to help them cover their childcare expenses and reconcile work and family life. The issue of work and life balance is viewed mainly from a childcare perspective and as a working mother's issue.

In 1997, the new socialist government announced a "new family policy," inspired by ideas of social justice and gender equity (Büttner et al., 2002). Emphasis was put on two priorities: improving work and family balance, and improving social and gender equity. State support focused on parents more than on families or on working mothers. The "freedom of choice" for mothers to work or to mother was progressively abandoned while European Union policy recommended an increase in employment rates in all countries. Hence, mothers were encouraged to work and the states to provide support by helping them to stay employed. Childcare support was still a priority on the political agenda. Emphasis was on indirect costs of children. Emphasis was also on values: norms of education for children and early socialisation, values attached to paid work and to family life, and gender equity. In France, the idea of an early and collective socialisation for children is well received. Public opinion still supports the notion of public services as evidence of state responsibility in education, health, and the well-being of children. However, work and life balance has become a priority on the public agenda, creating a challenge not only for family policies but also for working-time policies and for gender equity policies. The resulting emphasis of the different policy sectors is to change values in order to construct an environment more "child-friendly" and less work-oriented, for both men and women.

The new approach to work and family balance from the 1990s to the present developed in the context of a change in the parties in power. The change of government in 1997 has accelerated the process of change. The demands of the trade unions and the women's movement for childcare facilities, for better working-time regulations, and for time for families to give care have all been taken into account. In response to these social demands, policy objectives encompass a wider conception of human needs that emphasise personal autonomy, women's emancipation, and freedom of choice among different types of benefits. The state support for reconciliation of work and family life that was implemented in the 1980s has been reconstructed, not only in its objectives and content, but also in the form of governance, especially concerning state support to childcare.

Restructuring State Support to Childcare

Increasing involvement of women in paid work is undoubtedly one of the major changes in work and life patterns in all western countries. The change has been spectacular in France since the 1960s: women's activity rates have increased from 28.2% in the early 1960s to 48.3% in 2001, while men's activity rates grew from 58.4 to 61.8%. The rise in women's labour force participation is due mainly to the increase of mothers on the labour market, while at the same time, working life patterns have changed. Men and women stay longer in school and delay their entrance into employment. They also tend to retire earlier, since public employment programs have encouraged workers to leave paid work in the face of industrial restructuring and high unemployment. Under the age of 20, only 6% of women are in paid work, and only 7% of all women between ages 20 and 24. After age 55, they begin to retire; only 11.7% of all women 55 and older are in the labour force. The rates for men are rather similar, which means that the working life cycle is relatively short in France. The legal age for retirement is sixty, but a large proportion of employees quit the labour market earlier. The short length of working life is going to be problematic for the pension system, as the duration of retirement is expanding with the extension of life expectancy for both men and women, currently at 75.2 for men and 82.7 for women.

Resulting from these trends is a change in the employment profile of households as well as a reduction in the working-time gap between men and women. For an increasing number of women, working and mothering have to be reconciled: 81% of mothers with one child under 18 were in the labour force in 2000; 69% of mothers with two children; and 49% of mothers with three children or more (see Table 1).

Not only does the number of children affect the activity rates of mothers, but also the age of the last child appears to be determinant. With two children age six and over, roughly 82% of mothers are in the labour force, but when the second child is under three, the activity rate of mothers decreases to 55%. So the problem

Table 1. Activity Rates for Mothers Living with a Partner, by Number of
Children (Under Age 18), France, 2000.

	Activity Rate (%)
No child under 18	45.5
One child	
6–17	81.0
3–5	84.1
Under 3	79.2
Two children	
The youngest aged 6–17	81.7
The youngest aged 3–5	73.7
The youngest under 3	54.7
Three or more children	
The youngest aged 6–17	64.2
The youngest aged 3–5	52.4
The youngest under 3	32.8
Total	57.0

Source: Enquête sur l'emploi, mars 2000, INSEE, Paris.

of childcare for young children is acute for working mothers, and the demand for
state support to childcare remains strong.

The Demand for Childcare

According to the last time-budget survey in 1998–1999, more than 85% of dual
earner households with at least one child under pre-school age rely on external
childcare: 19% rely on informal unpaid services of a relative or a friend, and 67%
rely on one or more paid services (Guillot, 2002). So, among the 2.21 millions of
children under three years old in France, 36% were cared for either by a family
member (for three out of four) or in informal care by an unregistered person; 9%
were cared for in a collective public *"crèche"*; 19% by a registered childminder;
and 1.5% by a family helper in the child's home. The rest attend pre-school or other
forms of day-care centres. The choice of which type of childcare to use – whether
paid childcare services, informal unpaid care, or family care – depends on several
factors: on mothers' working time, on family income, and on the demographic
structure of the family that may or may not have help from older children or from
a grandparent. In dual earner families, childcare by a registered childminder is
the most common form of paid care: 45% of these families use such services.
Childminders are mainly used as carers for young children, and as carers for

children attending school or pre-school, for after school hours, and during vacations and Wednesdays. In general, there is a strong consensus on the responsibility of the state in childcare. The demand for state support was always very strong in France, and still is. The demand is conveyed by family associations, by trade unions, and by political parties of the left. The arrival of the socialists in power in the early 1980s after several decades of conservative governments gave a strong impetus to state support for childcare, with the aim of encouraging mothers to keep their jobs. Political parties from the right have always been reluctant to approve an increase of state support to collective childcare facilities, considering that the best carer is the mother at home. So, they usually encourage mothers of young children to leave their job for caring and then to return to the labour market after childrearing.

The "crèches" are preferred by parents of young children because of the quality of childcare (considered the best from a child development perspective) and because of the low cost for families, especially for low income families. But few parents can get a bed in "crèches" and roughly 43% have to find another solution. Although "crèches" and home care by paid helpers get the highest satisfaction rating among parents, there are not enough beds in the former, and the latter solution is too expensive for most parents.

Concerning pre-school age children (ages 3–6), 98% attend an "*école maternelle*" regularly although it is not compulsory, and 38% of children age 2–3 attend it regularly. Pre-school is not viewed as a childcare issue but as an educational issue. The "*écoles maternelles*" are under the control of the Minister of Education, and they are administered in the same way as schools (Letablier & Jönsson, 2003). Teachers receive the same training as those working in primary schools. School hours are the same whether pre-school or primary school: every day from 8 am to 4 pm, or 8 h 30 to 4 h 30, except on Wednesday and Saturday afternoon. In most schools, children can have a hot lunch on the site. However, working parents are facing the problem of after-school care during after-school hours and during school holidays. Usually, especially in large cities, after school hours care and daycare centers are available to parents. They are organised by local authorities and subsidized by the family policy fund. So, children are allowed to stay at school until 6 or 6 h 30, and are cared for by young carers appointed by municipalities. Other children who don't stay at school are cared for either by parents or relatives, or by childminders or babysitters.

State Support for Childcare

Since the early 1980s, state support to childcare has been a major focus of family policy, through the National Family Fund (*Caisse Nationale d'Allocations*

Familiales). First of all, there is broad consensus in France on the legitimacy of state intervention in childcare, and in providing families with support for the integration of work and family life. The families' demands on the state are strong; neither corporations nor the civil society are held accountable to the same degree (Letablier et al., 2003). Although the consensus on public childcare facilities remains very strong, the forms of state support have become more diversified since the 1980s under a variety of pressures: unemployment, high costs of public childcare such as *crèches*, and the necessity to reduce public expenditures. The families' demands have also changed: while a large number of parents consider that public collective childcare is the best from the children's point of view, care by a registered childminder responds better to their own constraints.

Different forms of state support to childcare have developed since the 1980s. In the first stage, state initiatives focused on childcare facilities and services such as collective day-care centres (crèches), and then moved to other forms of benefits aimed at compensating the costs to parents of individual forms of childcare. Since 1980, the number of childcare places in *crèches* has increased regularly – on average by 6,400 places per year between 1981 and 1996 – to reach a total of 203,000 in 2002[1] (*crèches collectives*[2] and *crèches familiales*[3]). Although state support to "crèches" slowed during the early 1990s, it became a priority again on the agenda of the socialist government in 1997. From the mid-1980s to the mid 1990s, priority was given to individual forms of childcare by registered childminders ("*assistantes maternelles*") caring for children in their home, or by a family helper caring in the children's home, or by parents themselves. Allowances were introduced to subsidise these different forms of childcare, as well as tax deductions for childcare costs and reductions of social contributions associated with the employment of a paid person. Parents who employ a registered childminder to care for a child under six receive an allowance called "allowance for families who employ a registered childminder" ("*Aide à la famille pour l'emploi d'une assistante maternelle agréée*" – AFEAMA) ranging from 130 Euros to 200 Euros per month according to the family income and to the number of dependant children. In addition, they are exempted from social contributions. Parents receive an "allowance to employ a family helper at home to care for a child" under three years old (*Allocation de garde d'enfant à domicile* – AGED) aimed at covering 75% of the social contributions due to social security. They are also eligible for tax deductions. In addition, a parent who gives up her (or his) job or reduces her economic activity to care for a child under three years old receives a parental leave allowance ("*Allocation parentale d'éducation*" – APE) of 485 Euros per month if the parent is caring full-time and 242 Euros if the parent is caring and working part-time. The allowance is given only after the second child and under specific conditions of previous employment.

In sum, the restructuring of state support to childcare has broadened childcare supply for parents, and at the same time has changed the public-private mix, resulting in a shift from collective public childcare facilities to individualised forms of childcare that are subsidised by public funds.

The Individualisation of Childcare

Over the last twenty years, state support to childcare has shifted from benefits in kind for collective childcare to benefits in cash allowed to parents. Cash benefits cover part of childcare costs for families. Geographic distribution of childcare benefits varies according to the number of beds in "crèches" and to family profiles. "Crèches" are more numerous in urban areas than in rural regions. And so for childcare at the child's home by a home helper, the solution is most attractive to high income families. In rural areas, childcare is mostly assumed by childminders and by mothers themselves who receive the parental leave allowance. Informal unpaid care is also more prevalent in rural areas and among families with the lowest income. In addition to state support, some local authorities can offer further benefits to support certain forms of childcare. The outcomes, however, result in spatial regional inequalities that compound social inequalities.

Employing a paid helper at home remains the most expensive childcare for families (roughly 1,200 Euros per month for one child). The allowance AGED serves the richest households, whereas AFEAMA serves families with lower income. Families who receive AGED have on average an income twice as high as families who receive AFEAMA and three times as high as families who receive the parental leave allowance or who have their child cared for in a *crèche*. The "crèche" is the lowest cost childcare for families with low income because the cost is means tested and the cost varies from 62 Euros per month for very low income families to 522 Euros for families with an income five times the minimum wage. The cost of a childminder is flat (roughly 400 Euros per month). In fact, the poorest families have a limited choice between the *crèche* if they can find a bed, and care by one of the parents receiving the parental leave allowance, while the richest families are those who benefit more from tax deductions although the allowance for care at home (AGED) is lower than other allowances.[4] Whereas they benefit the richest families more, tax deductions for childcare expenses were introduced to encourage employers to pay social contributions for the home helpers and to discourage the underground economy in childcare.

In 2003, half of children under three years old are cared for at the parent's home either by one of the parents or by a paid family helper, and the other half is cared for outside the home either at the childminder's home or in "crèches" or at pre-school

Table 2. Distribution of Children Under 3 According to the Childcare Programs, France, 2003.

	Children Attending Pre-School	Children Cared by a Childminder	Children Cared in a "Crèche"[a]	Children Cared by a Family Helper at Home	Children Cared by One Parent Receiving the Parental Leave Allowance	Children Cared by Mothers on Maternity Leave[b]	Children Cared by a Parent	Others (Unknown)[c]
Number	256,000	457,200	243,600	30,600	556,000	174,000	400,000	180,000
%	11.7	20.6	10.7	1.3	24.5	7.6	7.6	7.9

Note: Some children can be counted twice because they use two different types of childcare facilities.

Source: Adapted from Leprince (2003).

[a] There are only 203,000 beds in "crèches" but one bed receives on average 1.2 children.

[b] Six weeks before the expected date of birth and ten after. After the third child, leave is extended to 26 weeks.

[c] Estimation.

(Table 2). Roughly 20% of children under 3 attend a collective care (pre-school or "crèche"). In addition to pre-school which is free of charge, most childcare facilities are subsidized by the state or by local authorities.

Since 2002, the priority of the new government in power is not to make public investments in collective childcare. The priority is rather to increase the amount of the allowance for care at home (AGED) which is favourable to the richest families whose cost of employment of a family helper is being reduced. This orientation is consistent with the government objective of limiting the redistribution dimension of family policy in order to focus more on support to indirect costs of children, whose costs increase with parents' income.

In spite of the diversification of childcare facilities and benefits, the current system of childcare does not offer a real choice to parents of young children because childcare facilities are not equally spread throughout the country and because they have varying costs that do not make them accessible to all parents. Less well educated women are discouraged from working when they cannot find a bed in a *crèche* or when they cannot rely on relatives to care for a young child. The current system of state support to childcare is complex and the new government in power since June 2002 is planning a reform of childcare allowances. The project is to have a unique allowance (a childcare allowance) for all children under three whatever the employment status and the economic situation of parents. This allowance is supposed to replace the AFEAMA, the AGED and the parental leave allowance. At the same time, the government expects to involve other groups in the funding and organisation of childcare crèches and services.

Work and Family Balance: A Question of Time

The employment profiles of households in France differ from most other European countries. Just as France among EU countries has one of the highest rates of dual earner families, it is also, with Denmark and Portugal, the country where the gap in working time between men and women is the lowest (Franco & Winqvist, 2002). These patterns are due to the short working time of men and the relatively low level of women part-timers. Moreover, the average working time of part-timers is higher in France than in most other EU countries, especially the U.K., the Netherlands and Germany, where part-time work is a means of reconciliation of work and family life.

In France, the collective norm of a slightly less than 40-hour week is still very strong. More than 50% of men work 38–39 hours a week on average. This standard of working time is a result of strong state regulation. Very long working weeks are not usual, except for professionals, and flexible hours of work (in the evening, on the weekend) are less extensive in France than in most other countries although they are becoming more common.

Part-Time Work

In 2001, 16.4% of all workers worked part-time: 5% among men and 30.4% among women. Part-time work has been increasing over the last two decades, and especially among women. This is a new phenomenon in France where women used to enter the labour market on a full-time basis. Part-time work has not really been promoted as a mean of reconciliation between work and family life although trade unions and feminists opposed the idea as a tool for the subordination of women to a male breadwinner model of the family. The development of part-time work during the 1980s and 1990s was encouraged by policy measures aimed at sharing work in a context of high unemployment, and at increasing flexibility of work. Costs of part-time jobs for employers were reduced by a decrease in their social security contributions. Part-time jobs developed especially in the service sector where the need for flexibility was higher than in the manufacturing industry.

Working part-time is not always the result of a choice: 42.2% of men part-timers and 31.5% of women declare that they would prefer to work full-time if jobs were available. When the situation of the labour market improves, the proportion of involuntary part-time decreases, for men and for women alike (see Table 3). More than one woman out of three is not satisfied with her part-time job and is looking for longer hours of work. This attests to the norm that full-time work is still dominant in France. Only a limited proportion of part-timers choose this form of work in order to accommodate work and family life.

Table 3. Proportion in Part-Time Work, Men and Women, France, 1997–2001.

Part-Time Work (%)	1997	2001[a]
Total	16.6	16.4
Men	5.4	5.0
Women	30.8	30.4
Involuntary part-time[b] (%)		
Men	51.5	42.2
Women	36.7	31.5

Source: Enquêtes sur l'emploi, 1997 et 2001, Insee, paris.
[a] March 2001.
[b] Persons working part-time but looking for a full-time job or wanting to work more.

In short, the population of women working part-time is heterogeneous: some make the choice not to work full-time while others have no other choice than to accept shorter hours than they desire. For those who have chosen to work part-time, the reasons can be diverse: caring for young children or for a dependant partner or relative, being in training, or retiring gradually. But, in 50% of the cases, women make this choice for family reasons. Mothers who work part-time take over the largest part of domestic and parental responsibilities and duties.

By contrast with other European countries, part-time work in France is characterised by long part-time, and especially among women: 45.6% work more than 25 hours on average per week compared to 24.5% of women in the United Kingdom. Most mothers working part-time choose not to work on Wednesday when children don't go to school, and this is especially true of mothers employed in the public sector. When children are grown up, mothers come back to work full-time. The decision to work part-time as a means of reconciling work and family life is influenced by the level of income of the partner and by the number of dependant children. But, the higher a woman's wage, the lower her probability of working part-time (Bourreau-Dubois et al., 2001).

Working-Time Policies

The reduction in length of the legal working week was a priority on the political program of the left when it came into power in 1997. The option was a collective reduction of working time by law, instead of supporting individual forms of time reduction. The primary challenge of the "35 hours laws" (1997 and 2000) was work-sharing in a context of high and persistent unemployment. By reducing the average legal working week from 39 to 35 hours, the government expected to increase the number of jobs, and hence lower unemployment. In this sense, the reduction of working time was more an employment policy than a social policy aimed at improving the workers' well-being. However, improving work and family balance was also an objective of the laws:[5] *"to answer to the demands of the employees for more free time and a better work life balance"* (M. Aubry, Exposé des motifs de la première loi Aubry devant l'Assemblée nationale, décembre 1997).

Over time, the employment objective became less explicit and the goal of work and family balance gained a broader place in the political debate. For many employees, the trade off has been between time and money. Most employees have got more free time but their wages have not increased for several years. The impact of the reduction of working time on work and family balance has been documented in several surveys (Estrade et al., 2001; Fagnani & Letablier, 2003a, b; Méda & Orain, 2002; Pelisse, 2002). Research shows the positive impact of the law on work and family balance, especially for parents with young children. Roughly 60% of parents with a child under six say they are satisfied with the reduction in their working time[6] (Fagnani & Letablier, 2003a). Parents who say they are satisfied with the outcomes of the law in terms of work-family balance more often than others have good working conditions, a family-friendly employer, and good human resource management in their enterprise. Also, more frequently than the dissatisfied, they have regular working time and standard hours. Fathers, as well mothers, claim to spend more time with their children, especially when the reduction in their working time is calculated on a weekly basis.

However, the reduction in working time is not neutral in terms of gender equality. The rules governing working time that apply to all workers, both men and women, are considered to be more equitable than simply individualised arrangements that encourage part-time work. One of the outcomes of the restructuring of working time has been to establish a new pattern of male and female paid work and arrangements for care. Men and women are both involved in employment, mostly full-time, but they work shorter hours than in most EU countries. The working-time gap between men and women is being reduced: average weekly working-time for full-time workers is declining while part-time workers have increased their hours of work.[7] Although the average hours worked by full-time workers fell to 38.3 hours per week in the late 1990s, the average number of hours worked by part-timers continued to rise and was around 23.3 hours a week (INSEE, 2000). One of the outcomes of the laws has been to reinforce the norm of full-time work, and accordingly to increase the model of dual earner families composed of two "short" full-time workers[8] (70% of the dual earner families).

Time to Care for Families

The French welfare state recognises care as being both a state responsibility and a family responsibility. Policy makers have assumed this responsibility of the state by providing generous support and provisions for childcare and to a lesser extent for eldercare. The right of families to provide care has been written into labour regulations and into the tax and social security systems.

Most of the caring rights in the Labour Code concerns the leaves that employees are allowed to fulfill their care obligations towards children or dependant relatives. Maternity leave, paternity leave, and leave to care for a sick child are fundamental rights of workers. Enterprises can also provide care facilities to their employees that come in addition to these rights.

Maternity Leave

Every pregnant working woman is entitled to sixteen weeks maternity leave (six before the expected date of birth and ten after). The leave is extended to 26 weeks in cases of birth of a third child, of multiple births, of health problems due to pregnancy (two additional weeks before the delivery and four weeks after), or in cases of health problems with the new born child. Lay-offs during maternity leave are strictly forbidden. Employees cannot be fired during the four weeks following leave, and the return to work is guaranteed after the leave is up. The health insurance system pays a replacement wage (roughly 85% of the regular wage) during the maternity leave.

Paternity Leave

Since January 2002, fathers have been eligible for two weeks paid leave following the birth of a child.[9] Leave is paid for by social security as a replacement wage.[10]

Parental Leave

After maternity leave (or adoption), parents have the right to take parental leave or to work part-time (not less than sixteen hours a week) if they have been in the enterprise for at least one year. Parental leave is linked to employment rights but is not paid. Parents can apply for a parental leave allowance to the National Family Fund, which can be granted under specific conditions. The duration of parental leave is one year but can be extended twice until the child is three years old. One more year can be granted in case of illness or disability.

Leave to Care for a Sick Child

Every employee has the right to take unpaid leave to care for his (or her) sick child under the age of sixteen. Legally, periods of leave cannot exceed three days (or five days in specific cases), but this is a minimum and, in fact, most collective agreements have special arrangements. In the public sector, employees are allowed to take fourteen days a year to care for a sick child.

Parental Leave to Care for a Child with a Serious Illness

In cases of a serious disability or illness of a child under sixteen, every employee with at least one year of employment in the enterprise is entitled to paid leave to care for her/his child, or to work part-time. The level of the allowance depends on the duration of work in the enterprise and on the family structure. A similar period of leave is possible for employees needing to care for an elderly relative near death, child, or parent living in the same house or apartment.

Over the last five years, the responsibility of enterprises vis-à-vis the reconciliation of work and family life has been called for by policy actors and by trade unions.

Though employers are already involved in the funding of family policy, they are invited to take account of the family constraints of their employees and to be more family-friendly in their management. Not only employers have been involved in the improvement of the work and family balance, but also local authorities and the civil society. It is not only an issue for work and employment policies but also for urban policies. Over recent years, "Timing offices" (*bureaux des temps*) were introduced in several large cities in order to regulate the timing of transports, services, shopping, and childcare services with time of work. Thus, work and life balance in everyday life has become an issue for public policy, employment policy, family and social policy, and for urban policy as well.

Gendering Work and Life Balance

Although women's participation to the labour force is increasing and dual-earner families are becoming the norm, women continue to perform most domestic and parental work in the home. Time budget surveys show that men spend half as much time as women on domestic tasks and a third as much time caring for children. So, caring for children at home is still largely a women's activity (Algava, 2002). Involvement of women in paid work has not produced a symmetric involvement of men in unpaid work, even though the time spent by men on domestic tasks has slightly increased (Glaude, 1999).

Sharing Parental Responsibilities

Though the right to care is inscribed in social policies so as to promote gender equity in labour markets, the traditional gender culture, in terms of norms and values, continues to guide social practice, and to maintain an asymmetrical gendered division of labour at home. The burden is heavy, especially for women in low-income families or for single mothers, who cannot delegate part of their domestic tasks to others. Tax deductions offered to households who employ domestic helpers do not encourage men to take on any of the unpaid work in the home.

The collective reduction of working time has slightly increased fathers' participation in parental activities. Above all, it has permitted a negotiation of parental activities between parents in dual earner families, resulting in an increase of time dedicated by parents to their children and also in a reduction of childcare expenses (Fagnani & Letablier, 2003b).

Equality of opportunity among men and women has become a major issue on the European Union agenda and all European countries are obligated to implement this principle in their policies. European governments are encouraged to increase employment rates of their populations, and especially those of women. Accordingly, they are encouraged to develop childcare facilities and to implement gender equality in the workplace. Since the 1980s, the French government has put a special emphasis on gender equality in public policies: there is a minister (or a junior minister) for women's rights, and several laws on equal opportunities have been introduced. Although the principles behind policies have changed, the gender culture associated with the male breadwinner model of families still persists. The extension of the paternity leave in 2002 from three days to fourteen days after a child's birth was an attempt to change the largely feminine culture of care and to involve fathers in their parental responsibilities as soon as possible. Preliminary evaluations of the measure conclude that 40% of the fathers of a new-born took up the paternity leave during the first four months after the paternity leave was extended.

CONCLUSION

Work and family balance has been a major issue for public policies in France for a long time. The protection of the family life of workers has been a major issue for policies since the end the nineteenth century when laws were adopted to limit working hours, especially for women and children, in order to save the family as a value and to preserve family life. Regulations on working time have been in operation since that time, at first to preserve women's health and capacity to bear children during the period that population replacement was a national concern. But the need of families for time has always been the deeper issue. It is still on the political agenda even though there have been major changes in work organisation and family life. By the beginning of the 21st century, several policy domains are now understood to be relevant: employment, work organisation, working time, family and social policies, and urban policies. Policies have had to respond to the increasing number of dual earner families and to a demand for more state support to childcare and for more leisure for family and social activities. The restructuring of childcare policies in the late 1990s reflected the development of new principles driving the care issue. Childcare is no longer considered to be an issue for mothers only but is also considered a paternal responsibility. In an attempt to improve gender equality in the domestic sphere fathers are expected to be more involved in the education of their offspring. Following this line of argument, the reduction in working time, as well as the creation of a paternity leave, are attempts to promote a model of equal sharing of parental obligations in order to improve equal opportunities between men and women both in the labour market and within the family.

The two pillars of the policy for work and family balance are to support childcare on one hand and working-time policy on the other. This combination constitutes a singular dynamic among continental welfare regimes. What is distinctive about the French approach is the role of the state in regulating social life – family life as well as working life. Collective regulations take precedence over individual regulations. But in recent years a process of individualisation can be observed in the individualisation of childcare facilities and the individualisation of working time. Individualisation of childcare facilities is not privatisation because childcare is still highly subsidised by public support, even though new forms of partnership are being implemented at the local level. Individualisation of working-time schedules means that in the process of implementing the reduction, a large number of employees have had the opportunity to choose among diverse forms of reduction, whether daily, monthly, or annual according to their needs and wishes. But a problem remains for employees subjected to non-standard hours, who have no choice. Most of them who are in low skill jobs, with low salaries, would prefer to work longer hours and have higher income. For those who are parents of young children, finding suitable childcare is still a vexing problem.

NOTES

1. In addition, "*halte-garderies*" (68,000 places) take children occasionally, or for a few hours every day. They were set up to provide supplementary childcare.

2. *Crèches collectives* are publicly subsidised daycare centres where children under three years old are cared for by trained staff. They are supervised by the *Protection maternelle et infantile*, a statutory service responsible for the health care of children under six years old, and with supervisory responsibility for all public and private child care provision.

3. *Crèches familiales* organise childcare by registered childminders who are paid by the local authority and monitored by qualified state infant care personnel.

4. A childminder cares for several children in her home while a family helper works in her employer's home. Generally, the family helper not only cares for children but also cleans the house and prepares the meals. Most of them are immigrant women, and are not qualified. However, most of childminders are registered, which means that they have received the approval of family institutions (usually a physician appointed by a commission specialized in the children protection) to care for young children. The authorization is given according to conditions of housing and health. Since the late 1970s, a collective agreement rules work conditions and earnings of childminders. The number of children they are allowed to care for is limited and they are submitted to controls. On average, childminders care for 2.5 children. A limited number of childminders (8%) work in a "crèche familiale,"

i.e. in a collective place outside their house. Fifty percent of the childminders live in rural areas or in small towns. They are on average 44 years old (family helpers are rather young single women) and receive on average five hundred Euros per month.

5. The aims of the law reducing working time were presented by the Minister of Work and Social Affairs to the members of the Parliament in 1997 in the following order:

(1) sharing work in order to stimulate the job creation;
(2) improving firms' performances by reorganising work and increasing flexibility;
(3) increasing time dedicated to social and family life (*le temps libre*) in order to improve workers' everyday life;
(4) implementing negotiation at the firm level rather than at the branch level.

6. The survey was conducted in 2000 on a sample of 3,216 parents with a child under six, in different regions in France.

7. It should be added that part-time workers affected by the implementation of the laws are those who have increased their working time by more than thirty minutes, whereas part-time workers not covered by the law have increased theirs by only ten minutes.

8. "Long part-time is defined here as above 20 hours a week that is above a half full-time, and "Short" part-time under 20 hours. Long and short full-time hours are defined in comparison with other European countries: we define long full-time as being above 40 hours a week.

9. Fathers already had the right to take three days off work after the birth of a child. These three days are paid for by the employer. Paternity leave adds eleven days to the three days covered by health insurance.

10. The arrangements for payment for paternity leave differ in the public and private sectors. Employees in the public sector receive 100% of their former salary, while employees in the private sector receive less because an upper limit is set. In some cases, employers can add a supplement for employees who lose part of their income. The problem with this system is that fathers with the highest wages do not take leave. Such differences between public and private sectors are common in France.

REFERENCES

Algava, E. (2002). Quel temps pour les activités parentales? *Etudes et Résultats* 162. Paris: Drees, Ministère des Affaires Sociales et de la Solidarité.

Aubry, M. (1997). *Projet de loi d'orientation et d'incitation relatif à la réduction du temps de travail*. Exposé des motifs devant l'Assemblée Nationale par Madame M. Aubry, Ministre de l'Emploi et de la Solidarité. Paris: Assemblée Nationale (document No. 512, 11 décembre 1997).

Bourreau-Dubois, C., Guillot, O., & Jankéliowitch-Laval, E. (2001). Le travail à temps partiel féminin et ses déterminants. *Economie et Statistique*, 41–57, 349–350.

Büttner, O., Letablier, M.-T., & Pennec, S. (2002). *L'action publique face aux transformations de la famille en France*. Paris: Rapport de recherche No. 02, Centre d'études de l'emploi.

Esping-Andersen, G. (1990). *The three worlds of welfare capitalism*. Cambridge: Polity Press.

Estrade, H., Méda, D., & Orain, R. (2001). Les effets de la réduction du temps de travail sur les modes de vie. *Premières informations et premieres syntheses* 21–1. Paris: Dares, Ministère de l'emploi et de la solidarité.

Fagnani, J., & Letablier, M.-T. (2003a). La réduction du temps de travail a t-elle amélioré la vie quotidienne des parents de jeunes enfants? *Premières informations et premieres syntheses* 03–1. Paris: Dares, Ministère de l'emploi et de la solidarité.

Fagnani, J., & Letablier, M.-T. (2003b). S'occuper des enfants au quotidien: Mais que font donc les pères? *Droit Social, 3*, 251–259.

Franco, A., & Winqvist, K. (2002). Les hommes et les femmes concilient travail et vie familiale. *Statistiques en bref*, Eurostat, Thème 3, 9/2002.

Gauvin, A., & Jacot, H. (Eds) (1999). *Temps de travail, temps sociaux. Enjeux et modalités de nouveaux compromis*. Paris: Editions Liaisons.

Glaude, M. (1999). L'égalité entre les femmes et les hommes: Où en sommes nous? In: Conseil d'analyse économique (Ed.), *Egalité entre femmes et hommes: Aspects économique* (pp. 71–104). Paris: La documentation Française/CAE 15.

Guillot, O. (2002). Une analyse du recours aux services de garde d'enfants. *Economie et Statistique*, 213–230, 352–353.

Hantrais, L., & Letablier, M.-T. (1996). *Families and family policies in Europe*. London: Longman.

INSEE (Institut national de la statistique et des études économiques) (2000, 2002). *Enquêtes sur l'emploi*. Paris: Ministère de l'Economie, des Finances et de l'Industrie.

Knibiehler, Y. (1997). *La révolution maternelle depuis 1945: Femmes, maternité, citoyenneté*. Paris: Perrin.

Lanquetin, M.-T., Laufer, J., & Letablier, M.-T. (2000). From equality to reconciliation in France? In: L. Hantrais (Ed.), *Gendered policies in Europe: Reconciling employment and family life* (pp. 68–88). London: MacMillan.

Leprince, F. (2003). *L'accueil des jeunes enfants en France. État des lieux et pistes d'amélioration*. Paris: Rapport réalisé à la demande du Haut Conseil de la Population et de la Famille.

Letablier, M.-T., & Jönsson, I. (2003). Kinderbetreuung und politische Handlungslogik. In: U. Gerhard, T. Knijn & A. Weckwert (Eds), *Berufstätige Mütter in Europa, Alltagspraxis und Socialpolitik*. Frankfurt: Beck Verlag.

Letablier, M.-T., Pennec, S., & Büttner, O. (2003). *Opinions, attitudes et aspirations des familles vis-à-vis de la politique familiale en France*. Paris: Rapport de recherche No. 09, Centre d'Etudes de l'Emploi.

Méda, D., & Orain, R. (2002). Transformations du travail et du hors travail: Le jugement des salariés. *Travail et Emploi, 90*, 23–38.

Norvez, A. (1990). *De la naissance à l'école. Santé, modes de garde et préscolarité dans la France contemporaine*. Paris: PUF/Ined (Travaux et documents No. 127).

Pelisse, J. (2002). A la recherche du temps gagné. Les 35 heures entre perceptions, régulations et intégrations professionnelles. *Travail et Emploi, 90*, 7–22.

Rollet-Echallier, C. (1990). *La politique à l'égard de la petite enfance sous la Troisième République*. Paris: Presses Universitaires de France/Institut National d'Etudes Démographiques (coll. Travaux et documents No. 127).

10. THE INFLUENCE OF EUROPEAN UNION LEGISLATION ON LABOUR MARKET EQUALITY FOR WOMEN

Sabine Berghahn

ABSTRACT

This paper describes the legal progress made in European Community law and litigation with regard to women and their problems in labour life. The improvement of European legislation started in the 1970s and was fostered by the European Court of Justice. Gender equality thus was implemented in the legal systems of all the European member states. But the main problem still is translating law into practice. Therefore the top-down strategy of gender mainstreaming and some demands within the new amended "Equal Treatment Directive" (2002/73/EC) could bring further achievements in equality. Structural change, however, is impeded by the background presence of the male breadwinner regime.

INTRODUCTION

Changes in labour laws and their impact on international labour life patterns are hard to describe in a few words. My focus will therefore be on legal developments within the European Union (Berghahn, 2001a, b, 2002; Heide, 1999). The

Changing Life Patterns in Western Industrial Societies
Advances in Life Course Research, Volume 8, 211–230
ISSN: 1040-2608/doi:10.1016/S1040-2608(03)08010-9

Union (EU) includes states with differing societal and labour market structures; specifically, it includes various gender regimes with respect to the division of paid and unpaid work. Similarities and differences between the EU and other highly-industrialised nations, especially the USA or Japan, can thus be quite easily discerned.

First, a word of caution regarding the relationship between changes in industrial and social welfare laws and their empirical outcomes. It is very hard to produce knowledge about causal connections in this area. There has been little research in this field. Connections between legal changes and social changes can at best be established in studies on specific regions and issues and in research focussing on a few individual cases.

In this paper, however, I am concerned with the wider context, namely, the slow but steady progress towards a more egalitarian labour and social law in the member states and its influence on a quantitatively stronger and qualitatively improved participation of women in working life. The first part describes how the process of legislation and litigation was initiated in the European institutions and how it developed. The chapter also reviews specific pieces of European legislation and legal tools against discrimination, and suggests the reasons why it is so complicated to transform law into practice. The second part deals with specific strategies to achieve equality for women, such as gender mainstreaming, pay equity and affirmative action. A third part discusses variations in realisation of women's equal rights, particularly as influenced by the background existence of the male breadwinner model and systems of taxation.

ORIGINS OF GENDER EQUITY LEGISLATION IN THE EUROPEAN UNION

Article 119 of the Treaty of Rome has stipulated equal pay for men and women since the European Community's founding document was signed in 1957. But it was not until the beginning of the 1970s that the European Community (EC)[1] issued numerous further norms in the form of directives intended to ensure equal opportunities for women and men in the labour market and in working life generally.

Developments in the area of gender-sensitive labour and social welfare laws look at first glance very progressive, but there was nothing automatic about the reforms. Rather, they were achieved only through sustained efforts to implement and maintain this normative process. The principle of equal pay, which existed from the very beginning of the European Community, was largely neglected for a long time. Trade unions and employers frequently ignored it and the legislative bodies in the member states also failed to enforce the principle of equal pay.

The situation only began to change when a senior Belgian air hostess, Gabrielle Defrenne, began her campaign opposing the widespread discrimination against women in employment in the end of the 1960s. We have her to thank for a total of three decisions handed down by the European Court of Justice (ECJ) dealing with several aspects of unequal treatment, which Defrenne had to endure.[2] These decisions became historic, although she lost two of the three court actions. They were, however, the first cases dealing with questions of equal pay and equal treatment of women brought to the European Court of Justice by national courts. Pay discrimination at this time had been an especially compelling problem from the viewpoint of female workers and their organisations. Gabrielle Defrenne lost her first claim, because at the time when her law suit came before the ECJ (1970), there was no provision to prevent the Belgian airline Sabena from its habitual practice of discharging female stewardesses at the age of 40, whereas male stewards were allowed to remain in service on airplanes several years longer. She won the second claim and her employer Sabena had to pay her compensation because Defrenne had received a lower wage as a ground hostess than her male colleague who could continue his work in the aircraft service. The ECJ could only be helpful on behalf of the question of equal pay but not in the fight for equal retirement benefits and equal treatment in terms of not being discharged at a lower age. Thus, two of her three claims were rejected by the European Court of Justice because the regulations which prohibit such forms of unequal treatment had not been issued at that time. But her claims challenged the European Commission to draft and pass the first important directives.

When the European legislation process began in the 1970s, the women's movement was gathering strength in many parts of the world, and the discontent and protest it articulated prompted the European Commission to prepare several directives on equal pay (75/117/EEC), equal treatment in access to the labour market and working conditions (76/207/EEC), and equality in the statutory systems of social insurance (79/7/EEC) and in the systems of occupational insurance (86/378/EEC). Although these directives would require many significant changes to the laws of the member states, the Council of the EC agreed unanimously on these directives without veto. Later, in the 1980s and 1990s, it was less easy to pass further directives. The drafts then were often diluted and delayed.

The ideal of the liberal European market still remained the free and flexible worker, who was normally a man. As women were not free and flexible in the same way, the European institutions issued specific directives over the past three decades, for example on pregnant women and breast-feeding mothers at the workplace (89/391/EEC and 92/85/EEC), on parental leave (97/75/EC), on part-time work (97/81/EC), and the burden of proof (97/80/EC). The basic conditions to achieve equality, however, were fixed in the directives on equal pay (75/117/EEC) and equal treatment (76/207/EEC) that were passed in the 1970s and amended in 2002 (2002/73/EC). With the help of these rules the European Community established the basic conditions of protection and promotion of equality within its member states.

The Treaty of Amsterdam and the New Amended "Equal Treatment Directive"

In the Treaty of Amsterdam (1997) the former Article 119 became Article 141; the text and the meaning were also expanded. The article now covers not only equal pay for the "same" work, but also equal pay for "work of equal value." The concept of equal pay was defined more precisely, and there is now a secure justification for the member states of the Union to establish affirmative action, in Europe called "positive measures," for the implementation of "full equality." The member states may introduce new legal measures or retain existing ones, even though such measures bring specific advantages for the under-represented sex and thus formally violate the principle of equal treatment. Within Article 141, Section 4, the possibility for "affirmative action" is envisaged by the EC-Treaty itself, not as before only by an EC-Directive (76/207/EEC). The member states may make use of it, but they need not.

As of 2002, ten separate directives on equal opportunities for women and men in general and on several specific subjects of working life were issued. The most recent represented an important reform of an earlier one, 76/207/EWG from the 1970s, called the "Equal Treatment Directive." The new directive 2002/73/EC[3] entered into force on 5 October 2002 and must be executed by the member states within three years. The member states have to implement the issues of the directive, but they are free in choosing the exact structure of the regulation. Rather controversial were in particular the obligatory implementation of group action in all the member states (now Art. 6, Sec. 3), the introduction of a national body or bodies for the promotion, analysis, monitoring and support of equal treatment of all persons without discrimination on the grounds of sex (now Art. 8a, Sec. 2), and the reach of the provision which demands measures of promotion of equality by private employers (now Art. 8b, Sec. 2).

What began with the action of Gabrielle Defrenne was continued by many more female claimants bringing test cases, and by some male claimants too. National or regional courts frequently brought the most important questions of their suits to the European Court of Justice at Luxembourg to ask for a so-called "preliminary ruling" (Art. 234 ECT, former Art. 177).

Introduction of Legal Tools Against Discrimination

The main issue of equality legislation and justice was the fight against discrimination on the ground of sex. This meant in the first place direct discrimination, "where one person is treated less favourably on grounds of sex than another is, has been or would be treated in a comparable situation" (now defined in Directive 2002/73/EC, Art. Sec. 2). But beyond applying this to several cases the ECJ also developed the concept of "indirect discrimination," indicators to test whether it existed in a given case, and instruments to proceed against it (Bertelsmann, 1994, p. 169).[4] Indirect discrimination on the grounds of sex is held to exist if there are gender-neutral provisions which lead in practice to substantially unequal social results, unless there is a justification for this that is independent of the gender dimension.[5] By using this measure the ECJ established, for example, that the exclusion of part-time workers from the system of occupational pensions contravened EC-principles.[6] The court also voted against the exclusion of part-time workers from interim benefits after leaving the job where such benefits had been promised in union-employer agreements.[7] It further declared the requirement was contrary to EC law that part-time workers had to work twice as long as full-time workers before achieving promotion following a period of probation.[8] The court also held that part-time members of works councils were entitled to full pay when they took part in full-day training.[9] Of great significance was the judgement on the exclusion of part-time workers employed for under ten hours per week from sickness benefits. The problem was exemplified by some German cleaning women whose cases were brought to the ECJ in 1989 (Bertelsmann, 1994, p. 167).[10] The Court held that excluding these workers from sickness benefits was an illegal form of indirect discrimination. In 1986 the Court had already examined the evaluation of different job categories, in particular the criteria for "physically strenuous labour" and their gender specific implications.[11]

In emphasising the Court's decisions against indirect discrimination I do not intend to imply that direct discrimination on the ground of sex no longer exists. On the contrary: it is remarkable how long direct discrimination continued in practice. An example for this is an additional compensation for married male workers (the "wife bonus" or "*Ehefrauenzulage*") in the metallurgical industries of West Berlin (married female workers did not qualify for such additional payment). It was not until 1985 that the German federal industrial tribunal (*Bundesarbeitsgericht*) banned this regulation.[12] Direct discrimination also existed in the practice, commonly adopted by employers, of enquiring if a female job applicant was pregnant.[13] If the employer then found that the woman had falsely denied her pregnancy, he could dismiss her immediately. With the help of the directive 76/207/EEC and the ECJ, however, the member states were forced to abolish this practice. But it took rather a long time for the ECJ to assert itself with this principle. The highest German industrial court for example, the *"Bundesarbeitsgericht,"* tried to keep some exceptions, when a woman competes with other women, not with men, or when she could not even begin her work because of a special protection law in the case of a dangerous working place. It was not until 1992,[14] that the *Bundesarbeitsgericht* dropped the first mentioned exception, and took another 11 years (to 2003) to abandon the second exception.[15]

According to several European directives the member states generally had to implement measures to prevent discrimination and to provide sanctions when the principle of non-discrimination was violated. However, European legislation in this field impacted the actual practice in member states only after some delay, and individual states often avoided consistent regulations in their domestic legislation; loopholes frequently enabled employers to continue discriminatory practices.

It was therefore another slow process requiring many further judgments by the ECJ until the legislation of the member states reflected the standards of European equality law concerning equal treatment and adequate compensation in the case of discrimination. In the Federal Republic of Germany this process took about 18 years. In 1980 an article prohibiting labour market discrimination (§ 611a BGB) was established in the Civil Law Code. However, it fell far short of European standards, first, because the employer was only liable to pay compensation if he/she could be shown to have knowingly or negligently discriminated against female workers and, secondly, because the amount of compensation was ridiculously small. The article therefore became known as the "Porto-Paragraph," which means something like "refunding the postage." After the first judgements of the ECJ[16] in the 1980s, German courts granted compensation of between one and six months' wages, but in 1994 German legislation reduced this to a maximum of three months' wages. A new decision at Luxembourg[17] finally led to an amendment of this article in 1998. The standards of the ECJ – no-fault dependency and adequate compensation – were fulfilled at least at a minimum level. No-fault-dependency means that the discriminated person can get compensation not only if the damage was caused by the fault of the employer but also if the discrimination had been executed blamelessly (without knowledge but would do harm).

In this way the EC-Treaty, the directives and the judgements of the ECJ contributed to the implementation of equality and the enforcement of equal opportunities in the member states. The standards of equal treatment, and the ban on direct and indirect discrimination have forced the member states to transform the traditionally gendered aspects of their legal systems into a gender-neutral mode of regulation. Typical male jobs, such as officers in the armed forces[18] and night work,[19] were opened to women (2000 and 1991), and sexual harassment was declared to be a form of discrimination (see the directive 2002/73/EC).

The biggest winners were part-time workers of whom the vast majority are women (Eurostat, 2002). The ban on indirect discrimination substantially increased their rights and opportunities. The improvement in their legal position in European law has gone hand-in-hand with an expansion of part-time work in European countries, though not to the same extent in all countries (see Chaps 6 and 7 in this book.) The starting point for improvement was the fact that these women definitely had the status of workers with the same general rights as their male colleagues in full-time jobs.

The Main Problem of the European Laws: Translating Law Into Practice

A comparative research project was carried out in the early 1990s on the "Utilisation of Sex Equality Litigation Procedures in the member states of the European Community" by Judith Blom, Barry Fitzpatrick, Jeanne Gregory and others; their second report was delivered in 1995 (Blom et al., 1995). The research group looked at the twelve member states of the Union before the addition of Sweden, Finland, and Austria. Even though these empirical results are between eight and ten years old, it would be too optimistic to see them as being completely outdated by now. We should rather proceed on the assumption that the societal practice of equal opportunity is limping far behind the progress of law.

The results of the research from the 1990s are dispiriting. Blom et al. wrote: "The vast bulk of the national legislation was enacted in order to comply with European law, following EU membership or in anticipation of membership. This has resulted in an information gap: these relatively sophisticated laws were delivered to women from an authority outside their own governments and were only in small part (for example in the U.K. and Ireland) the product of national campaigns involving the women's movement. Consequently women initially had very little sense of ownership of this legislation and it is taking time for them to become aware of its significance" (Blom et al., 1995, p. 6). "Although the principle of equality has been acknowledged as a fundamental right in Community Law and enshrined within the national legal systems of all the member states, there are many factors, social, economic and political, as well as legal, which will facilitate or impede the realisation of this principle in practice" (Blom et al., 1995, p. 7).

The research group found that, in general, knowledge and understanding of sex equality laws were low throughout the Community, although in most member states the situation was showing signs of improvement. In Spain, Luxembourg and Portugal, however, awareness of the legislation seemed to be particularly low. The authors pointed out that cultural, social and economic factors in these countries create a climate which is generally antagonistic to the principle of equality (Blom et al., 1995, p. 6). In Denmark and the Netherlands there was a recent shift in political focus away from sex equality in the labour market towards family policies informed by the need to achieve a balance between work and family life. With respect to Germany the group pointed out that the old states that made up the former Federal Republic of Germany – and also in the meantime the new states created on the territory of the former German Democratic Republic after unification – have established equality agencies at the local and state level and have also required public bodies to establish equality ombudswomen. Reports from experts in the individual countries reveal a very wide spectrum of problems and political strategies to counteract discrimination. They provide ample evidence of the crucial importance of government initiatives in helping to increase awareness and promote positive attitudes in relation to sex equality.

The report shows that the existence of discrimination does not necessarily precipitate action to challenge it. On the contrary, an employee needs to be aware of her rights and feel reasonably secure in her employment – or to have already left – before she has the confidence to consider taking action (Blom et al., 1995, p. 8). There is, for example, evidence of widespread sexual harassment in all member states and although more women are now coming forward on this issue, it still remains a largely hidden area of discrimination, particularly in Spain and Greece.

In the Netherlands, the United Kingdom (U.K.) and also in Ireland a high proportion of cases are resolved without the help of ordinary courts, because of the existence of Equal Treatment Commissions (Netherlands, United Kingdom) or Equality Officers (Ireland). In other member states, where these quasi-judicial proceedings carried out by special commissions do not exist, the procedures for settling complaints are for the most part unsatisfactory. In Germany and the U.K., the level of settlements in sex equality cases is generally lower than in other areas of labour law; however, the research group had evidence of a high level of settlements in equal value cases (work of comparable worth) although these do not occur frequently.

These disappointing results are connected to the fact that even if the formal procedures for equality litigation are in place, in many member states the possibilities of enforcing an equality claim through the judicial process is limited by a number of factors. At all stages, from initiation of the complaint to the final award of compensation for the discriminatory treatment, the person has to fight on her own assisted only by her lawyer. The research group therefore came to the conclusion that a "group justice model" of equality would "enormously enhance the opportunities for effective utilisation of equality litigation across the Member States" (Blom et al., 1995, p. 21).

If we compare the findings from Blom et al. with the current situation of regulations in the European Union, the picture looks somewhat brighter today.

The new directive on equal treatment (2002/73/EC) demands from the member states that they implement the possibility of group action (Art. 6 Sec. 3). In the future, organisations and associations will be entitled to support individual complainants in their administrative or judicial procedure or even act on behalf of them.

RECENT DEVELOPMENTS AND STRATEGIES TO ACHIEVE EQUALITY IN EUROPEAN LAW

We have seen that the utilisation of equality laws has not come very far and has still to fight against many serious obstacles in practice. European equality laws do not work very efficiently, and some feminists have also expressed a fundamental criticism of the concept of "symmetric equality" in the law of the European Community (Schunter-Kleemann, 2001). Symmetric equality mainly means strictly equal treatment of women and men.

The Strategy of Gender Mainstreaming

Nevertheless feminists should be aware of the potential value of EU legal instruments and in particular how these are implemented through gender main-streaming.[20] Gender mainstreaming is a mostly top-down management strategy for institutions and enterprises that integrates the principle of gender equality into everyday practices. In the view of the Council of Europe (Council of Europe 1998, cited by Woodward, 2001, p. 6), gender mainstreaming is defined as the reorganisation, improvement, development and evaluation of policy processes, so that a gender equality perspective is incorporated in all policies at all levels and at all stages, by actors normally involved in policy making (Woodward, 2001, p. 6). More practically it means that the promotion of equal rights for both genders should be integrated into all political fields and programmes at all administrative levels. This begins with the preparation of proposals, plans and programmes, which must include a separate analysis of the effects on women and men of the decisions planned before those decisions are finalized (Woodward, 2001, p. 7). To achieve mainstreaming has become a kind of official mission for feminist thinkers and feminist agencies looking for the next step in progress for women in the advanced countries.

Gender mainstreaming is anchored in the Treaty of Amsterdam (1997) in Art. 3, Sec. 2 of the EC-Treaty. There is now an explicit requirement to demonstrate gender awareness in applications for support under the European Social Fund

(Woodward, 2001, p. 10). Since 1997 the so-called European guidelines of employment policy have been established and renewed annually by the member states. Each member country has to draw up a "National Plan of Action" according to the European guidelines. Within these guidelines there are four important pillars of action of which the enforcement of equality and equal opportunity for women and men is one of the four. Beyond this, the gender-equality goal is also embedded in each of the other three objectives: improvement of employability, development of entrepreneurship, adjustment of the companies and their employees to modern economic development (Maier, 2002, p. 66).

On the one hand, gender mainstreaming is held out as a new hope by "femocrats," as the women's movement activists, feminist academics and politicians are sometimes called. But on the other hand, the principle of gender mainstreaming has become increasingly controversial. Alison E. Woodward writes: "The flurry of definitions indicates part of the danger, as the same word means very different things in different governmental contexts. Some interpret the approach as meaning that vertical institutions for equal opportunity policy will necessarily disappear, thanks to the change in attitude in policy making that mainstreaming would bring about. The risk has become so potent that the European Commission femocrats have increasingly had to emphasise that gender mainstreaming involves an active dual or twin-track strategy. Specific policies addressing specific women's issues will continue to exist and, as the European Parliament (resolution A 4–0072/99) suggests, even be strengthened, at the same time as mainstreaming is promoted. The intention was that "resources to remedy gender inequality would be increased, but the risk is that with mainstreaming, gender issues might simply disappear" (Woodward, 2001, p. 11).

For the legal context, gender mainstreaming is supposed to be a politically helpful instrument, as long as it is not used as an excuse to weaken the traditional feminist strategy of equal opportunity and affirmative action. In most of the cases gender mainstreaming does not lead to a specific decision or result, because it is a merely "proceduralistic" strategy. The governments are bound by an obligation, but its substantial content then is vague and open to several interpretations and solutions. And we must keep in mind that gender mainstreaming is a top-down-strategy for the management of administrations and enterprises, not in the first step an instrument for the persons who are disadvantaged and treated unequally to improve their conditions. In the future it will therefore still be important to build and extend bottom-up structures, which favour equal rights litigation, i.e. to support networks for test cases and group action (class action) in European countries. This is especially important in those countries which have little experience of social and civil rights movements, where women will have the opportunity to make use of the growing body of case law and of the litigation process.

Equal Pay and the Concept of Indirect Discrimination

Since the process of legislation started with the subject of equal pay for men and women, probably most of the victories women won at the ECJ were achieved in this area.

Yet a special field where the litigation strategy could be improved is the fight for equal pay for work of equal value (comparable worth). This option results from the ban on indirect discrimination in European law. Meanwhile direct discrimination has largely been abolished and there are no regulations left which provide different rulings for women and men, except rulings about cases of pregnancy or maternity. As it is rather easy to abolish direct discrimination simply by removing those provisions that enshrine it, the vast bulk of indirect discrimination is left as the result of old traditions of unequal treatment and devaluation of female work. Thus, there is still a lot of structural inequality left in the legal systems of the member countries. Especially in the field of collective bargaining and union agreements the methods of classification and valuing of jobs are not yet gender-neutral but still favour male work as harder, heavier, or more demanding and therefore due higher pay. In the fight against this form of "doing gender" in labour agreements or individual contracts, the concept of indirect discrimination has a greater potential than has hitherto been realised. According to the ECJ, some EC-directives and related national laws, the instrument of tracing indirect discrimination makes it possible to mark union agreements as discriminating, if there is statistical evidence that they were built in disadvantage to one sex. For example, if most of the women in a company or in the reach of a specific union agreement happen to be put in lower wage groups whereas most of the men are found in the higher ranks of payment, it is a sign of discrimination unless the result can be explained by objective reasons that are not related to gender stereotypes.

While those instruments of litigation exist, nevertheless international comparisons reveal tremendous differences in the awareness of and activities against unequal pay for women. We should distinguish between the older conception which is based on individual court-centred litigation on one side and the newer conception of campaigning for "pay equity" on the other. In this latter strategy the procedure to evaluate the worth of labour and to bargain on pay is crucial. In Scandinavian states and also in France some steps have been taken in this direction: governments and trade unions are obliged to report on pay relations in regard to men and women. More and better steps have been taken in Canada and the U.S. (Winter, 1998).

The issue of equal pay for work of comparable value therefore is a field in which efforts have been made to apply the strategy of fighting against indirect discrimination. In this way it may be possible not only to achieve formal equality but to transform the idea into practice and actually to change working patterns by upgrading the value of female work and therefore improving the real conditions of life.

Affirmative Action

Whereas the development of European legislation and the decisions of the ECJ were regarded in the past as rather positive, especially in the 1980s, because the European institutions forced recalcitrant member states to take fundamental steps in the right direction, the jurisdiction of the European Court of Justice in the 1990s has been less enthusiastically received. In the view of feminist jurists the ECJ has partly undermined its own idea of equality. The "Kalanke" case,[21] in particular, prompted vociferous protest. For the first time at the ECJ this lawsuit dealt with explicit affirmative action legislation, the so-called "quota clause." The case came from the German city state of Bremen. The clause said that a female applicant for a regular position in the civil service should be favoured, if she had a qualification equal to that of her male competitor and if women were under-represented in the particular wage group or group of positions the person was applying for. In the case of Eckart Kalanke the German Federal Labour Court (*Bundesarbeits-gericht*) had referred in 1993 to the ECJ for a preliminary ruling under Article 177 EEC Treaty on the interpretation of Article 2, Sec. 1 and 4 of Council Directive 76/207/EEC.

The Case: Eckart Kalanke and Heike Glissmann were horticultural employees of the Parks Department at Bremen. The two persons applied for the post of a Section Manager in the Parks Department. The Staff Committee refused to give its consent to Mr. Kalanke's promotion, proposed by the Parks Department management. Reference to arbitration resulted in a recommendation in favour of Mr. Kalanke. The Staff Committee then stated that the arbitration had failed and appealed to the conciliation board which, in a decision binding on the employer, considered that the two candidates were equally qualified and that priority should therefore be given, in accordance with the Bremen Gender Equality Law (*Landesgleichstellungsgesetz*, LGG), to the woman. Eckart Kalanke claimed that he was better qualified than Heike Glissmann and that the quota system was incompatible with German and European law. But his application was dismissed by the Labour Court (*Arbeitsgericht*) and again, on appeal, by the Regional Labour Court (*Landesarbeitsgericht*). The Federal Labour Court then asked for a preliminary ruling on the question whether the LGG was compatible with European law, especially the directive 76/207/EEC. The ECJ answered that under the quota clause of Bremen, women are "automatically to be given priority" and judged it as a violation of the principle of equal treatment.[22]

The quota clause can indeed be classified as an exception to the strict rule of equal treatment, since it operates in favour of the under-represented sex in order to achieve equal opportunity for women. It establishes a priority for hiring a woman in the civil service when there are more men than women in comparable positions and the female applicant is equally qualified in comparison to the male applicant. At the time of the first quota decision, in October 1995, affirmative action was only covered by the old directive 76/207/EEC from the 1970s. The question then was, whether Art. 2, Sec. 4 of the directive 76/207/EEC, which stated an exception from the strict principle of equal treatment, would be seen as covering the quota clause. Art. 2, Sec. 4 stated that the directive "shall be without prejudice to measures to promote equal opportunity for men and women, in particular by removing existing inequalities which affect women's opportunities." The ECJ, however, found in 1995 that this provision only permitted a form of promotion, which gave a "specific advantage to women with a view to improving their ability to compete on the labour market and to pursue a career on an equal footing with men."[23] As the "derogation from an individual right" laid down in the Directive, Art. 2, Sec. 4, must be "interpreted strictly" the court found the Bremen quota clause went "beyond promoting equal opportunities" and overstepped the limits of the exception.[24] Therefore the ECJ rejected the quota clause in 1995 and gave a rather restrictive interpretation to admissible affirmative action.

Protest against this decision by many female politicians from different countries, by journalists, female trade unionists, and other activists led to an improvement within the Treaty of Amsterdam in 1997. The exception from the principle of equal treatment was then formulated as Section 4 of Article 141, to permit more serious measures in favour of the under-represented sex. Thus, the political development also led in 1997 to a new judgement in a case involving a quota regulation. The deciding case involved legislation passed by another of the German states, North Rhine-Westphalia. In this case, brought on behalf of a male person "Helmut Marschall," the ECJ held that the quota clause conformed to European equality law.[25] Although this case had to be resolved under the old version of the Equal Treatment Directive (76/207/EEC), the decision was quite different from that in the case of Kalanke.

The difference between the two pieces of legislation in Bremen and North Rhine-Westphalia was a so-called clause of individual hardship (*"persönliche Härteklausel"*). The new judgement of the ECJ allayed criticism of the earlier decision; the derogation clause under the directive was now interpreted differently. The equality law of North Rhine Westphalia had provided a quota with the same conditions for promotion but it contained an additional clause of individual hardship. Priority should be given to an equally qualified woman under the condition of under-representation of women, unless the personal consequences for the man result in greater hardship. It is obvious that the court had changed its opinion rather extensively and now judged the quota clause as permissible under European law. In 2000 the court continued its ruling by a further decision on the equality law of Hesse, another of the German states (case of Badeck et al.).[26] This law contains an affirmative action clause, which mainly refers to a specific procedure of bringing more women into the higher ranks of administration *(Frauenförderpläne)* if they are still under-represented there. This procedure was also judged as compatible with European law.

In the same year, however, a Swedish quota clause was again rejected (case of Abrahamsson et al.).[27] The clause had been included in a law on equal opportunities for women at universities, because their under-representation was very apparent in higher education, even in Sweden. On the basis of this law a woman could be appointed over a better-qualified male applicant, provided she had the necessary minimum qualifications for the position and was "not much less qualified" than her male competitor. In this case the ECJ insisted on the condition that the priority to the woman could be given only if the qualifications of the two competitors are exactly equal.

To summarise: The ECJ requires three conditions to be met if a quota clause in the field of access to jobs is to be deemed in accordance with European law: first, the person claiming priority must belong to the underrepresented sex; secondly, there must be a procedure for checking and verifying all individual aspects and potential hardships of each competitor, so that in case of tremendous hardship the job can be given to this person, even when belonging to the better represented sex; and third, the person must be (exactly) as well qualified as his or her competitor of the opposite sex. The European Court of Justice has, however, scrupulously refrained from indicating the criteria by which personal hardship is to be judged. It merely states that personal hardship cannot be adduced on the basis of criteria that in themselves are indirectly discriminatory, and leaves the precise scope of personal hardship to the case law of the individual member states. In so doing, the ECJ opens a "back door," since national courts are often supportive of the practice of companies and the civil service viewing the "breadwinner" role of the male job applicant as decisive. Such considerations will almost always result in indirect discrimination against women, and it is to be feared that, given the vaguely-worded decisions of the ECJ, employers and the national courts will opt for such a traditional interpretation.

Only a few member states make use of such clauses. These restrictions show after all how small and narrow the field is on which affirmative action can lead to new patterns in the labour market. Therefore there is no evidence that the very slowly increasing number and ratio of qualified women in higher positions of occupational life is the result of such legal measures. Perhaps more women will be employed in qualified jobs under the mandate of such clauses in Germany, Austria or Sweden, where quota legislation exists; but in other countries governments have shown themselves to be very reserved towards affirmative action.

The New Amended Directive on Equal Treatment: A Basis for Group Action

Thus, it remains the main field of activity of European anti-discrimination laws to prevent states and employers from discriminating against women and men on grounds of sex either directly or indirectly and to enforce equal treatment. After the Treaty of Amsterdam entered into force (in May 1999), women's interest groups and special experts of the European Parliament and the European Commission campaigned for a reform of the old directive 76/207/EEC, arguing that the progress represented by the renewed Article 141 in the EC-Treaty and a lot of improved details from the judgements of the ECJ should be included in the directive. Within the new directive 2002/73/EC, in force since October 2002, all forms of discrimination are now explicitly defined, among them sexual harassment. As only scant regard has been paid to the ban on discrimination until now, the new directive contains many principles which have been worked out by the ECJ in the past decades concerning such issues as non-discriminatory treatment of pregnant workers, or the criteria for effective compensation or reparation in the case of loss or damage sustained by a person as a result of discrimination.

In addition to the regulations about compensation and judicial or administrative procedures, including appropriate conciliation procedures, there is also a new obligation for the states to ensure that associations, organisations, or other legal entities may engage either on behalf of or in support of the complainant, with his or her approval, in any judicial and/or administrative procedure (Art. 6, Sec. 3). This means that in the future, group action (i.e. class action) will be possible in all countries of the EU. If, for example, a union agreement contains provisions which discriminate against women in an indirect manner, it can be challenged in court not only by individuals but also by women's interest associations. This will help to bring discriminatory practices to court in cases where the individual person directly affected does not dare to take legal action. In this way, a long-standing demand of feminist jurists will be fulfilled.

VARIATIONS IN REALISATION OF
WOMEN'S EQUAL RIGHTS

A further aspect of feminist discontent with the existing norms and the dispensation of the ECJ concerns the structures of the social security systems. In most of the member states one can still find hidden exclusions and indirect discriminations resulting from the model of the male breadwinner. One need only think of the division of benefits, of the dilemma in connection with the widow's pension, and the fact that more women than men are dependent on maintenance from their partner.

The Background Presence of the Male Breadwinner Model

Even though the judgements of the ECJ on subjects of social insurance and social welfare law are not uniform, it is clear that in this area the court has not shown the same determination to eradicate traditional forms of discrimination as it has in its decisions on labour law (Bieback, 1996/1997). The directive 79/7/EEC is seen as a rather weak foundation for measures against discrimination. There have been some disappointing judgements in the nineties, especially when the court accepted the justifications of its member state Germany for excluding part-time employees working very low hours (under 15 hours) from the social insurance system.[28] Even though this exclusion was regarded as a form of indirect discrimination, the court accepted the reasons for the regulation as "gender-neutral" and justified them by objective arguments. Nevertheless the exclusion of the part-time workers, of whom the majority were women, from social security benefits was obviously based on the traditional male breadwinner model. If the court had to decide about similar cases in the field of employment relations, it surely would not have accepted such arguments for the exclusion from equal payment. But in the field of social security systems the idea of sovereign member states and the EU-principle of subsidiarity were more dominant than the idea of the liberal market on which men and women should earn equal wages in order to prevent the competition between companies from being distorted by sex discrimination. Subsidiarity means in this context that if there is a competing competence for the EU and the member states to pass legislation, the power of ruling is given in the first place to the member states, because they are nearer to and more familiar with the particular problems.

Whereas the main issue of the early years of the European Community legislation and jurisdiction was to achieve equal conditions for economic competition, and equal rights and equal duties for workers of both sexes and employers in all the member states, the efforts to influence the structure of the different national security systems are not so strong. As it is very complicated and expensive to transform the statutory systems, the goal of the European Union is not adjustment of the different systems but only coordination of some aspects in order to guarantee the freedom of movement. In the field of the social security systems it seems as if the financing problems of the states in combination with the fact that men and women still play segregated roles in work and family are also influencing the decision making of the court in a traditional way. Therefore the ECJ does not intervene with the same intensity as in the field of direct conditions of employment.

In most of the social welfare systems in Europe many elements are still based on the idea that women do not need their wages for themselves or for their family as urgently as the male breadwinner does. Many individuals and institutions still assume that women, at least if they are married, are not supposed to be fully self-supporting breadwinners. In this view, there is no need to give them full pay and the full set of opportunities which is normally granted to male workers. This structural asymmetry is not mainly produced by labour law; rather, the working patterns of women are influenced more strongly by the system of taxation, by social security regulations, and in some respects also by family law.

In particular, the system of taxation and social contributions influences the personal decision of a family worker to take up a job as a second breadwinner in the family. Within the connections between family law and social security provisions there is another meaning of subsidiarity. Here the word means that the individual, who is not able to earn his/her living, only gets social benefits from the state at a minimum level if there is no husband or relative who has to pay maintenance for the person. As there are such duties of paying maintenance especially between husband and wife, the social security systems in most of the European countries still rely very solidly on the old principle of maintenance and subsidiarity. Where this principle is executed rather strictly, as in Germany, this means a structural disadvantage for women, because a married woman is unlikely to get access to these social benefits except at a minimum level when her husband has to pay for her maintenance. In this case she keeps being dependent on her husband even if she is already divorced and there is only a small amount of legal and social help for her to return to the labour market. Although the statutory regulations now are formulated in a gender-neutral manner, in most of the cases women are the dependent persons, as they have a structurally disadvantaged position on the labour market.

CONCLUSIONS

To give a summary: Without the development of European equality law the legal systems of the member states would not be so far advanced as they are by now. In most areas of labour law the impact of European legislation and jurisdiction helped women to enter the labour market and to improve their working conditions, especially as part-time workers. European law also managed to facilitate reconciliation between work and family, but only to a small extent. Women's work and life patterns are thus being influenced by the slow development of legal instruments and their use, although the realisation of equal rights is still limping behind the law, and legislation is in the best case following social change by a distance of some years.

The main issue of European equity law is simple as well as crucial: it says that women and men are to be treated equally and that discrimination on the grounds of sex is prohibited. A new amended directive (2002/73/EC) has entered into force recently and must be translated into national legislation within three years. It contains some hopeful provisions, such as the implementation of "group action" and of a national body to review the laws in practise and to support individuals and interest groups. The future potential of the principle of non-discrimination lies in the opportunity for interest groups to draw attention to hidden disadvantages for women. With the help of the existing tool to uncover "indirect discrimination" it will be possible to fight against discrimination which is still enshrined in the structure of many regulations and union agreements. Although there are great differences between the legal and social security systems in the European Union with respect to the "gender regime" within a society, many traditional similarities can also be found. With the exception of the Scandinavian states most of the European countries are still influenced by structural elements of the traditional male breadwinner model, which can be found particularly in the social security system and its connections to family law and taxation. As it is the feminist aim to weaken the male breadwinner model, it will be useful to develop a specific transformation plan for every different system. In this field the law of the European Union provides a wide framework, while the concept and the details of transformation must be designed in various and different ways as appropriate to each of the member states.

NOTES

1. Since the Treaty of Maastricht (1992) there has existed a European Union, as the political form of the European Community. The Treaty of Rome (1957) marked the founding of the European Economic Community, which since 1992 has styled itself the European Community. There are separate treaties on political cooperation (Treaty of the European Union) and economic and social cooperation (Treaty of the European Community). Since the Treaty of Amsterdam (1997) the Articles of the EC-Treaty are newly numbered, the former Art. 119 became Art. 141.

2. C-80/70, Defrenne I, 25.5.1971, Rec. 1971, p. 445; C-43/75, Defrenne II, 8.4.1976, Rec. 1976, p. 455; C-179/75, Defrenne III, 15.6.1978, Rec. 1978, p. 1365.

3. "Amending Council Directive 76/207/EEC on the implementation of the principle of equal treatment for men and women as regards access to employment, vocational training and promotion, and working conditions," OJ, 5.10.2002, 45. Vol., L 269, p. 15–20.

4. Applied by the ECJ for the first time to sex equality cases in: C-96/80, Jenkins, 31.3.1981, Rec. 1981, p. 911.

5. For the definition of indirect discrimination see Art. 2, Sec. 2 of the directive.

6. C-170/84, Bilka Kaufhaus, 13.5.1986, Rec. 1986, p. 1607.
7. C-33/89, Kowalska, 27.6.1990, Rec. 1990, p. I-2591.
8. C-184/89, Nimz, 7.2.1991, Rec. 1991, p. I-297.
9. C-360/90, Bötel, 4.6.1992, Rec. 1992, p. I-3589.
10. C-171/88, Rinner-Kühn, 13.7.1989, Rec. 1989, p. I-2743.
11. C-237/85, Rummler, 1.7.1986, Rec. 1986, p. 2101.
12. BAG, 13.11.1985, see *STREIT- feministische Rechtszeitschrift*, 1986, p. 132–134, with a remark by Ninon Colneric.
13. C-177/88, Dekker, 8.11.1990, Rec. 1990, p. I-3941; C-421/92, Habermann-Beltermann, 5.5.1994, Rec. 1994, p. I-1657; C-32/93, Webb 1994, 14.7.1994, Rec. 1994, p. I-3567; C-207/98, Mahlburg, 3.2.2000, Rec. 2000, p. I-549., C-438/99, Melgar, 4.10.2001, Rec. 2001, p. I-6915; C-109/00, Tele Danmark, 4.10.2001, Rec. 2001, p. I-7545.
14. Bundesarbeitsgericht, 15.10.1992, 2 AZR 227/92, STREIT, Vol.1–2, p. 51.
15. Bundesarbeitsgericht, press information 6.2.2003, 2 AZR 621/01.
16. C-14/83, Colson and Kamann, 10.4.1984, Rec. 1984, p. 1891; C-177/88, Dekker, 8.11.1990, Rec. 1990, p. I-3941.
17. C-180/95, Draehmpaehl, 22.4.1997, Rec. 1997, p. I-2195.
18. C-285/98, Kreil, 11.1.2000, Rec. 2000, p. I-69.
19. C-345/89, Stoeckel, 25.7.1991, Rec. 1991, p. I-4047.
20. European Commission: *Towards a Community Framework Strategy on Gender Equality (2001-2005)*, COM (2000) 335 final. See also Woodward (2001); Bothfeld/Gronbach/Riedmüller ed. (2002); Nohr/Veth ed. (2002).
21. C-450/93, Kalanke, 17.10.1995, Rec. 1995, p. I-3051.
22. C-450/93, Kalanke, 17.10.1995, Rec. 1995, p. I-3051, no. 16.
23. C-450/93, Kalanke, 17.10.1995, Rec. 1995, p. I-3051, no. 19.
24. C-450/93, Kalanke, 17.10.1995, Rec. 1995, p. I-3051, no. 21, 22.
25. C-409/95, Marschall, 11.11.1997, Rec. 1997, p. I-6363.
26. C-158/97, Badeck, 28.3.2000, Rec. 2000, p. I-1875.
27. C-407/98, Abrahamsson and Anderson, 6.7.2000, Rec. 2000, p. I-5539.
28. C-317/93, Nolte, 14.12.1995, Rec. 1995, p. I-4625; C-444/93, Megner and Scheffel, 14.12.1995, Rec. 1995, p. I-4741.

REFERENCES

Berghahn, S. (2001a). Auf Adlers Schwingen oder auf dem Rücken des Stiers? Zum Vorankommen von Frauen- und Gleichheitsrechten in der Europäischen Union. In: E. Kreisky, S. Lang & B. Sauer (Ed.), *EU. Geschlecht. Staat* (pp. 231–249). Wien: Facultas Verlag.
Berghahn, S. (2001b). *Ehe als Übergangsarbeitsmarkt?* WZB-Discussion Paper, FS I 01–207, Berlin.
Berghahn, S. (2002). Supranationaler Reformimpuls vs. mitgliedstaatliche Beharrlichkeit. *Aus Politik und Zeitgeschichte*, 33–34, 29–37.
Bertelsmann, K. (1994). Ein Weg zur Verwirklichung? – Der Europäische Gerichtshof und die Entgeltgleichheit. In: R. Winter (Ed.), *Frauen Verdienen Mehr* (pp. 163–184). Berlin: Edition Sigma.
Bieback, K.-J. (1996/1997). *Die mittelbare Diskriminierung wegen des Geschlechts. Ihre Grundlagen im Recht der EU und ihre Auswirkungen auf das Sozialrecht der Mitgliedstaaten.* Baden-Baden: Nomos Verlag. English version: *Indirect Sex Discrimination Within the Meaning of Directive*

(CE) 79/7 in the Social Security Law of the Member States, V/1333/96-EN, Brussels, European Commission, 1996.

Blom, J., Fitzpatrick, B., Gregory, J., Knegt, R., & O'Hare, U. (1995). *The Utilisation of Sex Equality Litigation Procedures in the Member States of the European Community*. Edited by the European Commission, Directorate-General V, Employment, Industrial Relations and Social Affairs, Equal Opportunity Unit, June 1995, Brussels.

Bothfeld, S., Gronbach, S., & Riedmüller, B. (Eds) (2002). *Gender Mainstreaming – eine Innovation in der Gleichstellungspolitik?* Frankfurt/New York: Campus Verlag.

Eurostat (2002). Beschäftigungsquoten und Arbeitskräfteerhebung der Gemeinschaft, www.europa. eu.int/comm/e (accessed June 26, 2002).

Heide, I. (1999). Supranational action against sex discrimination: Equal pay and equal treatment in the European Union. *International Labour Review, 138*, 381–410.

Maier, F. (2002). Gleichstellungspolitische Fortschritte durch Europäische Beschäftigungsstrategie und Gender Mainstreaming? In: F. Maier & A. Fiedler (Ed.), *Gender Matters. Feministische Analysen zur Wirtschafts- und Sozialpolitik* (pp. 61–87). Berlin: Edition Sigma.

Nohr, B., & Veth, S. (Ed.) (2002). *Gender Mainstreaming – Kritische Reflexionen einer neuen Strategie*. Berlin: Dietz Verlag.

Schunter-Kleemann, S. (2001). Euro-Club und Reglement der Geschlechter. In: E. Kreisky, S. Lang & B. Dauer (Eds), *EU. Geschlecht. Staat* (pp. 171–184). Wien: Facultas Verlag.

Winter, R. (1998). *Gleiches Entgelt für gleichwertige Arbeit. Ein Prinzip ohne Praxis*. Baden-Baden: Nomos Verlag.

Woodward, A. E. (2001). *Gender Mainstreaming in European Policy: Innovation or Deception?* WZB-Discussion Paper, FS I 01–103, Berlin.

11. THE WELFARE STATE AND TIME ALLOCATION IN SWEDEN, DENMARK, FRANCE, AND ITALY

Jens Bonke and Elke Koch-Weser

ABSTRACT

This chapter examines the allocation of time from a welfare state perspective, and asks whether the ordinary welfare regime models are appropriate for the understanding of diversity in everyday life between European countries. The study investigates the time-allocation of the working-age population in Sweden, Denmark, France, and Italy and explains the variation as a function of socio-economic characteristics and of differential policy constraints. Family obligations are still more important in southern and middle-European countries than in Scandinavian countries, and therefore, contribute to women's working-life and family-life dilemma. The empirical analyses re-examine data from national time-use surveys in connection with data from the European Community Household Panel.

INTRODUCTION

The present study was launched to compare the macro-micro interfaces prevalent in Denmark and Italy, which are assumed to be conditioned by two contrasting welfare state regimes described in the literature as "social-democratic" and "conservative" (the latter with a particularly Mediterranean family-based content).

Changing Life Patterns in Western Industrial Societies
Advances in Life Course Research, Volume 8, 231–253
© 2004 Published by Elsevier Ltd.
ISSN: 1040-2608/doi:10.1016/S1040-2608(03)08011-0

The statistical material upon which analyses are based are presented also for Sweden and France in order to better document and sustain the argument of diverging tendencies. The data are drawn from Time Budget Surveys and from data-sets produced by the European Community Household Panel. For further information about the data applied in this chapter, see Bonke and Koch-Weser (2001).

After a brief theoretical examination of welfare regimes in Europe, the first part of the paper traces characteristics of the four countries and the impact of public policy constraints upon the extent of labour force participation. Against this background, time allocation within couples of husbands and wives (or cohabiting partners) is analyzed as a function of labour supply and of number of children. Recurring to a causal model, determinants of household and market work are established. Next, the analysis explores the impact of these adopted solutions on personal satisfaction or eventual feelings of discontent. The report concludes with implications of the various forms of caring obligations for the gender-based division of labour, thereby touching on a particularly significant issue in the current welfare state debate.

THEORIES ON EUROPEAN WELFARE REGIMES

In the discussion of contemporary Western societies, welfare state theory has played an important role in identifying and explaining their development. It is generally believed that the modernization or industrialization process in capitalist societies and the political agency of social democratic parties or class alliances have been the basis for the establishment of the welfare state and, thereby, have made a significant contribution to the improvement of employees' working conditions. Furthermore, the welfare state has brought an immense increase in welfare expenditures, which has enforced its capacity to modify class and economic status differences.

In the literature, different typologies have been proposed to understand the differences and similarities between present welfare societies. Thus, Esping-Andersen (1990) distinguishes between three different welfare state regimes: the liberal, the conservative-corporative, and the social-democratic regime. The characteristics of the liberal regime are the minimizing of the role of the state, the individualization of responsibilities and risks, and the utmost promotion of the market. This means that social policy in liberal regimes gives low priority to citizens' entitlements and rights. The liberal regime has for the same reason been called a residual regime, which favours means-testing or income-testing of social assistance. The liberal model assumes that social services are a task for the market to regulate as an individual responsibility, which does not mean, however, that the state is not involved, since it contributes by giving tax-concessions to individuals or to group life insurance and benefit plans.

The social-democratic welfare regime is characterized by modern entitlement programs, which follow a more traditional social assistance system. This model had its roots in poor relief programs, as was found in Britain in the early days. The universalistic approach to risk-sharing has become its distinctive mark together with generous benefit levels and egalitarian ideals and rights based on citizenship (Esping-Andersen, 1990; Stephens, 1994). The social-democratic regime has made a great effort to de-commodify welfare through redistributive policies and, thereby, minimize market dependency. Furthermore, an infrastructure of care-giving was established in the 1970s and 1980s in the Nordic countries, especially aimed at day care for small children and aged people. These programs contributed to the increasing employment of women during that period.

Conservative regimes have been influenced by Christian-democratic or conservative coalitions in the postwar period that stress a mixture of status demarcation and familism. Their roots are less egalitarian and are built on a legacy that was authoritarian, status-based, or corporatist and relied on the principle of subsidiarity. The legacy of status privilege is seen in the special place accorded the public civil service, which is found in Austria, Belgium, France, Germany and Italy (Esping-Andersen, 1999).

In the southern European countries social policy based on familism is strong and is reflected in distribution of social benefits to the male breadwinner, which means that they have to be regarded not as individual benefits but as a family social wage. The family is the caregiver and is ultimately responsible for the family members' welfare. This social assistance will not be granted to adult children if their parents can support them; and only in case of family failure is social assistance given. In the liberal regime market failure is the factor that releases public social assistance.

In spite of this rich typology of welfare state regimes the family is rarely treated as an independent societal institution in welfare state theory, a fact that has raised criticism among feminist researchers (Daly, 1996). They claim that to understand the public systems of state welfare, the connection to welfare within the household/family system must be explicated, and this holds for the understanding of the structure of welfare policy as well. The welfare state is also heavily dependent on arrangements outside the formal economy and on services provided by women, and thereby relies on the immense amount of unpaid work within the family. Furthermore, the modern welfare state has not displaced effectively all the families' welfare responsibilities for which the family is still important provider of goods and services (Sainsbury, 1994).

To confirm the existence of the different welfare regimes, Esping-Andersen (1999) does some calculations based upon empirical data ranking the regimes by the degree of de-familization, including a Southern-Mediterranean regime among others. Thus, if the coverage of daycare institutions, public spending on family services, and homehelp are used as indicators, Esping-Andersen finds that the social-democratic regime is the most de-familized, followed by the conservative regime, the liberal regime, and the southern European model, which comes out as the least de-familized regime. The intensity of family welfare provision (indicated by the percentage of old people living with their children, unemployed youth living with their parents, and weekly unpaid hours) gives the same ranking, with the social-democratic countries as the most de-familized, the southern European countries as the least de-familized, and the conservative and liberal regimes in between.

Surprisingly, the more family-oriented a regime, the lower its fertility rate. Thus, familistic policy appears counterproductive to family formation. Italy and Spain have the lowest fertility rates and Denmark and Sweden the highest, indicating a positive correlation between fertility and women's paid employment. In familistic welfare states the choice for women is between having children and a labour market career, and the findings here show that the latter is preferred at the expense of the former (see Blossfeld, 1995; Esping-Andersen, 1999).

The welfare state typology used here refers to, as any other categorization, a particular period of time, for which reason it does not necessarily capture present trends in development, nor what is going to happen in the future concerning differences and similarities between the countries under consideration. In the following, we focus on the changes in the labour markets of Sweden, Denmark, France and Italy, during the 1980s and 1990s, as this is the period here covered empirically.

SOCIO-ECONOMIC CHARACTERISTICS OF THE FOUR COUNTRIES

In all the western countries a trend exists that is moving towards ever greater numbers of highly educated women and men. The percentage of women in higher education was the highest in Sweden in 1980 followed by Denmark, and with French and Italian women being somewhat behind. Ten years later, French women had passed Scandinavian women, while Italian women were still in last place, although the proportion of Italian women had also increased considerably. For men, the ranking is different. In 1980, Italian men had the highest educational level followed by men in Denmark and Sweden. In 1990, however, France had the highest percentage of men in higher education, while the other three countries were on a lower but rather similar level. This means that France invested heavily in human capital during the 1980s (UNESCO, 1994; see Bonke, 1999).

Working Patterns

Not surprisingly the relationship between education and entry into the labour market, i.e. participation rates, has been found to be positive for men and women from all the countries. The distribution of educational skills in the populations, however, is still very skewed, and significant differences between men and women appear. For the same reason, men in all the countries can expect to be permanently attached to the labour force from their youth until the age of retirement, while this is not generally the case among women. Only in Denmark and Sweden can women expect to be in the labour market to nearly the same extent as men are. In France, the level is lower than in the Nordic Countries, although French women exhibit something of a "Nordic" profile. In Italy, women appear to avoid employment during their childbearing years and interrupt their labour market career when they have children, and most of them do not reappear in the labour market.

As regards women's overall labour market attachment, or participation rates among 15–64 years olds, we find a rising trend. In the middle of the 1960s, 50% of Danish and Swedish women were in the labour market compared with around 80% in the middle of the 1990s. For French women the proportion increased from slightly under 50% to 60%. In Italy, where every third women was in the labour market 30 years ago, still less than 40% are to be found there today. In comparison, the variation in men's labour market participation is relatively small; the ranking is, however, the same as that for women (Borchorst, 1998; see Bonke & Koch-Weser, 2001).

A significant proportion of the labour force entrants have been women who have undertaken part-time work. The explanation of this phenomenon is that many of these jobs have been supplied in order to give individuals the opportunity to combine childcare and other household tasks with paid work. This "balance" factor has become particularly important, where the number of childcare facilities is inadequate or the division of labour between the spouses is pronounced.

The number of part-timers is in fact related to the total number of women in the labour market. In Italy, where female participation rates are low only a few women were part-time workers (4%) in 1994, while, on the other hand, many women workers in Denmark and Sweden were part-time (25 and 32%, respectively) (Bonke & Koch-Weser, 2001). Nonetheless, developments concerning part-time jobs are moving towards a similar rate with the result that in countries with many employed women, the number working part-time decreases. In Denmark, for example, the part-time rate decreased 7 percentage points in less than 10 years, while the opposite is occurring in countries with low employment rates of women.

Also the number of hours worked is different for women and men. Not only because of part-time work, the effect of which has decreased in some countries in recent years, as mentioned above, but also because of overtime and additional jobs, which are mostly the preserve of men. For this reason, the labour supply of women is lower than that of men, as indeed are potential career opportunities for women.

Public Services, Taxes and Family Structure

The working-life/family-life dilemma, which many women experience in modern welfare states, can be solved either by working fewer hours on the labour market, by having fewer children (a decrease in fertility), or by having access to day-care facilities for the child(ren) and by non-familial care arrangements for the elderly.

Most countries have expanded the number of daycare places available for pre-school children and improved leave entitlement for parents to meet women's demand for a career. Thus, leave arrangements make it possible to have a legitimate break in the career and at the same time to be compensated economically. Daycare facilities obviously contribute to an increase in women's participation rates and labour supply.

Referring to the middle of the 1990s in Denmark, France, and Italy, a specific period of leave was reserved for the mothers' (maternity leave), while in Sweden the leave could be shared freely between the parents (parental leave). The maternity leave was 24 weeks after birth in Denmark (a recent change allows for taking 48 weeks after birth), 12 weeks in Italy, and 10 weeks in France extended by 10 weeks for the birth of the third child and subsequent children. Only Denmark and Sweden provided paternity leave separate from maternity leave. Denmark provided 2 weeks for the maternity leave period and another two weeks for the parental leave. Sweden allowed 30 days of general parental leave, which was offset by the leave of the mother.

In all countries mothers and fathers were entitled to receive an allowance during their leaves, which, however, varied considerably. Multiplying the maximum leave period by the benefit rate gave the overall entitlement to leave, and not surprisingly France came out in first place. However, only French families with at least two children were entitled to the benefit. In comparison, the overall entitlement in Sweden was less than half that of the French, and the Danish was half again that of the Swedish entitlement (Friedberg & Rostgaard, 1999). In Italy, allowances for maternity leaves were 100% and for parental leave 38% of the worker's normal wage. This means that the incentives for spending time together with one's child and participating in the labour market at the same time will vary considerably among parents in the four countries.

The differences in leave periods and allowances between the countries are, however, much bigger than the supply of child care provision among pre-school children (excluding Italy from the comparison). That is, in Denmark, Sweden, and France, day care for pre-school children is provided for approximately every second child of pre-school age, with a smaller provision for children birth to 2 years than for children ages 3 to preschool age. Nonetheless, some variations appear. Denmark leads at providing daycare for 46% of small children and 80% of older children. Then follow Sweden and France with provisions for 42 and 35%, respectively, of children birth to 2 years old and 72 and 75% of children from age 3 to preschool (Friedberg & Rostgaard, 1999). In Italy, in 1988/1989, only 6% of children 0–2 years old were in child care, but 75% of 3–5 year olds were in kindergarten (*scuola materna*) (ISTAT, 1994).

In Denmark and Sweden, a daycare guarantee has been introduced, provided that resources are available. In France, an agreement between the Family Allowance Fund and the local authorities has expanded the provision of day care. There are also other differences between the Scandinavian countries and France. Public daycare is universally provided only for older children in the French system of nursery schools.

Care of older people is another social obligation of society. However, many nowadays are living on their own. Increasing life-expectancy, improving health conditions, and preferences for independent living explain the tendency in all four countries towards an increasing proportion of old people living apart from adult children or in old-age institutions. In Denmark, Sweden, and France, we found a decrease in the proportion of 65+ people living with adult children. In the two Scandinavian countries only 5% of the elderly live in inter-generational families, and 15% in France. In Italy, the tendency towards autonomy seems the least marked since nearly 40% of elders live in intergenerational families (Friedberg & Rostgaard, 1999).

This does not mean, however, that family members do not provide care for their parents. Even in the Scandinavian countries with relatively high levels of provision of formal care, spouses and children provide care to their parents, if in need of help. In Scandinavian countries the main source of care for the elderly, however, is home-help provided through the public sector. In Denmark, home-help is the prevalent form of care of elders displacing all other kinds of care, whereas in Sweden it counts less than help provided by either the spouse or the children. For older people in France home-help is only a supplement to informal care (17%) and in Italy it hardly exists at all; only 3% of people over 65 receive that kind of help. In all these countries voluntary organizations are of only negligible importance as suppliers of help for the elderly (Friedberg & Rostgaard, 1999).

The nature of the tax-system as well as the availability of public benefits are essential elements for gaining an understanding of the labour supply and time-allocation of women. The tax-system affects the level of work available on the labour market and, thereby, equality between the sexes. This is especially the case for single parents where the labour supply is undoubtedly influenced by an interaction that occurs between taxes and transfer payments, which in some countries means marginal tax-rates approaching 100%. This results in a lack of incentives for a single parent to supply sufficient time to the labour market and thereby become an independent breadwinner. Finally, if there is not a sufficient supply of daycare facilities for children and the elderly, and women still wish to work, the only available strategy for them to manage women's working life besides changes in the intra-familial distribution of time is to give birth to fewer children. Thus, we find decreasing fertility rates in the 1960s and 1970s simultaneous with increasing labor force participation rates for all four countries. Furthermore, for Denmark and Sweden, the participation rates continued to grow in the 1980s, while they flattened out in France and Italy. In that period of time the supply of daycare institutions increased considerably in the two Scandinavian countries and the fertility rates could thus rebound and return to their former levels. However, in France and, especially, in Italy, the fertility rates continued to decrease and are now as low as 1.2, which together with the Spanish fertility rate are the lowest for the European Countries. The supply of formal care facilities has evidently not been sufficient to meet the demand in France and Spain, although child minders working in private homes are now supported by the state in France (Letablier, 2003).

To summarize, a pattern appears to emerge whereby different welfare state regimes are associated with distinctive family forms. Two countries that are examples of this, Denmark and Sweden, have a "modern" family structure, where small households, high divorce rates, many women working part-time, public services, and considerable equal opportunities for two-earner families are the norm. At the other extreme, in Italy, the family structure is more traditional with big families still being the norm. Although the fertility rates are decreasing in Italy, low divorce rates, a small service sector, relatively low labour market participation rates for women, and many one-earner families remain common features in this economy. France is in between regarding the family structure and women's labour market participation rates. However, the childcare facilities are well-developed in France and women's employment is found to be on a more permanent basis. Here the demographic transition towards lower fertility rates appeared earlier than in Italy.

METHODS AND DATA

The empirical analyses in this paper regard two different sorts of data, from national time-use surveys and from the European Community Household Panel (ECHP). The first are gathered by a self-reporting diary technique, whereas the second are ordinary survey data gathered by interviews. The ECHP includes Denmark, Belgium, France, Germany, Greece, the Netherlands, Ireland, Italy, Portugal, Spain, UK, all covering the full period 1994–2001, and Austria (1995–2001), Finland (1996–1997), Luxembourg (1994–1997), and Sweden (1997–2001). However, only 1994-data are used here to come as close as possible to the years of the time-use surveys dating back to the late 1980s.

The Time-Use Survey

The time-use surveys for the four countries under consideration are similar in many respects. In the first place they all refer to the same period, i.e. the later part of the 1980s, when European countries embarked in their first round of costly time budget studies which only recently are being launched again. Furthermore, they all adopt representative samples of the whole population, and the survey techniques used in data collection are in accordance with main-stream methodology. That is, the data represent all days of the week, and for France, Italy and Sweden they cover the different seasons of the year as well. Since for Denmark the interviews were gathered during one month only, that data file does not capture seasonal variations.

Besides covering a rich set of socioeconomic variables, the time-use categories were also comparable, although the Danish study had only relatively few and pre-coded groups of activities. For all the studies, a primary activity was assumed to be going on at any point in time, and hence respondents had to assign priority to the one they thought the most important. In the Danish time-use survey this activity refers to fixed 15 minutes intervals, whereas in the other three countries open interval diaries were used. This means that short-time activities tend to be under-represented in Denmark.

In any case, time-use surveys give rich and reliable information on the allocation of time by different groups in the population, and thus offer a detailed picture of everyday life in the countries under consideration (Bonke, 2002).

An overview of the characteristics for these national time surveys is given in Bonke and Koch-Weser (2001). For further information, refer to Andersen (1987), ISTAT (1993), INSEE (1985), and Klevmarken and Olovsson (1993) for the Danish, Italian, French and Swedish time-use surveys, respectively.

In the case of France and Sweden, the following figures are recalculations on the basis of the information in the article "Patterns of Time Use in France and Sweden" by Anxo and Flood (1994, 1998), because the authors have had no access to the original data-sets. For Denmark and Italy calculations were done on the original data from the Danish and the Italian Time-Use Surveys.

In all samples the age range is 18–64 years and we find that there is only a minor variation in the average age for women and men. The age-distributions, however, differ from country to country, with relatively many young women in Denmark and France, relatively many middle aged women in Italy and Sweden, and relatively many old women in Denmark. Italian men, as well as women, up to 34 years of age very rarely (only 5%) live as singles in a household of their own. The educational levels of French and Swedish women and men are very similar to each other and differ less from each other than those of Italian and Danish men and women. The highest level of education is found in Denmark, where the difference between men's and women's education is also the greatest as well. The classification is not, however, very reliable, as only a three-level educational scale following the OECD-classification is used, for which reason the comparison here has to be taken with caution.

The labour supply figures mentioned here are all based on ordinary questions in the time-use surveys and correspond nicely to the figures to be found in the labour force surveys. However, results obtained from time-use research on household work often do not allow straightforward comparisons because of different activity classifications. In order to overcome the difficulty that the categorization of household tasks for France and Sweden is somewhat unusual (Gershuny, 1994), we have recalculated the French and Swedish data on the basis of information in the Appendices to the paper by Anxo and Flood (1994, Tables A1–A5).

The European Community Household Panel

Another data-set employed here is the European Community Household Panel (ECHP), which was established in the beginning of the 1990s as a unified data bank to monitor the development in the labour markets and in the different welfare systems constituting the European Community. The resulting micro-data regard labour market behaviour, the flow of money between households and the public sector, and housing.

The European Community Household Panel (ECHP) is a panel study including a Household Register, a Household Questionnaire, and an Individual Question-naire (Eurostat, 1996). By sampling households randomly and conducting joint as well as individual interviews with all family members born in 1977 or earlier, the sample becomes representative of both individuals and households without the need of any weighting procedure.

Another advantage of getting information on all members of the same household appears when analyzing the distribution of time in the family and the internal division of labor between women and men.

ALLOCATION OF TIME IN COUPLES

Time Diary Data on Family Structure and Labour Supply

There appear to be two basic arrangements in families where the husband is 18–64 years. In the "male breadwinner model" one partner is working full-time (defined as more than 34 hours per week) whereas the other one takes care of home and offspring (and in any case works less than 15 hours per week) as shown in Table 1. In the "gender equality model" both partners work full-time. The family's rationale in choosing the first one of these models tends to be that taking care of children corresponds to an investment in human capital compensating for foregone professional income whereas opting for the second model is driven by

Table 1. Time Use of Couples by Labour Supply,[a] 18–64 Years. Sweden, Denmark, France and Italy. Hours:Minutes Per Weekday 1984–1989.

	Male Working Full-Time – Female Non-Working		Male Working Full-Time – Female Working Full-Time	
	Man	Woman	Man	Woman
Sweden (1984–1985)				
Housework	1:06	4:33	1:03	2:25
Leisure	4:29	5:44	4:15	3:35
Care and needs	10:25	12:32	9:54	10:09
Denmark (1987)				
Housework	0:38	3:25	1:10	2:18
Leisure	6:00	6:38	6:21	5:12
Care and needs	10:08	11:10	10:02	10:34
France (1985–1986)				
Housework	0:45	5:52	0:48	2:28
Leisure	3:49	4:05	2:43	1:55
Care and needs	10:15	12:55	9:46	10:09
Italy (1988–1989)				
Housework	0:40	6:54	0:52	4:25
Leisure	4:27	3:47	4:18	2:47
Care and needs	11:08	12:25	10:57	11:12

Source: Elaborations of the original Danish and Italian datasets, see Andersen (1987) and ISTAT (1993). For Sweden and France, see Anxo and Flood (1998).

[a] Full-time: >34 hours per week. Non-working: <15 hours per week. For Denmark and Italy, the distributions of couples between the two categories are 17.1 and 60.8%, and 53.3 and 37.8%, respectively, whereas there is no such information for France and Sweden.

the idea that under-utilized competencies and skills constitute a loss in tangible (income) as well as intangible benefits (psychological satisfactions).

In the left section of the table, where the "male breadwinner" situation is at issue, it can be seen that, with the exception of Sweden and Denmark, men are practically absent from housework. In Sweden, men offer 19% of total housework time; in Denmark, they contribute 16%, in Italy 9%, and in France 8%. Housework rests therefore almost entirely on the shoulders of the women. Expressed in hours and minutes, the female load is least heavy in Denmark followed by Sweden, heavier in France and the heaviest in Italy (where women spend twice as much time in housework as in Denmark). With the exception of Italy, leisure is a little more available for women than for men as is also the time for care and needs, such as looking after children and physiological regeneration.

With respect to the "gender equality model" on the right side of the table, it can be seen that in Sweden, Italy, and France the fact that the wife also works full-time away from home and gains her own income does not at all increase the husband's availability to give her a hand in doing the housework. Only in Denmark does the male partner increase his contribution by half an hour. Working wives generally spend from 1 to 3 hours less time on housework when both their husband's and their own labour supply is full-time. The reduction is most pronounced in France and also in Italy, countries where double breadwinner families still hire domestic help (often immigrants). But such reduction in housework is not sufficient to make up for female full-time workers' absence from their home. In fact, to be able to support a full-fledged professional career, women workers must not only reduce their leisure time by 1 or 2 hours but also decrease time for the care of relatives and for personal needs from half an hour (Denmark) to almost 3 hours (France).

Compared to a family without children, parents with two children 18 or younger encounter organizational problems and face other responsibilities for their care. In particular, the couple need to decide how much time is to be invested in the children's upbringing and how much time allocated to earning the means for a better standard of living. As seen in Table 2, once there are two children, fathers in all countries tend to increase their time for market work in order to take care of extra costs of their family (in France an increase of 54 minutes; in Sweden, 44 minutes; in Denmark, 20 minutes; while in Italy there is no change). None of the fathers, however, increases his contribution to household work.

Unlike the fathers' behaviour, that of mothers varies among the four countries according to policy regulations and availability of childcare that either encourage or discourage maternal labour force participation. Everywhere mothers face more housework when they have children: 15 minutes more in France where there is long-standing public support, 23 and 34 minutes more in Sweden and

Table 2. Time Use of Couples (18–54 Years) by Number of Children < 18 Years.[a] Sweden, Denmark, France, and Italy. Hours:Minutes Per Weekday 1984–1989.

	Couple With No Children		Couple With 2 Children	
	Man	Woman	Man	Woman
Sweden (1984–1985)				
Market work	4:24	2:44	5:08	3:25
Housework	1:16	3:18	1:19	3:41
Leisure	5:21	5:08	4:34	4:22
Care and needs	10:16	11:13	10:51	11:34
Denmark (1987)				
Market work	5:18	4:14	5:38	3:39
Housework	0:58	2:14	0:50	2:48
Leisure	7:13	7:01	5:34	5:16
Care and needs	9:37	10:11	9:58	10:36
France (1985–1986)				
Market work	5:09	2:56	6:03	2:55
Housework	1:15	4:10	1:04	4:25
Leisure	4:39	4:01	4:21	3:22
Care and needs	10:40	11:15	10:45	12:02
Italy (1988–1989)				
Market work	6:25	2:52	6:21	1:48
Housework	0:46	4:51	0:44	6:11
Leisure	4:35	4:07	4:17	3:14
Care and needs	10:40	11:11	11:10	12:03

Source: Elaborations of the original Danish and Italian datasets, see Andersen (1987) and ISTAT (1993). For Sweden and France, see Anxo and Flood (1998).

[a] For Denmark and Italy, the distributions of couples between the two categories are 34 and 29%, and 16 and 9%, respectively, whereas there are no such information for France and Sweden.

Denmark, but as much as 1 hour and 20 minutes more in Italy where indeed, therefore, fertility has dramatically fallen over recent times, turning the country demographically into one of the oldest worldwide.

Yet, more family responsibility due to children does not necessarily imply significant maternal reduction in labour force participation. In fact, in France childless wives and women with two children contribute the same amount of time to market work and in the Nordic welfare regimes mothers' market work is only a half hour less than that of childless wives. But in Italy mothers market work is over an hour less than that of childless wives, which suggests, in terms of foregone income, the economic cost of children.

As is to be expected, in all cases couples with children need more time for looking after them and for restoring their own energies by a sufficient amount of sleep. Less obvious is the need for leisure. Generally not only the mother, but both partners, when they have two children, have less free time. In Italy, the loss of free time is negligible for men and small for women, while in Denmark for each parent the loss surpasses one and a half hours.

In summary, the following empirical life style models emerge:

In Denmark, having two children rather than none means for the husband 5% more and for the wife 18% less market work, for him 14% less but for her 25% more housework, as well as for both about 20% less leisure.

In Italy, by contrast, having two children has practically no impact at all on the time the husband accords to market work, housework or leisure, but for the wife it means a 37% reduction in presence on the labour market, 27% more housework, and 20% less leisure.

European Household Panel Data Regarding the Determinants of Labour Supply

In the European Community Household Panel questions on labour market attachment are used for an overall classification of individuals (being out of the labour force, unemployed, employed part-time, or employed full-time). The actual number of hours spent on paid work is used as well as the degree of satisfaction with work hours. For individuals not working full-time, explanations for not seeking a job or working only part-time are given, such as housework, looking after children or other persons, education or training, personal illness or disability, inability to find a full-time job, or other obligations preventing full-time work. Finally, all individuals are asked specifically if care obligations for children or other persons are preventing the preferred level of paid work, and, thus, indirectly if other formal or informal care arrangements are available as partial substitutes. In the following analysis, only Denmark, France, and Italy are included, as Sweden did not participate in the ECHP-project before 1996.

The first striking observation is that more than three out of four men over 16 years old in Denmark, France, and Italy are in the labour market, while that proportion holds for women only in Denmark. Only about half of all French women are employed, and no more than two out of five Italian women participate in the labour force. Thus, the proportion of active women to active men is very high in Denmark (91%), moderate in France (78%), and the lowest in Italy (55%). Even after accounting for the high proportion of part-time working women in Denmark, the probability of finding a woman working full-time in Denmark is double that of finding a corresponding woman in Italy, and 40% higher than in France. The number of hours full-time working women perform is, however, higher in Italy and France than in Denmark, whereas Danish, and Italian, full-time working men work more hours than corresponding French men do (Table 3). For women, the low proportion of full-timers might mean a more homogeneous group of career-oriented women working hard to reach their aims.

In all countries there is little difference between men or women in level of satisfaction with the number of working hours. However, big differences between the countries appear in overall patterns. Less than two-thirds of Italian full-time workers are satisfied, whereas this holds for more than three out of four French full-time workers. In Denmark, the corresponding figures are as high as 83%. For part-time workers the differences between the countries are even bigger, as 45% of such Danish women are satisfied with their working schedules relative to 18% of French women, and for Italy, only 5% find it satisfactory to work 21 hours a week, although this is what every tenth Italian woman does often as undeclared *lavoro nero* work. There are similar differences among men, but the prevalence of dissatisfaction is in any case smaller, as relatively few men are working part-time in the three countries.

Being unsatisfied with the number of hours worked as a part-time man is usually due to the spending of time on education, training, being ill, etc.; only 4–5% of French and Italian men and no Danish men mention housework as a restriction on their supply of more hours to the labour market. Not surprisingly, women more often refer to housework as the reason why they do not work full-time. Every third French woman says so compared with every fourth Italian woman. By contrast, Denmark has the lowest proportion of housewives among the EU countries, 4% relative to 26% in France and 44% in Italy. Housewifery here includes ordinary housework as well as child caring obligations and caring for others, which are the most common arguments given for being a housewife and for not seeking a job on the labour market – an argument made more often in France than in Italy and Denmark.

However, if the focus is on care obligations only, a majority of French housewives (70%) mention this as the reason for their status, while this is the case for a minority of Italian (35%) and Danish women (33%). For other non-employed wives the picture is different, as only 2% of such French women find that care obligations are preventing paid work, while the corresponding figures are 14% for non-employed Italian women and 11% of Danish women.

The findings confirm the thesis raised in this study, that child care obligations and housework have different implications for the labour supply of women in the three countries, the different organization of the welfare states being the explanation.

Table 3. Labour Supply, Reasons for Not Seeking a Job or Working Part-Time, and Satisfaction with Working Hours. Denmark, France, and Italy. Respondents ages 16–74 Years 1994.

	Non-Employed		Housewives		Unemployed		Part-Time Employed		Full-Time Employed	
	Men	Women	Men	Women	Men	Women	Men	Women	Men	Women
Denmark										
(N: 1824/1674) percentages	21.9	24.6	0.1	4.2	3.0	3.2	2.6	14.5	72.4	53.5
Number of hours paid work	6.9	0.6	0.0	3.5	4.3	0.0	33.5	24.4	50.1	39.1
Not jobseekers (percentages)	96.5	96.1	100.0	91.6	1.9	0.0	–	–	–	–
Reason for not seeking a job or for working part-time (percentages)										
Housework	0.5	1.5	–	80.0	–	–	0.0	30.8	–	–
Other reasons[a]	99.5	98.5	–	20.2	–	–	66.7	23.8	–	–
Satisfied with number of hours paid work (percentages)	–	–	–	–	–	–	33.3	45.4	83.1	83.8
Care obligations preventing preferred paid work[b] (percentages)	3.6	11.1	–	33.3	0.0	4.0	0.0	4.3	1.3	6.2
France										
(N: 4302/3750) percentages	29.6	19.0	1.3	25.9	4.0	6.2	2.5	10.5	62.6	38.3
Number of hours paid work	1.0	0.0	0.0	0.0	3.6	0.0	21.8	22.3	46.3	40.6
Not jobseekers (percentages)	99.5	99.4	98.2	95.9	5.8	4.3	–	–	–	–
Reason for not seeking a job or for working part-time (percentages)										
Housework	0.0	0.9	0.0	55.2	–	–	3.6	36.0	–	–
Other reasons[a]	100.0	99.1	100.0	44.8	–	–	75.0	46.1	–	–

Satisfied with number of hours paid work (percentages)	0	–	–	–	–	–	21.4	17.9	78.1	76.4
Care obligations preventing preferred paid work[b] (percentages)	0	2.3	0	69.9	0	0	0	2.9	0.7	1
Italy										
(N: 4728/4018) percentages	27.3	16.5	0.1	44.3	2.6	3.9	3.6	9.0	66.4	26.3
Number of hours paid work	5.2	0.1	0.0	0.0	9.1	0.0	31.0	21.1	50.6	40.3
Not jobseekers (percentages)	99.5	98.8	100.0	90.2	6.6	7.7	–	–	–	–
Reason for not seeking a job or for working part-time (percentages)										
Housework	1.0	8.6	–	83.4	–	–	5.1	25.0	–	–
Other reasons[a]	99.0	91.4	–	16.6	–	–	86.5	70.5	–	–
Satisfied with number of hours paid work (percentages)	–	–	–	–	–	–	8.3	4.5	62.9	63.0
Care obligations preventing preferred paid work[b] (percentages)	6.5	13.7	33.3	34.8	2.1	10.4	1.5	6.0	2.1	3.4

Note: – less than 25 respondents in the distribution.

Source: European Community Household Panel, un-weighted data, see Eurostat (1996).

[a] Including study, training, community, military service, retirement, own illness, injury, incapacitation, believe no suitable work available, already found work, other possibilities.

[b] "Do looking after children or other persons prevent you from undertaking paid work which you otherwise would do?"

CARING OBLIGATIONS

In any society, caregiving is the key activity for maintaining and strengthening interpersonal relationships within and between generations. For the society the choice is between providing support for family care and providing access to paid professional care delivered by private or public institutions. For the individual, the choice is between spending time on caregiving one's self or paying for care given by others either directly or through the tax system. Where family provision is preferred, income has to be forgone. If instead external provision is to be obtained, earning income is required.

To show the effects of the strategies chosen in the different welfare regimes under consideration, Table 4 compares the amount of care for children and others performed by married or cohabiting women and men in 1994 (ECHP data). Child care means care given to one's own or to someone else's children, and care for other persons means special help for those who require it because of old age, illness, or disability. In both cases care is offered without pay. The most striking finding is that only every fourth French woman finds that she has daily childcare obligations, while every third Danish woman does, and two out of three Italian women find that they have such an obligation. This is indeed astonishing, as the fertility in Italy is now lower than in Denmark and France. The only reasonable explanation is that Italian children leave their homes later than other children because of the *mammone* syndrome, which means that their parents are expected to take care of them and do so. That French women surpass Danish women might be due to the employment of nannies and *au pairs* in France, who help parents meet their care obligations. For men, childcare also scores the lowest in France, whereas there is no significant difference between Danish and Italian men in the proportion giving childcare.

In caring for others, Italian men and women are the most engaged. Every seventh Italian woman (13.6%) reports such care as a daily obligation compared with only every twentieth French and Danish woman (5.8 and 5.7%). In France and Italy, the proportions of men giving care to others are half that of women (2.9 and 6.8%), while the difference between Danish men and women giving daily care to others is fairly small, 4.0% for men and 5.7% for women.

The time women spend on childcare does not vary so much. In all the countries more than two-thirds spend more than 4 hours a day, which means that this is a heavy burden for these women. That three-quarters (75.7%) of Italian women are giving more than 4 hours daily to childcare means that childcare consumes a large part of their working day and results in limited opportunities for participation in the labour market. In comparison, relatively few Italian men give that many hours a day to child care. When compared with French and Danish men, Italian men

Table 4.   Distribution of Care Work. Denmark, France, and Italy. Respondents ages 16–74 Years, 1994.

	Child Care		Care for Others	
	Men (%)	Women (%)	Men (%)	Women (%)
Denmark (N: 1824/1674)				
Caring obligations	30.2	36.1	4.0	5.7
Distribution by hours per day				
<2 hours	31.3	13.1	75.3	87.2
2–4 hours	37.6	17.5	8.2	4.3
>4 hours	31.1	69.4	16.5	8.5
	100.0	100.0	100.0	100.0
France (N: 4299/4356)				
Caring obligations	12.5	26.6	2.9	5.8
Distribution by hours per day				
<2 hours	39.2	12.6	63.4	62.0
2–4 hours	32.4	20.1	17.9	14.9
>4 hours	28.4	67.3	18.7	23.1
	100.0	100.0	100.0	100.0
Italy (N: 4728/4013)				
Caring obligations	29.4	63.0	6.8	13.6
Distribution by hours per day				
<2 hours	36.6	6.1	46.3	28.2
2–4 hours	41.7	18.2	28.6	34.4
>4 hours	21.7	75.7	25.1	37.4
	100.0	100.0	100.0	100.0

Source: European Community Household Panel, un-weighted data, see Eurostat (1996).

are again found to be at the bottom of the distribution who give more than 4 hours a day to child care (21.7%) vs. 31.1% for Denmark and 28.4% for France.

However, when it comes to care for others, employed Italian men offer more time than French men, who again are supplying more time to that activity than Danish men. While only every fourth Danish man spends more than 2 hours on care for others, the corresponding figures for French men are one out of every three, and for Italian men one out of every two on a randomly chosen day. For women this burden varies widely. In Denmark, 12.8% of women offer more than 2 hours a day to other caregiving relative to 37.9% of French women, and 71.8% of Italian women.

The care burden determines the available time for other purposes, including paid work; Table 5 shows who contributes most to childcare and care for others

Table 5. Sharing of Caring Between Women and Men. 16–74 Years, 1994.

	Denmark		France		Italy	
	Child Care	Care for Others	Child Care	Care for Others	Child Care	Care for Others
Wife > husband	63.1	33.5	84.5	62.5	73.5	62.8
Wife = husband	15.8	58.1	8.5	35.4	2.0	10.9
Wife < husband	21.1	8.4	7.0	2.1	24.5	26.3
	100.0	100.0	100.0	100.0	100.0	100.0

Source: European Community Household Panel, un-weighted data, see Eurostat (1996).

given that there is a care obligation to fulfil for at least one of the spouses. France comes in as the most old fashioned country concerning the sharing of child care between partners. In 84.5% of all French couples women do the most, and only in 7.0% are the roles the opposite with the man as the main caregiver. In Italy, the corresponding figures are 73.5% who are traditional families where the wife does more child care than her husband, and 24.5% are "post-modern" families where the husband does the major part of the childcare within the family. Denmark is found to be the most gender-neutral country with 63.1% traditional families and 21.1% "post-modern" ones, which gives a percentage of 15.7 of egalitarian families in Denmark relative to 8.5% in France and only 2.0% in Italy.

Finally, care for others is also distributed rather equally between Danish spouses (58.1%), whereas in France only every third (35.4%) family shares that obligation equally, and no more than every tenth (10.9%) in Italy. Furthermore, only every third Danish family is to be considered as a traditional one with respect to care for others, while two out of three French and Italian families with such care obligations let the woman do most of the work.

These findings are in accordance with what one should expect assuming a correlation between care obligations, the supply of public care arrangements, and the functioning of the labour markets. That is, the arrangement of the welfare state and its generosity as well as the social responsibility of the labour market are critical in shaping men's and women's everyday life and, thereby, the distribution of welfare in modern societies.

CONCLUSION

The comparative analysis of nationally representative data for four different European countries has clearly shown that there are differences in the complexity of welfare regimes, when defined as institutional set-ups that vary in the amount of choice that is offered to citizens.

Denmark's "social-democratic" welfare regime, aimed at decommodification of social services, has produced high labour force participation among women whereas Italy's "conservative" regime has the lowest rates. Public service provisions sustaining the family (leave entitlements and day care for children, support of the elderly, subsidies for paying domestic help, etc.) are amply developed in Scandinavian countries, but are to some degree also available in France. These arrangements are least available in Italy where, after a long period of Christian-democratic government, the family is still largely expected to provide for itself. Furthermore, Nordic countries offer ample part-time schemes to parents, while in Italy part-time work is very seldom chosen and when present is usually disadvantageous to the worker.

Concerning time allocation, Denmark shows patterns similar to Sweden, and Italy resembles France. In the two Scandinavian countries, time for overall work – probably due to more rationally managed household chores – is reduced in favor of leisure activities. In France and Italy, on the other hand, market work and in particular household work (comprising care for the old and for the younger generation) absorbs a disproportionate amount of the available time and diminishes participation in recreational and cultural life. In addition, differences in the patterns of male/female division of work are much less pronounced in Nordic countries where, as compared to France and Italy, indices of market work masculinization and of family work feminization are relatively low. But what is most significant is that, with perhaps the exception of Denmark, husbands are everywhere scarcely available to assure a better market work/family work equilibrium for their wives. Neither the fact that both members of the couple work full time, nor that in addition there are children to care for, appears to persuade men to put into household work more than token shares of the average 24-hour weekday.

In sum, having focused on major North-South divergences, we conclude that where the welfare model assumes a "social-democratic" service-oriented slant, more degrees of freedom are achieved in the direction of gender neutrality and individual decision-making. On the contrary, in "conservative" welfare regimes with additional Mediterranean familistic characteristics, females with professional ambitions and levels of education now surpassing males may strive for equality on the labour market, but they remain severely constrained by the amount of social and private responsibility assigned to families. Women in Southern Europe choose market work in order not to forego professional income that is indispensable for stabilizing their families' otherwise declining social status. Facing insufficient public support in the family realm, not surprisingly, has placed Italy in a difficult demographic situation. With its increasingly postponed and foregone marriages and its dramatically reduced fertility rates, this country now finds itself leading in negative population growth and has become one of the first countries worldwide where old people outnumber the young.

What can be underlined is that Denmark and Sweden in the 1980s provided their male and female citizens with relatively ample margins of choice in designing their life projects. In contrast, in France to some extent, but most clearly in Italy, the fundamental paradox emerges that the prevalent familistic social policy gives families insufficient support and provides few incentives for achievement-oriented female life-projects. Familistic welfare regimes thereby risk undermining the very premises on which the family as an institution is based.

REFERENCES

Andersen, D. (1987). *Den danske befolknings tidsanvendelse 1987. Teknisk dokumentation af undersøgelsens database*. Arbejdsnotat. København: Socialforskningsinstituttet.

Anxo, D., & Flood, L. (1994). *Patterns of time use in France and Sweden*. Memorandum No. 205. Gothenburg: Gothenburg University, School of Economics and Commercial Law.

Anxo, D., & Flood, L. (1998). Patterns of time use in France and Sweden. In: I. Persson & C. Jonung (Eds), *Women's Work and Wages* (pp. 91–121). London and New York: Routledge.

Blossfeld, H.-P. (Ed.) (1995). *The new role of women: Family formation in modern societies*. Boulder: Westview Press.

Bonke, J. (1999). Education, work and gender. An international comparison. In: O. Hufton & Y. Kravaritou (Eds), *Gender and the Use of Time* (pp. 297–318). The Hague: Kluwer.

Bonke, J. (2002). Paid work and unpaid work – questionnaire information vs. diary information. Copenhagen: The Danish National Institute of Social Research. Working Paper.

Bonke, J., & Koch-Weser, E. (2001). The welfare state and time allocation – Denmark, Italy, France and Sweden. Copenhagen: The Danish National Institute of Social Research. Working Paper 09:2001.

Borchorst, A. (1998). Køn, vetfaerdsstatsmodeller og familiepolitik. In: J. Elm Larsen & I. Hornemann Møller (Eds), *Socialpolitik. Socialpaedagogisk Bibliotek*. København: Munksgaard.

Daly, M. (1996). *The gender division of welfare: The British and German welfare states compared* [Ph.D. thesis]. Florence: European University Institute. EUI.

Esping-Andersen, G. (1990). *The three worlds of welfare capitalism*. Cambridge: Polity Press.

Esping-Andersen, G. (1999). *Social foundations of postindustrial economies*. Oxford: Oxford University Press.

Eurostat (1996). *The household panel newsletter*. Luxembourg: Eurostat. Theme 3. Series B.

Friedberg, T., & Rostgaard, T. (1999). *Caring for children and older people: A comparison of European policies and practices. Social security in Europe* (Vol. 6). Copenhagen: The Danish National Institute of Social Research 98:20.

Gershuny, J. (1994). *Economic activity and women's time use. Time use of women in Europe and North America*. Geneva: UN, Economic Commission of Europe.

INSEE (1985). Paris: Enquête Emploi du Temps.

ISTAT (1993). Roma: *L'uso del tempo in Italia. Indagine multiscopo sulle famiglie. Anni 1987–1991* (Vol. 4). Roma: Istat.

ISTAT (1994). Roma: *Il mondo dei bambini, Indagine multiscopo sulle famiglie. Anni 1987–1991* (Vol. 9). Roma: Istat.

Klevmarken, N. A., & Olovsson, P. (1993). *Household market and nonmarket activities: Procedures and codes 1984–1991*. Stockholm: The Industrial Institute for Economic and Social Research.

Letablier, M.-T. (2003). Work and family balance: A new challenge for policies in France. In: J. Z. Giele & E. Holst (Eds), *Advances in Life-course Research: Changing Life Patterns in Societies* (Vol. 8, pp. 165–188). Oxford: Elsevier.

Sainsbury, D. (Ed.) (1994). *Gendering welfare states*. London: Sage.

Stephens, J. (1994). The Scandinavian welfare states: Achievements, crisis and prospects. In: G. Esping-Andersen (Ed.), *Welfare states in Transition*. London: Sage.

PART IV:
THE ROLE OF INDIVIDUAL AGENCY AND CHOICE

12. PUBLISHING AND THE NEW MEDIA PROFESSIONS AS FORERUNNERS OF PIONEER WORK AND LIFE PATTERNS

Sigrid Betzelt and Karin Gottschall

ABSTRACT

The cultural industries as part of the growing knowledge-based services sector seem to promise a chance for pioneer work and life patterns since they distinguish themselves by specific working patterns. As our study on the German situation in publishing and new media professions shows, these are characterized by flexible employment forms and a low degree of gender-segregation. The workforce is mostly academic, with high shares of well-educated women. Moreover, we could identify several innovative collective risk-management strategies to cope with radicalised market conditions, reflecting changed demands of a young and gender-mixed labor force. However, the positive image of these occupational fields is only partly justified. Even such "modernized" strategies of professional organizations are based on gendered understandings of professional work that play down certain discriminatory structures and social inequality.

Changing Life Patterns in Western Industrial Societies
Advances in Life Course Research, Volume 8, 257–280
Copyright © 2004 by Elsevier Ltd.
All rights of reproduction in any form reserved
ISSN: 1040-2608/doi:10.1016/S1040-2608(03)08012-2

INTRODUCTION

During the last decades most capitalist societies witnessed a structural change from an industrial economy to a service economy accompanied by rising female employment rates and a pluralisation of family structures. Despite visions of labor losing its core function for modern societies, paid work still remains the basic foundation of individual and household welfare and social inclusion. Women especially insist on greater economic autonomy and professional development as a means to enhance gender equality.

Furthermore, the shift to services implies a broader transformation of work: Manufacturing as well as service work become more flexible and knowledge-based. Jobs are less characterized by career stability and corporatist regulation. Apart from the so-called "standard employment relationship," characterized by socially secured, lifelong full-time work, new forms of employment like temporary work and self-employment gain importance. In consequence the traditional work and life patterns relying on a spatial, temporal, and moral separation of "paid work" (as dependent work) and "private life" as well as the traditional biographical patterns come under pressure. These changes pose a challenge to the gender contract safeguarding a male breadwinner and a dependent female carer, a model still inherent in most West European post-war welfare regulations (Gottschall & Bird, 2003).

The social impact of the transformation of work is controversial. While some authors highlight the civilian potential of the way "towards a new modernity" (Beck, 1992; Beck et al., 1994), others are more sceptical especially with respect to creating a new work and life balance (Carnoy, 2002; Hochschild, 1996; Sennett, 1998). A third strand of discussion contained in comparative welfare state research underlines the role and quest of political re-regulation of education, work, and social services (Crouch et al., 1999; Esping-Andersen, 2002). But we still know little about the driving forces behind emergence of new patterns of work and life and the interaction of more general features like individualization and globalisation within specific national settings. To ground the general debate in a nation-specific context, more empirical examples are necessary.

This is our starting point. In this chapter we will take a closer look at the cultural industries as one of the expanding knowledge-based service sectors, with more or less equal representation of males and females, that comprises a mostly academic workforce. In this sector flexible forms of employment and work, namely self-employment and full-time and part-time work, are frequent; and non-standard work and life patterns can be expected. The expansion of the sector itself, which comprises the production and dissemination of cultural goods like printed matter and literature, music, visual arts, cinema and photography, radio and television, games and sporting goods (UNESCO, 2000), can be found throughout most OECD countries. We will refer to the significance and push and pull factors of this development as a general feature in West European countries. Germany is an interesting case, since unlike the liberal market conditions for all kinds of jobs and services in Great Britain or the U.S., German labor and product markets are characterized by strong corporatist and institutionalized regulation extending at least to the public part of the cultural sector. This study draws on recent empirical research on particular subsectors of the cultural industries in Germany, namely, journalism, book publishing, and graphic design.[1] Since the 1990s, with a growing number of private investors, publishing, film, and the media industries are exposed to turbulent and uncertain market conditions. Based on secondary analyses and expert interviews we will first present findings on *working conditions and institutional regulations*, focusing on individual arrangements of risk-management as well as reactions of professional associations and trade unions. Turbulent markets with cut-throat competition not only enhance social polarisation but at the same time create a demand for professional interest groups to protect professional standards. *Two case studies* of graphic designers and certain media professionals give a more detailed insight into innovative strategies of these collective actors. Finally, we turn to the question of *gender and work and life arrangements*. Undoubtedly working conditions and career paths in the cultural industries are less gendered compared to the traditional liberal professions. But it can be shown that even the innovative policies of professional associations in this field are not free of discriminatory effects. On the one hand, they address the cultural professional as a worker who is free of family duties; yet on the other, they rely on private resources to cushion incalculable market risks. This seems in line with the findings of international studies on work and life patterns of dual-career couples (Blossfeld & Drobnic, 2001) and supports a rather more sceptical than optimistic view on the egalitarian potential of new forms of work and life.

RISING SOCIO-ECONOMIC SIGNIFICANCE OF THE CULTURAL INDUSTRIES

Up until recently, the economic and labor market aspects of the arts and cultural sector were of secondary significance to the welfare state. Throughout the OECD, world culture was considered rather as a public service meant to promote the aesthetic understanding of the nation's citizens than as an area that should be subject to market criteria. This has changed during the last two decades with two independent but interacting processes: the commodification of culture accompanied by a cut-back of public expenditure in cultural services, on the one hand, and the "culturalisation" of the economy, promoted by new management strategies and a better educated workforce, on the other hand. Nowadays the so-called cultural economy is addressed not only as a "prime mover for globalisation processes" (Krätke, 2002, p. 1) with regard to the world's urban systems in which cultural production clusters concentrate, but also as a motor for job growth of service economies (European Commission, 2001; Leadbeater & Oakley, 1999; UNESCO, 2000).

Indeed, in most advanced western societies the cultural sector, including the new digital media production, expanded during the last decades and thus became a still small but significant part of the changing feature of the former industrial society. As a reassessment of the employment figures in OECD countries in the time period 1986–1998 shows, the services contributed to a continuous and overall employment growth while industry and agriculture still produced employment losses (OECD, 2000, p. 125). Within the service sector, cultural services (as part of the personal services in the OECD classification) still have a small but rising share of employment.[2] The same holds true for the EU countries in the nineties. Following a recent sophisticated report on the job potential in the cultural sector, from 1995 to 1999, the cultural sector in the EU experienced an average annual rate of employment growth of 2.1%, covering currently about 7.2 million workers. The growth was concentrated in those areas where the demand for content creation is greatest, while employment stagnated in the characteristically industrial areas such as the printing industry. Within the cultural sector, employment figures for cultural occupations strongly grew, whereas non-cultural occupations (such as administration) tended to decrease. As to the future development of employment the report predicts that the rapidly increasing digitization of cultural products will result in declining significance of the traditional cultural media, such as books and printed matter, whereas new media such as internet websites will come to the fore (European Commission, 2001).

Moreover, the cultural sector clearly displays some characteristics that are discussed as a future profile of a broader range of knowledge-based work. *First* cultural industries are characterised by *a high share of freelancers and small companies* (European Commission, 2001). They thus contribute to the general trend of an increasing share of (non-agricultural) self-employed in most post-industrial countries.[3] Although the size of growth and the sectoral distribution of self-employment vary throughout Western Europe in accordance with country-specific institutional settings and "entrepreneurial cultures," especially for post-industrial countries there is evidence that knowledge-intensive services (like finance/insurance, business services, culture, and education) form a significant part of the recent so-called "modern" growth particularly of single person self-employment (Leicht, 2000; Luber & Leicht, 2000).

Second the cultural sector shows a *high share of academically educated women* ranging from 40 to 50% of the total workforce.[4] Interestingly enough, this feature does not correspond to the historically well-known occupational pattern of "feminization equals downgrading." Rather, it seems to follow the more recent trend of highly educated women seeking professional advancement and at the same time working conditions offering flexibility to combine work and family. The growing influx of women in self-employment as well as in traditional male professions like medicine and law are points in case (Lohmann, 2001; McManus, 2001). As to the cultural professions there are indications that women are not only attracted by "soft factors" like the positive image of the sector as creative, young, dynamic, egalitarian, entrepreneurish and simply "cool." Of relevance are also the "hard facts" of good job prospects and the promise of a creative professional career with rather flexible working hours and employment forms, especially self-employment, which seemingly allow for a better work-life-balance than traditional industrial production (Gill, 2002; Haak & Schmid, 1999; Leadbeater & Oakley, 1999; Rehberg et al., 2002). A study on the book publishing industry in the U.K. showed that barriers to the top level of corporate hierarchies (the glass-ceiling effect) as well as difficulties in combining work and family promote the transition or entry into self-employment (Fraser & Gold, 2001; Granger et al., 1995). In a study on freelance journalism in Germany, women stressed the fact that as freelancers, being able to control and limit the volume of their work, they could much better combine work and family in order to secure professional continuity (Wirths, 1994).[5]

Greater control can also be based on a less gender-segregated distribution of working-time schemes, incomes, and qualification levels in this occupational field which do not follow the traditional pattern of male breadwinner/female housewife and caregiver but rather imply dual-earner patterns.[6] As the available statistical data for Germany suggest, female as well as male journalists or graphic designers are spread along the whole range of different working-time patterns: from under 30 hours a week, to 30–45 hours, to over 45 hours. For example, 40% of male journalists in Germany work part-time (less than 31 hours).[7] The same heterogeneity can be observed with respect to the income distribution which ranges from rather low earnings, which are quite frequent, to medium incomes, and peak revenues of a small professional elite. Even though women are represented in the lower income groups slightly more often, the observed strong social differentiation is not primarily based on gender; rather, the peak income group is composed of about the same proportions of men and women (Brasse, 2002).[8]

Corresponding to these findings is a *third characteristic* of cultural work that is the *emergence of a new type of more flexible work*, implying new work and life patterns. As already mentioned, cultural occupations traditionally have been practised in specific employment forms like freelancing which allow (and require) more flexibility in terms of working hours, income, and place of work. Individual transitions between in-house work, freelancing, or complete self-employment have always been quite normal and frequent. The training sequence is far from being standardized but allows diverse and complex qualification tracks. The flexibilised production regime in the media world requires a high degree of self-management in everyday life as well as in the life course. These features soften the demarcation line between "work" and "not work," especially in an institutional setting where dependent work as well as the traditional professions are highly regulated as in Germany (Gottschall, 2002). While these characteristics can already be studied in the cultural industries they are not unique to them. On the contrary, the de-standardisation of work, qualification tracks, and work and life patterns along with a corresponding new demand on self-management competencies is currently discussed as a more general transformation of work of post-modern societies and can also be found in other more or less modern industries like telecommunication, software, and e-commerce (Felstead & Jewson, 1999; Pongratz & Voß, 2002).

All in all, the employment model of the cultural professions might imply the *chance for a pioneer role for new and de-gendered work and life patterns*. How far these chances can actually be realized is a question awaiting further research. In fact, there is little known about the implications of the specific, highly flexible employment model in the cultural professions for the social structure of the labor force and the arrangements of work and life in everyday and biographical perspective. The available quantitative data on employment and household forms of cultural professionals are not at all satisfying, either on the national level or on a comparative international level. This is partly due to a lack of scientific and official recognition of the sector's impact on employment, and partly to the absence in the official statistics of standardized definitions for the highly heterogeneous and dynamic field of "cultural industries" and "cultural professions."[9]

In the following account we draw on recent findings of a mostly qualitative cross-sectional analysis of self-employment among selected cultural professions (journalists, editorial workers, translators, graphic designers) in Germany. We are using secondary data, the results of a standardized questionnaire, and expert interviews with key representatives of professional organizations and trade unions that focus on working conditions, forms of collective and individual risk-management, and their impact on work and life patterns.

TURBULENT AND CUT-THROAT MARKETS CHALLENGE THE COLLECTIVE ACTORS

The generally intensified globalisation processes of markets in the nineties had particularly strong effects on the cultural industries as one of the most booming branches. Accompanied and accelerated by the digitization of production processes in the media, the markets for cultural products became international, and competition among large media groups and smaller firms increased rapidly. New competitors from the Far East (Hong Kong) appeared on the global markets (UNESCO, 2000) causing turmoil. Despite booming demand and economic expansion, rationalization and internal restructuring on a large scale were used to cut costs and stay competitive in Germany as well as in other Western countries. As a result, in-house employment was replaced by freelancers or completely eliminated through outsourcing. Moreover, public broadcasting was privatized, new private radio and TV stations emerged, and public institutions cut jobs by partly outsourcing their business. Electronic communication, especially the Internet, initially brought brand-new and unexpected opportunities for the media market, though in the end it did not realize the tremendous profit margins that had been expected.

With respect to the supply side, increasing numbers of well-qualified university and college graduates, among them many women, entered the external labor markets, leading to increased competition among employees. For many newcomers as well as experienced workers, freelancing and self-employment became the only way to enter or to stay in the marketplace and thus was and still is to some extent involuntary.

INCREASED SOCIAL POLARIZATION

Due to the changed economic environment at the beginning of the 21st century working conditions in the cultural industries appear to have worsened. Freelancers, in particular, are facing higher economic risks due to increased competition and cost-cutting policies of the firms who hire them. Moreover, rapid technological change such as digitization calls for continuous training to keep up with the most recent electronic products (Kotamraju, 2002). Freelancers must manage these requirements at their own expense, which can become difficult especially when the needed training must be undertaken on the worker's own initiative within a tight schedule. Fortunately the financial cost has risen only slightly, thanks to lower prices of electronic equipment and software.

With regard to *income distribution*, the few available studies on the situation in Germany indicate a broad spread between relatively low earnings of freelancers especially in the print media, and top incomes of a privileged professional elite, in film and TV.[10] The net hourly incomes of freelancers in the entire German media industry in 1997 ranged between about €7 in the public relations segment and €8 in film production (Rehberg et al., 2002, p. 87).[11] The data on freelancers in the relatively well-paid subsegment of private television, radio, and digital media show monthly gross incomes between less than €450 up to over €5,000 (Satzer, 2001, p. 21). In the print media, however, data from 1998 show clearly lower income levels; here 34.7% of the real freelancers earned up to €1,000 monthly gross income, nearly one-third were in the medium class up to €2,500, and only 5% had peak incomes of more than €4,000 per month (Grass, 1998, p. 74).

These data must, of course, be seen in connection with working hours. Despite heterogeneous working-time patterns, long working hours of 45–60 hours per week are normal to earn one's living as self-employed, at least in periods of full employment. In 1997, two-thirds of freelancers in the media sector worked 40 hours or more, compared to 37% of in-house employees. More than one-third (37%) of freelancers worked over 50 hours, against 7% of in-house employees (Rehberg et al., 2002, p. 86). However, strong flexibilization according to the needs of the production process has led to "bulimic careers" (Pratt, 2000, p. 432) or "feast and famine cycles" (Leadbeater & Oakley, 1999, p. 27) of freelance media workers. Periods of hard work, sometimes on multiple jobs simultaneously, and long hours including night and weekend shifts alternate with slack periods when only a small job or none at all is at hand. The claimed (or hoped for) greater autonomy of the self-employed with respect to working hours often becomes merely theoretical, being mainly dependent on the cyclical demand for services with tight deadlines. Only a small, well-established elite of highly specialized professionals seems to really enjoy the privilege of self-direction and autonomy today.

What these working conditions mean for *female* cultural professionals can only be supposed on the basis of the recent empirical studies in Germany and the European Union. These suggest that women in the media industry are working under even more unfavourable conditions than their male colleagues (Brasse, 2002; Gill, 2002; Rehberg et al., 2002; Satzer, 2001). For female self-employed cultural workers the German data show lower incomes in spite of their average higher formal education levels, and longer hours for the same earnings as men (Rehberg et al., 2002; Satzer, 2001).[12] The study of Rehberg et al. (2002) on the situation of women in the German media industries reveals that freelance women workers on average earn only 90% of the net hourly wage of their male colleagues, despite their generally higher formal skill levels (Rehberg et al., 2002, p. 87). In general, these women work only slightly fewer hours than men. For example, in the booming Bavarian media industries women work on average 44 hours (men: 50 hours). In the entire German film industries women average 46 hours (men: 47.5), although the average for the whole German media industry shows a bigger gender disparity (women, 37 hours; men, 46 hours). In a comparative European study on new media workers,[13] Rosalind Gill and her team found that women work on fewer simultaneous jobs that are less lucrative than men's, resulting in such low incomes that they are pushed into other occupations like teaching to earn their living. Gill's study on this "most modernized" group of media workers shows gender income disparities of 40%. The average yearly net income for women was €10,000, against €16,000 for men (Gill, 2002, p. 79). Moreover, many more women than men work from home. But this gender difference does not mirror a female preference for combining work and family, as is often thought. Female new media workers, like their male peers, would prefer to have a rented studio or workshop in the cultural quarter of the city to combat isolation, but they cannot afford it (Gill, 2002, pp. 82, 84).

Nevertheless, it would be simplistic to state that the observed *social polarization* of cultural professions is predominantly to the detriment of women as a social group. According to our own evaluation of data, for example, the gender proportions are nearly equal among private broadcasting journalists in the peak income classes of over €4,500 per month.[14] Despite evident gender disparities, gender appears to be *not* the main demarcation line of social differentiation in this occupational field, but variables such as age, work experience, skill level, or sector are at least as relevant.

Summing up, the market conditions for cultural professionals in the globalized and digitized new century can be described as highly competitive and risky for the individual, demanding high and specialized skill levels, while the material rewards for many freelancers appear to be rather modest. Nevertheless, cultural workers appear to remain in this industry because of the non-material compensations that are connected to high intrinsic motivation and a strong identification with the work.

To better understand the labor market dynamics of cultural professions and their impact on individual and collective actors the broader context of their specific work regulation modes has to be considered.

REGULATION AND INDIVIDUAL NEGOTIATION IN NETWORK STRUCTURES

From a sociological and social-political perspective the regulation of work is seen in the broader context of national institutional frameworks, in particular as influenced by the state and its effect on market conditions for labor, industry, and services. In the specific case of Germany, cultural professions are particularly interesting since they may represent a new type of work regulation of growing importance, thus playing perhaps a pioneer role for changes in the German employment system (Gottschall & Betzelt, 2001). Beyond such nation-specifics, the regulation modes of cultural professions may also indicate general tendencies of rapidly changing high-skilled labor markets in advanced western societies, if recent developments in the traditional professions are considered.[15]

Regarding the German employment system, cultural professions neither comply with the image of the real self-employed, as represented by the traditional professions (doctors, lawyers), nor do they conform to the image of the "standard employment relationship," represented by the dependent employee. They are neither subject to the "institutionally secured self-regulation" of the professions (characterized by control of access, state guaranteed monopoly for rendering services, and private social security provisions secured by high income), nor do they have access to a "corporatist regulation mode," relevant for the majority of dependent employees and guaranteeing them a limited but nevertheless long-term protection of occupational status, qualifications, and social security.

In the German welfare system, unlike in other western countries, the regulation of both corporations and professions is closely associated with the state as a legal regulator, a guarantor of social security, and an employer (Lane et al., 2000). This does not hold true for cultural professionals who are exposed to stronger and more immediate market risks. In terms of risks and chances they take an intermediate position between the professions and the standard employment relationship. In contrast to dependent employees, cultural professionals have the privilege of determining their own working hours and volume as well as the balance between their work and life spheres. In contrast to the true professions, however, this privileged status is not anchored in an institutionally secured economic monopoly. Rather, each cultural professional's market value must constantly be reproduced anew in the relevant networks through the control of communication, trust, and reputation. This negotiation through network structures makes the labor markets for cultural professions more open and flexible, but also more risky than labor markets in which the supply of labor and the demand for services is institutionally regulated, as in the case of doctors. Market success in the cultural professions is predicated primarily on individual cultural and social capital and is at the same time susceptible to risk in the case of changes in market conditions (Gottschall & Betzelt, 2001; Haak & Schmid, 1999).[16]

Furthermore, due to the relative modernity of these professions, there is a lack of traditional collective forms of professional control regarding qualification standards and the regulation of prices for their services. The exposed position of cultural professionals, that is closely dependent on the labor supply and demand for cultural services, implies both challenges and opportunities for the constitution of professionalism and social security. Therefore, the "opportunities and risk profile" of cultural professions typically moves within a range from privilege to precariousness.

CHALLENGES AND OPPORTUNITIES FOR COLLECTIVE ACTORS IN THE MEDIA INDUSTRIES

Cultural professions and the collective representation of heterogeneous interests have to act within these open markets and individualized regulation modes. They face particular challenges due to increasing social differentiation within this sector and a threat to their professional standards (Betzelt, 2001). Professional organizations have to cope with the need of maintaining or claiming standards for professional quality and prices that are not legally fixed against the superiority of large corporations. As voluntary societies they compete for members, and they have to organize a highly heterogeneous, fragmented occupational group with varying skill levels, who are also subject to rapid technological innovation.

Moreover, the situation of collective actors is even more complicated since these harsh working conditions go hand in hand with an increasingly *individualized* workforce that at least partly identifies itself with the positive entrepreneurial, dynamic and "cool" image of the sector. Hence, in this modernized environment traditional membership organizations that are built on honorary commitment of their members and strong ties of collective professional identity are apt to experience particular difficulties. On one hand, the secular trend of declining membership in mass organizations like trade unions or traditional voluntary associations is of concern in this particular occupational field. But on the other hand, the growing attractiveness of modernized professional organizations in the journalistic and creative field can be observed.[17] There is an obvious demand for professional interest groups even though the idea of collective organization is generally fading. Two examples of innovative professional strategies in Germany are described below.

Innovative Risk-Management Strategies: Two Examples

Our two examples of modernized professional organizations belong to different occupational subgroups and represent different basic orientations: The first represents today's largest professional association of designers in Germany and organized freelancers who work in the various fields of design. The second example represents a "modernized" trade union for freelance and employed journalists in private broadcasting, film, multimedia, new electronic media, and advertising agencies. Despite their dissimilar membership bases, organizational culture, and professional rather than trade union orientation, both examples illustrate certain common elements in their strategies. They engage in innovative forms of lobbying on behalf of knowledge-workers who are presently facing rapidly changing market conditions and work requirements. The analysis is based on expert interviews with the key representatives of the two organizations, complemented by findings from a semi-structured questionnaire on basic organizational data, and documentary material from the associations.

Professional Association of Designers: "Modernism Wins the Day"

Since the 1990s, the traditionally male dominated graphic design industry has increasingly come under pressure due to several developments. First, more people with varying skill levels are entering the industry: graduates from arts schools and colleges, newcomers from technical occupations, or the self-taught, among them more and more women. Simultaneously, the demand for services has changed: the traditional arts and craft qualification has lost its value due to digitization and accelerated production cycles. In addition to technical competence, the complete "one stop-shop" solution – from planning and conception to product delivery – is in demand. In this more competitive environment management skill, corporate-style structures, and a cooperative project-oriented working style has competitive advantage and is in greater demand. This situation puts pressure on traditional professional associations and small elite outfits because they still adhere to the relevance of high formal qualifications such as a diploma as an entry requirement, and because they implicitly stick to the model of the individual creative professional that is typically male.

For instance, the oldest and once most established professional association, Bund Deutscher Graphikdesigner – *(BDG)*, has continuously lost stature during recent decades. This traditionally structured organization suffers from a drastic decline of members and now mainly consists of elderly male professionals. It has been outrun by a modernized, more socially inclusive professional association, *Allianz Deutscher Designer – (AGD)* that spun off from the BDG twenty-five years ago and since then has increasingly gained ground. It was established by active members of the traditional graphic design society (BDG) who were dissatisfied with its antiquated structures and methods, and who also aimed at forming a modern, alternative association that could meet today's demands for an interest group of design professionals, particularly of those who work as freelancers. Consequently, and reflecting changing market conditions, the access to the *Allianz* is not limited to credentialist criteria, but is open to various skill levels, specializations, and occupational fields in commercial design. The only criterion for becoming a member is having a freelance status, i.e. not being employed in-house. To assure that qualifications are sufficiently high for being accepted into the association, the board of directors operates in an informal way to exercise some control; this approach corresponds to the generally informal regulation modes in the field of cultural professions. Such a socially inclusive strategy follows the post-industrial trend to evaluate professional profiles in a flexible and individualized way which is different from the old concept of a clearly fixed, and collectively defined "profession." The new concept implies that the professional has a more or less individual-specific bundle of competencies and skills (Stooß, 1999).

The *Allianz* has meanwhile grown into the largest professional design association in Germany (over 3,000 members), with a nearly gender-balanced membership (47% women). Most members are between 30 and 50 years old and thus represent professional newcomers as well as more established associates. As a lobby of freelancers, the association is not primarily serving corporatist professional interests, such as maintenance of qualitative, credentialist standards. Rather, the association focuses primarily on the *individual economic success* of its members. It offers its associates *specialized services* that enable them to succeed in changing markets: for instance, individual consulting and training in price calculation and self-marketing, or legal aid. To promote up-to-date qualification levels, continuing education courses are offered at a discount. Beyond mere individual support, *networking* is another strategy for collective risk-management. The association's board continuously creates events to stimulate such networks and specifically cultivates internal social-professional communication in order to strengthen project-based business cooperation between members. At the same time, and this is another sign of the heterogeneity of collective actors in the cultural professions, *traditional risk-management* strategies are also pursued. The designers' alliance promotes "wage agreements" for freelancers[18] and publishes a catalogue of recommended fees and prices for design services. In addition, it is lobbying to improve copyright protection for design work, which in Germany has a much weaker legal status than, for example, protection for authors.

The organization's specifically tailored services for freelancers in the field of design are congruent with the demands of a dynamic and open market for knowledge-based services. This accomplishment is only possible as a result of *professionalized management* on a full-time basis and within an effective, centralized organization. Nevertheless, membership fees are not extraordinarily high but are rather modest in light of the relatively insecure and low level of most members' incomes. Summing up, the innovative designers' association Allianz reflects the dynamic structure of the profession and can be seen as an effective agent of the collective interests of its member base now and in the future.

Trade Unionist Network of "New Media" Freelancers:
"Continuity via Change"

Journalists constitute the biggest and most professionalized group within
the cultural professions. Direct employment in publishing houses and television is traditionally just as common as freelancing. The co-existence of a
traditional professional association with a comparatively strong trade union
results in several complementary rather than competitive forms of professional
representation.

Since the 1970s both the largest professional association *Deutscher Journa-
listenverein – (DJV)* and the huge services *Verdi* trade union (which absorbed the
former *IG Medien*), have represented the interests of both dependent employees
and self-employed journalists in a complementary rather than competitive way. In
the prosperous seventies, they together succeeded in implementing not only wage
agreements for dependent workers in radio and TV stations and the print press,
but also agreements for freelancers. Those freelancers who worked predominantly
for just one large publisher or public broadcaster were guaranteed minimum
fees and extensive social security provisions. Furthermore, a special form of
social security for freelancers was achieved in 1983 with the introduction of a
nation-wide *special social insurance scheme for artists* (although in Germany,
access to public social security is normally reserved for dependent employees
only) (Betzelt & Schnell, 2003; Gottschall & Schnell, 2000).[19]

These social-political achievements, which had succeeded in a specific historical
era during the reign of a social-liberal government and in a period of economic
growth, have since then come under continuous economic pressure. The changing
market conditions of the 1990s, especially privatization of public broadcasting,
job cuts, and the advent of online journalism, watered down the once established
standards. In private television and radio, in the new electronic media and in the
former Länder of the German Democratic Republic, agreed minimum fees and
social security provisions for freelancers have never been effective. There are
clear indications of involuntary self-employment and growing income insecurity
and social inequality.

At the same time, especially in the *new electronic* and *privatized audiovisual
media* the individualization of the labor force proceeded quickly, mainly due to
the young age of workers in these fields. Such individualized initiative makes
collective action especially difficult for *trade unions* which are built on the idea of
solidarity and a collective workforce identity. Particular problems for organizing
the new media workers are the strong identification of freelancers with "their" TV,
or radio station, fluctuating customer/employer relationships, and the widespread

self-image of the journalists in the new media as "autonomous" professionals rather than dependent employees.

Given increased competition and uncertainty in the new media, to counteract the increased market forces in this difficult arena, the trade union of the industry – more or less with its back to the wall – explored new strategies which actually proved to be quite successful. A special service organization called *"Connexx"* was founded in 1999 to represent the interests of freelancers in private broadcasting, film, audiovisual media, and the Internet. It works like a kind of "special task force" for these interest groups within the large services trade union, *Verdi*, yet has great autonomy and its own budget. Connexx is essentially a trade unionist consultancy which works on two levels: first, a "virtual" level, represented by an Internet website which delivers a whole lot of information relevant both to freelance and in-house workers in the media industry, such as legal information or special business news.[20] The second operating level of Connexx is currently represented (March, 2003) by five offices in different cities which cover big regional clusters of the media industry[21] and are each staffed with one or two professional experts who give advice to media workers on all kinds of problems regarding the working conditions in the field. Altogether, nine media professionals work within Connexx, five women and four men. Despite being part of a larger trade union, Connexx nevertheless works quite autonomously and has established an internal division of labor along the lines of individual expertise. This strong autonomy, together with the professional know-how of the Connexx people and special operating strategies, distinguish Connexx from traditional forms of trade unionist organizations. These innovations have been a success: Within two years after its founding it had recruited 1,500 new young members of both sexes from all over Germany.[22] Due to this enormous growth the trade union granted Connexx more resources in 2002 for adding personnel. Meanwhile Connexx enjoys an excellent reputation in the field.

One essential factor in the development of Connexx was that some former professional freelancers with long experience in the special field of private film and broadcasting played a decisive role in its formation and right from the start came into responsible full-time positions in its management. This recruitment of full-time personnel from young insiders in their early thirties, who spoke the same language and lived the same lifestyles as the larger membership distinguished Connexx from traditional trade unions and made it quite popular. Another innovative aspect of Connexx was to focus not on single occupations or professions but to organize in an inclusive manner. Connexx was interested in appealing to all the freelancers, who worked in private and new media and IT (Information Technology), regardless of qualifications and skills. Connexx thereby took account of fluid skill profiles and market dynamics. Moreover, it offered services not only to union members, but also initial consultation to non-members. The special know-how of the Connexx-people and their reliability was used as a public relation strategy to promote the idea of a modern type of trade union.

The main strategy of Connexx with regard to *"true" freelancing*, i.e. relatively autonomous work for different customers, aims at establishing an acceptable level of fees for journalistic work in the private and new media. These services support the individual economic success of self-employed media workers and offer specific legal aid (such as fee contracts, copyright for electronic sources) as well as legal protection, further training opportunities, technical information, relevant news, newsletters, etc. Great store is set in up-to-date publication of all information and immediate availability of individual consulting made possible by the intensive use of electronic media (Internet, electronic mail), telecommunication, and by efficient organizational structures (flat hierarchies, networking, and cooperation).

A further innovative element of Connexx is that they also use scientific expertise to learn more about their "modern" interest groups of electronic media workers. On behalf of Connexx, several empirical surveys among media workers in the respective fields have been carried out to learn more about the working conditions, the social composition of the workforce, and the demands on trade union representation.[23] This attempt at founding "modern" trade unionist work on a scientific basis has made clear not only the general lack of data about the conditions of work in new media, but also the great interest of professional associations in contacting new groups of workers.

With respect to those media workers who are actually *not self-employed* but depend on one broadcaster or firm, Connexx pursues at the same time the more traditional trade union strategy of establishing works councils within local business enterprises. Despite the "modern" character of the market segments and the young clientele, this policy has also been successful due to worsening working conditions after the economic crash of many new media firms.[24] Media workers with less autonomy are moreover advised to assert their social security rights with their employers.

All in all, Connexx stands for a fruitful attempt to reconcile traditional trade unionist goals – collective representation of workers' interests to industrial management – with modernized professional strategies for new groups of a highly skilled labor force for whom no collective bargaining is likely. The main innovative driving force is to adapt to post-industrial trends without losing solidarity; thus Connexx aims at strengthening bargaining power and market position of the *individual*, but also fights for *collective* rights and social security provisions.

Common Innovative Elements in Both Types of Collective Strategy

Both kinds of collective actors have managed to develop new strategies which answer to changed demands for representing the interests of new working groups. They have established modern, effective internal structures and they work with professional, specialized staff. Their organizations do not emphasize traditional criteria for membership such as fixed occupational characteristics, but are more socially inclusive in order to take account of workers' changing skill profiles and of changing markets. Consequently, the growing memberships are mainly young, with relatively high shares of females and heterogeneous skill specializations and fields of activity.

Their strategies aim at supporting the individual economic success of freelance professionals. For this purpose, the organizations offer specialized services for their members, and, as a marketing strategy, partial benefits to non-members also. They use and support networking as a new way of succeeding in the markets as freelancers. At the same time, they pursue more traditional strategies with regard to collective representation, such as setting standards for quality and prices of their knowledge-based services.

In summary, the new strategies have in common that they neither follow the model of trade unionist lobbying typical of dependent workers, nor do they use the protectionist lobbying model of professional associations that is typical of the classic professions. Rather, the forms of collective representation among cultural professions in Germany can be described as *hybrid*: they contain components similar to those of trade unions aimed at protection from market risk, and elements similar to those of professional associations for securing professional autonomy. It seems that the most successful organizations are those that address *the risks as well as the opportunities* of the market, and, unlike the traditional associations, are more socially inclusive.

Hence it seems that despite difficult conditions for freelance work in the cultural industries, successful "modernized" solutions have been developed by collective associations. However, a closer look at the question of social equality and gender in the field gives a somewhat less positive impression.

BETWEEN DE-GENDERED WORK AND RE-GENDERED WORK AND LIFE ARRANGEMENTS

What do the results so far suggest about the implications of collective risk-management strategies for gendered work and for sustainable patterns of work and life for both genders? On the basis of our study, the preliminary answer is ambiguous: Regarding the *work sphere*, cultural professions are less gendered with respect to the distribution of working hours and income than standard employment or classical professions. And their collective associations reflect the more or less equal gender-mix of the labor force quite adequately. The implicit normative professional ideal, particularly of the more recent organizations, carries no overt male connotation; instead the ideal – the *individualized autonomous self-employed* – seems to be gender neutral. However, this normative orientation also contains a certain idea of the *relationship between the private and the public*. With respect to private circumstances, the worker is seen as independent of family ties: a professional worker is not a parent and does not care for family members. Parenthood remains a private issue. This interpretation, drawn from the implicit ideas of the interviewed professional representatives, is also suggested by the fact that none of them – male or female – *explicitly* raised the subject of family duties of their own accord. Our questions about whether their professional organizations offered their members any support for reconciling work and family were met with some surprise, and they explained that this was outside the scope of the organization's duties and rather an individual private matter.

While such an expectation marks a boundary between the private and the public, there is another side of the coin where this border dissolves. As a necessary precondition, the image of the autonomous self-employed worker is based on a particular model of dual-earner partnership in the household: One partner has to cushion the incalculable aspects and risks faced by the other in the market place, whether the loss of income, or overlong working hours that require support with everyday reproductive work. The highly flexibilised working process of the media industries requires individual support by reliable private partners who possibly have complementary working hours and receive stable incomes. The collective actors take these private individual solutions for granted; the risks are implicitly seen as a natural element of working as a cultural professional, and hence are not seen as a field of collective responsibility or risk-management.

At this point the question arises what this model means for the everyday division of labor in partnerships as well as for the *arrangements of work and life* in the life-course. Recent findings of other studies in the field indicate that the employment form of freelancing under radicalised market conditions possibly can only be kept up during certain stages of the life-course or within specific private household constellations. If that is the case the limitations appear to follow quite familiar gender-stereotyped patterns. Several empirical findings for Germany and for some EU countries prove that freelance women in the media sector more often than men correspond to the *type "young and childless"* (Brasse, 2002; Gill, 2002; Rehberg et al., 2002).[25] According to these data, mothers are clearly under-represented among freelance media workers, in particular in the new electronic field. It seems that "professional freelancing" for women is an acceptable or attractive employment form only so long as they can (and are willing to) match the "male" professional ideal. This would imply a *short-term career* for the expert who is a single-person entrepreneur in a highly competitive market – at least for female (or male) professionals who take on care obligations. The same interpretation is suggested by statements in our expert interviews. *Health or age reasons* were the usual motives for an individual's leaving (or wishing to leave) the freelancing form of employment.

International studies also point out that with regard to private partnership among female and male professionals, dual-earner households are quite frequent, yet they do not necessarily go along with an egalitarian division of labor. Instead, we find women making the trade-offs between work and family in the sense of *dual-earner/female part-time caregiver* or *dual-earner and paid caregiver patterns* that draw new class-specific demarcation lines between women (Blossfeld & Drobnic, 2001; Crompton & Birkelund, 2000; Gottschall, 2002; Hochschild, 2000). At the same time, new patterns of heterosexual partnerships are also developing among academics such as the *dual-career couple* where both partners follow their individual professional career track and both do household work and child care. This promises perhaps more egalitarian arrangements than the traditional model of "male breadwinner/female housewife." Initial findings show, however, that the division of labor within this modernized arrangement is definitely not free of old gender-specific asymmetries. In particular, the immense internal "costs" of coordinating and synchronizing two professional careers remain a responsibility typically taken on by the female partner (Behnke & Meuser, 2002).

The general *gender neutrality* of the collective associations in the field of cultural professions and their neglect of the impacts of new self-employment forms on work and life arrangements hides other specific *structures of social inequality* in the media industry (Gill, 2002). The regulation of open labor markets by informal social mechanisms in professional networks implies a lack of transparency with respect to power structures, hierarchies, and subjective assessment of the quality of creative work. Access to lucrative jobs and allocation of work are granted through informal personal contacts outside of formal organizations and hierarchies. This can lead to mechanisms of social exclusion which in a still somewhat male-dominated occupational field is of concern to women. In the "old boys networks" of modernized professional freelancers everyday sexism is nevertheless present (Gill, 2002; Rehberg et al., 2002). However, in the media sector with its glamorous, young and dynamic image, a new meritocratic and egalitarian discourse prevails that makes these discriminatory social structures invisible. As a result, any signs of discrimination are ignored as a potential cause for political action by the collective organizations.

A preliminary conclusion of our analysis is that some scepticism is in order regarding the role of modernized professions in pioneering new work and life patterns. They indeed provide new career opportunities for highly-skilled women, offering comparatively autonomous working conditions despite increased individual risks in their radicalised competition for global markets. But these new professions and market segments are built on long established societal and economic structures, and therefore it is not really surprising that well-known gender-asymmetries persist in the new employment forms and work and life arrangements. This study has concentrated on the part of collective actors in these new fields of the cultural professions; a future task of great interest will be further research on how *individual* actors – male and female – live and interpret the social changes they are part of, and especially to what extent they are helping to bring about the de-gendered patterns of work and life that appear to be the trend of the future.

NOTES

1. The Research project "*New Forms of Self-Employment in Cultural Professions*" (*2001–2003*) is funded by the German Research Foundation (DFG). The professional groups include journalists, graphic designers, editorial freelancers, and translators. Research methods include secondary statistical analyses and a standardized online-survey of cultural workers in Germany focusing on the social structure and market situation of cultural professions. Furthermore, we carried through a standardized questionnaire and 17 expert interviews with representatives of professional associations and other relevant institutions. Forty guided in-depth interviews with cultural workers to be evaluated until the end of 2003 are focusing on professional identity and individual strategies of risk-management (area: five German cities where cultural industries are clustered).

2. The OECD sector classification differentiates agriculture, industry, and producer services, distributive services, personal services, and social services. According to these data in 1998 all services had a 76% share of total employment, with the social services as the leading sector (35.5%), followed by distributive (19.6%), personal (12.3%) and producer services (12.2%) (OECD, 2000, p. 124, Table 3. C.1).

3. For example, self-employment as a percentage of total employment increased from 1983 to 1997 in the U.K. from 9.3 to 11.8%, in Germany from 7.4 to 9.3% (Luber & Leicht, 2000, p. 111).

4. Despite a severe lack of reliable data there are indications of relatively high shares of women among cultural professionals at least in some segments and in several European countries. For example, Leadbeater and Oakley (1999, p. 21) numbered the proportion of female workers in the British cultural sector at 45%, estimating even higher figures in the younger industries of the media world. The European Commission study reports (2001, p. 121f) a female share of 38.7% for the large (and heterogeneous) occupational group of "writers and creative or performing artists" (according to the International Classification of Occupations ISCO 1988, no. 245; see International Labour Office, 1990). For the occupational group of "artistic, entertainment and sports associate professionals" (among them

commercial designers, radio and TV announcers and others; ISCO 347), the EU-average proportion of women is 43.1%. Different figures are observed with regard to a sectoral classification. For Germany, Rehberg et al. (2002, p. 61) number the share of female workers in the entire media industry at 47% which is 3 percentage points more than in the whole economy.

5. The general employment trend of rising self-employment in several service sector branches gave rise to debate in labor market policy on the one hand emphasizing a cyclical "push" effect of unemployment and outsourcing policies of public and private companies, and on the other hand, the optimistic view of a historical revival or new "pull" effect of entrepreneurial ambitions. As the findings on women in self-employment suggest, the reasons for becoming self-employed might be more complex than the push-and-pull argument suggests.

6. The available German occupational studies referring to the cultural sector suggest that dual-earner patterns prevail (cf. Grass, 1998; Leicht & Lauxen-Ulbrich, 2002; Rehberg et al., 2002; Satzer, 2001).

7. These and the following data are derived from a special evaluation of the Sample Census 1999 that has been carried out by the Federal Statistical Office (Statistisches Bundesamt) on our behalf.

8. These results are derived from a special gender-sensitive evaluation of data by order of the mentioned DFG-research project, based on a survey of users of the trade unionist network "Connexx" (see below).

9. For example, no comparative data on incomes in cultural professions are at hand, and only rough averages are given with respect to working hours in EU-countries (European Commission, 2001, p. 126).

10. For Germany we refer to the study of women in the media industry by Rehberg et al. (2002), the survey of freelancers in private television and broadcasting by Satzer (2001), and the EU-comparative study of Gill (2002).

11. All cited figures are converted from German marks into Euros.

12. In some segments, like the film industry or publishing, gender income disparities are even much higher: In the film industry, women earn on average 55% less than men, in publishing the average income difference between women and men is 18% (Rehberg et al., 2002).

13. The studied countries were Austria, Finland, the Netherlands, Spain, and the U.K. The EU-project, which was coordinated at the London School of Economics, carried out an online-survey and semi-structured interviews with freelance new media workers, and organized conference discussions with project-based workers (Gill, 2002, pp. 76–77). The occupational field of new media work comprises "content creation" such as digital animation, web design, multimedia authoring, web broadcasting, and digital arts and design (Gill, 2002, p. 71).

14. Women 11.1%, men 12.5% (Brasse, 2002).

15. At least in recent findings and discussions of the sociology of professions a rising importance of market risks and economic dependency for professions is reflected (Evetts, 2003; Lane et al., 2000).

16. The decisive role of informal network structures for the regulation of "cultural" labor markets has also been analysed for other western societies (e.g. Baumann, 2002; Blair, 2001; Krätke, 2002).

17. Most of the interviewed occupational organizations indeed show growing numbers of members; some organizations even experienced a membership growth by some 100% within a few years.

18. Such agreements are concluded between the designers' "alliance" and an employers' association of design studios. Since neither association can claim to function as representative agency for its groups these agreements are rather toothless instruments compared to collective wage settlements between trade unions and employers.

19. This scheme gives freelance artists and journalists, who have a maximum of one employee, access to health and pension insurance. The enormous rise in the number of participants in this scheme over the years shows that this provision of social security has mitigated the social risks associated with the low average incomes of cultural professions and has facilitated continuity of professional activity (Gottschall & Schnell, 2000).

20. The website covers subjects such as legal aid, market situation, and working conditions in the media industry, present trade unionist issues etc., see http://www.connexx-av.de.

21. These regions are Hamburg/Hannover (north), Berlin/Brandenburg and Leipzig (east), Cologne/Düsseldorf (west), and Stuttgart/Munich (south).

22. Regarding the age structure, approximately 70% of workers in the electronic media are younger than 40 years, which is mirrored in the recently recruited membership, too. With regard to gender, both men and women are represented among the members, while men still seem to have a slight (estimated) advantage. The media trade union has roughly 34% of its members who are female. These data are drawn from our expert interviews and the questionnaire. The growth in membership is also remarkable since the membership dues in *Verdi* are higher than for other trade unions and even for some professional associations.

23. The data of these surveys have also been used by the DFG-research project (Brasse, 2002; Satzer, 2001).

24. For example, works councils were established in the well-known global enterprise "Pixelpark" due to the effective help of Connexx.

25. The average age for female freelance workers in the Connexx study is 34 years, for men 37. Only 15% of women had children, against 35% of men (Brasse, 2002). Rehberg et al. (2002) calculated that nearly half of all female workers in the Bavarian media sector are younger than 35 years (men: 42%). Two-thirds of the female media workers did not have children. The average age of new electronic media workers (Gill, 2002) is between 25 and 35 years; only a handful of the sample had children; none of them were women. Also other occupational studies support this trend (e.g. Grass, 1998).

REFERENCES

Baumann, A. (2002). Informal labour market governance: The case of the British and German media production industries. *Work, Employment and Society, 16*, 27–46.

Beck, U. (1992). *Risk society: Towards a new modernity*. London: Sage.

Beck, U., Giddens, A., & Lash, S. (Eds) (1994). *Reflexive modernization*. Cambridge: Polity Press.

Behnke, C., & Meuser, M. (2002). *Zwei Karrieren, eine Familie – Vereinbarkeitsmanagement bei Doppelkarrierepaaren*. Dortmund: Universität Dortmund.

Betzelt, S. (2001). Self-employment in cultural professions: between privilege and precariousness. Paper presented at the 5th Conference of the European Sociological Association (ESA) 'Visions and Divisions', Helsinki (30 August).

Betzelt, S., & Schnell, C. (2003). Die Integration "neuer" Selbstständiger in die Alterssicherung: Modelle, Erfahrungen und Probleme in Deutschland und vier europäischen Nachbarstaaten. *Zeitschrift für Sozialreform, 49*, 249–270.

Blair, H. (2001). You're only as good as your last job: The labour market in the British film industry. *Work, Employment and Society, 15*, 149–169.

Blossfeld, H.-P., & Drobnic, S. (2001). *Careers of couples in contemporary societies*. Oxford: Oxford University Press.

Brasse, C. (2002). *Zusatzauswertungen der "Connexx-Studie"*. (unpublished tables). Dortmund: Prospektiv GmbH.

Carnoy, M. (2002). *Sustaining the new economy. Work, family, and community in the information age*. New York: Russel Sage Foundation.

Crompton, R., & Birkelund, G. (2000). Employment and caring in Britain and Norwegian banking: An exploration through individual careers. *Work, Employment and Society, 14*, 331–352.

Crouch, C., Finegold, D., & Sako, M. (1999). Are skills the answer? *The Political Economy of Skill Creation in Advanced Industrial Countries*. Oxford: University Press.

Esping-Andersen, G. (2002). *Why we need a new welfare state*. Oxford: University Press.

European Commission. DG Employment and Social Affairs (2001). *Exploitation and development of the job potential in the cultural sector*. München: MKW Wirtschaftsforschung GmbH München.

Evetts, J. (2003). The construction of professionalism in new and existing occupational contexts: promoting and facilitating occupational change. *International Journal of Sociology and Social Policy* (Special Issue: Health professions, gender and society. Shifting relations in times of institutional and social change) (pp. 22–35).

Felstead, A., & Jewson, N. (1999). *Global trends in flexible labour*. London: MacMillan.

Fraser, J., & Gold, M. (2001). 'Portfolio workers': Autonomy and control amongst freelance translators. *Work, Employment and Society, 15*, 679–697.

Gill, R. (2002). Cool, creative and egalitarian? Exploring gender in project-based new media work in Europe. *Information, Communication and Society, 5*, 70–89.

Gottschall, K. (2002). *New forms of employment in Germany: Labour market regulation and its gendered implications*. Detroit/USA: Wayne State University, College of Urban, Labour and Metropolitan Affairs.

Gottschall, K., & Betzelt, S. (2001). *Alleindienstleister im Berufsfeld Kultur – Versuch einer erwerbsoziologischen Konzeptualisierung. ZeS-Arbeitspapier 18–2001*. Bremen: Zentrum für Sozialpolitik, Universität Bremen.

Gottschall, K., & Bird, K. (2003). Family leave policies and labour market segregation in Germany: Reinvention or reform of the male breadwinner model? *Review of the Policy Research, 20*, 115–134.

Gottschall, K., & Schnell, C. (2000). 'Alleindienstleister' in Kulturberufen – Zwischen neuer Selbständigkeit und alten Abhängigkeiten. *WSI-Mitteilungen, 53*, 804–810.

Granger, B., Stanworth, J., & Stanworth, C. (1995). Self-employment career dynamics: The case of "unempolyment push" in U.K. book publishing. *Work, Employment and Society, 9*, 499–516.

Grass, B. (1998). Arbeitsbedingungen freier Journalisten. Bericht zu einer Umfrage unter Mitgliedern des DJV. *Journalist, 11*, 65–80.

Haak, C., & Schmid, G. (1999). *Arbeitsmärkte für Künstler und Publizisten – Modelle einer zukünftsfähigen Arbeitswelt?* Berlin: Wissenschaftszentrum Berlin, Querschnittsgruppe Arbeit & Ökologie.

Hochschild, A. R. (1996). *Time bind*. New York: Metropolitan.

Hochschild, A. R. (2000). Global care chains and emotional surplus value. In: W. Hutton & A. Giddens (Eds), *On the Edge. Living with the Global Capitalism* (pp. 130–146). London: Jonathan Cape.

International Labour Office (Ed.) (1990). *International standard classification of occupations: ISCO-88*. Geneva: International Labour Office.

Kotamraju, N. P. (2002). Keeping up: Web design skill and the reinvented worker. *Information, Communication and Society*, *5*, 1–26.

Krätke, S. (2002). Global media cities in a worldwide urban network. *GAWC-Globalization and World Cities Study Group and Network. Research Bulletin 80*. Edited and posted on the web on 15. March 2002, http://www.lboro.ac.uk/gawc/rb/rb80.html

Lane, C., Potton, M., & Littek, W. (2000). The professions between state and market. A cross-national study of convergence and divergence. ESRC, Working Paper 189. Cambridge: University of Cambridge.

Leadbeater, C., & Oakley, K. (1999). *The independents. Britain's new cultural entrepeneurs*. London: Demos.

Leicht, R. (2000). Die "neuen Selbständigen" arbeiten alleine. Wachstum und Struktur der Solo-Selbständigen in Deutschland. *IGA Zeitschrift für Klein- und Mittelunternehmen/Sonderdruck*, *48*, 75–90.

Leicht, R., & Lauxen-Ulbrich, M. (2002). *Soloselbständige Frauen in Deutschland: Entwicklung, wirtschaftliche Orientierung und Ressourcen*. Mannheim: Institut für Mittelstandsforschung, Universität Mannheim.

Lohmann, H. (2001). Self-employed or employee, full-time or part-time? Gender differences in the determinants and conditions for self-employment in Europe and the U.S. Working Paper Nr. 38. Mannheim: Mannheimer Zentrum für Europäische Sozialforschung.

Luber, S., & Leicht, R. (2000). Growing self-employment in Western Europe: An effect of modernization? *International Review of Sociology*, *10*, 101–123.

McManus, P. A. (2001). Women's participation in self-employment in western industrialized nations. *International Journal of Sociology*, *1*, 70–97.

OECD (2000). The OECD employment outlook. Paris: OECD Publications.

Pongratz, H. J., & Voß, G. G. (2002). *ArbeiterInnen und Angestellte als Arbeitskraftunternehmer? Erwerbsorientierungen in entgrenzten Arbeitsformen. Forschungsbericht an die Hans-Böckler-Stiftung. Projekt Nr. 2000–182–3*. München/Chemnitz: Unpublished research report.

Pratt, A. (2000). New media, the new economy and new spaces. *Geoforum*, *31*, 425–436.

Rehberg, F., Stöger, U., & Sträter, D. (2002). *Frauen in der Medienwirtschaft: Chancen und Hemmnisse für Frauenerwerbstätigkeit in einer prosperierenden Zukunftsbranche*. München: Reinhard Fischer.

Satzer, R. (2001). *Nicht nur Traumjobs – Vom Arbeiten und Verdienen in den Medien. Studie im Auftrag von connexx.av (verdi). Dokumentation der Ergebnisse*. Frankfurt/M.: Connexx.av.

Sennett, R. (1998). *Corrosion of character. The culture of new capitalism*. New York: W.W. Norton.

Stooß, F. (1999). Arbeitsmarkt Kultur. Eingrenzung – Struktur – Entwicklung. In: Deutscher Kulturrat (Ed.), *Weiterbildung in künstlerischen und kulturellen Berufen* (pp. 153–204). Bonn: Deutscher Kulturrat.

UNESCO Institute for Statistics (2000). International flows of selected cultural goods 1980–1998. Report. Paris: United Nations.

Wirths, S. (1994). *Freiberuflerinnen im Journalismus. Selbstverständnisse, Arbeitsformen, Probleme und Strategien*. Hamburg: Lit Verlag.

13. ECONOMIC RELATIONS BETWEEN WOMEN AND MEN: NEW REALITIES AND THE RE-INTERPRETATION OF DEPENDENCE

Annemette Sørensen

ABSTRACT

Women's lives and opportunities in the advanced industrialized countries have changed dramatically during the last decades of the 20th century. One of the important changes is that women's economic power has increased considerably, with women's labor force experience and earnings capacity much closer to that of men's than has ever been the case. In this paper I focus on how these changes have affected economic relations between men and women who share a household. Of special interest is how women's greater earnings affect their partnership, spouses' dependence on and independence of each other, and the meaning of their economic contributions to household income. Is there a new gender regime, where women's income no longer should be considered a threat to the stability of the partnership, where women's economic dependence no longer has the meaning it did when few women made significant contributions to family income, and where men increasingly are dependent on women's income?

Changing Life Patterns in Western Industrial Societies
Advances in Life Course Research, Volume 8, 281–297
© 2004 Published by Elsevier Ltd.
ISSN: 1040-2608/doi:10.1016/S1040-2608(03)08013-4

INTRODUCTION

It is the argument of this paper that changes in women's educational, economic and occupational opportunities during the last decades of the 20th century have had profound implications for gender relations within families and for the meaning of economic equality and inequality between spouses. My main point is, that when societal conditions change, what previously may have been oppressive and restrictive may no longer be so or be perceived so. The revolution in women's lives has changed society in profound ways, and these changes spill over into the family (Nock, 1998). Specifically, women's economic dependence on their partner may no longer be the key to the perpetuation of women's subordinate status (Chafetz, 1990; Sørensen & McLanahan, 1987), in part because their dependence at a given point in time may be the result of purely voluntary choice (Hakim, 2000), in part because the level of married women's economic dependence has declined as has the length of time a married woman is completely dependent on her spouse. This has made an increasing proportion of married men highly dependent on their wife's earnings, thus increasing the interdependence of spouses (Oppenheimer, 1997a; Sørensen, 2001). It is commonly argued that men have been slow to "respond" to the new roles and contributions of their wives, especially when it comes to taking on their fair part of housework and childcare. This may be so, but it does not necessarily mean that nothing else has changed. What I try to argue in this paper is that economic relations between men and women who share a household have changed qualitatively, forcing us to rethink the meaning of a measure of gender inequality such as women's economic dependence on their spouse or partner.

In his book on *Marriage in Men's Lives*, Steven Nock (1998) makes the important point that:

> Few women or men object to dependence per se, rather, it is the nature of such dependencies that is the problem, especially the extent to which they are perceived or experienced as inequitable, unfair, or excessively restrictive (p. 134).

In other words, we need to look more closely at the nature of the dependencies between men and women who live together, and we need to be open to the possibility that what looks pretty similar, for example, that the vast majority of married or cohabiting women still are economically dependent on their partner, may in fact represent a quite different situation than it did twenty or fifty years ago. It is very likely, for example, that many more couples today *perceive* the wife's earnings to be important, even when she earns less than he does. As Sen (1990) has argued, perception biases against women is an important source of male power in the family. As such biases begin to disappear, women and men may become more equal partners, even when some economic inequality remains.

THE CHANGING NATURE OF WOMEN'S
ECONOMIC POWER

It is well established that women's position in the labor market has improved rapidly during the last decades of the 20th century. Women's labor force participation, their hours of work and the continuity of their employment has become much more like men's than has ever been the case. This is in part because women's educational qualifications have improved bringing their earnings capacity considerably closer to that of men's, but also societal efforts to eradicate barriers in the labor market and reducing discrimination have played a role. Contributing further to women's stronger position in the labor market are that women's interest in employment and occupational careers has become stronger as their opportunities have improved (Goldin, 1990; Jackson, 1998) and the fact that in industrialized countries the "right to be thought of as an equal is a right that women today have seized upon with a grip far surer and unyielding than at any other time in history" (Kittay, 1999, p. 184). The consequence has been that the gender gap in wages has become considerably smaller (Blau & Kahn, 1992) in all industrialized countries, and that women's earnings have increased considerably (Bernhardt et al., 1995; Cotter et al., 1999). These changes in women's position in the labor market have had dramatic effects on the family economy, especially on the relative contributions of men and women to household income, and thus on women's economic dependence on their spouse or partner.

In previous work, it was proposed to measure women's economic dependence as the difference between the husband's earnings and the wife's earnings divided by their combined earnings (Sørensen & McLanahan, 1987). The measure ranges from 1 to −1, with 1 indicating that the woman has no earnings and is completely dependent on financial support from her spouse, and with −1 indicating that the man is completely dependent on his wife for support. If the dependence measure is zero, there is complete earnings equality. There is a linear relationship between this measure of dependence and the woman's relative contribution to family income. Such a measure ranges from 0 to 1, with 0.5 indicating perfect equality, and 0 and 1 complete dependence of the wife and the husband, respectively. As the woman's contribution to family income exceeds the man's, we move from a situation where she is the dependent to one where he is dependent on her. I have in earlier work thought of the measure of economic dependence as a measure of equality between partners, but this is really only so long as very few women earn more than their spouse or partner. If that becomes commonplace, then a decline in women's economic dependence may signal an increase in men's dependence, and thus not a decline in inequality between partners. As we shall see below, several countries are now in this situation, and I have therefore decided not to describe a decrease in women's economic dependence as synonymous with an increase in equality. It can be, but it is an empirical question whether it in fact is. In the remainder of the paper, I therefore focus on the degree of women's economic dependence or their relative contribution to family income.

Previous research has shown that married women's economic dependence declined precipitously between 1940 and 1980 in the United States (Sørensen & McLanahan, 1987), a decline that was also observed in the Netherlands, for example (Van Berkel & De Graaf, 1998). Until 1970, the decline was brought on almost exclusively by the decline in the completely dependent wife, but beginning around 1970 in the USA we see an increase in the proportion of couples making about equal contributions to family income and couples where the wife earns more, such that in 1997 (see Table 1) only 20% of white and 16% of African-American women were fully dependent on their spouse or partner, while 29% of white women and 39% of African-American women contributed as much or more to household income as did their partner.

The figures presented in Table 1 also show the extent to which women are economically dependent in seven European countries in the early to mid-1990s (see also Bianchi et al., 1999). It is evident that there is a great deal of variation across countries. The mean dependence ranges from a high of 0.63 in the Netherlands in 1991 (the same as the USA average in 1970) to a low of 0.15 in Finland in 1995. In other words, if we assume that couples pool and share incomes, Finnish women living with a spouse or partner received only 15% of their share as an implicit transfer from their partner, while the corresponding figure for a woman from the Netherlands was 63%. In the Nordic countries women are considerably less dependent than in the other European societies with mean dependence scores ranging from 0.15 to 0.23. It is interesting to note that women's economic dependence among African-Americans in the USA is at the same low level as in the Scandinavian countries. This is a result of the longstanding need for African-American women to contribute to the financial support of their families, a need brought on by African-American men's relatively low earnings (Landry, 2000).

In countries with a low mean dependence score, it is rare for married or cohabiting women to have no income and not unknown for men and women to contribute about the same to family income. In Finland, for example, women contribute about the same as their spouse in 18% of the cases, and in Denmark fully 21% of couples have about equal earnings. In the United States, African-American women contribute the same as their spouse in 17% of the cases, and 22% earn more than their partner. In general, there is a negative association between the average level of women's economic dependence and the percentage of couples with equal earnings. It is also the case, however, that lower mean dependence for women is associated with a higher proportion of couples where she earns more than her spouse or

Table 1. Women's Economic Dependence on their Partner.

Country	Mean Dependence	Woman has No Earnings (in %)	Woman Earns Less (in %)	Equality in Earnings (in %)	Woman Earns More (in %)	Woman Sole Earner (in %)
Denmark 1992	0.22	12.2	50.4	21.3	10.5	5.6
Finland 1995	0.15	12.1	44.5	17.6	16.7	9.1
Norway 1995	0.22	13.4	53.4	14.0	10.1	9.1
Sweden 1995	0.23	8.7	57.9	15.5	12.3	5.5
Germany 1994	0.39	33.5	39.2	9.6	6.3	11.5
The Netherlands 1991	0.63	48.0	38.4	6.6	2.7	4.2
United Kingdom 1995	0.36	25.8	46.3	12.5	5.0	10.3
USA, AA 1997	0.24	16.4	44.4	17.1	14.9	7.2
USA, W 1997	0.37	20.0	51.0	13.5	11.3	4.2

Note: Couples with positive income from earnings.

Dependence = (man's earnings − woman's earnings)/(couple's earnings).

Source: Luxembourg Income Study: own calculations.

partner. So, a decline in women's economic dependence does mean that more couples move towards equality; but such a decline also brings an increase in the proportion of couples that are unequal because the woman has the higher earnings.

Theories About the Consequences of Less Economic Dependence for Women

The decline in women's economic dependence has been celebrated by feminists as emancipatory and liberating for both women and men (e.g. Chafetz, 1990; de Beauvoir, 1953; Myrdal, 1946), and as strengthening the foundation for true love between partners (Jasso, 1988). Chafetz, for example, sees women's economic dependence as the key factor in maintaining gender stratification, and she argues forcefully that for gender stratification to decline, it is necessary for women's economic dependence on their partners to be reduced. Central to her argument is that less dependence provides women with power to make decisions about family, work, and training that will strengthen their position in the world outside the family.

Other theories see women's higher earnings as a threat to marriage or partner-ship; women will lose interest in marriage because they can support themselves, and both men and women will be more likely to leave unsatisfactory marriages. This independence thesis finds proponents both in sociology (from Parsons, 1949 onwards) and economics (Becker, 1981). Parsons argued that if both partners were employed and pursuing a career, conflicts would ensue and thus threaten the relationship. Central to Becker's argument is that as women become more eco-nomically independent of men, the gain to marriage is reduced for both sexes. The complementarity and interdependence that exist in partnerships where one spouse specializes in market production and the other in domestic activities dissolves if both spouses are employed full time and share housework (Becker, 1981). This view has been challenged by Oppenheimer (1997a), on both theoretical and empirical grounds. In a thorough review of the empirical literature, she found inconsistent support for the independence theory of Becker, and no strong support for alternative views. On theoretical grounds she suggests that while women's earnings provide financial independence, they also raise family income and the standard of living. An increase in both spouses' gain to marriage is thereby possible. As more women make substantial contributions to family income, men may become more interested in marriage because they are no longer expected to be the sole provider for the family and because they have an opportunity to share in their wife's earnings. It is thus possible that as a society moves towards more earnings equality between spouses, both women and men will have some financial independence, yet at the same time remain quite dependent on each other. Independence for women may then not undermine interdependence between spouses, but rather strengthen it. Rather than independence or dependence, the true issue may be the positive effects of interdependence.

One may ask why there are so many different ideas about the effects of less economic dependence of women and such inconsistent empirical support for any of them. I suspect that one reason is that until very recently there were very few couples where partners contributed equally to family income and even fewer couples where the woman was the main earner. It is only within the last ten to twenty years that there has been meaningful variation among couples in the extent to which the woman depends on her spouse or partner for financial support. If there are severe restrictions on the variations of an independent variable in a statistical model, it is difficult to find significant effects, and variations from sample to sample in the range of the measure of women's economic dependence may explain why some studies find one effect or another, while others do not. We should expect that more recent studies in societies with more variation in the dependence measure, would show more consistent effects.

There is also evidence that women increase their labor supply in *anticipation* of a future marital breakdown. Women who subsequently divorced were significantly more likely to have increased their work hours during the three years prior to divorce, while there was no evidence that labor force participation increased the risk of divorce (Johnson & Skinner, 1986). If such adjustment in women's employment behavior is not taken into account, then it will, of course, seem that women who are employed and work more hours have higher risks of divorce.

A third explanation for the lack of strong empirical support for any one theory is that there may be some truth to each of them, and that what is required is to determine the circumstances or conditions under which women's increased earnings have an independence effect, an income effect, a strengthening influence on love, or a positive impact on the interdependence of spouses and partners. My hypothesis is, that as more and more women make substantial contributions to family income, Oppenheimer's theory will find more support, and Becker's and Parsons' less.

In the remainder of the chapter, I review recent research exploring whether there is support for such a thesis and whether we are beginning to see evidence suggesting that there has been a change in the meaning of women's continuing economic dependence on their partner.

THE EFFECT OF WOMEN'S EARNINGS ON MARRIAGE AND DIVORCE RATES

The Beckerian argument that women's increased earnings and education will reduce the gain from marriage and therefore reduce the rates of marriage has, as shown by Valerie Oppenheimer (1997a), received mixed support in the empirical literature (see also Sayer & Bianchi, 2000). A number of studies have demonstrated that once school enrollment is taken into account, women's educational attainment, and thus their earnings capacity, has a small *positive* effect on the rate of marriage (Blossfeld & Huinink, 1991), but only in societies where it is relatively easy for women to combine marriage and employment (Blossfeld, 1995). In an important recent paper, Sweeney (2002) reports the results of an analysis comparing the experiences of successive birth cohorts to see whether the effects of women's earnings, education and employment status have changed over time. She suggests that "models that were designed to explain marriage before the revolutionary economic changes of the 1960s and 1970s may be inappropriate for understanding marriage formation in more recent historical periods" (Sweeney, 2002, p. 133) and that the nature of the marital bargain may have changed (Oppenheimer, 1988). Her central hypothesis is that the effect of women's economic prospects on the rate of entry into first marriage is becoming more positive over time. Her results provide strong support for this hypothesis. Women's earnings and employment status have significantly higher positive effects on marriage rates for younger cohorts, net of school enrollment which has a strong negative effect. Marriage is delayed because more women spend longer time enrolled in school, but once schooling is completed women's economic prospects increase their chance of marriage. As Sweeney (2002) points out, her analysis does not provide a direct test of Becker's theory which implies that it is the *gap* between potential spouses' earnings that determines the gain to marriage. It would, however, seem reasonable to assume that the gap between women's and men's earnings would be lower in the younger cohorts, where women's earnings has the greatest effect on marriage rates, thus providing indirect evidence against Becker's theory.

Recent research on divorce provides more evidence seemingly in favor of the independence hypothesis, suggesting that women's lower economic dependence indeed does increase the risk of divorce. Using data from the Panel Study of Income Dynamics, South (2001) examines the effect of women's hours worked and education on the risk of divorce and finds fairly convincing support for the hypothesis that these effects are positive and are *increasing* over time. Indeed, he finds no effect of women's labor supply in earlier periods, leading him to the following observation: "Ironically, then, while the predictions derived from the models of Parsons (1949) and Becker (1981) were unlikely to have been correct when these theorists first developed them, they appear to have become validated under recent conditions" (South, 2001, p. 241). This is, of course, completely at odds with my expectation, and exactly the opposite of Sweeney's conclusion with respect to marriage.

However, as Oppenheimer (1997b) points out in her critique of similar findings reported by Ruggles (1997), the observed association between the risk of divorce and women's economic independence "reflects a disenchantment with specific marriages rather than marriage per se" (Oppenheimer, 1997b, p. 470). Whereas the independence thesis sees women's economic independence as causing divorce by lowering the gain to marriage, an alternative view sees marital unhappiness as the cause of divorce and that women's economic independence makes it easier to leave an unhappy marriage. Very few studies have been able to distinguish between these two explanations, because marital satisfaction or happiness is rarely included in the analysis. Two recent studies have, however, done exactly that, and the results are very interesting, providing strong support for Oppenheimer's view. Using data from the National Survey of Household and Families, Schoen et al. (2002) found, in accord with earlier studies, that marriages in which the wife was employed full-time were at considerably higher risk of divorce than other marriages. However, when marital happiness was included in the model, the story became quite a different one. For couples where both partners reported that they had a happy marriage, the wife's employment status had no effect on the risk of divorce, but if one or both spouses were unhappy with the marriage, the woman's full-time employment increased the odds of divorce. This lends strong support to the view that women's economic independence facilitates the dissolution of unhappy marriages, but has no such effect on happy marriages.

Using data from the same study, Sayer and Bianchi (2000) found an initial positive effect of the wife's contribution to family income on the risk of divorce, but once they controlled for the wife's gender ideology, this effect was no longer significant. Wives who professed a modern gender ideology were more likely to divorce (husband's gender ideology had no effect), and wives who contribute more to family income were more likely to reject a traditional role for women. The wife's commitment to the marriage, her feeling that the marriage was in trouble and that the marriage was an unhappy one had positive effects on the risk of divorce and further reduced the effects of the wife's contribution to family income.

It is evident that the story about women's lower economic dependence and decisions regarding marriage and divorce is a complex one, and that even the most recent research leaves many questions unanswered. It will be important for future research to begin to specify the circumstances under which women's increased earnings influence such decisions as exemplified by the conditioning effects of marital happiness on divorce risks, and of school enrollment on marriage decisions. I also think that it should be acknowledged that women's increased earnings do provide options for women that they did not previously have, including options for delaying marriage or not marrying, and for getting a divorce when the marriage does not work out, just as the feminists predicted. The real split between the proponents of the independence thesis and their adversaries is whether women's economic independence has a *causal* effect on the gains from marriage, including marital happiness, or whether it simply provides opportunities to women for making choices that are not dictated by the need for economic support and for men to make choices not dictated by a commitment to support a wife.

There is surprisingly little research on this, but there is some evidence that there has been a decline in marital happiness and satisfaction over time (Glen, 1991) and that at least some of this should be attributed to the changes in women's lives. In a comparison of two marriage cohorts, one married between 1969 and 1980, the other between 1981 and 1992, it was found that the younger group reported significantly higher levels of marital conflict and problems and lower levels of interaction and commitment to the marriage (Rogers & Amato, 1997). Much of the difference in marriage quality could be attributed to the fact that it was more common in the younger cohort for the wife to be employed while there was a preschool child in the home. One of the ways in which married women's economic dependence has declined is, of course, that they return to work very soon after a child's birth. This suggests that a direct effect of women's lower economic dependence under some circumstances is that the burden of daily life becomes high, influencing the couple's relationship. Once that happens, separation is more likely if the woman is employed, that is if she is not completely dependent on her partner. (It is striking that South's study referred to earlier found an effect of the wife's full-time employment on the risk of divorce *only* for the period 1985 to 1992 and not for earlier periods (South, 2001, p. 239).)

There is also some evidence supporting the notion that women with non-traditional gender role attitudes report less happiness, less interaction, more dis-agreements, more problems and a higher proneness to divorce (Amato & Booth, 1995). The findings reported earlier that gender ideology could account for the positive effect of the wife's contribution to family income on divorce (Sayer & Bianchi, 2000) also supports this view. In addition, there seems to be a negative relationship between economic dependence and commitment to marriage (Nock, 1995; Sayer & Bianchi, 2000). In a study of "equally dependent spouses," Nock (2001) found that when couples became equally dependent over a period of five years, i.e. where the wife's earnings increased so that she contributed between 40 and 60% of the family income, the wife's commitment to marriage declined and the risk of divorce increased. The analysis did not take into account the possibility that the increase in the wife's earnings may have been the result of an anticipation of a marital breakdown (Johnson & Skinner, 1986). If there indeed is a link between women's employment and earnings and marital commitment and quality,

then it should come as no surprise that the effect of women's independence has increased over time (South, 2001) in studies that do not take marital satisfaction and
commitment into account. This will be so because a higher proportion of younger
marriage cohorts will show less commitment to marriage and experience more
problems in the marital relationship (Schoen et al., 2002).

What these scattered pieces of evidence suggest is that we cannot reject the
possibility that women's greater earnings and earnings capacity indeed may
have some negative effects on the marital relationship. Couples for whom this
is the case would then be at greater risk of separation and divorce, a risk further
increased by the fact that both spouses earn an income.

Men's Dependence on Women's Earnings

Women's greater financial independence clearly also has implications for men,
and one of them is that as women earn more money, men come to depend on that
income. They do so even if they are not economically dependent on their spouse in
the sense defined earlier. The point brought home so forcefully by Oppenheimer
(1997a) is that, when women begin to earn good money although less than their
husband, men enjoy the benefits of that income; they come to rely on it and will
experience an economic loss were they to lose it because the marriage dissolved or
the wife lost her job. As women contribute more to family income, both partners
gain some financial independence, but also economic interdependence and a
sharing of economic risks which was absent in the partnership that relied
exclusively on male earnings.

In earlier work (Sørensen, 2001), I have shown that the low economic dependence of women in the Nordic countries (see Tables 1 and 2) makes Nordic men
more dependent on their partners' income than men in countries where women are
more dependent on their spouse. I examined the mean decile position for couples
in the distribution of gross household income under two conditions: (1) counting
their combined earnings and transfer income; and (2) subtracting the partner's
earnings from the combined earnings. This provides a very crude measure of
how much change there would be in the couple's financial position if one income
were to disappear, and everything else remained constant, including the need
for income.

In societies where women contribute more to family income, men risk a greater
decline in economic status if they lose their partner's income than do men in less
egalitarian societies. For women, the opposite is the case. The more women earn
compared to their partner, the less they move down the economic ladder, should
his income disappear. This means, of course, that the discrepancy between men

Table 2. Mean Decile Position in the Distribution of Gross Household Income.[a]

Country	Mean Decile Position. Couple's Earnings + Transfer Income	Mean Decile Position if Partner's Earnings were Zero	Mean Decile Decline (Women/Men Ratio)
Denmark 1992			
Men	6.5	4.2	2.3
Women	6.4	2.8	3.6 (1.5)
Finland 1995			
Men	5.4	3.7	1.7
Women	5.2	2.7	2.5 (1.5)
Norway 1995			
Men	4.8	3.4	1.4
Women	4.6	2.1	2.6 (1.8)
Sweden 1995			
Men	7.1	4.9	2.2
Women	6.9	3.4	3.5 (1.6)
Germany 1994			
Men	5.6	4.1	1.5
Women	5.5	1.8	3.7 (2.5)
The Netherlands 1994			
Men	6.1	4.9	1.2
Women	6.1	1.8	4.3 (3.6)
United Kingdom 1995			
Men	5.4	4.2	1.2
Women	5.3	2.2	3.1 (2.6)

Source: Table 5 in Sørensen (2001).
[a] Based on the couple's earnings and transfer income and the respondent's earnings and transfer income. Couples with income from earnings or transfers.

and women's economic decline is smaller, and that men as well as women in egalitarian societies are apt to suffer economic decline were they to lose their partner's earnings. These expectations are well supported by the data. In the Netherlands, for example, men on average would move 1.2 deciles down in the household income distribution if they lost their spouse's earnings. But women would move fully 4.3 deciles down if they lost their husband's earnings, more than three times as much as for men. This pattern of a relatively modest risk for men and a much higher risk for women is also seen in Germany and the United Kingdom, although women there are somewhat better off than in the Netherlands with risks that are about 2.5 times that of men's. In Finland and Norway, women on average would experience a decline of 2.5 and 2.6 deciles, respectively, if they lost their husband's earnings. Men's risk is somewhat less, reflecting their higher earnings, with a mean decline of 1.7 and 1.4 deciles. In Denmark and Sweden, gender differences are also relatively small with women's risk being about 1.5 times that of men's, but the average decline for both men and women is somewhat higher than in Finland and Norway. In other words, Danish and Swedish partners are somewhat more dependent on each other's earnings for maintaining the current economic status than is the case in Finland and Norway.

As more men depend on their wives' earnings, men's economic risks associated with a divorce increase. This is clearly shown in a recent study of men's financial circumstances following a marital separation, which found a strong association between the woman's contribution to family income prior to separation and change in the man's nominal income as well as in standard of living (McManus & Diprete, 2001). All men experienced a decline in nominal income but if they had contributed 80% or more to the pre-separation family income the average decrease after taxes and transfers was 28% while it was fully 38% for white men who contributed between 60 and 80%. For men who contributed about the same as their partner, the decrease in post tax and transfer income was fully 45%. Change in men's standard of living is also strongly related to the pre-separation composition of family income. White and black men who contributed 80% or more of the family income, experienced a slight increase in standard of living once taxes and transfers had been taken into account. But men who contributed between 40 and 60% of pre-separation family income experienced a decline of about 20% in their living standard.

By demonstrating the direct link between the observed financial consequences of separation and divorce and women's contribution to family income, this study makes it very clear that as women's economic dependence declines, men share more equally in the financial risks associated with breaking one household into two. It is also evident that this is the case, even for men whose wives were economically dependent on them in the sense that they contributed less than half of the household income.

The Role of Women's Preferences

In Chapter 4 in this volume, Catherine Hakim presents her preference theory arguing that women's situation today in all modern societies is such that they to a great extent can act on their preferences regarding family, employment, and careers. It is an appealing idea, although the empirical evidence remains sketchy. But if more and more women indeed are able to act on their preferences, then we need to re-evaluate what it means to depend economically on a spouse. Hakim suggests that there are three distinct groups of women, each with a different set of preferences. Adaptive women prefer to combine employment with family obligations without any fixed priority to either. Work-oriented women see employment and career as central to their lives, with family work taking a decidedly second place. Home-oriented women give priority to family life and responsibilities once they are married. The adaptive group is considerably larger than the other two. Based on data from the United Kingdom, Hakim (2000) estimates that between 40 and 80% of women belong in the adaptive group, and 10–30% in either of the other two groups.

If a home-oriented woman acts on her preferences, she would choose not to be employed and to work exclusively for the family. She would be completely dependent on her spouse for economic support, but since it's her choice, it probably is not an oppressive situation but the fulfilment of a dream. It remains a risky choice, however. If she, for some reason could not act on her preference and had to earn money, this might be more of a problem for her. An adaptive woman may choose employment for some time, and then return to the domestic sphere, depending on the needs of her family. She will most likely earn less than her husband at any time, but in periods she is employed she will contribute meaningfully to family income. She would, in other words, move back and forth between being completely dependent and somewhat dependent. Again, as long as her situation reflects her preferences, the variation in economic dependence would not be a concern to her. It is for the work-oriented woman that high levels of economic dependence will be problematic, because it would signal that she had not been able to realize her preference, namely to work full-time over her lifetime. It seems then that if it indeed is the case that women have clear preferences for the balance between work and family in their life, and that most can realize these preferences; then economic dependence would be oppressive only for the minority of work-oriented women who cannot realize their preferences.

As women become more able to realize their preferences for how to combine work and family, we should then expect their economic dependence to reflect to a large extent these preferences. This means that one should not view women's economic dependence as a coercive arrangement that precludes women from making other choices. As Steven Nock (1998) has pointed out, inequity in marriage is not dependence per se. The inequity in traditional marriage is the coercive and unilateral nature of so many enforced dependencies (Nock, 1998, p. 135). Economic dependence in marriage continues to be gender biased in the sense that many more women than men depend on their partner for economic support. But the variation in women's economic dependence today is great, and not all should be attributed to coercion, but rather to a mixture of choice and gender inequalities in the labor market.

CONCLUSIONS

At the outset of this chapter I asked whether we have entered a new gender regime where women's income no longer should be considered a threat to the stability of partnerships, where women's economic dependence no longer has the meaning it did when the majority made little or no contribution to family income, and where men, although still out-earning their partner, are increasingly dependent on their wives' income and are sharing more equally the risk associated with a dissolution of the partnership. The answer is a tentative yes. Women continue on average to depend on their male partner for economic support, but the last three decades have seen an unprecedented increase in the proportion of women who make substantial contributions to family income. There is a concomitant decline in the fully dependent wife. The norms and expectations have definitely shifted, so that most women today expect to be in the labor force for most of their adult lives. Towards the end of the 20th century, a significant proportion of women contribute as much or more to household income as does their partner. As a result, fewer women are at the high financial risk that economic dependence implies, and an increasing proportion of men depend on their wife's earnings for their current standard of living. Women's increased earnings mean greater interdependence between men and women who share a household, more equality in the financial risks associated with the dissolution of the marriage, and for men better insurance against the risks posed by unemployment, layoffs, and illness. It also seems reasonable to conclude that women have not lost interest in marriage (and men may have gained some) due to women's greater earnings as would be predicted from the gain-to-marriage perspective. Indeed, the effects of women's economic prospects on marriage rates have become increasingly positive over time.

It is in the area of the couple's relationship that the evidence seems to point in the direction of some changes that should be attributed to changes in women's economic role and power. The research is not particularly strong, but it suggests that just as there have been changes in the economic foundation of marriage (Sweeney, 2002), relations between partners are changing in the direction of less commitment to each other, more conflicts, and less interaction. The most important effect of women's newfound independence may then be not on the gain to marriage but on the conflict level in marriage. This may be a transitional phenomenon as men adapt to women's new roles. More and better research is needed in this area. It will be especially important to specify the conditions under which modern couples manage to create strong, lasting relationships that exploit the advantages of more equal contributions to the financial support of the family. It will also be important to identify the conditions that lead in the opposite direction to separation and divorce.

REFERENCES

Amato, P. R., & Booth, A. (1995). Changes in gender role attitudes and perceived marital quality. *American Sociological Review, 60*, 58–66.

de Beauvoir, S. (1953). *The second sex.* New York: Knopf.

Becker, G. S. (1981). *A treatise on the family.* Cambridge, MA: Harvard University Press.

Bernhardt, A., Morris, M., & Handcock, M. S. (1995). Women's gains or men's losses? *American Journal of Sociology, 101*, 302–327.

Bianchi, S. M., Casper, L. M., & Peltola, P. K. (1999). A cross-national look at married women's earnings dependency. *Gender Issues, 17*, 3–33.

Blau, F. D., & Kahn, L. M. (1992). The gender earnings gap: Learning from international evidence. *American Economic Review, 82*, 533–538.

Blossfeld, H.-P. (1995). *The new role of women.* Boulder, CO: Westview Press.

Blossfeld, H.-P., & Huinink, J. (1991). Human capital investments or norms of role transition? How women's schooling and career affect the process of family formation. *American Journal of Sociology, 97*, 143–168.

Chafetz, J. (1990). *Gender equity, an integrated theory of stability and change.* Newbury Park, CA: Sage.

Cotter, D. A., Hermsen, J. M., & Vanneman, R. (1999). Systems of gender, race, and class inequality, multilevel analyses. *Social Forces, 78*, 433–460.

Glen, N. D. (1991). The recent trend in marital success in the United States. *Journal of Marriage and the Family, 53*, 261–270.

Goldin, C. (1990). *Understanding the gender gap. An economic history of American Women.* New York: Oxford University Press.

Hakim, C. (2000). *Work-lifestyle choices in the 21st century, preference theory.* Oxford: Oxford University Press.

Jackson, R. M. (1998). *Destined for equality. The inevitable rise of women's status.* Cambridge, MA: Harvard University Press.

Jasso, G. (1988). Employment, earnings, marital cohesiveness, An empirical test of theoretical predictions. In: M. Webster & M. Foschi (Eds), *Status Generalization, New Theory and Research* (pp. 123–167). Stanford, CA: Stanford University Press.

Johnson, W. R., & Skinner, J. (1986). Labor supply and marital separation. *The American Economic Review, 76*, 455–469.

Kittay, E. F. (1999). *Love's labor. Essays on women, equality, and dependence.* New York: Routledge.

Landry, B. (2000). *Black working wives. Pioneers of the American family revolution.* Berkeley, CA: University of California Press.

McManus, P. A., & Diprete, T. A. (2001). Losers and winners, the financial consequences of separation and divorce for men. *American Sociological Review, 66*, 246–268.

Myrdal, A. R. (1946). *Nation and family. The Swedish experiment in democratic family and population policy.* London: K. Paul, Trench, Trubner & Co.

Nock, S. L. (1995). Commitment and dependence in marriage. *Journal of Marriage and the Family, 57*, 503–514.

Nock, S. L. (1998). *Marriage in men's lives.* New York: Oxford University Press.

Nock, S. L. (2001). The marriages of equally dependent spouses. *Journal of Family Issues, 22*, 755–775.

Oppenheimer, V. K. (1988). A theory of marriage timing. *American Journal of Sociology, 94*, 563–591.

Oppenheimer, V. K. (1997a). Women's employment and the gain to marriage, the specialization and trading model. *Annual Review of Sociology, 23*, 431–453.

Oppenheimer, V. K. (1997b). Comment on "The Rise of Divorce and Separation in the United States, 1880–1990". *Demography, 34,* 467–472.

Parsons, T. (1949). The social structure of the family. In: R. N. Ashen (Ed.), *The Family, Its Function and Destiny* (pp. 123–167). New York: Harper & Row.

Rogers, S. J., & Amato, P. R. (1997). Is marital quality declining? The evidence from two generations. *Social Forces, 75,* 1089–1100.

Ruggles, S. (1997). The rise of divorce and separation in the United States, 1880–1990. *Demography, 34,* 455–466.

Sayer, L. C., & Bianchi, S. M. (2000). Women's economic independence and the probability of divorce. *Journal of Family Issues, 21,* 906–943.

Schoen, R., Astone, N., Rothert, K., Standish, N. J., & Kim, Y. J. (2002). Women's employment, marital happiness, and divorce. *Social Forces, 81,* 643–662.

Sen, A. (1990). Gender and cooperative conflicts. In: I. Tinker (Ed.), *Persistent Inequalities. Women and World Development* (pp. 123–149). New York: Oxford University Press.

Sørensen, A. (2001). Gender equality in earnings at work and at home. In: M. Kautto, J. Fritzell, B. Hvinden, J. Kvist & H. Uusitalo (Eds), *Nordic Welfare States in the European Context* (pp. 98–115). London: Routledge.

Sørensen, A., & McLanahan, S. S. (1987). Married women's economic dependency, 1940 to 1980. *American Journal of Sociology, 93,* 659–687.

South, S. J. (2001). Time-dependent effects of wives' employment on marital dissolution. *American Sociological Review, 66,* 226–245.

Sweeney, M. M. (2002). Two decades of family change, the shifting economic foundations of marriage. *American Sociological Review, 67,* 132–147.

Van Berkel, M., & De Graaf, N. D. (1998). Married women's economic dependence in the Netherlands, 1979–1991. *British Journal of Sociology, 49,* 97–117.

14. WOMEN AND MEN AS AGENTS
OF CHANGE IN THEIR OWN LIVES

Janet Zollinger Giele

ABSTRACT

This chapter focuses on the ways that personal biographies of individuals are related to their gender roles. Using biographical methods, the chapter develops a conceptual scheme for linking past experience to current life patterns. Modern work-centered women and the new care-oriented men are different from their traditional counterparts in their identity, social networks, goals and ambitions, and strategies for combining education, work, and family life. They are likely to seek out roles that allow them a greater degree of crossover in working and caring. A question for the future is how such preferences form and how they shape the broader gender contract of the larger society.

INTRODUCTION

The rising labor force participation of women has quickened over the last three decades in all the western industrial societies. Widespread changes in work and family patterns have appeared in every country, from the social-democratic Scandinavian countries, to conservative Mediterranean societies, and capitalistic and market-oriented nations like the United Kingdom and United States. In the Nordic Countries, the U.K., and the U.S., where the trend is most advanced, women now represent between 45 and 50% of all employed civilians (OECD, 2003). In the face of such widespread change in women's roles, the implicit division of

Changing Life Patterns in Western Industrial Societies
Advances in Life Course Research, Volume 8, 299–317
ISSN: 1040-2608/doi:10.1016/S1040-2608(03)08014-6

labor between women and men (the "gender contract") appears to be changing. Traditional norms of what constitutes male and female roles are being challenged. The question for this chapter is who leads the change, who the pioneers are, and how do their distinctive life course patterns contribute to their roles as innovators.

The upward trend in women's employment is accompanied by wider changes in women's roles: They have more education and more options in their family life. Fewer marry, more divorce, and their families are smaller. There are also some modest changes in men's roles: earlier retirement, shorter working hours for some, and greater participation in unpaid care work in the household and community (Bianchi & Mattingly, 2003). Despite these common themes, however, there are important differences between and within countries in the extent and speed of these changes. Families range from the traditional pattern of male breadwinner and female homemaker, to a mixed pattern where both husband and wife are working between part-time and full-time, and at the other end of the spectrum couples who share not only the work of earning an income but also the work of caregiving. A range of gender roles exists in every country even when policies are clearly weighted toward one pattern more than others.

The question of this chapter is who are the gender innovators: for example, mothers who are especially committed to breadwinning or fathers who are unusually involved in caregiving. Contemporary observers like Hochschild (1989) portray many families living within the present gender arrangements who feel time pressure and a simmering sense of injustice because women are doing a "second shift" of child care and housework while their husbands have time to relax and perform relatively pleasant and occasional chores that seem less onerous. Other reporters, however, like Coltrane (1996) and Bianchi and Mattingly (2003) show the rise in men's family involvement and the growing sense that fathers as well as mothers should be (and actually are) more involved with their children.

The developing field of life course research suggests that the life experiences of innovators are somehow distinctive. To produce social change, individuals have to depart from the norm and substitute constructive alternative patterns. In the process, they must exercise their own *agency* in the face of powerful social forces that otherwise would reproduce the existing social order. Mayer (2003) sees such a task as being at the center of the sociological study of the life course, which should be to bring back the person rather than focus only on the impact of environment. In his terms, the important questions concern how individuals of a given biological and psychological makeup are selected into a given role: ". . . how do they cope differentially with developmental tasks, and what are the consequences of specific life course experiences . . ." (p. 477).

To identify how individuals change their own gender roles, it is necessary to view persons as agents rather than mere pawns. Many studies have focused on the current work arrangements, time availability, and gender ideology that predispose some women and men towards a sex-typed division of household labor as compared with one that shares "male" and "female" tasks and flexibly allocates duties between women and men (Hochschild, 1989). This chapter assumes that the gendered division of labor is neither innate nor fixed but open to negotiation and change. The focus here is on the elements in the life course of individuals that predispose them toward either more ascribed or more flexible gender roles. Who are the innovative women, what is their distinctive life experience that makes them look for a different kind of partnership with husband or partner? Similarly, who are the new men and what is unusual about their lives, that leads them to a search for a different and broader role that includes duties usually labeled as feminine?

Just how difficult it is to accomplish change in gender roles is suggested by Scott Coltrane (1996), one of the leading sociologists of fatherhood. Coltrane (1996) notes that the average mother still does over three-quarters of the housework (cooking, cleaning, and laundry). But this gender-segregated division of labor is no longer so taken for granted. Coltrane points to several conditions that have promoted the sharing of family work: more equal earnings, more similar employment schedules, and gender ideologies that have become more egalitarian. He further suggests that "child-centered fathering appears to pull men into doing more of the housework." But then, why doesn't society ask men to do more? Instead it reinforces a pattern where a focus on the father's role as breadwinner reproduces the distance of fathers from their families and a pattern of male dominance.

This chapter addresses these questions by a combination of deductive and inductive strategies. The deductive analysis begins with life course theory and frames the question of innovative gender roles as an instance of a more general process by which innovation occurs in typical life patterns. Four universal factors are present in all human biography: (1) *location* in a particular time and place; (2) *linked lives* that stem from participation in social institutions and groups; (3) *agency* that expresses individual goals; and (4) *timing of life events* that represent strategic adaptations (Giele, 2002; Giele & Elder, 1998).

The inductive challenge is to describe the distinctive shape given each of these four elements in the life of an individual. This is done by drawing on existing studies of traditional and modern gender roles in order to gather clues about what factors seem to have been most important in shaping the lives of the new career-oriented women and the new care-oriented men. Important clues to understanding the sources of innovation among the women can be found by comparing traditional homemakers and those married women who combine families and careers. The data for such a comparison are drawn from my interviews with married dual-career mothers and homemakers in the United States as well as from a wider literature. In the case of men, parallel insights can be gleaned from a comparison of full-time breadwinners with "new men" who reject the stereotypic masculine ideal. Information on the men comes from the growing body of research on men's and fathers' roles.

BIOGRAPHY AND CHANGING GENDER ROLES

If the implicit gender contract in modern society is indeed being restructured, as suggested by current trends in time use and women's employment, a fundamental question is how such change takes place. Why in some instances does a couple solidify their breadwinner-homemaker division of labor, while in others the marriage may dissolve, the wife may work part-time or full-time, or both partners may share the breadwinning and homemaking functions equally?

One important set of answers points to the social and economic environment and the incentives that promote one path of action compared with another. Gornick and Meyers (2003) document the work, family, child care, and income policies of various countries and the types of behavior that they reward. Buchmann et al. (2003) reveal the subtle aspects of firm size and a woman's previous work history that either encourage her to return to a career after time out for child rearing or discourage her by relegating her to a lower status position. Sorensen (2003) highlights the importance of bargaining and negotiation within the marriage. Bonke and Koch-Weser (2003) document the variation in cultural ideals and expectations across EU countries and demonstrate that work and family life patterns of women and men are roughly correlated with national family ideals and traditions.

While "external" or "environmental" influences are undoubtedly important in shaping the national distribution of work and family patterns, it appears that individual preferences are critical for the individual's choices within any given country. Hakim (2000, 2003) suggests that much has to do with a woman's preferences for an independent, adaptive, or career-oriented mode. Bielenski and Wagner (2003) show that individual preferences on the whole favor more paid work on the part of women but that high unemployment in Europe as well as national family ideals and policies keeps them from realizing their preferences. Accordingly we need to examine what factors shape individual preferences besides the prevailing cultural climate.

In her 1989 book *The Script of Life in Modern Society*, Marlis Buchmann describes the challenge to the individual that is created by the shifts in modern social institutions of education, work, and family life:

> Overall, the life course regime in advanced industrial society is characterized by tension inherent in the relationship between standardization and re-standardization of the life course. Increasing bureaucratically determined status allocation coexists with growing discontinuity/flexibility and

diversification of life course patterns supported by the shifting cultural imagery of the private and public spheres. Individuals confront these conflicting tendencies as they devise their plans and attempt to put them into action. Current transformations of the life course regime thus highlight the dialectics between autonomy and action constraint (pp. 69–70).

Buchmann then sets out a conceptual framework for linking change in modern society to changes in the institutionalized life course. Persons and social organizations interact in a context of social and cultural change. The individuals develop their own biographical orientations and strategies to adapt to the demographic, technological, political, and economic changes that surround them. Their personal solutions add up to distinctive patterns that typify their age cohort. Over the long term the cultural expectations of individuals are constructed and reconstructed and reflected back to others in a never ending reciprocal process.

The matching of external demands and internal response can be understood as the construction of the individual life course whereby the person converts general cultural and social influences into particular form. Adult outcomes are the result of a complex layering of experience in which both childhood socialization and later opportunities play a part. The story of the connection between these early and later parts of life is what social scientists mean by the *life course*. Life course patterns are adaptations to circumstances, or what Thomas and Znaniecki ([1918–1920] 1927) termed "the solution of a situation," in which the person reacts to objective conditions with pre-existing attitudes and defines the situation in a way to cope with it successfully.

The challenge for this chapter is to specify this process in terms of gender roles. What are some of the characteristic biographical strategies by which traditionalists and innovators adapt to new challenges in the society? What forms do these biographical strategies take in the case of women and in the case of men?

FOUR FACTORS THAT SHAPE THE LIFE COURSE

To describe the precursors of the types of male and female life course patterns that lead to innovative gender roles, it is useful to have a conceptual framework for categorizing the various kinds of social context and types of influence that appear to be most critical. Four arenas for interaction between the environment and the individual (ordered from macro to micro) are found in the work of a number of social theorists: (1) temporal and cultural location; (2) institutional framework and social networks; (3) goal-oriented groups and activities; and (4) individual role expectations (Bronfenbrenner, 1979; Giele & Elder, 1998). Associated with each level is both an aspect of social structure and the internalized personal representation of that level as it is experienced by the individual. Thus, historical and cultural location is experienced by the person in terms of the definition and legitimation of *personal identity*. Institutional and social ties are experienced as membership in *social networks*. Involvement in goal-oriented collectivities such as the family or workplace give rise to a greater or lesser sense of *personal agency*. Finally, individual role transitions and obligations are realized in the *timing of life events* and roles that represent the concrete demands of the immediate environment.

Elsewhere I have described how one can "listen" to life stories with an ear for what is distinctive about particular life careers (Giele, 2002). It is possible to "hear" the structure of a social environment and the individual's response through the vehicle of biography and personal life history. Each life story can be coded according to the four different aspects of the social structure that shape the self: cultural, social, personal, and temporal. Depending on how each of these inter-changes is "solved," the person's actions will either reinforce or challenge the existing social structure. Table 1 below suggests how such personal orientations might be related to the prevailing gender roles if one were to observe those who challenge it and favor change.

As outlined in Table 1, the life course framework can be used to hypothesize what will be distinctive in the lives of gender innovators. Through their background and upbringing in a particular time and place, their distinct *personal identity* is likely to include an enhanced sense of self as somewhat unusual but naturally different from most other people of the same age and sex. Whether because of social class background, race, religion, disability, or unusual talent, the pioneers are comfortable with being different and departing from the norm, especially as it relates to the definition of normal womanhood and manliness.

Table 1. Relation of the Life Course to Innovation in Gender Roles.

Social Structural Level	Life Course Component	Characteristics of Innovators
Culture, time and place	Personal identity	Distinctive self-image as being different, pioneering, outstanding, out of the ordinary
Institutions, groups, social networks	Linked lives	Quest for equal status and rewards in male-female relationships
Individuals, human agency	Goals, priorities, ambition, attainments	*Females:* High value on career achievement
		Males: High value on intimacy and nurturance in husband-father role
Aging, change, timing of life events	Adaptation (with precocity, delay, or average timing)	Resourcefulness and inventiveness with respect to combining work and family roles

With respect to *social relationships*, one would expect gender innovators to resist patriarchal partnerships where the husband typically takes charge, earns more income, spends little time at home, and expects his wife to do the child care and household chores. One would expect the new women and men (if they don't stay single) to look for a different kind of partner who is ready to share both breadwinning and child care. The innovative women will likely be as well or better educated as their husbands and make similar or even greater incomes. The men will likely be comfortable with, and probably even proud of, a wife who is as well educated and capable of earning a significant part of the household income as themselves.

If the personal goals of the traditional woman are defined principally in terms of her ambitions for her home and family, one would expect that the *agency* of the new women is going to be relatively more invested in their paid work and in achievement outside the home than that of other women. Even if they are married, or have children, the new women will try to achieve in the world of paid work without sacrificing their families and will try to fulfill their responsibilities to their families without sacrificing their careers. One would expect innovators in the male role, on the other hand, to resist pouring all their energies into breadwinning and to look for satisfaction in supporting their wives' interests and spending time with their children and families.

The characteristic *adaptive strategy* of those who innovate in their gender role is likely to be resourcefulness in devising new schedules and dividing the labor of work and care. Pioneers have to be invested and flexible in devising new life strategies and timetables to accomplish their goals. They have to overcome resistance and skepticism on the part of their families and co-workers who subscribe to conventional gender role expectations. In the timing of their major life events such as school completion, marriage, and child bearing, as well as in their day-to-day schedule of working hours, the innovators are likely to devise novel arrangements that help them reach their goals.

With these hypotheses in mind, it now remains to examine what is actually known of innovators who define women's roles more broadly to make a larger place for market work and career achievement. Similarly, we ask what is known about those men who strive to give greater emphasis in their lives to nurturance and caregiving.

FEMALE INNOVATORS WHO REDEFINE WOMANHOOD

Against the backdrop of the mid-century "feminine mystique" that defined women's primary place as in the home, innovation in female roles is now generally understood to mean a life pattern that includes multiple roles in both market and non-market work. The multiple-role pattern legitimates women's activity in the public realm of paid work as well as their activity as wives and mothers in the family. Since 1970 some version of this multiple role pattern has become the norm among educated women in the United States (Giele, 1998). Within the multiple role pattern the most extreme innovative examples of innovation are likely to be found among those women who have reached the top echelons of occupational achievement while also marrying and having children. However, innovators (such as those who start their own home-based businesses or women who enter the male-labeled occupations such as construction workers or real estate and insurance sales) can also be found in mid-range and blue-collar occupations where women contribute to breadwinning and have help from husbands or others who share the work of the home. In other words, this analysis does not assume that innovation is confined to the highly educated or the professional class, among either women or men.

By examining biographies and accounts of innovators we can discern some of the precursors in the life course of those who innovate in their performance of the feminine role. The life stories of innovators appear to share some remarkably similar characteristics: (1) in their sense of being very different from other people; (2) in their choice of marriage partners who will share the household work and in some cases take the primary caregiver role; (3) in their driving ambition to be productive and to reach the top levels of achievement in their field; and (4) in their inventiveness at surrounding themselves with whatever resources are needed to make their multiple role pattern work out successfully. In presenting the evidence for each of these themes, I first draw on my own interviews in 2001 and 2002 with more than forty educated women and then on the observations of others.

Distinctive Background and Self-Image

During my interviews to compare life course experiences of dual career and homemaker mothers, it almost immediately struck me that the self-image of the dual career women was that of a different kind of individual, a person who came from an unusual background and was not afraid to challenge convention. The dual-career mothers' departure from the norm stemmed from a variety of sources. Examples included unusual brilliance or talent; membership in a minority group; working class background and upward mobility; having had a mother who was in a traditional role but was unhappy in it; a distinct identity compared to one's siblings; or a disability or handicap.

My first interview was with a 45-year-old Boston law partner in a small firm who came from a small city in the Midwest, the rural heartland of America, where she was a member of a tiny Jewish community in the midst of a Christian majority. Even in high school she had sat through the Christmas pageants and songs in order to "defend her First Amendment rights," by which she meant the American constitutional right to freedom of speech with its traditional separation of church and state. My very next interview was with a 35-year-old lawyer in a large Boston law firm. She revealed that she was a lesbian and pregnant at the time. She explained that she had eagerly accepted my request for an interview because she figured I "wouldn't get many people like her." In the space of a few more interviews, I encountered a 35-year-old entrepreneur and mother of two who with her husband had just sold their telecommunications start-up for over two hundred million dollars; she turned out to be the daughter of a policeman, and when asked whether she had any disabilities, revealed that she was legally blind! A fourth example was an African-American marketing executive in a *Fortune 500* company, both of whose parents had doctorates. This woman was very conscious of her privileged status growing up in a wealthy Boston suburb to which black inner city kids were being bussed as part of an effort to achieve racial integration and equality.

By contrast, the homemaker interviews generally conveyed the identity and self-image of women who thought of themselves as being much like other women of the same age and class. They did not perceive themselves as being especially different or unusual. Even those who were not fully engaged in full-time motherhood and housework, or were struggling with the question of whether they should go back to work, did not seem to see their lives as setting them apart.

Kathleen Gerson (1985) in her comparison of career-oriented and domestically oriented women also found differences in identity that helped shape a woman's role ideology. The choice of the career-oriented women might stem from any one of several types of early experience: having domestic responsibility for siblings that made them conscious of the costs of the domestic role; an unhappy mother who had never worked; upward mobility; or a high ambition for occupational achievement. Domestically-oriented women, on the other hand, might have started out in a career but gave it up when they encountered the joys and responsibilities of mothering. Most common, however, was the equation of domesticity with normality. According to Gerson, "the most common response among this group with traditional baselines was that they and everyone around them just assumed marriage and childbearing" (p. 61). Research by Karen Pyke (1994) on women who became full-time homemakers in a second marriage helps to round out this picture. In their first marriage, these women actually preferred the domestic role but were not able to realize it. In other words they valued the more conventional role for themselves and chose it when they had a chance.

Choice of an Equal Partner

Just as life course theory would predict, there is considerable evidence that the distinct identity and self-image of the dual career mothers is reinforced by their social networks and the opinions of those around them. In my interviews with the 35- and 45-year-old college-educated women graduates of the late 1970s and 1980s, I found that the career-oriented women in general did not "marry up." Instead they either married an equal in education and income potential or they married "down." They clearly were, and felt themselves to be, ahead of their time in both looking for and finding a partner who respected their achievements and facilitated their careers at the same time as being willing to help with child care, cooking, and housework.

The Jewish lawyer from the American heartland had married a husband in academic research with a schedule flexible enough to permit him to share in child care and household management. The lesbian lawyer's partner had agreed to stay home to care for their baby. The husband of the lawyer-entrepreneur, who was an engineer, took their first child to the office with him; the two of them for the preceding decade had shared in work for the company and work for the home. The 40-year-old black marketing executive was explicit in saying she had deliberately chosen a husband (a former chef) who would be willing to share family work and even take the lead in domestic responsibilities. He was at the time of the interview the primary parent who was at home with the children while she traveled. He also represented the family in school and community affairs.

The contrast between the life stories of the dual career mothers and those of the homemaker college graduates is quite striking. The relationships of homemaker mothers with their husbands appear to involve much more specialized roles in breadwinning or family work. This is most evident in the smaller proportion of household income brought in by the woman compared to the man. But the differentiated role pattern also appears in communication patterns and involvement with the children. The husband is more distant and less involved than in the dual-career couples. Here again, to understand the contrasting situation of the homemakers, it is helpful to refer to the observations of Pyke (1994) on women who chose the domestic role in their second marriages. Unlike the employed mothers who were rewarded for their achievements outside the home, Pyke's interviewees had the opposite experience of having their market work *devalued* by their husbands in the previous marriage.

Research of Maurer et al. (2001) in fact suggests that a partner's approval is critical for reinforcing cross-gender behavior. The authors found a significant relationship between a partner's approval and a woman's participation in the breadwinner role. Gerson (1985), on the other hand, locates the decisive factors in job opportunities and the success of a marriage. Her career-oriented women (not all of whom were married or had children) were pushed off a traditional path by social circumstances whereas the domestically oriented women were more likely to be insulated from forces that drove other women out of the home.

Driving Ambition in the World of Work

Even with a distinctive sense of self and approval from partner and peers, a woman is unlikely to be an innovator in the woman's role unless she has an unusual motivation to break the conventional mold. Many of the dual career college graduates whom I happened to interview in 2001–2002 were at or near the top of their fields given their relative youth (ages 35 and 45). A number of them had total household incomes well over $100,000 and several over $200,000 (in the top 5% of the nation overall). Their own contribution to the family income was near one-half and in several cases greater than half. But aside from occupational status or income, what was especially noticeable was their driving ambition and their full-time intense commitment to their work along with their concern for children and families. A number of them were in "male" types of occupation such as lawyer, entrepreneur, engineer, or professor. While they were devoted to their families, they seemed just as devoted to their work, as though they would not think of giving up one for the other, but that they considered both equally necessary to a happy and productive life. Similarly, Gerson (1985, pp. 64–65) observed the high occupational ambitions of her career-oriented women that left little room for traditional feminine pursuits. Often these ambitions led outside the usual sphere of "women's work" to male-dominated fields.

The life stories of the homemaker women were quite different in plot and intensity. The respondents spoke more slowly, packed in less information, and narrated a tale that had more instances of failure and drift than the case with the dual-career women. One homemaker, who had been a Summa Cum Laude graduate of her college, went straight to graduate school in art history, but left after a year. She explained her decision by saying, "I found that I just wasn't that ambitious. I didn't want to work 18 hours a day." She went on to recount the achievements of several of her male peers who went on to head major national museums and programs in the arts. But she did not seem to envy them or have any regrets. Rather she revealed a different kind of ambition that was directed toward family and children. Having wanted a family, she persisted through years of infertility treatment to adopt one child, then have a successful pregnancy of her own, and finally to adopt a second child, a sibling of the first. In her pantheon of values she had accomplished a rare achievement, but one outside the world of career success.

Corroboration for several of these themes comes from Pyke's (1994) study of remarried women who chose to abandon market work in order to realize a domestic role in their second marriage. They also had experienced frustration and blocked job opportunities in the world of paid employment. Gerson's (1985, p. 189) full-time mothers virtually all "viewed work, no matter how rewarding, as a poor substitute for the mothering experience."

Resourcefulness and Flexibility

Even with the distinctive identity, peer support, and unusual ambition that it takes to challenge gender norms, there is yet a fourth critical ingredient in the life course of those who turn out to be innovators in the feminine role. They need the resources of education and time, or the quality of resourcefulness to strike out on a different path. The dual career mothers were inventive and daring in finding the means to accomplish their goals. Like the woman lawyer from the American heartland who placed advertisements for a nanny in the Minneapolis newspapers, they were willing to hire outsiders to help at home. Like the black marketing executive, who had two offices in New England and one in New York, they were willing to engage in commuting marriages. Even when parental leaves were still relatively uncommon, the graduates of the 1970s (the 45-year-olds) had been willing to request them and use them. In a quite different type of resourcefulness, the lesbian lawyer and her partner investigated various means of having a child and finally chose artificial insemination. The young mother and entrepreneur who was legally blind had had a full-time household helper for about a decade to help not only with household and child care but also with driving and other matters of logistics and household management. Gerson (1985, p. 187) observed this quality nearly two decades ago: even then the women committed to work had developed "new arrangements for rearing children, new beliefs about their care, and new conceptions of men's and women's capacities . . . ."

In this comparison, homemakers were also very resourceful people, but for different ends. One woman, a musician and computer programmer, had stayed home after her first child was born. She had undertaken a phenomenally strenuous and unconventional program of home schooling for her three children. The would-be art historian who invested years in treatments for infertility demonstrated remarkable resourcefulness in the adoption process by working out an open and trusting relationship with the birth parents so that they approached her about adopting another one of their children, which she did.

Among the homemakers observed by Pyke (1994) the matter of difference in resources between the job-oriented and domestically-oriented women was even more stark. None of the domestically-oriented women had graduated from college as compared with one-third of the job-oriented women. Gerson (1985) also found the career-oriented to be somewhat better educated. But she also noted that for those committed to domesticity, "security remains rooted in a strict sexual division of labor that maintains a clear separation between parenting and economic responsibilities" (p. 187).

In sum, it is possible to characterize the innovators in women's roles as having had a distinctive set of life experiences and personal goals that set them apart from the women who take a more traditional path. Their distinct sense of who they are and the support from their surrounding family and friends enables them to persevere against the discouragement and frustration that they inevitably encounter. Their personal goals and definition of what constitutes a satisfying life, together with their particular form of resourcefulness and inventiveness, provides the energy and drive that carries them forward despite resistance from the larger society.

"NEW MEN" WHO REDEFINE MASCULINITY

Next we turn to the innovators who are developing an alternative template for the male role. For these men the challenge is to find a larger place for nurturance and care over against the traditional male focus on provision and protection. The question is how such an orientation comes about.

An explanatory framework put forward by Coltrane and Adams (2001) describes the process by which certain men become active participants in household and care work of the family. The central theory is that the increase in women's employment results in a cutback of women's hours spent in child care and domestic work. This affects the relative power of husbands and wives. As women's occupational resources come to resemble those of men, there is more sharing of housework Also, as fathers become more involved in parenting, they are more likely to be drawn into household work.

Maurer et al. (2001) provide another general explanatory approach that focuses on the partner's opinion of on-gender or cross-gender behavior. They find that partner's approval or disapproval is significantly related to adoption or rejection of cross-gender behavior. A husband is unlikely to engage in child care and housework unless his wife encourages, approves, and reinforces that behavior.

R. W. Connell (1995) provides a third slant on the topic by identifying distinctive characteristics of men who take a feminist perspective and treat women as equals. Connell probes the life histories of a small group of Australian men who reject conventional masculine success in their occupations or professions and adjust their way of life to give a greater place to typically feminine concerns. These men want to express their feelings, cultivate more intimate relationships, and engage in more activities like cooking that are typically done by women. Connell finds that such men have typically had a very affectionate and respectful relationship to their mothers that they are able to use as a model of mature relationships with women. The capacity to identify with their mothers enables them to empathize with and live out their egalitarian ideals in their dealings with women.

Let us see how these various theories and the accompanying evidence can be decoded in light of the four dimensions of life course experience.

Feminist Values and Masculine Identity

The clearest statement of the ideology of the new men comes from the Australian sociologist R. W. Connell (1995). In his interviews with men who had changed their life pattern deliberately to follow a less professionally or business-oriented and more family-involved way of life, he discovered an incipient feminist ideology among these new men. They had found "another side of life," one that involved "giving to people, looking after people." Their focus was on face-to-face interactions and on being able to find depth in emotional relationships through caring for people and nature. According to Connell (1995, p. 133), "Those qualities of openness and caring are supposed to be put to work in new-model personal relationships" which are not to be oppressive, dominant, or sexist. This capacity for reframing nurturance and care is based on a "re-alliance" with the mother during the post-Oedipal period by the undoing of Oedipal masculinity and the formulation of a new and more complex masculinity that is not regressive.

Whether or not it is always the same, the distinctive ideology of new men is mentioned by all the major authors as being important. This ideology appears to be an aspect of identity and a necessary ingredient in the more egalitarian relationships of these men with their wives and in their above average participation in child care and household work. Pyke and Coltrane (1996) mention husband's ideology along with other conditions (husband's fewer hours of paid work and wife's demanding working hours) as one of the best predictors of a husband's participation in household work.

In a study of men's changing participation in family work, Coltrane and Adams (2001) using longitudinal data from the National Survey of Families and Households, found that men's egalitarian ideology predicted their higher participation in household work whereas men who believed in separate spheres participated less. Educated men also participated more, suggesting differences in attitudes associated with social class. Attitudes about child-rearing further affect a father's involvement in household work. Those who believe in nurturant and child-centered fathering help more with housework and child care. On the other hand, those who have a more adult-centered and distant relationship with their children are likely to help less (Coltrane & Adams, 2001).

Social Networks and Mutual Dependence in Marriage

It is likely that a man's feminist ideology is the result of a two-way interchange with those around him. Not only is he likely to choose a partner who shares his views; he is also influenced by the attitudes and behavior of the partner he chooses. The findings of Coltrane and Adams (1996) support these hypotheses. In their study of men who made above average contributions to child care and housework, especially in driving them to extra-curricular activities, were more likely to help with household work.

Nock (1998) lists three positive effects of the marriage relationship on men: (1) encouragement of stable work and steady earnings; (2) integration of the individual into other regular social affiliations such as fraternal organizations and religious groups; and (3) encouragement of investment in the family rather than in non-family pursuits. It is but a short step to extend these principles to the egalitarian marriage and its role in helping to shape the new men. Thus, it seems probable that there is something in the men's relationships with their children, spouses and peers – their social networks and "linked lives" – that encourages and reinforces any initial predisposition they had toward an egalitarian division of household labor. Something about their social milieu is rewarding them for feminist rather than patriarchal behavior. Gerson (1993, p. 274) concludes her interview study of 138 middle class and blue collar men by concluding that, "Those who are able to forge stable marriages with a woman who prefers domesticity may decide to work harder to bolster their position as family breadwinners. Those who become committed or attracted to a work-committed woman may opt to share breadwinning and caretaking."

Connell (1995, p. 133) finds this alternative orientation of the new men is so profound that they even change their relationships with other men. All of his respondents were heterosexual men, yet they deviated from stereotypic masculinity in wanting their relationships to be "more open, more close, more trusting, more caring, more physically caring...." Their ideal social ties thus tended toward recognition and acceptance of mutual dependence and a rejection of domination and hierarchy.

Personal Goals and the Priority of Nurturance and Care

Infused with egalitarian ideals and supported by peers and family involvements, the new men behave differently in the way they exhibit their masculinity and carry out their roles as fathers and breadwinners. Steven Nock (1998, p. 6) contends that "Marriage changes men because it is the venue in which adult masculinity is developed and sustained." Masculinity is precarious and must be sustained in adulthood, and for that reason "Normative marriage is the only way by which *most* males can become 'men.'" Historically, at least since the nineteenth century, masculinity has implied three things: that a man be the father of his wife's children; that he be the provider for his wife and children; and that he be the protector of his family.

Unlike those men who equate masculinity with domination and strict separation of the provider and protector roles from close personal involvement in family life, the new men fulfill their masculinity not only through breadwinning but also by spending relatively more time in child care and household work. Conversely, more traditional men are likely to equate mature manhood mainly with being a good provider, as demonstrated by many of the men interviewed by Gerson (1993).

Resourcefulness and the Pragmatic Use of Time

The new men do not stand on ceremony: that is, they don't refuse to help with domestic chores and humble tasks of child care just because they are not usually defined as "a man's job." Instead they are resourceful and pragmatic and give help when they see that help is needed. Therefore a key element in the life course of the new men is the nature of the adaptive challenges that they face and the character of their response.

According to Coltrane (1996), there are two key life course factors related to time and timing that distinguish the involved fathers and husbands. Their wives work many hours in paid employment, and the men themselves have time available (either by choice or circumstance) to be able to substitute their own time by sharing the household work or giving the child care that is needed.

An inevitable question is which comes first, a man's ideology, the approval of his family and friends, his own priorities and goals, or the barriers and opportunities in his environment. The answer differs with the person. Coltrane (1996), Pyke (1994), Coltrane and Adams (2001), and Pyke and Coltrane (1996) all describe a dynamic where men with modern egalitarian attitudes encounter challenges (wife's breadwinning and shortage of household time) to which they respond in innovative ways by becoming more active fathers and more active contributors to domestic work. Their wife's approval and the intrinsic rewards of spending more time with their children help to cement the new behavior and establish a consistent tie between their ideals and preferences about the best ways to fulfill the husband-father role.

POLICIES, PREFERENCES, AND THE CHANGING GENDER CONTRACT

As more women enter the work force and take on a double burden of paid work and caregiving, it is increasingly common to ask how things might change to redistribute the labor more justly to the benefit of women, men and children. Previous chapters in this book have given particular attention to the weight of culture and social policy in shaping the sexual division of labor. The change envisioned by many is a change in the gender contract that would allow women to combine paid work and family work more easily and would allow men to reduce their hours of market work and increase their involvement with children and domestic life.

This chapter shares much the same vision, of a new more equitable division of labor between women and men. The emphasis here, however, is not on the policies that are needed to encourage such a change but on the signs that the change is already occurring on a small scale within individual households and couples. The aim of this analysis is to pinpoint the distinctive life histories that prefigure the innovative roles of women and men.

Four aspects of life experience turn out to be characteristic of the pioneers: (1) a distinctive personal identity; (2) approval from families and peers; (3) ambition of women for careers and of men for more intimate relationships; and (4) resourcefulness and inventive strategies for developing the practical means to achieve these ends.

Career-oriented mothers redefine womanhood to make a place for their commitment to work. They are able to sustain their alternative vision because of a distinctive self-image, choice of an equal partner in marriage, driving ambition for occupational achievement, and resourcefulness and flexibility in devising new strategies for combining childrearing with career advancement.

The "new men" redefine masculinity to include a larger place for fatherhood and domestic involvement. They have a distinct and secure identity in being able to combine feminist values with masculinity. They are supported in their roles by mutual dependence in their marriage. Their personal goals give a high priority to the expression of feelings and nurturance and care of others. Their commitment to this alternative definition of the male role is cemented by their pragmatic use of time to help out where needed at home and to make a place for fatherhood along side the breadwinner role.

In sum, the gender contract of the future is already being forged in pioneering households of the American women and men described in this research. Certain individuals by dint of their life experience are working out the new division of labor between husbands and wives, fathers and mothers. These experiments are occurring at the same time as efforts to establish family-friendly policies in the workplace and the community. What will be interesting for the future is the relative importance of the voice of innovators compared with that of more conventional women and men. At the moment it seems likely that both sets of voices will continue strongly for some time to come.

ACKNOWLEDGMENTS

For support in completing the interviews with educated women, I thank the Murray Research Center of Harvard University for the Research Support Award, the Mazer Fund of Brandeis University, and the Family and Child Policy Center of the Heller School. For assistance with the interviews and data management over the past two years, I thank Jennifer Eidelman, Donna Einhorn, and Meg Lovejoy.

REFERENCES

Bianchi, S., & Mattingly, M. (2003). Time, work, and family in the United States. In: J. Z. Giele & E. Holst (Eds), *Advances in Life-course Research: Changing Life Patterns in Western Industrial Societies* (Vol. 8, Chap. 5). London: Elsevier.

Bielenski, H., & Wagner, A. (2003). Employment options of men and women in Europe. In: J. Z. Giele & E. Holst (Eds), *Advances in Life-course Research: Changing Life Patterns in Western Industrial Societies* (Vol. 8, Chap. 7). London: Elsevier.

Bonke, J., & Koch-Weser, E. (2003). The welfare state and time allocation in Sweden, Denmark, France, and Italy. In: J. Z. Giele & E. Holst (Eds), *Advances in Life-course Research: Changing Life Patterns in Western Industrial Societies* (Vol. 8, Chap. 11). London: Elsevier.

Bronfenbrenner, U. (1979). *The ecology of human development: Experiments by nature and design.* Cambridge, MA: Harvard University Press.

Buchmann, M. (1989). *The script of life in modern society: Entry into adulthood in a changing world.* Chicago: University of Chicago Press.

Buchmann, M., Kriesi, I., & Sacchi, S. (2003). Labor-market structures and women's paid work: Opportunities and constraints in the Swiss labor market. In: J. Z. Giele & E. Holst (Eds), *Advances in Life-course Research: Changing Life Patterns in Western Industrial Societies* (Vol. 8, Chap. 8). London: Elsevier.

Coltrane, S. (1996). *Family man: Fatherhood, housework, and gender equity.* New York: Oxford University Press.

Coltrane, S., & Adams, M. (2001). Men's family work: Child-centered fathering and the sharing of domestic labor. In: R. Hertz & N. L. Marshall (Eds), *Working Families: The Transformation of the American Home* (pp. 72–99). Berkeley: University of California Press.

Connell, R. W. (1995). *Masculinities*. Berkeley: University of California Press.

Gerson, K. (1985). *Hard choices: How women decide about work, career, and motherhood*. Berkeley: University of California Press.

Gerson, K. (1993). *No man's land: Men's changing commitments to family and work*. New York: BasicBooks.

Giele, J. Z. (1998). Innovation in the typical life course. In: J. Z. Giele & G. H. Elder, Jr. (Eds), *Methods of Life Course Research: Qualitative and Quantitative Approaches* (pp. 231–263). Thousand Oaks, CA: Sage.

Giele, J. Z. (2002). Life course studies and the theory of action. In: R. A. Settersten & T. J. Owens (Eds), *Advances in Life-course Research: New Frontiers in Socialization* (Vol. 7, pp. 65–88). London: Elsevier.

Giele, J. Z., & Elder, G. H. (1998). Life course studies: Development of a field. In: J. Z. Giele & G. H. Elder, Jr. (Eds), *Methods of Life Course Research: Qualitative and Quantitative Approaches* (pp. 5–27). Thousand Oaks, CA: Sage.

Gornick, J., & Meyers, M. (2003). Welfare regimes in relation to paid work and care. In: J. Z. Giele & E. Holst (Eds), *Advances in Life-course Research: Changing Life Patterns in Western Industrial Societies* (Vol. 8, Chap. 3). London: Elsevier.

Hakim, C. (2000). *Work-lifestyle choices in the 21st century: Preference theory*. Oxford: Oxford University Press.

Hakim, C. (2003). Lifestyle preferences vs. patriarchal values: Causal and non-causal attitudes. In: J. Z. Giele & E. Holst (Eds), *Advances in Life-course Research: Changing Life Patterns in Western Industrial Societies* (Vol. 8, Chap. 4). London: Elsevier.

Hochschild, A. R. (1989). *The second shift: Working parents and the revolution at home*. With Anne Machung. New York: Viking.

Maurer, T. W., Pleck, J. H., & Rane, T. R. (2001). Parental identity and reflected-appraisals: Measurement and gender dynamics. *Journal of Marriage and Family, 63*, 309–321.

Mayer, K. U. (2003). The sociology of the life course and lifespan psychology: Diverging or converging pathways? In: U. M. Staudinger & U. Lindenberger (Eds), *Understanding Human Development: Dialogues with Lifespan Psychology* (pp. 463–481). Boston: Kluwer Academic Publishers.

Nock, S. L. (1998). *Marriage in men's lives*. New York: Oxford University Press.

OECD (2003). Female labour. *OECD Observer*. No. 235. December 2002 (published on March 6, 2003).

Pyke, K. D. (1994). Women's employment as a gift or burden?: Marital power across marriage, divorce, and remarriage. *Gender and Society, 8*, 73–91.

Pyke, K., & Coltrane, S. (1996). Entitlement, obligation, and gratitude in family work. *Journal of Family Issues, 17*, 60–74.

Sorensen, A. (2003). Economic relations between women and men: New realities and the re-interpretation of dependence. In: J. Z. Giele & E. Holst (Eds), *Advances in Life-course Research: Changing Life Patterns in Western Industrial Societies* (Vol. 8, Chap. 13). London: Elsevier.

Thomas, W. I., & Znaniecki, F. ([1918–1920] 1927). *The Polish peasant in Europe and America*. New York: Knopf.

AUTHOR INDEX

319

SUBJECT INDEX

women's earnings, 283, 286–288, 291
women's economic dependence, 281–287, 290, 293–295
women's economic dependence declines, 293
women's economic independence, 289, 290
women's economic power, 281, 283
women's economic role, 295
women's educational attainment, 288
women's educational qualifications, 283
women's employment behavior, 184, 287
women's employment preferences, 140
women's income, 12, 281, 295
women's labor force experience, 281
women's labor force participation, 3, 115, 167, 174, 180, 182, 283
women's labour force participation, 89, 194
women's lifestyle preferences, 87, 88
women's movement, 192, 194, 213, 217, 220
women's overall labour market attachment, 235
women's paid work, 165, 167
women's preferences, 88, 143, 151, 293
womens's work, 12
work and care regimes, 51, 60
work and family, 3, 6, 7, 9, 11–17, 19, 20, 31, 47, 74, 77, 79, 95, 97, 104, 106, 115, 116, 133, 152, 155, 175, 178, 180, 189–194, 197, 200–207, 218, 226, 227, 261, 265, 274, 275, 294, 299, 302, 304, 315
work and family balance, 97, 189, 192, 193, 200, 202, 203, 205–207
work and family obligations, 175, 180
work and family years, 115
work and life, 119, 171, 182, 189–191, 193, 194, 205, 227, 257, 258, 259, 261, 262, 266, 273–276
work and life balance, 189–191, 193, 205, 258
work and life patterns, 119, 171, 182, 190, 194, 227, 257, 258, 259, 261, 262, 276
work full-time, 85, 103, 106, 151, 158, 160, 161, 184, 201, 202, 241, 245, 294
work life balance, 202, 261

work orientations, 70, 73
work plans, 70, 71, 72
work relations in the United States, 23
work-centred, 76–79, 81–87
work-centred women, 76, 81, 83–85, 87, 299
work-family balance, 76, 203
work-family policies, 14
workforce, 11, 29, 52, 82, 115, 123, 142, 146, 257, 258, 260, 261, 267, 270, 272
working conditions, 33, 66, 139, 165, 171, 173, 182–184, 203, 213, 227, 228, 232, 259, 261–264, 267, 271, 272, 276
working full-time, 86, 241, 244
working hours, 8, 16, 59, 76, 120, 121, 123–127, 129, 133, 137, 138, 140, 143, 146–151, 153–158, 160–162, 166, 167, 175, 179, 180, 183, 184, 189, 206, 245, 246, 261, 262, 264, 266, 274, 277, 300, 305, 312
working life patterns, 194
working mothers, 109, 192, 193, 195
working time, 7–9, 16, 17, 19, 46, 47, 52, 54, 55, 58, 59, 63, 64, 66, 119–131, 133, 134, 138–141, 146, 147, 151–155, 157, 158, 160, 161, 166, 189–191, 193–195, 200, 202, 203, 205, 206, 207, 208, 261, 264
working time arrangements, 119–121, 124, 125, 139, 146
working time pattern, 122
working time policies, 54, 189, 190, 193, 202
working time preferences, 16, 139, 141, 147, 151, 153, 160, 161
working time regulations, 46, 52, 54, 55, 63, 66, 194
working wives, 242
working women, 77, 78, 83, 175, 191, 244, 245
working-time arrangements, 119, 120, 121, 124, 139, 146
working-time regimes, 119, 121, 126, 130
work-life balance, 261
work-oriented women, 294
workplans, 71